BRITAIN AND
THE GREAT WAR
1914–1918

In Memory of

My Grandfather
Private J. Sheldon
7th Battalion North Staffordshire Regiment
1880–1918
and
My Friend
Group Captain J.G. Bishop DFC
1916–1983

Britain and the Great War
1914 – 1918

J.M. BOURNE

Senior Lecturer in Modern History
University of Birmingham

Edward Arnold
A division of Hodder & Stoughton
LONDON NEW YORK MELBOURNE AUCKLAND

© 1989 John Bourne

First published in Great Britain 1989
Reprinted 1991 (with corrections)

Distributed in the USA by Routledge, Chapman and Hall, Inc.
29 West 35th Street, New York, NY 10001

British Library Cataloguing in Publication Data

Bourne, J.M.
  Britain and the great war 1914–1918.
  1. World war 1. Role of Great Britain
  I. Title
  940.3'41

  ISBN 0-7131-6592-8

Typeset in 10/11 Paladium by Colset Private Limited, Singapore.
Printed and bound in Great Britain for Edward Arnold, a division of
Hodder and Stoughton Limited, Mill Road, Dunton Green,
Sevenoaks, Kent TN13 2YA by Bookcraft, Avon

Contents

Preface

The Great War ended a lifetime ago. The ranks of its survivors become thinner with each passing year; the time cannot be far away when there will be none left at all. The war has surely passed into history. Detachment, however, is difficult. Even at this distance, the bitter struggle on the Western Front continues to fascinate and to appal and to provoke controversy and recrimination. The popular image of the war is fittingly captured by one of those principally responsible for planting it in the national consciousness, A.J.P. Taylor, in his phrase 'brave, helpless soldiers; bungling, incompetent generals; nothing achieved'. The war is still overwhelmingly seen as pointless, mismanaged and futile. This view came to be held quite commonly by 1930, but it was in many respects strengthened by the experience of the Second World War, the inevitable and heroic struggle against evil and tyranny, successfully concluded at far less cost in British lives than the Great War, not only a military but also a moral triumph. In the face of this, the writings of even the most persuasive and articulate revisionist historians have proved ineffectual. The Great War retains its sinister memory. At Armistice Day parades the sense of sorrow and shock is still tangible. The hurt remains.

Books about the Great War abound and continue to proliferate.[1] One may perhaps be forgiven for thinking that there is nothing left to be said. This is not the case. Volume is not a measure of quality. There have been many recent books about the war which display ability and insight.[2] But there have been many more which seek only to exploit the public's seemingly endless fascination with military trivia and are content to repeat uncritically the assumptions and prejudices which found clearest definition in the film *Oh! What a Lovely War* (1969).[3] Despite steady scholarly interest in the war, research has been lopsided. Professor Marwick's *The Deluge. British Society and the First World War* (1965) stimulated much able work on domestic aspects of the war, and this remains a fruitful area of activity.[4] Elsewhere, it has been a different story. The influence

1. See K. Simpson, 'An annotated bibliography of the British army, 1914–1918', in I.F.W. Beckett and K. Simpson, eds., *A Nation in Arms. A Social Study of the British Army in the First World War* (Manchester, Manchester University Press, 1985), pp. 238–66.
2. Notably, A. Ashworth, *The Sociology of Trench Warfare* (London, Macmillan, 1980); P. Fussell, *The Great War and Modern Memory* (London, Oxford University Press, 1975); J. Keegan, *The Face of Battle* (London, Jonathan Cape, 1976); E.J. Leed, *No Man's Land. Combat and Identity in World War I* (Cambridge, Cambridge University Press, 1979); D. Winter, *Death's Men. Soldiers of the Great War* (London, Allen Lane, 1976). I have deliberately avoided reading Trevor Wilson's epic *The Myriad Faces of War: Britain and the Great War 1914–1918* (Cambridge, Polity, 1986) until after the completion of this book.
3. This film, directed by Richard Attenborough, was based on Joan Littlewood's stage production at Stratford-East in 1966.
4. Important recent works include: L.M. Barnett, *British Food Policy During the First World War* (Boston, Mass., Allen & Unwin, 1985); K. Burk, ed., *War and the State. The Transformation*

of Liddell Hart has inhibited rather than encouraged a fundamental reassessment of British military performance. Many of the war's leading figures – Kitchener, Wilson, Robertson, Cowans – await adequate assessment. Among Army commanders, there are no modern biographies of Plumer or Rawlinson or Horne.[5] And only now is the transformation of the British army from a small, colonial *gendarmerie* into a modern, mass army, capable of taking on and beating the German Army in the field, receiving the attention which it deserves.[6]

My own motives for adding to the stock of First World War literature are entirely personal and belong to the realm of autobiography.

As a child (I was born in 1949) the Great War was a familiar source of difficulty and confusion. I can still recall with pain the memory of being publicly humiliated by my teacher for being the only child in my class of six-year-olds who was not wearing a Poppy. I was never allowed to buy one. This injunction stemmed ultimately from my formidable grandmother, Louisa Sheldon. Although she died when I was barely three I remember her vividly and with great affection. When I was old enough to inquire, I learned that my grandmother's objection was to the three words at the centre of a Poppy – 'Earl Haig Fund'. She was bitter about my grandfather's death during the war and seemed to hold Haig responsible for it. She saw the Poppy as a way of extorting money from the poor and gullible for Haig's private gain. Even after I realized the essentially irrational nature of my grandmother's belief (my grandfather never served under Haig's command) and of the libel which it inflicted on Haig's memory, I felt trapped by its granite immovability. To this day, I cannot buy a Poppy without an immense psychological effort and without a residual sense of guilt and betrayal. Haig was a scapegoat for my grandmother, as he has been for many others. Her real quarrel was with her husband.

My feelings towards my grandfather, Jesse Sheldon, encapsulate in a personal way many of the deepest British responses towards the Great War – sorrow, bewilderment, pride. I have always felt a tremendous sense of loss in not having known him. I am sure that this was because he was a soldier and because he died in the greatest war our country has ever fought. I never knew my other grandfather – and namesake – either, but I feel no sense of loss about him. He was the same age as Jesse in 1914. He, too, was a collier, but he did not go away to war. Just as part of me cannot forgive Jesse for going, part of me cannot forgive Ginger for not having gone. I place no flowers on his grave. I do not take

of British Goverment, 1914–1919 (London, Allen & Unwin, 1982); D. French, British Economic and Strategic Planning, 1905–1915 (London, Allen & Unwin, 1982) and British Strategy and War Aims, 1914–1916 (London, Allen & Unwin, 1986); B. Waites, A Class Society at War: England 1914–1918 (Leamington Spa, Berg, 1987); J.M. Winter, The Great War and the British People (London, Macmillan, 1986); D. Woodward, Lloyd George and the Generals (London and Toronto, Associated University Presses, 1983).

5. Plumer destroyed all his papers. Recent biographies of Byng and French are both excellent. J. Williams, Byng of Vimy: General and Governor-General (London, Leo Cooper at Secker & Warburg, 1983); R. Holmes, The Little Field Marshal: Sir John French (London, Jonathan Cape, 1981).

6. Especially, S. Bidwell and D. Graham, Fire-Power. British Army Weapons and Theories of War, 1904–1945 (London, Allen & Unwin, 1982) and T. Travers, The Killing Ground. The British Army, the Western Front and the Emergence of Modern Warfare 1900–1918 (London, Allen & Unwin, 1987). The collection of essays edited by Beckett and Simpson (see above, note 1) is also important.

my sons to visit it. His life was decent but mundane. He lived long enough to see most of his children into adulthood. I have my father's mature memories of him. But Jesse is a mystery. He left me only his swagger cane with its North Staffordshire Regiment crest – no photographs, no letters, none of his medals.[7] He died when my mother was six and disappeared from her life when she was two. She remembers little more about him than his waxed moustache and his military funeral, though her recall of my grandmother's memories of him has been entirely borne out by the surviving archival record.[8]

My grandfather was born in 1880 in the small North Staffordshire mining village of Brown Edge, on the road between Burslem and Leek. He was a collier from the time he left school. When the war broke out he was thirty-four and had a wife and five children, the youngest of whom, my Aunt Maud, was less than a month old. On 28 August 1914 Lord Kitchener raised the upper age limit for volunteers from thirty to thirty-five. Jesse enlisted the following day and became part of 'K2' – 'the second hundred thousand'. I cannot record this event without a sense of wonder and incomprehension. My grandfather's act was, by any standards, one of gross irresponsibility. And yet it is why I love him and treasure his memory.

For the first year of the war his service was little more than an extended camping holiday, a welcome respite after twenty years down the pit. He was stationed successively on Guernsey, with the Tyne Garrison, and on Cannock Chase. But in September 1915 reality intervened. He was sent to join the 7th North Staffords – a 'K1' battalion – who had been on Gallipoli since August. He remained with them for the rest of his war. After Gallipoli he fought in Mesopotamia and was present at the capture of Baghdad by General Maude in March 1917. In July 1918 he was invalided to India. He returned to England in September and was honourably discharged from the army on medical grounds at Whittington Barracks, Lichfield, on 19 October 1918. He died ten days later and was buried with full military honours in Burslem Municipal Cemetery on Armistice Day. His grave is maintained by the Commonwealth War Graves Commission. He was thirty-eight. He left my grandmother with five children, four of them girls, to scratch a living through the mean years of the Depression. She put her faith in hard work, self-help, the Independent Labour Party and a ferocious sense of family, which her grandson has inherited.

It was as an act of family piety, as an attempt to find out about my grandfather, that I first took an interest in the history of the Great War. By the age of sixteen I had exhausted the not inconsiderable resources of the City of Stoke-on-Trent Libraries Department. I found no lack of material to reinforce ingrained family prejudices about the purpose and conduct of the war. The British soldiers

---

7. My grandfather was awarded the 1914–15 Star, the British War Medal and the Victory Medal ('Pip, Squeak and Wilfred'). He did not live to receive any of them personally. The medals were lost in 1935. My mother succeeded in obtaining official replacements in 1986. I have also been able, thanks to the kind help of Lt. Col. Brian Hanley, to read his battalion's War Diary in the Staffordshire Regiment Museum at Whittington Barracks, Lichfield, where my grandfather began and ended his military career.

8. Service records of soldiers of the Great War are kept at the Ministry of Defence Records Office, Bourne Avenue, Hayes, Middlesex. They have suffered badly but some, including my grandfather's, have survived. A useful guide to documentary material relating to soldiers who served in the Great War is N.H. Holding, *World War I Army Ancestry* (Plymouth, Federation of Family History Societies, 1982). I should like to thank Miss Helen Berry for drawing this to my attention.

were 'lions led by donkeys'.[9] The war was either the result of miscalculation or of a wicked conspiracy. It solved nothing and sowed the seeds of another – and worse – war. Then came the publication, in 1963, of John Terraine's biography of Douglas Haig.[10] I expected this book to be a hatchet job and read it to gain more material for my family's world view. Despite deeply ingrained layers of prejudice against Haig, I found Terraine's arguments uncomfortably convincing. A visit to the battlefields in 1972 completed my conversion. To stand on the low hills round Ypres, on the eminence of Vimy Ridge above Arras and in the German front line trenches on the Somme was to gain for the first time a real understanding of the war and of the immense achievement of the British army in ejecting the Germans from their field fortress. I came away with the firm belief that there was more to the war than I had ever thought and that one day I would write a book about it. This is that book.

At the centre of any book on the Great War must be the British army and its massive and unprecedented demands on the whole of British life. From the British point of view the importance of the First World War lies in two things: it was the first time that Britain put a truly national army into the field (I remain unconvinced by arguments to the contrary); and it was the only time in which that army bore the principal share of the military burden (at least from mid-1916 onwards) against a major military and industrial power. Out of these fundamentals grew the military, political, social, economic and emotional impact of the war. It was the urgent need to create a modern, mass army in the face of a national tradition which was wholly unmilitary (even anti-military) and an industrial structure inferior to that of Germany which was the motive force behind the other changes. The army's struggles and failures and the massive casualties which it suffered give the war its drama and its haunting place in British memory. The military struggle cannot be relegated to 'noises off'. At the same time, to write a narrow military history would be to limit discussion of the war's true significance and importance: modern industrialized war is not merely a matter of military conflict, but of organization, planning and management, involving the whole of society and its political and economic resources.

The distinctive features of the book are therefore its attempt to discuss the military, the political, and the social and economic aspects of the war, and the primacy which it gives to the military struggle as the mechanism by which British government, politics, economic life and national values were changed. It is divided into three parts. The first deals with the military history of the war, the second with its politico-military conduct at the highest levels, and the third with its social, economic and emotional impact, particularly on the lives of ordinary people. The first footnote of each of the ten main chapters is designed to provide a guide to relevant further reading in lieu of a bibliography.

A work of synthesis depends greatly upon the research of others. I am grateful to the many scholars whose work I have read in the preparation of this book and whose ideas have informed my understanding of the Great War even when I have disagreed with them. Some may be dismayed by my views. I have tried

---

9. This phrase is usually attributed to General Max Hoffman (see A. Clark, *The Donkeys* (London, Hutchinson, 1961), endpapers), but seemingly without justification (see J. Terraine, *The Smoke and the Fire. Myths and Anti-Myths of War 1861–1945* (London, Sidgwick & Jackson, 1980), p. 171.
10. J. Terraine, *Douglas Haig. The Educated Soldier* (London, Hutchinson, 1963).

hard not to distort or misrepresent theirs. Responsibility for errors and omissions remains mine alone.

Many friends and colleagues have been generous in sharing with me their time and expertise. I wish to thank Vivian Allan, Dave Betts, Roger Bickle, Kate Brebner, Leslie Brierley, Bob Bushaway, Richard Dunk, Dani Gempton, Chris Grady, John Grenville, Eric Hopkins, Ian Houghton, Don Huffer, Martin Killeen, Jerzy Lukowski, Geoffrey Martin, Tony Nicholls, Richard Shackleton, Tom Shippey, Jack Simmons, Michael Stevenson, Michael Ursinus, Sally-Ann Vardy, Neil Werrett, Graham Winton, Chris Wreghitt and Alexander Zervoudakis. Over the years I have been privileged to discuss the war with some of its veterans. I should particularly like to thank George Allen MM (late Royal Warwicks, stretcher-bearer), George Burcombe (late Royal Field Artillery), William Henry Harper (late Cheshire Regiment (Bantams) and Machine Gun Corps), Harry Harrison (late Royal Field Artillery), the sixth Earl of Harrowby (late Royal Field Artillery) and Frank L.J. Vodrey (late Royal Engineers). Kate Brebner and Ian Houghton read the book in typescript and made helpful suggestions. Jerzy Lukowski submitted my prose to the kind of scrutiny that is possible only from a Classically-educated Pole born in Guildford. I am enormously grateful to him. My greatest thanks of all go to three people: Barbara, Peter and Tom. Without their love and understanding this book would never have been finished.

List of Illustrations

List of Maps

Prologue

The nations slithered over the brink into the boiling cauldron of
war without any trace of apprehension or dismay.

David Lloyd George[1]

The First World War had causes, but no objectives.

Correlli Barnett[2]

At the heart of all British perceptions of the First World War lie the casualties.
These were massive[3] and unprecedented in the British national experience. It
was the casualties which made it 'the Great War'. The sorrowful war cemeteries
dotted along the whole length of the old Western Front bear mute witness to
Churchill's judgement that 'the price of victory was bought so dear as to be
undistinguishable from defeat.'[4]

It was not only the size of the casualties, however, which contributed to the
retrospective[5] sense of 'futility'. It was the absence of any seemingly sane reason
to justify such a scale of human sacrifice. The war did not appear to be 'about
anything', or, at least, not about anything important. This was recognized even
during the course of the war itself. The cost of the military means eventually
inflated the political ends. A discredited diplomatic abstraction like 'the balance
of power' may have been enough to sustain the commitment of small,
mercenary armies, but the mass slaughter of citizen soldiers required something
more substantial. The war thus became 'a war to end all wars' and 'a war to
make the world safe for democracy'. Cynicism inevitably filled the gulf between
war-time rhetoric and post-war reality. And from this perspective the war
seemed at best a mistake, the result of bungling and miscalculation by 'small
men in great places', and at worst the result of a squalid diplomacy of secret
covenants secretly arrived at, behind which there stood the sinister shadow of
the armaments' manufacturers and international bankers. Not only had
millions died; they had also died in vain.

The gap between the human and material costs of the war and its apparent

1. D. Lloyd George, *War Memoirs* (2 vols., London, Odhams, [1938]), I, p. 32.
2. C. Barnett, *The Swordbearers. Studies in Supreme Command in the First World War*
   (Harmondsworth, Penguin, 1966), p. 35.
3. The most recent estimate of United Kingdom dead is 723,000. See J.M. Winter, *The Great War
   and the British People* (London, Macmillan, 1986), p. 74.
4. Quoted in J. Terraine, *The Western Front 1914–1918* (London, Hutchinson, 1964), p. 38.
5. Contemporary views were not necessarily the same. These are the subject of Chapter 10,
   below.

futility of purpose and achievement proved to be a powerful incentive to study of the origins of the war. Its causes remain one of the most intensively investigated subjects in modern history.[6] Much of the debate, inspired by the notorious 'war guilt' clause of the Treaty of Versailles, has been concerned with allotting blame for the war between the major protagonists. The balance of modern scholarship has firmly placed the responsibility where it was laid by the victors at Versailles – with the ambitions and fears of the governing élite of Imperial Germany.[7]

British policy has emerged relatively unscathed. Successive British foreign secretaries have been seen as 'high-minded champions of sanity and peace', struggling honourably to maintain the fabric of European diplomacy and civilization in the face of mounting odds. The only real criticism of British foreign policy is that it lacked clarity and that the studied ambiguity of the *entente* with France was an encouragement to German aggression.[8] But, ultimately, wherever the political and moral responsibility for the outbreak of the First World War rests, it was the British decision for war which was the most vital. British involvement turned a European war into a world war and made subsequent American intervention possible, with incalculable consequences for Europe and the world.

War is an act of state. Britain did not go to war in 1914 because of original sin or because of the destructive aggression of the male psyche. Few statesmen have been less personally aggressive than Sir Edward Grey. Few British Cabinets have been less warlike than that of Mr Asquith. Much less did Britain go to war because of popular demand. Neither was British intervention the result of a disinterested attachment to principles of natural justice and international law, although the incompetence and insensitivity of German policy allowed Britain 'the enormous advantage of being able to enter a war in the role of selfless guardian of European treaties'.[9] Nor was the decision forced on the government by a conspiracy of pro-French militarists at the War Office[10] or of anti-German

---

6.   The literature is immense. The best general account is probably J. Joll, *The Origins of the First World War* (London, Longman, 1983). For Britain, see Z.S. Steiner, *Britain and the Origins of the First World War* (London, Macmillan, 1977) and K.M. Wilson's brilliant *The Policy of the Entente: Essays on the Determinants of British Foreign Policy, 1904–1914* (Cambridge, Cambridge University Press, 1985). For a short and trenchant review of the literature, see F.R. Bridge, *1914: The Coming of the First World War* (London, Historical Association, 1983, revised 1985).

7.   See especially, V.R. Berghahn, *Germany and the Approach of War in 1914* (London, Macmillan, 1973); F. Fischer, *Germany's Aims in the First World War* (London, Chatto & Windus, 1967) and *The War of Illusions. German Policy from 1911 to 1914* (New York, Norton, 1975); I. Geiss, *July 1914. The Outbreak of the First World War. Selected Documents* (London, Batsford, 1967).

8.   J.A.S. Grenville, 'Foreign Policy and the Coming of War', in D. Read, ed., *Edwardian England* (London, Croom Helm, with the Historical Association, 1982), p. 164.

9.   G. Ritter, *The Schlieffen Plan* (London, Oswald Woolf, 1958), p. 88.

10.   This thesis can be seen at its most striking in Paul Johnson's splendid polemic *The Offshore Islanders* (Harmondsworth, Penguin, 1975), pp. 497–519. 'General Henry Wilson was at the centre of a web of intrigue which committed Britain, in 1914, to a vast land-war fought on behalf of French interests.' For an antidote, see K.M. Wilson, 'To the Western Front: British war plans and the "military entente" with France before the First World War', *British Journal of International Studies*, III (1977), pp. 151–68, and 'The British Cabinet's decision for war, 2 August 1914', *British Journal of International Studies*, I (1975), pp. 148–59; also, T. Wilson, 'Britain's "moral commitment" to France in August 1914', *History*, LXIV (1979), pp. 380–90.

diplomats at the Foreign Office.[11] Most important of all, perhaps, the war was not the inevitable result of fundamental and irreconcilable differences between Britain and Germany.[12]

Britain went to war on 4 August 1914 because the Cabinet decided that it must. This was a political decision taken by politicians. It was made with distaste, even with trepidation, for reasons which seemed clear and compelling at the time – the defence of British 'interests'. Failure to defend these interests would result in shattering consequences for national morale and prestige and for the safety and prosperity of the Empire. What British interests were and why they were threatened by a German victory in Europe lie at the heart of British entry into the First World War.

Britain, by 1914, was the greatest imperial power the world had ever seen. The years after 1880 had witnessed massive extensions of territorial control in Africa and the Pacific. The Empire was commonly regarded not only as a reflection of Britain's power and influence in the world but also as a cause of that power and influence. It was therefore seen as central to British interests. Few were prepared to dispute this. Many more looked to greater Imperial unity and a more systematic exploitation of Imperial economic resources as the surest guarantee of British security and prosperity in an increasingly competitive world.

In reality, the Empire was a shambles, without common institutions, common language, common culture, common religion or common purpose. Its 'citizens' ranged from the hardy and independent farmers of the Queensland outback and the Canadian prairies to the stone-age tribesmen of the highlands of New Guinea and the Kalahari Desert. This ramshackle edifice was held together principally by the Royal Navy and its maintenance of maritime supremacy. The only significant Imperial military reserve was the British-officered Indian Army. The British army was tiny by European standards and was mainly deployed in small dispersed units as a colonial police force. 'We are attempting to maintain the largest Empire the world has ever seen with armaments and reserves that would be insufficient for a third-class power', wrote the War Office official, Sir Henry Brackenbury, in 1899.[13] Large parts of the Empire were not only undefended but also indefensible.[14] This was apparent to some from the early 1890s. Lord Salisbury, most lucid and realistic of modern British statesmen, acknowledged it in his 'Mediterranean Agreements' with Italy and the abandonment of the Straits in 1895, which began the era of prudent Imperial retreat. The bitter experiences of the Boer War forcibly impressed the awareness of this need even on less perceptive minds.

The impact of the Boer War on British strategy and diplomacy was little short of revolutionary. The war had demonstrated the bankruptcy of the Empire's military arrangements. Under the inspiration of Balfour, Esher and Haldane, there followed fundamental reforms in the recruitment, education, training,

11. See Steiner, *Britain and the Origins of the First World War*, Chapter 8.
12. For the most comprehensive analysis of Anglo-German hostility, see P.M. Kennedy, *The Rise of the Anglo-German Antagonism, 1860–1914* (London, Allen & Unwin, 1980).
13. Quoted in J. McDermott, 'The revolution in British military thinking from the Boer War to the Moroccan Crisis', in P.M. Kennedy, ed., *The War Plans of the Great Powers* (London, Allen & Unwin, 1979), p. 101.
14. For an idea of the difficulties, see Lord Hankey, *The Supreme Command* (2 vols., London, Allen & Unwin, 1961), I, pp. 30–9.

equipment, conditions of service, tactical doctrine and management of the British army, with important consequences for its ability to undertake large-scale operations against modern military powers.[15]

Diplomatic changes were even more profound. The Boer War had strikingly exposed the Empire's vulnerability and given full rein to the jealousy which it inspired. There seemed to be only two ways to remedy the problem: by increasing the Empire's military resources or by limiting its liabilities. The first would require higher taxation and conscription at home and the greater military participation of the white Dominions abroad. Higher taxation was unpalatable and conscription virtually politically impossible, especially to the post-1905 Liberal governments, despite the crusading zeal of Lord Roberts and the National Service League.[16] Though there were fine words and good intentions on both sides, increased Imperial military co-operation got little further than the entirely nominal designation of an *Imperial* General Staff in 1907. The Empire remained a drain on Britain's military and naval resources. Imperial liabilities would therefore have to be limited. In practice, this meant finding mutually acceptable compromises with the Empire's potential enemies.

The search for an acceptable diplomatic solution to the Imperial dilemma was begun by the Conservative Foreign Secretary Lord Lansdowne. The Hay–Pauncefote Treaty with the United States in 1901 effectively abandoned the Western hemisphere to the Americans. It was a recognition by Britain that military conflict with the United States could not be contemplated and would result in national disaster. The second step, the Anglo-Japanese Alliance of 1902, was much more significant and dramatic, seeming to abandon the hallowed nineteenth-century traditions of 'splendid isolation' and the avoidance of 'entangling alliances'.

The Anglo-Japanese Alliance provided for British neutrality in a war between Russia and Japan and for British support for Japan in a war between Russia and Japan in which Russia was joined by another European power. Britain undoubtedly did well out of this arrangement. It greatly simplified naval strategy and allowed the concentration of naval resources in home waters. (The Australian and New Zealand soldiers were escorted across the Indian Ocean on their way to Egypt in 1914 by Japanese warships.) It gave Britain a counter to Russian ambitions in Asia and the far east. And it removed the threat of Japanese hostility to the British empire, the consequences of which were so vividly demonstrated a generation later with the ignominious collapse of British power in the far east in the face of the small, but superbly led, Japanese armies. For all that, the Alliance was a cynical agreement which made a far eastern war much more likely and contributed greatly to the long-term destabilization of the area. It was indicative of the anxiety of the British government to purchase a period of Imperial quiet even at the risk of a Russo-Japanese war.

Russia's only potential European ally in a war with Japan appeared to be France. France was also one of Britain's greatest Imperial rivals, especially in Africa. Relations between the two countries had not been good and occasionally threatened to break out into armed conflict. The advantages to Britain of a

15. For these developments, see E.M. Spiers, *The Army and Society, 1815–1914* (London, Longman, 1980), pp. 265–84.
16. Only three Liberal MPs were among the 105 Members of Parliament who allowed the journal of the National Service League to reveal their support for it, see Wilson, *Policy of the Entente*, p. 54.

diplomatic *rapprochement* with France were readily apparent. France, hostile to German ambitions in Europe but fearful of German power, was also anxious for increased diplomatic support. The result was the Anglo-French Entente of 1904.

The Entente was concerned solely with outstanding colonial issues of mutual concern, some of which now appear remarkably trivial.[17] The most important agreement was that which dealt with respective spheres of interest in Egypt and Morocco. The Entente was made without consideration for the European balance of power. It was certainly not intended by Britain to be anti-German. It was another significant step in Britain's determination to lessen the potential for Imperial conflict, which it was desirous above all to avoid. French policy was not so innocent. The price demanded of Britain was much more than acquiescence in French influence in Morocco. It was the diplomatic isolation of Germany. The Germans, themselves, made this situation much worse by their arrogant conduct over the Moroccan crises of 1905 and 1911, which brought France and Britain much closer together and led to the settling of the practical arrangements for military co-operation in a war with Germany.[18]

There remained the problem of India. India was at the heart of the British Empire and of British Imperial concerns. The greatest threat to India was posed by Russia. Contemplation of Russia as an Imperial enemy gave the recently-founded Committee of Imperial Defence nightmares. Defence of the North-West Frontier posed insuperable problems of 'distance, terrain, supply and . . . manpower'.[19] The army was very far from sanguine about its ability to defend India successfully against a Russian invasion without either conscription or a German alliance.[20] As neither of these seemed to be remotely possible, the army began to contemplate the advantages of a continental strategy and a *rapprochement* with Russia at the price of British support for Russia and France in a war with Germany. The frontiers of India would be more effectually defended on the banks of the Meuse than at the Khyber Pass.

The Liberal Foreign Secretary, Sir Edward Grey, showed equal concern with the fate of India and the threat of Russia.[21] Only diplomacy could provide India with the margin of safety which her armies could not achieve. Russia's defeat by Japan in 1905 removed any immediate threat and gave Grey his opportunity to extract from Russia a favourable understanding on matters of mutual imperial concern. The Anglo-Russian Convention of 1907 was solely designed to lessen the potential for imperial conflict between Britain and Russia in Asia.[22] Such an agreement had been a fundamental aim of British policy since the 1890s.[23] The

17. For the development of political and military relations between Britain and France, see S.R. Williamson Jr., *The Politics of Grand Strategy: Britain and France Prepare for War, 1904–1914* (Cambridge, Mass., Harvard University Press, 1969). The best account of French foreign policy during the crucial period of the *entente* is C.M. Andrew, *Théophile Delcassé and the Making of the Entente Cordiale* (London, Macmillan, 1968).
18. The agreements which constituted the Entente (and also the Anglo-Russian Convention of 1907) are reprinted in M.C. Hurst, *Key Treaties for the Great Powers, 1814–1914* (2 vols., Newton Abbot, David & Charles, 1972), II, pp. 756–65, 805–9.
19. McDermott, 'British military thinking', p. 108.
20. *ibid.*
21. The best account of Grey's career is K. Robbins, *Sir Edward Grey. A Biography of Lord Grey of Fallodon* (London, Cassell, 1971).
22. See B.J. Williams, 'The strategic background to the Anglo-Russian Entente of August 1907', *Historical Journal*, IX (1966), pp. 360–73.
23. Wilson, *Policy of the Entente*, p. 71.

revival of Russian power and Russian activities in Persia aroused new British fears and determined the Foreign Secretary to maintain good relations with Russia at all costs.[24] The Convention was not aimed at Germany, or at anyone else. There was never a 'Triple Entente' between Britain, France and Russia designed to encircle Germany. At the heart of British interests was the security of the Empire. It had become increasingly clear that the nation's imperial interests could only be defended by coming to a mutual understanding with the Empire's most serious potential enemies. Those potential enemies were France and Russia – not Germany. But, ultimately, the price of Russian and French understanding was bought at the cost of a deterioration in Anglo-German relations, a deterioration which the Germans did little or nothing to arrest and much to advance.[25]

An Anglo-German alliance was not without influential supporters. Joseph Chamberlain and Lloyd George had both, at various times, advocated its merits. But the courtship proved difficult and wearing and seemed doomed to frustration. The failure to arrange a match was accompanied by much recrimination, misunderstanding and pettiness, in which the tortured personality of the Kaiser played a not insignificant part. The real reason for the failure, however, lay not in mutual hostility but in mutual incompatibility.[26] Britain wished, above all, to secure her Empire without increasing her military resources. The main threat to the Empire came from France and Russia. Germany was certainly not going to fight a war in Europe against France and Russia for the sake of maintaining the British Empire. Germany feared a two-front war with France and Russia. The tiny British army could do nothing significant to redress the military balance in Europe. As the Kaiser observed, the only balance was his 'thirty army corps'. Germany had little of practical value to offer Britain in her imperial dilemma and asked little of Britain except that she look the other way and leave the continental giants to their own affairs. The two countries thus drifted apart and into conflict.

The diplomatic crisis of July 1914, which followed the assassination of Archduke Franz Ferdinand on 28 June, posed grave problems for Sir Edward Grey. Britain had no desire to go to war with Germany. She had little to fear from her directly. The much-vaunted Anglo-German naval race was over by 1912. Britain had won, and both sides knew it.[27] Germany was a major trading partner as well as a major trading rival. Many Britons professed distaste for German militarism and for the swaggering conceit of the Kaiser, but the world was full of unpleasant and unsatisfactory régimes and this was not a reason for going to war. Britain, however, could not afford the luxury of neutrality. At the Foreign Office, the ever-percipient anti-German Eyre Crowe analysed the problem. 'Should this war come and England stand aside,' he wrote, 'one of two things must happen: Either Germany and Austria win, crush France and humiliate Russia . . . [Then] what will be the position of friendless England? Or France and Russia win. What would then be their attitude towards England? What about India and the Mediterranean?'[28] The threat to the Empire was now

24. Grenville, 'Foreign Policy', pp. 176–7.
25. Wilson, *Policy of the Entente*, p. 98.
26. Steiner, *Britain and the Origins of the First World War*, p. 243.
27. M. Howard, 'The Edwardian Arms Race', in Read, ed., *Edwardian England*, p. 160.
28. Quoted in Wilson, *Policy of the Entente*, pp. 79–80.

in Europe. The signs from Russia were not encouraging. The day before Crowe's minute, on 24 July 1914, the British Ambassador in St Petersburg had warned 'If we fail [Russia] now we cannot hope to maintain that friendly co-operation with her in Asia that is of such vital importance to us.'[29]

Britain's best interests lay in a peaceful resolution of the Balkans Crisis, and Grey made strenuous efforts towards this end. As it became clear that these efforts would be unavailing, Britain had nowhere to go. The reality of the situation was not lost on the Foreign Secretary. After the fateful decision was taken, he summarized the reasons for going to war. 'If we did not stand by France and stand up for Belgium against this aggression, we should be isolated, discredited and hated; and there would be before us nothing but a miserable and ignoble future.'[30]

By August 1914 the 'policy of the *entente*', the pursuit of colonial bargains to preserve the British Empire on the cheap, had brought Britain to the very brink of war. All room for manoeuvre had gone. For those senior members of the Cabinet most closely associated with the conduct of foreign policy, a choice between war and peace existed only in theory. The real question was not whether Britain went to war, but whether she went to war under a Liberal government or under a coalition.[31] To men who were party politicians as well as statesmen, this was an important matter.

A British decision to enter a European war was unlikely to meet with universal approbation in the Liberal party. The party had a strong radical wing, which was non-interventionist, even pacifist. There was significant pacifist sentiment in the Cabinet. A few Liberal Members were outspoken sympathizers of Germany; many more were hostile to Russia. A declaration of war was inseparable from the reputation and future of Liberalism. There was a genuine danger of dividing the Cabinet, the party and the country, and this in turn would have had grave, possibly disastrous, consequences for the successful conduct of military operations. Asquith and those of his Cabinet colleagues who were fully convinced that Britain could not afford to flinch from a declaration of war were saved by the German Army.

German violation of Belgian neutrality allowed Sir Edward Grey to cloak British foreign policy in an aura of moral respectability and traditional strategic concern for the independence and integrity of the Low Countries. In a masterly speech to the House of Commons on 3 August 1914, Grey, with a skill which made him appear almost guileless, rallied parliamentary and public opinion behind the ultimatum to Germany to respect Belgian neutrality. British policy was portrayed as a principled stand against unprovoked German aggression in defence of international obligations and the rights of small nations.[32] For those waverers who prefered their politics without humbug, like the Little Englander Colonial Secretary, Lewis Harcourt, there was also sufficient talk of British 'interests' and of the vital importance of preventing German possession of Belgium and the entry of a German fleet into the English Channel.[33] Britain could go to war for France and appear to do so for Belgium. It was, of course,

29. Quoted in Bridge, *1914*, p. 23.
30. Quoted in Steiner, *Britain and the Origins of the First World War*, p. 245.
31. Bridge, *1914*, p. 39.
32. 5 *Hansard*, LXV, 1809–1827.
33. For Harcourt's view of the *casus belli*, see C. Hazlehurst, *Politicians at War, July 1914 to May 1915. A Prologue to the Triumph of Lloyd George* (London, Jonathan Cape, 1971), p. 114.

sophistry, but crucial sophistry none the less. British policy may have hit the buffers, but neither the nation nor the Liberal party had been derailed.

The principal political beneficiary of the German violation of Belgian neutrality was David Lloyd George. Lloyd George was in a difficult position. He was the leading radical in the Cabinet and heir apparent to Asquith. He had made his reputation by his courageous opposition to the Boer War. He had been a leading champion of closer co-operation with Germany. But he had become increasingly suspicious of German policy and hostile to German intentions. His speech at the Mansion House on 21 July 1911, at the height of the Second Moroccan Crisis, had sent an unambiguous signal to the German government of British determination to support the French position even at the risk of war. This had been a landmark not only in Lloyd George's attitude to foreign affairs but also in the general orientation of British foreign policy. The march of the German armies through Belgium let Lloyd George off the hook. He could follow the Cabinet line with a clear conscience, without apparent repudiation of pro-claimed political principles and without alienating his radical constituency. Denied his leadership, the Liberal party's irreconcilable opponents of British belligerency proved incapable of effective concerted action.[34] Only three (relatively unimportant) members of the Cabinet resigned. The Liberal party and the nation could go to war united.

Few members of the Cabinet, if any, thought they were committing the British people to a total war of attrition. Grey, in particular, was prone to sonorous predictions of the doom of industrial civilization, but he was massively and culpably ignorant of military realities.[35] Britain had sent expeditionary forces to the continent before. There was nothing new in that. It was not expected that Britain's military role would be great. Grey certainly expected it to be primarily naval. It took the dramatic eruption on to the domestic political scene of Lord Kitchener to disabuse the politicians of these comforting illusions. The Empire, which had been acquired in 'a fit of absence of mind', run on the cheap, and sustained by a now-bankrupt diplomacy, was soon to extract a price from the British people which was almost beyond imagining.[36]

At 11 p.m. on 4 August 1914 the British ultimatum to Germany expired. At the Admiralty, with strains of 'God Save the King' drifting down from the Mall and through the open windows on the warm summer air, Winston Churchill despatched telegrams to the Fleet, already at its battle stations. 'Commence hostilities with Germany.' Within a few days a British army would set foot on the continent of Europe for the first time in almost a hundred years, and for the first time as the friend of France. It had begun.

34. For the party political manoeuvrings and Lloyd George's rôle in them, see Hazlehurst, *Politicians at War, passim*.
35. He was not alone in this. Correlli Barnett has accused statesmen of all the combatant nations of believing that the war 'would be a matter of six weeks' autumn manoeuvres with live ammunition', see *The Swordbearers*, p. 29.
36. Grey did not grasp this. His speech to the House contains the phrase 'if we are engaged in war, we shall suffer but little more than we shall suffer even if we stand aside'. Characteristically for a Victorian Liberal, his fears were primarily for trade.

PART I

'One Great and Continuous
Engagement':
A Military History of the Great War

1

'The Manoeuvre for Position' 1914[1]

'We'll do it! What is it?'

Motto of the BEF[2]

'. . . this German Army is a superb fighting maching.'

Major-General Henry Wilson[3]

The epic battles of 1914 were the product of a century of social, economic and political change, which had accelerated with increasing rapidity during the forty years after 1870. If the scale of the war was to be unprecedented, this was not least because Europe itself was more populous, more materially powerful and more coherently organized than ever before. The massive and sustained rise in

1. For the military history of 1914, see British Official History (henceforth *OH*), *Military Operations France and Belgium 1914* (2 vols., London, Macmillan, 1925). These volumes were compiled by the Official Historian, Brigadier-General Sir James Edmonds. For the status and reliability of the Official History, see J. Luvaas, 'The first British official historians', in *The Education of an Army* (London, Cassell, 1965). This question is also treated by D. French, ' "Official but not History"? Sir James Edmonds and the Official History of the Great War', *Journal of the Royal United Services Institute for Defence Studies*, CXXXI (1986), pp.58–63. Secondary studies include: D. Ascoli, *The Mons Star: the British Expeditionary Force 5 August–22 November 1914* (London, Harrap, 1982); K. Caffrey, *Farewell Leicester Square: the Old Contemptibles 12 August–19 November 1914* (London, André Deutsch, 1980); T. Carew, *The Vanished Army* (London, William Kimber, 1964) and *Wipers: the First Battle of Ypres* (London, Hamish Hamilton, 1974); A. Farrar-Hockley, *The Retreat to Victory* (London, Batsford, 1960); E. Owen, *1914: Glory Departing* (London, Buchan & Enright, 1986). Accounts written by participants are plentiful. French's memoirs, *1914* (London, Constable, 1919), are thoroughly untrustworthy, but nevertheless revealing. For Haig, see his *Private Papers* ed. R.N.W. Blake (London, Eyre & Spottiswoode, 1952). Wilson's official biographer, Sir Charles Callwell, quotes uninhibitedly from Wilson's pungent diary, *Field-Marshal Sir Henry Wilson, His Life and Diaries* (2 vols., London, Cassell, 1927). E.L. Spears's account of his rôle in *Liaison 1914* (London, Heinemann, 1930) is a brilliantly written epic. For the worm's-eye-view, see Lieutenant-General Sir T. Bridges, *Alarms and Excursions* (London, Longman, 1938); A. Corbett-Smith, *The Retreat from Mons* (London, Cassell, 1917); J.M. Craster, ed., *'Fifteen Rounds a Minute': the Grenadiers at War August to December 1914* (London, Macmillan, 1976) is moving as well as important; F. Hawkings, *From Ypres to Cambrai* (Morley, Elmfield Press, 1974); J.L. Jack, *General Jack's Diary* ed. J. Terraine (London, Eyre & Spottiswoode, 1964); F. Richards' classic *Old Soldiers Never Die* (London, Faber & Faber, 1933); and H.A. Stewart, *From Mons to Loos. Being the Diary of a Supply Officer* (Edinburgh & London, Blackwood, 1916).
2. Major Tom Bridges (4th Dragoon Guards), quoted in Caffrey, *Farewell Leicester Square*, p. 44.
3. Callwell, *Wilson*, I, p. 185.

European population,[4] and the more efficient use of labour through the mechanization of agriculture and industry, left a 'surplus' of young adult males for military service. The revolution in food production made it possible for the first time to sustain mass armies in the field indefinitely. Railways permitted the rapid movement of millions of soldiers and their supplies; and the electric telegraph provided a rudimentary instrument of command and control.[5] First the breech-loading (1871) and then the magazine-loading (1884) rifle, the belt-fed machine gun (1884) and the quick-firing rifled cannon (1891) transformed the rapidity, range, accuracy and lethality of military fire power and ensured that in any future war scientists and engineers would be as important as soldiers. The irrational but potent force of nationalism gave increased political authority and moral legitimacy to the State and allowed it to make far greater demands upon its citizens than anyone had previously imagined.

The winds of change blew only fitfully over Great Britain. Her burgeoning population, crammed into the neat terraced streets of the industrial towns, resulted in no improvement in her military resources. Between 1870 and 1914 France, with a smaller population than Britain, increased the number of men under arms from less than 500,000 to an incredible 3,200,000. In August 1914 Britain was able immediately to put into the field a mere 80,000 men. The application of science to industry in the last third of the nineteenth century, 'the second industrial revolution', had found British industry wanting and unable to sustain the technological and economic supremacy of the great mid-Victorian heyday.[6] This left her with an industrial structure in many respects markedly inferior to that of Germany and for which there was a high price to pay once the war began. Patriotism, a sense of community, a self-disciplined obedience to law and convention there was in abundance, but the cutting edge of nationalism was absent, except in Ireland where it was as great a cause for concern as the war itself. The concept of the State in Britain remained ambivalent and ambiguous, its power constrained by a political tradition which was liberal, utilitarian and individualist.[7] The capacity of the British State to demand sacrifices for the greater good was untested; the willingness of the subjects of the Crown to abandon their inveterate and appealing imperviousness to political grandiosity unknown.

These gloomy forebodings found no echo in Britain's small professional military forces. Among the officers and men of the Royal Navy and the British Expeditionary Force, there was only certainty – in their equipment, their moral and racial superiority and their cause. As one soldier confidently exclaimed shortly before his disembarkation at Le Havre, 'We'll soon give them f——Belgiums what for!'

4. M. Van Creveld, *Supplying War. Logistics from Wallenstein to Patton* (Cambridge, Cambridge University Press, 1977), p. 109.
5. M. Van Creveld, *Command in War* (Cambridge, Mass., Harvard University Press, 1985), p. 152.
6. For this, see M.W. Kirby, *The Decline of British Economic Power Since 1870* (London, Allen & Unwin, 1981) and A.L. Levine, *Industrial Retardation in Britain 1880–1914* (London, Weidenfeld & Nicolson, 1967).
7. For this, see R. Currie, *Industrial Politics* (London, Oxford University Press, 1979), especially p. 19.

Plans

The Great War was thoroughly planned. The German Army had a plan, perhaps the most famous plan in military history since the Trojan Horse.[8] The French Army had lots of plans, but had finally settled on Plan XVII.[9] Even the British army[10] had a plan. The Royal Navy pretended to have a plan. The British government had no plan at all, but thought it prudent to adopt one. The plan which the government adopted was that of the British army. This has been the cause of much dispute and recrimination and many have seen in it the seeds of all future disasters.

The British army's plan was a simple one. It was to mobilize the British Expeditionary Force with the utmost rapidity upon the declaration of war and to assemble it on the left flank of the French armies in the neighbourhood of Maubeuge, near the Belgian border, thirteen miles south of Mons. The BEF was to conform to the movements of the French Army in its violent assault on the invading Germans, the focus of which was to be many miles to the south in Lorraine. The reasoning behind this plan was less simple.

The essence of British military planning in the years before the Great War was to find an effective role for the small British Expeditionary Force of six infantry divisions and a cavalry division. The British Expeditionary Force was one of the principal achievements of the great reforming war ministry of R.B. Haldane.[11] The expeditionary force was deliberately created to give the British government the capacity to intervene militarily in a continental war. It was maintained at a level of war-readiness unusual in British military history and detailed plans for its mobilization laid down in the years after 1908. The expeditionary force's size, however, bore no relationship to its intended role in a continental war between armies numbered in millions.[12] The size of the force was principally determined by the military needs of the Empire. The BEF was simply the largest formation that could be made out of the units left at home after the demands of Imperial policing had been met.

The military reasoning for placing the BEF on the left flank of the French armies in France was severely Clausewitzian in its logic. The British army would be 'the decisive force, at the decisive place, at the decisive time'.[13] This belief was based upon General Henry Wilson's calculations of the number of divisions which France and Germany would put into the field and of the space which each would occupy along the likely battle front from Verdun to Maubeuge.[14] The six British infantry divisions would extend the shorter French line (calculated at 37 to 39 divisions) beyond that of the Germans (calculated at 40 divisions), making

8. See G. Ritter, *The Schlieffen Plan* (London, Oswald Woolf, 1958).
9. The best account of the politics behind the acceptance of Plan XVII is D. Porch, *The March to the Marne: the French Army 1871–1914* (Cambridge, Cambridge University Press, 1981).
10. The extent to which the British forces were an army rather than an Army will be discussed below, especially in Chapter 7.
11. For Haldane, see E.M. Spiers, *Haldane: an Army Reformer* (Edinburgh, Edinburgh University Press, 1980).
12. S.R. Williamson Jr, *The Politics of Grand Strategy. Britain and France Prepare for War 1904–1914* (Cambridge, Mass., Harvard University Press, 1970), p. 100.
13. See Wilson's paper 'Appreciation of the Political and Military Situation in Europe', reprinted in C. Hazlehurst, *Politicians at War July 1914 to May 1915* (London, Jonathan Cape, 1971), pp. 307–20, and especially p. 319.
14. K.M. Wilson, *The Policy of the Entente: Essays on the Determinants of British Foreign Policy 1904–1914* (Cambridge, Cambridge University Press, 1985), p. 62.

it difficult, if not impossible, for the Germans to outflank the French position and affording decisive security for the French Army during its advance into Lorraine.

Wilson's original calculations were made in 1911. By 1912 he *appeared* to have changed his mind. In a gloss to his 'Appreciation of the Political and Military Situation in Europe', he observed that 'This paper was written in September 1911 since when the position of affairs on the Continent has altered considerably, and it can no longer be claimed that our 6 Divisions will make the numbers decisive.'[15] But, later, this did not prevent him from railing against the Liberal government's cowardice and incompetence in failing to send all six infantry divisions to the front immediately upon the outbreak of war. 'If the Cabinet had sent 6 divisions instead of 4,' he wrote in his diary after the Battle of Mons, 'this retreat would have been an advance and defeat would have been a victory.'[16] This remark must set a record for fatuousness even by Wilson's own high standards. His private fear that six divisions were 'fifty too few' to take to a continental war was nearer the mark.[17] Whatever his doubts, however, they did not cause him to alter his plans or his advice to the government. A belief in the decisiveness of Britain's military contribution remained the driving force behind Wilson's thinking; and Wilson remained the driving force behind the formulation and implementation of British military strategy. By August 1914 the ultimate test of his strategy and his planning was at hand. The final decision lay with the government.

On 5 August 1914 the Prime Minister, Mr Asquith, called one of the most remarkable meetings in British constitutional history. The meeting began at 4 p.m. in the Cabinet Room at No. 10 Downing Street. But it was not a Cabinet meeting. Some of those who attended were members of the Committee of Imperial Defence, founded in 1902 by A.J. Balfour and charged with responsibility for co-ordinating British defence policy and planning.[18] But it was not a meeting of the Committee of Imperial Defence. The personnel invited were predominantly military.[19] Asquith had gathered round him almost everyone with relevant strategic expertise and an opinion on the appropriate use of British military resources. It was a council of war. The purpose of this extraordinary gathering was to decide what to do next.

The shambolic discussions of this body bordered on the comic.[20] Henry Wilson, in an uncharacteristic fit of charity, described it as 'An historic meeting

15. The gloss was added on 17 October 1912. The annotated copy was that given to the Secretary of State for War, Colonel J.E.B. Seely.
16. Callwell, *Wilson*, I, p. 167.
17. Wilson, *Policy of the Entente*, p. 63. Haig commanded 59 divisions during the Battle of the Hundred Days in the second half of 1918.
18. See N. D'Ombrain, *War Machinery and High Policy: Defence Administration in Peacetime Britain 1902–1914* (London, Oxford University Press, 1973). Also, J.P. Mackintosh, 'The role of the Committee of Imperial Defence before 1914', *English Historical Review*, LXXVII (1962), pp. 490–503.
19. Those who attended the meeting were Asquith, Grey, Churchill, Haldane, Lord Kitchener, Prince Louis of Battenburg, Sir John French, Sir Ian Hamilton, Sir John Cowans, Sir Stanley von Donop, Sir Douglas Haig, Sir James Grierson, Sir Archibald Murray, Colonel Maurice Hankey, Colonel St G. Gordon, and Henry Wilson.
20. There are numerous accounts: Lord Grey of Fallodon, *Twenty-Five Years* (2 vols., London, Hodder & Stoughton, 1925), II, pp. 62–7; Churchill, *The World Crisis 1911–1918* abridged and revised edition (London, Thornton Butterworth, 1931), pp. 137–8; French, *1914*, pp. 3–5; Haig, *Private Papers*, pp. 68–9; Callwell, *Wilson*, I, pp. 158–9.

of men, mostly entirely ignorant of their subject'.[21] The decision which they eventually took, however, was of undoubted importance. It was to send the British Expeditionary Force to France to fight on the left flank of the French armies and to conform with their movements.[22]

This decision was not forced on the government by logistical inevitability. There was no surrender to the tyranny of the timetable. Wilson himself spoke of the 'flexibility of the French railway system for switching'.[23] Alternative plans were available.[24] Military considerations were secondary; political considerations were paramount. The chief constraint on British freedom of action was not the planning (or the scheming) of the General Staff, but the political imperatives arising out of the *entente* with France. These imperatives were reinforced by the balance of informed military opinion which held that the left flank of the French armies in France was not only the best place for the expeditionary force to be sent but also the only safe place. Sir Douglas Haig was horrified by Sir John French's 'reckless' suggestion that the British army could operate 'with advantage' against the flank of the 'powerful and still intact' German armies in Belgium and saw it as further evidence of his superior's unfittedness for supreme command in modern war.[25] Henry Wilson's carefully designed plans for mobilization were allowed to proceed.[26] The British army began its march 'to the Western Front'.

Mobilization

Eighteen months after the outbreak of war, Colonel Maurice Hankey, indefatigable Secretary of the Committee of Imperial Defence, found himself among a church congregation being collectively harangued by the preacher for the country's decadent lack of preparedness.[27] As one of those principally responsible for British preparations, Hankey was not amused. He knew the truth. And the truth was very different. 'Altogether,' concluded the Official Historian Sir James Edmonds, in a famous judgement, 'Britain never yet entered upon any war with anything approaching such forwardness and forethought in the preparation of the scanty military resources at the disposal of the War Office.'[28]

Britain's preparations for war were manifold. The creation of the Committee of Imperial Defence (1902) and of a General Staff (1904)[29] provided Britain with

21. Callwell, *Wilson*, I, p. 159.
22. The decision taken at the Council of War was subject to re-discussion and ratification by the Cabinet the following day (6 August).
23. Callwell, *Wilson*, I, p. 158.
24. See K.M. Wilson, 'To the Western Front: British war plans and the "military entente" with France before the First World War', *British Journal of International Studies*, III (1977), pp. 151–68.
25. Haig, *Private Papers*, pp. 68–9, 70.
26. With the exception that two of the six infantry divisions were retained at home, partly through fears of a German invasion, partly because of the situation in Ireland, and partly because of concern about the possibility of domestic disorder. They were soon released, the 4th Division reaching Le Cateau on 24 August, and the 6th reaching the Aisne on 16 September. They formed III Corps (Major-General W.P. Pulteney).
27. Lord Hankey, *The Supreme Command* (2 vols., London, George Allen & Unwin, 1961), I, pp. 174–5.
28. *OH 1914*, I, p. 18. For Hankey's view of British preparedness, see *Supreme Command*, I, pp. 136–50.
29. See J. Gooch, *The Plans of War: the General Staff and British Military Strategy 1900–1916* (London, Routledge & Kegan Paul, 1974).

a potentially effective machinery of defence planning for the first time in her history. At the Admiralty, Lord Fisher rode roughshod over ancient sensibilities and dragged the Royal Navy unwillingly into the twentieth century. The experience of the South African War and the recommendations of the committees of inquiry chaired by Lord Esher resulted in thoroughgoing reforms of the army.[30] Haldane's tenure of the War Office (1905–12) saw the creation of the Territorial Army, the Officers' Training Corps and the British Expeditionary Force. The passage of the Official Secrets Act (1911) and the formation of MI-5 and MI-6 laid the foundations of the modern British 'intelligence community'.[31] Above all, the actions of the government and the army were made the subject of detailed, coherent and specific planning.

The mobilization of the machinery of state was ordered and co-ordinated by the War Book, drawn up in the aftermath of the Second Moroccan Crisis of 1911 ('Agadir'). Credit for this has generally been awarded to Maurice Hankey, but the work of detailed planning and preparation belonged principally to Major Adrian Grant Duff of the Committee of Imperial Defence.[32] Each government department had a chapter in the War Book which gave full details of the actions which it was to take in the event of war, together with a summary of the 'corresponding and simultaneous' action to be taken by other departments. These actions were sub-divided into a 'Precautionary' and a 'War' stage. Large departments also had an 'Internal War Book' which assigned responsibility for each detail to its various sections.[33] By August 1914 the War Book was in a state of readiness and had become, in Hankey's words, the ' "Watch and Station Bill" of the British Empire'.[34]

At the War Office preparations were equally well advanced. They were the principal achievement of the Director of Military Operations, Major-General Henry Wilson. Wilson had four major tasks: to assemble at their base depots throughout the United Kingdom the constituent elements of the expeditionary force together with their arms and equipment and the reservists from civilian life necessary to bring battalions and regiments up to war strength; to move them by rail to Southampton, the principal port of embarkation; to carry them safely over the Channel to Boulogne and Le Havre; and to move them again by train and road to their place of deployment in France. All this was to be accomplished at maximum speed for fear that the decisive force at the decisive place would otherwise be too late to affect the result of the fighting with possibly disastrous results for France and for the alliance.

The first stage required the storage of large amounts of arms, equipment, wagons and ammunition to await the emergency for which they were designed. Thousands of telegrams recalling army reservists to the colours had to be prepared and despatched. This necessitated the involvement of every major post office in the country. The movement of units in stage two was a massive exercise in logistics, made possible only by the co-operation of the civilian railway companies and their staff. The transfer of enormous numbers of men, equipment and animals across the Channel needed large numbers of merchant

30. For Esher, see P. Fraser, *Lord Esher: a Political Biography* (London, Hart-Davis, 1973).
31. See D. French , 'Spy-fever in Britain, 1900–15', *Historical Journal*, XXI (1978), pp. 355–70.
32. See Sheila Sokolov Grant, 'The Origins of the War Book', *Journal of the Royal United Services Institute for Defence Studies*, CXVII (1972), pp. 65–9.
33. Hankey, *Supreme Command*, I, pp. 118–23.
34. *op. cit.*, I, p. 123.

ships 'taken up from trade' and the vital (though grudging) protection of the Royal Navy. The final stage required liaison with French military and civilian authorities, the provision of interpreters and of a double cypher for communication between the British and French armies. Here, Wilson's fluency in French and his uninhibited admiration for the French Army was a unique asset, however dubious it may have been in other respects.

Mobilization was frequently practised from 1908 onwards and mobilization tables, railway timetables and shipping dispositions constantly revised and improved in the light of experience. In the Aldershot Command of Lieutenant-General Sir Douglas Haig the last revision of mobilization orders before the outbreak of war was on 2 March 1914. 'All our arrangements were ready,' Haig wrote in his diary, 'even to the extent of having the telegrams written out. These merely had to be dated and despatched.'[35]

On 29 July 1914, under the terms of the War Book, observation of the 'Precautionary Stage' began. The political and diplomatic implications of this made Asquith nervous. Some important measures, such as the examination of ships entering British ports, were held in reserve and it was publicly stressed by the War Office that nothing in 'the nature of mobilization' had begun.[36] Delay, however, also had its dangers. France and Germany announced general mobilization on 1 August, the day of British naval mobilization. It was essential to British army strategy that the expeditionary force was put into the field alongside the French as soon as possible. Preferably, the mobilization of the two countries should coincide. Wilson became apoplectic with fury and anxiety at the government's prevarication, but he did not have long to wait.

British general mobilization began at 4 p.m. on 4 August 1914. General Haig, whose Aldershot Command was soon to become I Corps of the British Expeditionary Force, received his one-word telegram 'Mobilize' signed with the code-word 'Troopers' at 5.03 p.m. 'These orders were put in force and acted upon without friction and without flurry,' Haig noted in his diary.[37] Henry Wilson's administrative Rolls-Royce was at last on the road.

From 5 August, counted as the first day of mobilization, Wilson's plan began to unfold. All Commanding Officers received a set of documents containing movement orders for their units. Adjutants prepared nominal rolls, pay books and the sinister 'dog tags' for use 'on active service'. Officers were requested to pay their mess bills before departure. Armourers began sharpening swords. Quarter-masters began opening their reserve stores of equipment. Axles were greased, harness soaped. Reservists began to arrive. The Territorial Army was embodied by Royal Proclamation for the task of home defence. The troop trains began to roll. Three hundred and fifty arrived at Southampton within forty-eight hours.

Mobilization was remarkably swift. War found Private Frank Richards, an old sweat reservist of the 2nd Royal Welch Fusiliers, drinking in the Castle Hotel at Blaina in Monmouthshire. He arrived at the regimental depot in Wrexham on 5 August at 9 p.m., sailed from Southampton at 2 a.m. on 10 August, and arrived in Rouen to an ecstatic welcome at 3 p.m.[38] Less than a fortnight later his

35. Haig, *Private Papers*, p. 67.
36. Hankey, *Supreme Command*, I, pp. 156, 157.
37. Haig, *Private Papers*, p. 68.
38. Richards, *Old Soldiers*, pp. 9–10.

heavy army boots were ringing down the *pavé* of northern France in full retreat from the might of the German First Army.

At Maryhill Barracks, Glasgow, the mobilization of the 1st Cameronians was completed within the four days allowed for it. Only one reservist out of 600 failed to appear. Everything not needed for active service was sent to the depot in Hamilton. Officers' kit was weighed to the regulation allowance. Exercises were conducted. Then, between 11 p.m. and 1 a.m. on the night of 13/14 August, the battalion slipped away without either ceremony or attention. On 17 August it detrained at Busigny, six miles south-west of Le Cateau, at 9.30 a.m. and took up its position in the 19th (Independent) Infantry Brigade on 22 August, the day before the battle of Mons.[39]

The bulk of the expeditionary force disembarked either at Boulogne or Le Havre between 9 and 14 August. Men and animals (even infantry divisions had over 5,000 horses) were moved by train to the concentration area round Le Cateau, where GHQ was established on 20 August. From Le Cateau units moved by train or by foot to Maubeuge, where they took their place in the allied line on the left of the French Fifth Army of General Charles Lanrezac. Through every town and village their progress was marked by cheering women, children and old men. The absence of young men was noted by many in the army and was a sober reminder of the purpose for which they had come.

By 22 August the BEF was over 90,000 strong, divided into two corps, each of two divisions,[40] with a cavalry division[41] and an independent infantry brigade formed from lines of communication troops. It had over 300 guns. Each infantryman wore the 1902 pattern khaki service dress with 1908 Mills pattern equipment. Many had surrendered their caps and badges to adoring French children and some had taken to wearing handkerchiefs or even straw hats as protection from the sun. Both infantry and cavalry were armed with the formidable Lee-Enfield rifle, sighted to 2,000 yards and with a ten-round detachable magazine, capable of sustained speed and accuracy in skilled hands. For a war in which close-order combat was not only thought likely but also necessary, the infantry were armed with the 1907 sword pattern bayonet and the cavalry either with lances or with the controversial 1908 pattern sword, in the design and development of which Douglas Haig played an important part. The army's morale was exemplary.

The Commander-in-Chief of the British Expeditionary Force was Field Marshal Sir J.D.P. French, a small, florid cavalryman who had made a dashing reputation in the South African War.[42] French exuded charm and confidence. He was comfortable in the company of politicians, especially Liberals, and was a close friend of Winston Churchill. He was popular with ordinary soldiers and treated them with a tolerant and humane affection. His career had flourished in the reformed Edwardian army. Although the Curragh Mutiny[43] had given rise to

39. Jack, *General Jack's Diary*, pp. 22–5.
40. I Corps (Lieutenant-General Sir Douglas Haig), consisting of 1st Division (Major-General S.H. Lomax) and 2nd Division (Major-General C.C. Monro); and II Corps (General Sir H. Smith-Dorrien, succeeding Lieutenant-General Sir J. Grierson, who died of a heart attack on 17 August), consisting of 3rd Division (Major-General H.I.W. Hamilton) and 5th Division (Major-General Sir C. Ferguson Bt.).
41. Commanded by Major-General E. Allenby.
42. For French, see R. Holmes, *The Little Field Marshal: Sir John French* (London, Cape, 1981).
43. The Curragh Mutiny occurred in March 1914. Fifty-seven officers of III (Cavalry) Brigade,

some doubts about his character and judgement there were few to question and none to dispute the wisdom of his appointment.[44] In 1914, at the age of 62, he seemed at the height of his powers and the country looked to him for decisive success.

The prospects of decisive success, however, were not enhanced by the choice of French as Commander-in-Chief. There was a darker side to his character. He was devious and indiscreet and careless with money and other men's wives. He had a vicious temper when crossed. Bluster and bonhomie hid a personality which was wilful and capricious and subject to swift and unpredictable changes of mood when under pressure. He lacked the true self-confidence of the great commander, the ability to maintain mental equilibrium amid chaos and confusion and the strength to act alone.[45] These were serious weaknesses given the awesome task which his army was about to confront.

On 21 and 22 August 1914 the British Expeditionary Force advanced alongside the French Fifth Army and crossed the frontier into Belgium. On 23 August, a sunny Sunday morning, in a landscape reminiscent of the English Black Country, the Great War began in earnest for the British army. Another Belgian town was about to achieve the immortality of Waterloo and to win a special place among the battle honours of the British army. Mons.

Battle

Of all the battle plans which were implemented in the summer of 1914 the most important was that of the Germans. To some, the Schlieffen Plan remains the finest expression of 'pure' military genius in modern history, an infallible blueprint for total victory ruined by the tempering and mismanagement of lesser men.[46] In reality, its 'magic' was a myth. 'Schlieffen's formula for quick victory amounted to little more than a gambler's belief in the virtuosity of sheer audacity,' wrote Liddell Hart. 'As a strategic concept it proved a "snare and delusion" for the executants, with fatal consequences that were on balance inherently probable from the outset.'[47] This was small comfort for the BEF, which as a direct result of Schlieffen's great enveloping movement round the left flank of the French armies now found itself blocking the main axis of the German advance led by General Alexander von Kluck's First Army, over 300,000 strong.

Neither side planned or intended the Battle of Mons. The Germans had no idea even that the British army had landed in France. Throughout 1914 they displayed an astonishing ignorance about the strength and position of the BEF, a situation which owed much to the remarkable ineffectiveness of their cavalry and intelligence services. On the morning of 23 August this ignorance was

---

commanded by Brigadier-General H. Gough, declared that they would prefer to accept dismissal if ordered to coerce Ulster into Home Rule. The Brigade was stationed at the Curragh Camp, near Dublin.

44. Haig, as we have seen, was an exception.
45. For the psychology of command, see N.F. Dixon, *On the Psychology of Military Incompetence* (London, Cape, 1976). French is discussed on pp. 83–5.
46. One of the best accounts of the implementation of the Schlieffen Plan is C. Barnett, *The Swordbearers. Studies in Supreme Command in the First World War* (Harmondsworth, Penguin, 1966), Part I.
47. B.H. Liddell Hart, 'Foreword', to Ritter, *Schlieffen Plan*, p. 4.

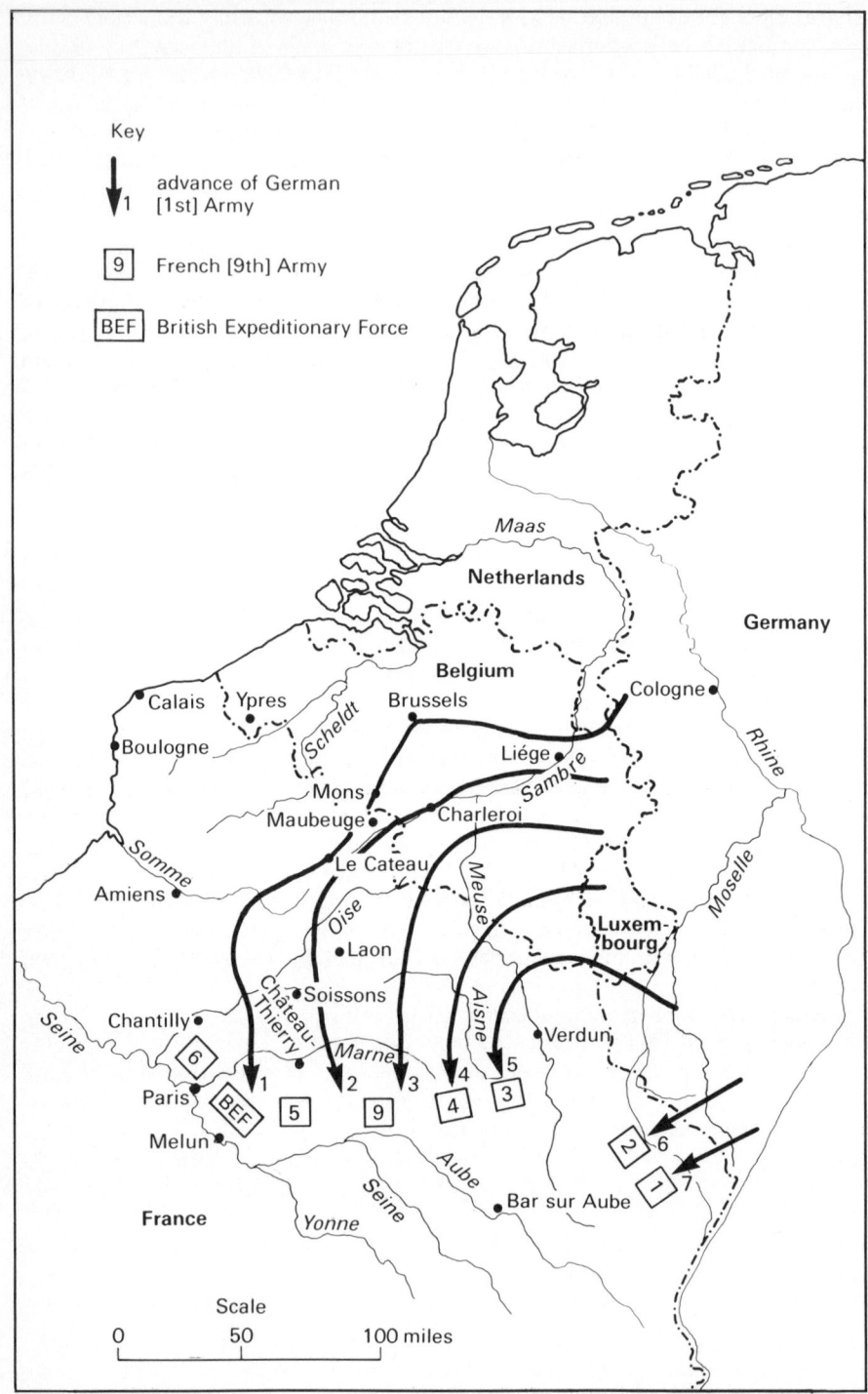

Map 1   The Western Front on the eve of the Battle of the Marne, c. 5 September, 1914

shared by the townspeople of Mons who were still going about their business as the first British volleys smashed into the dense masses of fieldgrey.

The Battle of Mons is of little military interest. The German Army blundered into Sir Horace Smith-Dorrien's II Corps drawn up along the Mons–Condé canal. Superior British musketry and battle-craft inflicted serious losses on the Germans.[48] So great was the Germans' numerical superiority, however, that the British had no choice but to withdraw. And retreat was made certain by the shattering defeat of the French Fifth Army at the Battle of Charleroi on 21–23 August.

The Battle of Mons had important results. It confronted the British Expeditionary Force with the true magnitude of its task and with the prospect of annihilation; and it fundamentally undermined Field-Marshal French's faith in the integrity and competence of his ally. For the next fortnight French faced two formidable enemies – the German Imperial Army and General Lanrezac.

French's first meeting with Lanrezac at Rethel on 17 August was not propitious. The meeting has since become shrouded in legend. French characteristically attached little importance to it in his obscure and unreliable memoirs.[49] But others saw in it the seeds of many future Anglo-French misunderstandings and tensions.[50] General Lanrezac was a man of formidable intellect, over-endowed with the dangerous gift of sarcasm. He had no faith in the professional judgement of his Commander-in-Chief, General Joffre, and thought the French battle plan absurd and potentially disastrous. When the early events of the war confirmed the rightness of his scepticism he could find no response other than 'I told you so'. His intellectual pessimism collapsed into defeatism; the result was failure and disgrace.

In the formal instructions which he received from Lord Kitchener on 14 August French was ordered to co-operate fully with the French Army. No one appeared to have told General Lanrezac that the same courtesies were expected of him. His actions after the Battle of Charleroi threatened the existence of the British Expeditionary Force, which was not informed of the French withdrawal.[51] When the British Commander-in-Chief learned of the French retreat he was horrified to find his own army with both flanks in the air and faced by the possibility of encirclement. His reaction was one of anger and panic. It was some time before he regained his composure and only after grave damage had been done to Anglo-French relations, to British civil–military relations and to French's relations with his subordinates. The repercussions were felt right into 1915.

The summer of 1914 was one of the finest of the century. August was suffocatingly hot. For the British Expeditionary Force, at least two-thirds of whose members were civilians less than three weeks before, the Retreat from Mons became a nightmare. The cobbled roads of northern France were murderous to feet still achingly unfamiliar with army boots. The heat was exhausting. Confusion was total. Worst of all was the sense of shame.[52] Whenever the army had stood to fight – at Mons, at Le Cateau, in the woods of

48. German losses, on British calculations, were about three-and-a-half times as great (c.6,000 to 1,642).
49. French, 1914, pp. 36–7.
50. See Spears, Liaison, pp. 72–80.
51. op. cit., pp. 172–5.
52. See Stewart, Mons to Loos, p. 24.

Villers-Cotterets – it had proved its moral and tactical supremacy over the Germans, but still the retreat continued and none could say when it would end. Ordinary soldiers could not understand it and their officers could not explain it to them. But for the foresight and initiative of the Quartermaster-General, Sir William Robertson, in dumping food at strategic crossroads the retreat might well have become a rout. Strain was severe on all ranks. Sir Archibald Murray, French's feeble Chief of Staff, suffered a temporary nervous breakdown, though French appears not to have noticed. In the aftermath of the Battle of Le Cateau, Colonel Boileau, GSO1 of the 3rd Division, broke down completely and shot himself. At one point, on 31 August, Field-Marshal French contemplated taking his army out of the line and retiring to the coast to re-equip and refit. It took an unhappy visit from Lord Kitchener to prevent this.[53] The BEF stayed in the line but the passage of every day reduced its military effectiveness.

By the end of August the French supreme commander General J.J.C. Joffre was forced to recognize the total collapse of his plans and the hopes of his country. At that moment he achieved greatness. The decisions which Joffre took in the early days of September were not intellectually difficult. But this was not a Staff Exercise. The Battle of the Marne was more than an astute military manoeuvre. It was a moral triumph, a triumph of will, on the part of a man who had seen his plans laid waste within days of the outbreak of war, who had seen his basic beliefs about the strength and dispositions of the German Army proved false, and who had watched helpless as his armies in Lorraine suffered a catastrophic national defeat. Joffre's decision to create a new army – the Sixth, under General Maunoury – to the west of Paris and to take the German First and Second Armies in flank changed the course of history. It also marked the end of the BEF's long and dispiriting retreat.

By 1 September the BEF was at Melun, twenty-five miles south-east of Paris. It had retreated further than any other part of the Allied line. On 4 September, in the absence of Sir John French (who was visiting his troops), General Murray made plans for a further retreat of ten to fifteen miles. This caused consternation both to Henry Wilson and to the French, for on that same day General Joffre had risen from his seat in the shade at Bar-sur-Aube and made the historic decision to counter-attack on the left. Under pressure from General Galliéni, the Military Governor of Paris, Joffre fixed the time of the attack for 6 September, one day earlier than he had intended. At 10.00 p.m. on 4 September 1914 he issued his General Order, beginning with the momentous words 'The time has come'. But it was far from clear that the time had come for the BEF. Sir John French's return to GHQ had not produced decisive action. French continued to prevaricate and the retreat planned by Murray was allowed to proceed. By the evening of 5 September the 2nd Grenadier Guards, in the British rear, were as far south as Fontenay. They were destined to go no further.

With less than thirty-six hours to go before the battle which would decide the fate of France and of Europe, the co-operation of the BEF in the French counter-attack was still in doubt. British support was vital. Joffre decided that he was the only man who could arrange it. He drove the 115 miles from Bar-sur-Aube to Melun to see Sir John French personally. The two commanders met in the Louis Quinze salon of the Château de Vaux-le-Pénil at 2 p.m. It was the most important meeting of the war so far. Joffre was at his most commanding.

53. See French, *1914*, pp. 99–101, for a bitter account of this visit.

Accounts of his speech differ. But whatever he said it worked. French suffered one of his characteristic changes of mood. He flushed and began to cry. He attempted to reply in French but could not find the words. He turned to Henry Wilson and said 'Damn it, I can't explain. Tell him that all men can do our fellows will do.' The Retreat was over.

The effect of French's decision on his army was electric. 'We marched towards the rising sun,' exulted the former Secretary of State for War, Colonel J.E.B. Seely, who remembered Sunday, 6 September 1914 as the happiest day of his life. 'A marvellous change has come over the situation,' Captain James Jack of the 1st Cameronians wrote in his diary on 7 September. 'We have been chasing the Germans back for the past two days. . . . This totally unexpected news almost passed belief after the long depressing retreat; all faces were bright as we marched 16 miles north-east.'[54] Even more heartening was the fact that the 19th Brigade had begun to take prisoners. The tide had turned.

It did not, however, turn quickly enough. Owing to French's prevarication the BEF began the Battle of the Marne ten miles south of the start line envisaged in Joffre's General Order. From that moment the BEF was rarely up with the game and there appeared to be little determination on the part of the high command to remedy the situation. Even regimental officers commented unfavourably on the lack of vigour in the pursuit.[55] Despite his emotional acquiescence in Joffre's request for support at Melun, French remained deeply worried about the state of his army, especially after reflecting on the 'disastrous' losses suffered by II Corps at Le Cateau. Lord Kitchener's injunction that 'the greatest care must be exercised towards a minimum of losses and wastage' began to take on increased significance. But the worst was yet to come.

Even before the Allied counter-attack the Germans had begun to realize the precariousness of their position. On 5 September Colonel Richard Hentsch, emissary of the German Supreme Command, ordered the German First Army to halt its advance. Von Kluck was less than five miles from the outposts of the BEF. His soldiers had achieved prodigies of physical exertion and the forty days allowed for 'victory in the west' were not yet up. But the cruel truth was that the Schlieffen Plan had failed and the German Army was now in a trap. By 8 September, with a thirty-mile gap between the German First and Second Armies, Colonel Hentsch made his second appearance upon the stage of history and the complete withdrawal of the German right wing began.

Retreat intensified the fatigue of the German armies. In advance weary soldiers could be inspired by the thought that soon they would 'rest in Paris'. Now, Paris was fading into the distance behind their backs. The German First Army had marched nearly 200 miles. It was time to stop and fight. On 12 September the First and Second Armies crossed the River Aisne and began to dig in. Trench warfare had begun. Two days later *Generaloberst* Helmuth Johannes Ludwig von Moltke, hapless inheritor of a great name and a ruinous strategy, was removed from the supreme command of the German armies and replaced by the Minister of War, Erich von Falkenhayn.

Despite its undoubted importance, the Battle of the Marne remains somewhat intangible to the British. The BEF saw comparatively little fighting. Its pursuit of the retreating Germans was ponderous and unsatisfactory. The Aisne was

54.   Jack, *General Jack's Diary*, p. 48.
55.   *op. cit.*, p. 49.

1 The beginning of trench warfare. 1st King's Own (Royal Lancaster Regiment), 12th Bde, 4th Div., 'dug in' at Ste Marguerite on the Aisne, 22 September 1914 (*The Trustees of the Imperial War Museum, London*)

different. It was a 'real battle'.[56] The BEF suffered over 20,000 casualties. In some ways, the army adapted itself with astonishing speed to the changed conditions of warfare. In 2nd Grenadier Guards a system of reliefs, familiar to later stages of trench war, was established as early as 18 September.[57] In other respects, the battle exposed for the first time the BEF's material inadequacies, its lack of entrenching equipment, of heavy guns, and of high explosive. Above all, it highlighted the dilemma implicit in Sir John French's instructions from his government. Sympathetic co-operation with his ally in order to achieve the ends of British policy *and* preservation from serious loss of the country's precious military resources were becoming increasingly incompatible. How incompatible it was left to the 1st Battle of Ypres to demonstrate.

At the end of September Field-Marshal French forced General Joffre to agree to the transfer of the British army from the Aisne to Flanders. French's logic and his insistence were persuasive. Now that the BEF was receiving reinforcements, French wished to regain his power of independent initiative on the left flank of the French armies and to simplify his logistical arrangements with his bases on the Channel coast.[58] The decision was an important one.[59] Its immediate effect was to place the BEF once more across the axis of a major German offensive.

56. Caffrey, *Farewell Leicester Square*, p. 204.
57. Craster, ed., *'Fifteen Rounds a Minute'*, p. 93.
58. For the correspondence with Joffre, see French, *1914*, pp. 164–74.
59. See below, p. 27.

By the middle of October the German armies, in their attempt to outflank the Allied line in the so-called 'race to the sea', were placed in a pronounced salient on the Franco-Belgian border round Ypres, Armentières and Neuve Chapelle. It was from this salient that Falkenhayn launched his attack to capture Calais and Boulogne, the last major attempt by the Germans to win a decisive victory in the west in 1914.

The 1st Battle of Ypres (18 October–18 November) was extremely bitter and massively confused. In the BEF the major burden fell this time on Sir Douglas Haig's I Corps. The rapidity and accuracy of British musketry had a devastating effect on barely trained German volunteers attacking in dense masses. German casualties were enormous. On 3 November a company of the Oxford and Bucks Light Infantry found 300 Germans dead in front of a position which they had just taken over from the 2nd Grenadier Guards.[60] British casualties were also severe. The battle was a graveyard for the old British regular army. Even more than on the Aisne the BEF began to realize the cost of the struggle between manpower and firepower. 'The Germans are fighting this war with guns and machine guns,' Lieutenant-Colonel Wilfred Smith noted in the battalion War Diary of 2nd Grenadier Guards in November, 'and jolly good they are too.'[61] Between 18 October and 19 November 2nd Grenadiers lost 8 officers killed or died of wounds and 6 wounded; and something like 400 Other Ranks killed and wounded.[62] The battalion's second-in-command, Major George 'Ma' Jeffreys, was the only combatant officer left who had been out in France from the beginning. The battle was equally hard on newcomers. The GOC of the 7th Division, Major-General 'Tommy' Capper, described himself on 1 November as a 'curiosity – a Divisional Commander without a Division'.[63]

The crisis of the battle came on 31 October. Four shells fell on the Hooge Château where the commanding officers and staffs of the British 1st and 2nd Divisions were meeting in conference. General Lomax, GOC 1st Division, was fatally wounded and seven other senior officers killed. This was a bad blow to the Corps commander, Douglas Haig, at whose insistence Lomax had moved his headquarters to the chateau where Haig thought he would be more 'comfortable'. To make matters worse the Germans broke through the depleted British line at Gheluvelt on the Menin Road and seemed poised to advance on Ypres. The situation was saved by a gallant charge of the 2nd Battalion Worcestershire Regiment, under the command of Major E.B. Hankey, made on the initiative and at the express instructions of Brigadier-General Fitzclarence, commanding 1st (Guards) Brigade. Gheluvelt was recaptured and the British line re-established. This was probably the last decisive act of the old pre-war, peacetime-trained regular army in the Great War. It was a fitting climax.

Bitter fighting continued after 31 October. The British line bent but it never again broke. The scarred battalions of the BEF often existed only in name, being reduced in many cases to 200 rifles or less. In some places the line was held by the superb marksmen of the cavalry fighting dismounted. The mood was one of grim determination, a fierce refusal not to be beaten after coming so far and suffering so much. The mood of the Commander-in-Chief was equally grim but not always so determined. 'Now there's nothing for it but to go up and be killed

60. Craster, ed., 'Fifteen Rounds a Minute', p. 93.
61. op. cit., p. 132.
62. op. cit., p. 144.
63. op. cit., p. 126.

with I Corps,' French melodramatically announced on 31 October. But he stayed where he was, and reinforced by regular draughts from General Ferdinand Foch's bottomless well of optimism his nerve held. Ragged, dirty and profoundly tired, the BEF badly needed a rest and relief from 'those horrible shells'.[64] 'My one thought was how soon I could get my battle-worn troops relieved, and given a few days rest out of the trenches and shell fire,' wrote Douglas Haig on 5 November.[65] He did not have long to wait. Amid mutual exhaustion and worsening weather the battle petered out in the middle of November.

The British Expeditionary Force suffered 50,000 casualties at Ypres. In the three and a half months of fighting between 23 August and 18 November the BEF lost more men than the total strength of the army at the outset of the campaign. More than half those who earned the right to wear the 'Mons Star' became casualties. One in ten died. Losses among officers and NCOs were especially heavy. 'No good officer has the right to be alive during a fight like this,' remarked Major-General Capper. Britain's small reservoir of trained manpower was virtually exhausted. The German Army's bid for a swift and total victory in the west had been frustrated, but there was no end in sight. 'And so the year goes out in wind and rain and sobs,' Henry Wilson wrote in his diary on 31 December 1914.[66] For the British, however, the crying had only just begun.

Much has been claimed for the BEF in 1914. 'But for the small British force,' wrote General Spears in 1930, 'final and irremediable defeat would have overtaken France.'[67] As a witness to many of the most dramatic events of 1914 Spears's verdict commands respect. As a judgement on the course of the war as a whole it is irrefutable. Without British military, naval, political, moral, financial and economic support, France would certainly have been defeated by Germany. The French always feared this. That is why they wanted Britain as an ally in the first place. But whether, without British military support, France would have suffered a 'final and irremediable defeat' *in 1914* is more doubtful. For all its immense gallantry, professionalism and sacrifice, the British miltary contribution in 1914 was puny in comparison with its own later efforts and in comparison with those of the French. The battles fought by the French army were infinitely greater in scale and magnitude than any fought by the British. And so were the French losses. Two-fifths of the casualties suffered by France during the whole of the war were inflicted in 1914. A tenth of the officer corps was killed. Even Ypres, where the single greatest British contribution was made, was a predominantly French battle, something only grudgingly recognized in most British accounts of the war. France survived in 1914 because General Joffre kept his nerve at the moment of supreme destiny and retrieved salvation from the wreckage of his country's hopes.

The large number of books on the British battles of 1914 testifies to their continuing appeal to the British imagination. This is out of all proportion to their military importance. The reason for this is to be found principally in public perceptions about the nature of battle. Battles should ideally be on a human

---

64. *op. cit.*, p. 96. The phrase was used by Lieutenant-Colonel W.R.A. Smith on 21 September.
65. Haig, *Private Papers*, p. 77.
66. Callwell, *Wilson*, I, p. 198.
67. Spears, *Liaison*, p. 373.

scale. They should take place in a relatively confined space and occupy a limited amount of time. They should be clear-cut in their result and decided by identifiable individual acts of heroism. This was how battles were painted by generations of war artists in the great Victorian and Edwardian illustrated press.[68] This is how they were painted in 1914.[69] Dease and Godley holding the bridge at Nimy against two battalions of German infantry, the heroic action of 'L' Battery, Royal Horse Artillery, at Néry, the charge of the Worcesters at Gheluvelt, Haig and his staff calmly riding up the Menin Road to steady their men at Ypres evoked memories of the Alma, of Waterloo and Albuera, even of Horatius and the Spartan heroes at Thermopylae. It is, perhaps, no accident that the finest lament for the 'Old Contemptibles' was written by a Classicist – A.E. Housman, in his 'Epitaph on an Army of Mercenaries'.

The Aisne is less well remembered because it does not conform to this stereotype. It looks uncomfortably forward to another kind of battle fought on the shattered uplands of the Somme – vast, impersonal, unceasing, inconclusive, the war of the troglodyte, the war of the machine, a landscape devoid of colour and incident for the graphic artist, the stuff not of legend but of despair.

The performance of the British Expeditionary Force in 1914 demonstrated the strengths and weaknesses of the British army. At the small unit level its courage, discipline and professionalism were exemplary and provided a vindication of pre-war reforms in training and tactical doctrine. Man for man it was probably the best army in the field. As an Army, however, it can barely be said to have existed. The reasons for this were deeply rooted in the historical experience of the British army as a colonial police force and in its curious regimental system which remained, even after the Edwardian reforms, the prime focus of loyalty for the British regular officer. Individuals, units, even branches of the army performed with distinction, but there was an overall lack of orchestration and co-ordination. In the field, problems began at the top.

It is difficult to discover Field-Marshal French in the act of generalship. Smith-Dorrien fought Mons and Le Cateau with little help and some hindrance from his Commander-in-Chief. Ypres was essentially Haig's battle. French's one decisive intervention was the transfer of the BEF from the Aisne to Flanders. This was made on his own initiative and despite opposition from the masterful Joffre. In later years Asquith was given to saying that French's action was one of the greatest of all services to the Allied cause and by itself justified his appointment.[70]

Staff work at GHQ was often poor. General Murray's orders, happily often rendered nugatory by events, were miracles of opacity, devoid of context, and a source of consternation and confusion to those who received them.[71] In the early stages of the war, especially during the Retreat, communications were a shambles. The few available wireless sets were used solely for communication

68. See the interesting article by R.T. Stearn, 'War and the Media in the 19th Century: Victorian Military Artists and the Image of War, 1870-1914', *Journal of the Royal United Services Institute for Defence Studies*, CXXXI (1986), pp. 55-63.
69. See, for example, the plates facing p. 145 in Caffrey, *Farewell Leicester Square*.
70. See C.R.M.F. Cruttwell, *British Strategy in the Great War* (London, Cambridge University Press, 1936), pp. 29-30.
71. A.H. Farrar-Hockley, *Goughie: the Life of General Sir Hubert Gough* (London, Hart-Davis-MacGibbon, 1975), p. 129.

between GHQ and the Cavalry Division.[72] Telegraph communication between Corps HQ and GHQ was sporadic and sometimes dependent upon the vagaries of the French civilian system. This threw up some curious anomalies. Although it was often impossible to make contact with GHQ, General Gough was able to send a comforting telegram to his wife in London from the post office at Homblières after the Battle of Mons.[73] A network of motor-cycle despatch riders and staff officers in cars attempted to make up for these technological inadequacies, but their task was not made easier by the repeated failure of GHQ to report changes of location to subordinate formations or by the frequent absences from GHQ of Field-Marshal French, whose tours of the line may have done wonders for his own morale but which seem to have had little impact on the troops who received his visits with the puzzled enquiry 'Oo's the ole bloke, then?'

The battles of 1914 were 'soldiers' battles'. The key decisions were made 'at the sharp end' among formations of company level or even below. Command and control at the highest level was often irrelevant and sometimes impossible. The army had proved its gallantry and its resourcefulness. It remained to be seen whether it had the capacity to achieve the level of all-arms' co-operation necessary to defeat the German Army in the field.

'The King's Ships'

No British institution entered the war with greater self-confidence, a greater sense of destiny or a greater burden of public expectation than the Royal Navy.[74] Naval power was widely believed to be the supreme instrument of international relations. The rise of the British Empire provided ample evidence for such a belief, but it was powerfully reinforced by the influential writings of the American naval theorist Captain Alfred Thayer Mahan. 'Those far distant, storm-beaten ships, upon which the Grand Army never looked, stood between it and dominion of the world,' Mahan wrote of Nelson's fleet.[75] It was a captivating judgement. The Royal Navy would vanquish the Kaiser as it had vanquished Bonaparte. The lavish expenditure of public money on a modern, fast, all big-gun fleet capable of defeating the German Imperial Navy in a single victory of total annihilation, a second Trafalgar, sharpened anticipation of a decisive naval contribution to the outcome of the war. In 1914, however, and in the war as a whole, the fortunes of the Royal Navy were dogged by bad luck and doomed to frustration.

The Navy's 'plan' for winning the war amounted to little more than a set of platitudes and faith in the past. The belief that naval supremacy gave complete freedom of strategic manoeuvre to land Britain's small army at some point where it could inflict damage on the enemy out of all proportion to its size did

72. A.J. Smithers, *The Man Who Disobeyed: Sir Horace Smith-Dorrien and his Enemies* (London, Leo Cooper, 1970).
73. Farrar-Hockley, *Goughie*, pp. 126–7.
74. The best general account of the Royal Navy during the war is R. Hough, *The Great War at Sea 1914–1918* (Oxford, Clarendon Press, 1983). A.J. Marder's brilliant study *From the Dreadnought to Scapa Flow* (5 vols., London, Oxford University Press, 1961–70) is indispensable. See also P.M. Kennedy, *The Rise and Fall of British Naval Mastery* (London, Allen Lane, 1976).
75. A.T. Mahan, *The Influence of Sea Power Upon the French Revolution and Empire 1793–1812* (2 vols., London, Sampson Low, 1892), II, p. 118.

not survive the mauling it received at the famous meeting of the Committee of Imperial Defence on 23 August 1911.[76] Admiral Fisher continued to indulge fantasies about landing a British (or a Russian) army on the 'thirty miles of hard sand' along the Pomeranian coast less than 100 miles from Berlin, but not even his own advisers could tell him how this was to be done in the face of minefields, torpedo boats and modern coastal defences – not to mention the German High Seas Fleet. The Royal Navy was left with the rôle of chaperon to the British Expeditionary Force during its deployment across the Channel – and with the strategy of blockade.[77]

Blockade was central to the 'theory' of naval power. The denial of seaborne commerce to an enemy could be a potent instrument of war, especially perhaps in the case of industrialized economies with their reliance on trade in raw materials and manufactured goods and on international structures of credit. Mahan clearly believed that the blockade was fundamental to the defeat of Napoleon. But in the early years of the twentieth century new developments conspired to undermine its effectiveness. In naval technology, the electromagnetic mine, the torpedo, the submarine and the big coastal gun made close blockade of the Nelsonic type extremely hazardous, if not impossible. Any blockade would have to be a distant one. This presented its own considerable logistical and tactical problems. The system which the Royal Navy was forced to operate was in reality one of 'contraband control' rather than a true blockade, and even this was seriously constrained by international agreements on the definitions of contraband and the rights of neutrals which had steadily eroded the power of belligerents to wage an effective campaign of economic pressure. One of the more remarkable contributions to this process was the British-sponsored Declaration of London (1907).[78] Hankey, who led a campaign of opposition to the Declaration within the defence establishment, denounced it in characteristically restrained language as 'a dubious instrument'. But even without British acquiescence in 'short-sighted' international agreements, her freedom to impose rigorous control, examination and confiscation of neutral ships was limited by the need to maintain the goodwill of the most important neutral – the United States of America. Within months of the outbreak of war most of the pious resolutions of the Declaration of Paris (1856) and the six Hague Conventions relating to naval warfare were jettisoned along with many other comforting prewar assumptions, but the problem of American opinion and American power remained.

The purpose of the blockade, however, was not only to disrupt the German economy but also to force the German High Seas Fleet into a fight in which it would be annihilated. Admiral Fisher had dedicated his life to the construction

---

76. For an account of this, see Churchill, *World Crisis*, pp. 51–4. See also M. Howard, *The Continental Commitment* (London, Maurice Temple Smith, 1972; Harmondsworth, Pelican, 1974), pp. 45–7.

77. For the blockade, see A.C. Bell, *A History of the Blockade of Germany and the Countries Associated with her in the Great War 1914–1918* (London, HMSO, 1937). This is the Official History. It was kept on the secret list and not published for general readership until 1961. Supervising K.Burrows's unpublished BA dissertation 'The Economic Blockade of the Central Powers 1914–1918 — Its Aims, Methods and Effects' (Birmingham University, 1983) helped greatly to clarify my own ideas on the subject.

78. See Hankey, *Supreme Command*, I, pp. 94–102. The Declaration, in effect, restricted 'blockade' to 'close blockade', which was impossible, and narrowed definitions of contraband making 'distant blockade' ineffectual.

of a fleet capable of inflicting such a defeat.[79] By 1914 it appeared that he had succeeded. For a man of such volcanic energy, Fisher could show remarkable patience when it mattered. And patience was all that did matter. The policy of 'steady pressure' might be slow but it would be sure. There would be a day when the German fleet would have to come out to fight and when it did it would be smashed.[80] A conclusive British victory at sea would be the decisive battle of the war. It would have an immense effect on German morale and neutral opinion. Economic warfare could be waged with much greater ruthlessness. The Royal Navy would be able to enter the Baltic and land Russian armies near the heart of Germany. The war would be as good as over.

Unfortunately, patience was not prominent among the virtues of the navy's political head, and Fisher's erstwhile friend and patron, Winston Churchill. The explosive chemistry of their relationship, following Fisher's recall to office from retirement in October 1914, exercised an increasingly malign influence on naval and political affairs during the next seven months of the war.

The chart room at the Admiralty was Churchill's spiritual home. His imagination, his sense of history, his appetite for decision was inspired by the global responsibilities and awesome power which were reflected on its walls.[81] His conduct of naval affairs in 1914 was marked by a restless ambition which regularly took him beyond the confines of his departmental brief and by a gradual and reluctant awareness that some of his senior professional advisers and commanders were beginning to doubt whether all was well with the Royal Navy.

The navy could claim substantial achievements in 1914. The BEF was transported to France without the loss of a man or ship. The French Atlantic coast was made safe from enemy interference. German deep-sea merchant shipping was brought to a standstill. Enemy commerce raiders were remorselessly hunted down. Admiral Sturdee's victory over von Spee's squadron at the Falkland Islands on 8 December removed a major surface threat to British trade and communications and was sufficiently annihilating for public taste.[82] In the cold and inhospitable waters to the north of the British Isles the blockade ships kept vigil. The High Seas Fleet remained imprisoned in port and showed little desire for assaulting its jailer. The happy capture by the Russians of the German naval cypher books meant that the British Grand Fleet was likely to enjoy forewarning of German moves to dispute command of the sea. 'Steady pressure' had been applied.

But there were shadows. The withholding of two infantry divisions from immediate despatch with the BEF was at least in part due to the Royal Navy's

79. For Fisher, see A.J. Marder, *Fear God and Dread Nought: the Correspondence of Admiral of the Fleet Lord Fisher of Kilverstone* (3 vols., London, Cape, 1952–9). Fisher's papers, admirably edited by P.K. Kemp, have been published by the Navy Records Society, *The Papers of Admiral of the Fleet Sir John Fisher* (2 vols., London, Navy Records Society, 1960, 1964).

80. See 'Memorandum by the First Sea Lord on the Position of the British Fleet and its Policy of Steady Pressure' (25 January 1915), printed in M. Gilbert, *Winston Churchill. Volume III Companion. Part I, Documents, July 1914–April 1915* (London, Heinemann, 1972), pp. 452–4.

81. Churchill's tenure of the Admiralty in 1914–15 inspired some of his finest prose, even though his account is in the nature of an *apologia*. See *The World Crisis* (London, Thornton Butterworth, 1923), vols. 1 and 2.

82. See G. Bennett, *Coronel and the Falklands* (London, Batsford, 1962).

unwillingness to give guarantees of its ability to prevent German forces landing on the east coast. This remarkable private caution was in stark contrast to an uncompromising public optimism. Failure to prevent the flight of the *Goeben* and *Breslau* into the Sea of Marmora had brought Turkey into the war on the side of the Central Powers and had given early warning of the Fleet's poverty of communications and the lack of initiative of some of its commanders.[83] German bombardment of Hartlepool, Whitby and Scarborough inflicted a damaging blow on public confidence in the navy and raised the cry for more decisive action. This found no echo in the mind of the Commander-in-Chief of the Grand Fleet, Sir John Jellicoe. He was unsure even of the security of his base at Scapa Flow in the Orkneys and preferred to keep his ships at sea, sometimes dangerously remote from the likely arena of battle. The outline of his tactical methods for fighting a major fleet action, which he sent to the Admiralty on 30 October 1914, was prudential and revealed his doubts about the Fleet's capacity to achieve the crushing victory which was expected of it.[84] Churchill's extraordinary conduct in organizing the operations at Antwerp and the disaster which overtook Admiral Cradock's cruisers at Coronel sowed the first poisonous seeds of doubt about the First Lord's character and judgement.

Churchill, himself, however, had no doubts. The Royal Navy had won command of the sea. He did not believe that this in itself would be decisive. The important thing was to *exercise* the command which had been established. Sturdee's victory convinced Churchill that the whole balance of naval power had moved in Britain's favour. 'For the first time we saw ourselves possessed of immense surpluses of ships of certain classes, of trained men and of supplies of all kinds, and were in a position to use them to the best advantage,' he later wrote.[85] 1915 would be the year of the navy.

83. See D. Van der Vat, *The Ship that Changed the World: the Escape of the Goeben to the Dardanelles in 1914* (London, Hodder & Stoughton, 1985).
84. See *The Jellicoe Papers*, ed. A. Temple Patterson (2 vols., London, Navy Records Society, 1966, 1968), I, pp. 75–7.
85. Churchill, *World Crisis* (abridged edition), p. 255.

2

'The First Clash of Battle' 1915[1]

Tell them at home, there's nothing here to hide:
We took our orders, asked no questions, died.

H.W. Garrod[2]

It will become a war between peoples which is not to be
concluded with a single battle but which will be a long, weary
struggle with a country that will not acknowledge defeat until
the whole strength of its people is broken: a war that even if we
should be the victors will push our own people, too, to the
limits of exhaustion.

Helmuth von Moltke[3]

At the end of 1914 the war entered a new phase. The plans of all the combatants
lay in ruins. After the 'manoeuvre for position', however, clear advantage
rested with the Germans. Their attempt to win a decisive victory in the west
'before the leaves fall' had been frustrated, but they had achieved a degree of
success which was to influence the whole course of the war until the spring
of 1918.

The German Army was in occupation of most of Belgium and large parts of
northern France, including many areas of industrial importance. At its closest
point the German line was only forty miles from Paris. 'Les Boches sont à
Noyon,' Clemenceau daily reminded his fellow countrymen on the front page of
Le Chien Enchaîné. National necessity and national pride demanded that the
French Army should take the offensive to expel the invader, despite its savage
losses. The French could expect little effective support from their allies. The
performance of the British army had been an uncomfortable surprise, but it was
still small and poorly equipped for the kind of positional warfare which now

1. For the military history of 1915, see British Official History, *Military Operations France and
   Belgium* (2 vols., London, Macmillan, 1927, 1928). Volume 1, compiled by Brigadier-General
   Sir James Edmonds and Captain G.C. Wynne, deals with Neuve Chapelle and Second Ypres.
   Volume 2, compiled by Edmonds, deals with Aubers Ridge, Festubert and Loos. Secondary
   accounts are few and poor. A. Clark, *The Donkeys* (London, Hutchinson, 1963), has had an
   influence out of all proportion to its merits; deep down a rather shallow book. P. Warner, *The
   Battle of Loos* (London, William Kimber, 1976) is an uninspired account. Gallipoli is treated
   separately, below.
2. H.W. Garrod, 'Epitaph: Neuve Chapelle', first published 1919, in D. Hibberd and J. Onions,
   eds., *Poetry of the Great War: An Anthology* (London, Macmillan, 1986) p. 52.
3. H. von Moltke to his wife, 29 January 1905, quoted in C. Barnett, *The Swordbearers*
   (Harmondsworth, Penguin, 1966), p. 40.

seemed inevitable. The Russian Army had been dealt a series of humbling blows and appeared ripe for defeat.[4] Germany's strategy would be to exploit the prospects for victory in the east and to stand on the defensive in the west. The German Army in France and Flanders was free to retreat to positions of tactical advantage, to reinforce them with all the considerable ingenuity of its field engineering, and there to await the inevitable French attack. 'No position in war is stronger than a strategic offensive coupled with a tactical defensive,' wrote Correlli Barnett.[5] And it was such a position which the French Army would have to assault in 1915.

As the new year began the most pressing problem for the British government was to decide whether the British army would assault it with them.

On 7 and 8 January the War Council[6] gave formal consideration to 'THE POSSIBILITY OF EMPLOYING BRITISH FORCES IN A DIFFERENT THEATRE [FROM] THAT IN WHICH THEY ARE NOW USED'.[7] The most influential voice in the War Council's deliberations was that of the Secretary of State for War. 'Kitchener *was* military opinion,' declared Churchill, who nevertheless did his best to dispute the title. Asquith himself described Kitchener's appointment as a 'hazardous experiment',[8] but there was no doubt that it produced an instantaneous effect on British conduct of the war.[9]

During the first week of August 1914 the British government took three crucial decisions. On 2 August it was decided to send an ultimatum to Germany demanding respect for Belgian neutrality. This constituted a declaration of war. On 5/6 August it was decided to send the British Expeditionary Force to France to fight on the left flank of the French armies. This was the origin of the 'Western Front'. And on 7 August, after the most perfunctory discussion, it was decided to raise a great new volunteer army. This was the vital decision and it was taken solely as a result of Kitchener's initiative.[10]

Britain had declared war before. Expeditionary forces had been sent to Europe before. But never had Britain attempted to raise an army capable of challenging the Continental Powers at their own game. Even before a shot was fired, the kind of war which ministers like Grey envisaged was fundamentally changed.

The decision was vital for two reasons. A mass army made possible the mass casualties which have dominated subsequent British perceptions of the war. And without this mass British army the Allies would almost certainly have been defeated.

Kitchener's thinking in the early days of 1915 convinced him that the British Expeditionary Force must remain on the Western Front and co-operate to the

4. For the Eastern Front, see N. Stone, *The Eastern Front, 1914–1917* (London, Hodder & Stoughton, 1975). Churchill's *The World Crisis. The Eastern Front* (London, Thornton Butterworth, 1931) is still valuable. It was reprinted as *The Unknown War, The Eastern Front* (London, Keystone Library, 1937).

5. Barnett, *Swordbearers*, p. 117.

6. For the constitutional position of the War Council, see below, Chapter 5.

7. See F-M Viscount French, *1914* (London, Constable, 1919), pp. 313–18.

8. J.A. Spender and C. Asquith, *The Life of Herbert Henry Asquith, Lord Oxford and Asquith* (2 vols., London, Hutchinson, 1922), II, p. 105.

9. There is no really satisfactory biography of Kitchener, but see G.H. Cassar, *Kitchener: Architect of Victory* (London, William Kimber, 1977).

10. Viscount Grey of Fallodon, *Twenty-Five Years*, (2 vols., London, Hodder & Stoughton, 1925) II, p. 69.

best of its ability in the plans of the French Army. If he was a 'Westerner', however, it was not because he lacked the vision to see beyond the sandbagged confines of No Man's Land. He took a global view of strategy in which the fate of Russia and the course of the war in the east was a fundamental concern.[11]

Kitchener was virtually certain that the German lines in the west were unbreakable.[12] But if he was wrong and the French succeeded in breaking them, it was important for the BEF to be in at the death if Britain wished to have a voice in the post-war settlement. If he was right and the task proved beyond the capacity of France it would increase her need for armed support with which to resist a German attack. In the event of a stalemate in which neither side had the power to achieve victory a British presence on the Western Front would be the surest guarantee of maintaining a level of military activity necessary to prevent Germany from concentrating decisive force against Russia in the east.

Accordingly, on 9 January 1915, Field-Marshal French was informed in a War Council memorandum that his own proposal for a British advance along the Belgian Coast with the capture of Zeebrugge as its object was denied. He was to remain in the line and to co-operate fully with General Joffre. The future use of the New Armies being raised in England was, however, still to be decided. 'Certain possible projects for pressing the war in other theatres [would] be carefully studied during the next few weeks.' The War Council had, characteristically, compromised. Out of the compromise developed the main lines of British military policy for the rest of the year.

The prospect of military initiatives elsewhere cheered those members of the government who believed that 'chewing barbed wire' on the Western Front was a wasted use of limited resources. Chief among these was Winston Churchill, who pursued with ever greater determination the plans which resulted in the ill-fated Dardanelles adventure.

In the Ypres Salient and in the dreary mining villages along the Franco-Belgian border the British Expeditionary Force prepared itself to pay the price of executing Lord Kitchener's grand strategy with inadequate manpower and supplies of heavy artillery and high-explosive ammunition.

The Western Front

The British army's experience on the Western Front in 1915 was conditioned by two things – the insistent need of the French for support in the implementation of their strategy and the inadequacy of the BEF's material resources for the successful prosecution even of this subsidiary role.

In the west in 1915, as in 1914, the French Army bore the brunt of battle. General Joffre's plan was to attack the shoulders of the great German salient between Arras and the River Aisne, to rupture the German line and to seize the initiative in open warfare. This involved the French Army in massive offensives in Artois and Champagne during the spring and autumn.

Joffre looked to the British Expeditionary Force for full co-operation in these attacks by offensive action of its own designed to prevent the Germans from transferring men and materials from quiet sectors of the front to stem the

11. K. Neilson, 'Kitchener: a reputation refurbished ?', *Canadian Journal of History*, XV (1980), pp. 207–27.
12. Sir G. Arthur, *The Life of Lord Kitchener* (3 vols., London, Macmillan, 1920), III, pp. 85–6.

French assaults. For the French, this seemed little more than they had a right to expect; for the British, it was more than enough to stretch their resources to the limit, to destroy what remained from 1914 of their reserves of trained manpower and to provoke fundamental questioning of many cherished national beliefs.

From the outbreak of war in August 1914 until the Battle of Messines in June 1917, British strategy on the Western Front remained subservient to that of the French. The dominance of the French military contribution to the alliance, the continuing threat posed by Germany to the independence and integrity of France and Belgium and the wavering fortunes of Russia made this an inescapable reality. This was never more true than in 1915. British offensives were fought for the sake of the French and often on the ground and at the time of French choosing. They were essentially 'political' offensives. The BEF's resources of manpower and firepower were far too inadequate for it to make a significant military contribution to the defeat of Germany. The melancholy consequences of this were wholly predictable.

The British Commander-in-Chief, Sir John French, was a more than willing collaborator in French strategy, but even he saw the dangers. Neither French nor his Army Commander, Douglas Haig,[13] thought that Neuve Chapelle or Loos were sensible places to attack. And they were right. The location of the British offensives offered no significant strategic opportunities and considerable tactical disadvantages. Haig, in particular, believed that an attack in Flanders held out the best hope for success and would allow the British army to act with greater independence and initiative.

Field-Marshal French tried hard to impress these objections on General Joffre. He failed.[14] Joffre was interested only in action. 'You cannot lose time in war,' Maurice Hankey observed.[15] Time was the last thing which Joffre could afford his ally. Nor was he interested in allowing the British greater independence and initiative. He had no expectation that the BEF could defeat the German Army. Only the French Army could do that. The BEF's role was to act as an effective distraction. It mattered less where the British attacked; it was more important that they fought. And the sooner the better.

British acquiescence in the imperatives of French strategy was reluctant and fearful. It was also explicit in its awareness of the cost. 'We must act with all our energy and do our utmost to help the French even though . . . we [suffer] very heavy losses indeed,' Kitchener informed Sir Douglas Haig on 19 August.[16] The probability of heavy losses was made more certain by the wholly inadequate resources with which the BEF was required to discharge its responsibilities to the alliance.

The material weakness of the BEF had been apparent for some time. 'What we want out here are *men*, *guns* and ammunition – not cigarettes and mufflers!'

---

13. On 26 December the infantry formations of the BEF were divided into two Armies. The First (I, IV and Indian Corps) was commanded by Haig; the Second (II and III Corps) by Smith-Dorrien.
14. F-M Earl Haig, *The Private Papers of Douglas Haig*, ed. R.N.W. Blake (London, Eyre & Spottiswoode, 1952), p. 100.
15. Quoted in J.F. Naylor, *A Man and an Institution. Sir Maurice Hankey, the Cabinet Secretariat and the Custody of Cabinet Secrecy* (Cambridge, Cambridge University Press, 1984), p. 56.
16. Haig, *Private Papers*, p. 102.

Brigadier-General Hubert Gough wrote angrily to his wife in November 1914.[17] The heavy fighting round Ypres had revealed serious shortages of howitzer and field-gun ammunition.[18] 'Our arrangements do not contemplate battles lasting a month!' declared Major J.L. Mowbray in his diary on 25 October.[19] The expenditure of shells was prodigious and far greater than any of the combatant armies had expected or were prepared for. Even in a three-day battle like Neuve Chapelle (10–12 March 1915), the duration of which was deliberately limited by recognition of the paucity of ammunition available, the British army fired more shells than in the whole of the South African War. No one was more horrified by this than Lord Kitchener, whose reputation was founded on his ability to win wars off the cuff and on the cheap. He had always believed that the war would be a long one. By 1915 neither he nor his field commanders were in any doubt that it would be expensive as well, both in money and in lives.

Government response to the army's needs was slow and uncertain. It took the 'shell scandal' of May 1915, contrived by Sir John French for his own – largely dishonourable – reasons,[20] to make the issue public and to stimulate demands for effective action. The foundation of the Ministry of Munitions under David Lloyd George was to have far-reaching political and social consequences, but it made little difference to the situation in 1915. At no time did the BEF have the quantity or quality of guns and ammunition to wage war with any prospect of success against the German Army heavily entrenched in positions of great tactical strength. This situation was neither of the army's making nor of its choosing. There is no doubt, however, that it sealed the fate of many gallant men and of their Commander-in-Chief.

The British offensive battles of 1915 were necessarily experimental. The problems with which the BEF was confronted were unprecedented in the army's history.

Responsibility for tactical conduct of the battles was given to the First Army commander, Sir Douglas Haig. This owed much to the coolness and resolution which he had displayed at Ypres, but was also indicative of the strains and tensions within the British high command on the Western Front, and which ran like a *motif* through the campaign of 1915.

The Commander-in-Chief, Sir John French, harboured a violent hostility to his Second Army commander, Sir Horace Smith-Dorrien. French never forgave Smith-Dorrien for the bloody rearguard action which he had fought on his own initiative at Le Cateau on 26 August. Despite the plaudits which he showered on II Corps in the immediate aftermath of the battle, French had come to believe that it had carelessly jeopardized the survival of the whole expeditionary force. From that moment Smith-Dorrien was a marked man. The German gas attack on Second Army at Ypres on 22 April gave French the opportunity to rid himself of an unwelcome subordinate and he effected Smith-Dorrien's ignominious dismissal five days later.

Haig's army made four assaults on the German line in 1915: at Neuve Chapelle (10–12 March), Aubers Ridge (9 May), Festubert (15–27 May) and

17. A.H. Farrar-Hockley, *Goughie: the Life of General Sir Hubert Gough* (London, Hart-Davis, MacGibbon, 1975), p. 149.
18. 'The Diary of Major J.L. Mowbray' (in the possession of the Royal Artillery Institution, Woolwich), p. 48.
19. *op. cit.*, p. 45.
20. For the 'shell scandal', see below, Chapter 5.

Map 2   The Western Front in 1915

Loos (25 September–8 October). Haig brought to their planning and preparation all the professional meticulousness on which he prided himself. Every aspect of battle was deliberated in detail. Assaulting troops were withdrawn to rear areas for special training. Attacks were thoroughly rehearsed. Tactical units were given specific objectives. Care was taken to ensure that each infantryman had a clear understanding of what was expected of him. Consideration was given to the vexed problem of infantry–artillery co-operation and expedients devised. Advantage was taken of new developments. Neuve Chapelle was the first battlefield in the history of war to be surveyed in its entirety by aerial photographic reconnaissance. Chlorine gas was used at Loos. Despite the BEF's limited resources, overwhelming concentration of force at the point of assault was achieved. The result was failure.

By the autumn of 1915 the unpalatable truth was that the BEF had suffered a series of clear tactical defeats. And it was doubtful to what extent the strategic purpose of distracting German attention from the French offensives had been achieved. Only Loos can be considered a major battle. The others were mere pin-pricks which contributed little to the support of French attacks. No significant gains of ground were made. The human costs were high.[21] The German attack at Ypres in April demonstrated their continuing, unpredictable and dangerous capacity for seizing the initiative.

The BEF's failure was not total. On the first day at Neuve Chapelle and on part of the front on the first day at Loos, Haig's troops overran the German front line and effected deep penetrations into the enemy position. On neither occasion could the impetus be sustained. The Germans were able to re-group and counter-attack. The line stabilized, casualties mounted. Once battles entered the attritional stage, the BEF's lack of material resources compelled a halt to offensive action.

Both failure and success held important lessons for the future. Attempts to distill wisdom from the bitter experience of battle, however, met with mixed fortune. Lessons mis-learned as well as lessons learned helped shape the conduct of war in 1916.

The key lessons appeared to concern the artillery. Artillery would be the chief weapon of offence. The recipe for success was long preliminary bombardments, limited objectives and wide fronts of assault.

Long preliminary bombardments, requiring ample supplies of heavy guns and ammunition, could alone ensure sufficient damage to the enemy front line for the infantry to assault it without incurring crippling casualties. The tragic failure at Aubers Ridge on 9 May was an important influence. Haig, himself, summarized the response in the immediate aftermath of the battle. 'The defences in our front are so carefully and so strongly made, and mutual support with machine-guns is so complete,' he wrote in his diary on 11 May, 'that in order to demolish them a *long methodical bombardment* will be necessary by heavy artillery (guns and howitzers) before Infantry are sent forward to attack.'[22] Infantry was dethroned as queen of the battlefield and relegated to the role of 'mopper up' for the artillery. Artillery would conquer; infantry would occupy.

---

21. Official British casualty figures were: Neuve Chapelle, 12,892; Aubers Ridge, 11,629; Festubert, 16,648; and Loos, 50,380. British casualties in the defensive battle of 2nd Ypres were 59,275.
22. Haig, *Private Papers*, p. 93.

The pre-war tactic of fire *and* manoeuvre was replaced by the concept of fire *then* manoeuvre. It was a crucial mistake.

Limited objectives would ensure that the infantry did not out-distance its protective umbrella of artillery fire. Neuve Chapelle and Loos provided clear evidence of the ability of the British infantry to storm the German front line, but without the support of artillery they were left desperately vulnerable to the German machine-guns carefully concealed 800–1,000 yards to the rear if they attempted to maintain the impetus of the assault. It was better to take a line at a time, consolidate, bring up the artillery and begin the systematic demolition of the second line.

Wide fronts would protect the flanks of any break-in from enfilade artillery fire. The very narrow frontages of the spring battles had been necessitated by limited supplies of ammunition. At Loos the use of gas had made possible an attack on a six-division front, but even that had proved inadequate. A front of at least twenty-five miles was considered necessary.

Important lessons were not learned. The desperate gallantry of the British and Indian infantry floundering on the slopes of Aubers Ridge expunged the memory of Neuve Chapelle where a short bombardment had succeeded with dramatic effect. Festubert demonstrated the importance of the element of surprise even when the artillery bombardment appeared to have reduced a defence position to rubble, but this was ignored.

Most crucially of all, infantry tactics fell into abeyance. '[There was] no effort to limit that solid target of frail human bodies offered by successive lines of men all walking across no-man's land simultaneously and unprotected,' wrote Captain G.C. Wynne.[23] The spectre of the Somme was already apparent.

At Neuve Chapelle the possibility of a genuine breakthrough had been lost because the high command learned too late of its opportunity and was unable to commit reserves to an effective exploitive manoeuvre.

At Loos, in order to avoid this, Haig requested Sir John French to place an adequate reserve close to the rear of the First Army's attacking divisions and under Haig's command. This was not done. The spectacular success of the 15th (Scottish) Division, which penetrated the German position to a depth of 3,000 yards by 09.00 hours on the first morning of the battle, was not exploited. The 21st and 24th divisions were not released from GHQ reserve until well after dark. Their movement forward was a nightmare. By the time they were committed to the attack they were cold, hungry, tired and confused, and all chance of success had gone. They suffered heavily.

The huge casualty bill and the miniscule gains of ground disturbed British public opinion. Sir John French sensed trouble. He resorted to his customary tactic when cornered. He lied. The publication of his despatch on the battle in *The Times* on 2 November contained fundamental inaccuracies about the release of the reserves. French refused to make corrections even after receiving a letter of protest from Haig. This squalid episode contributed further to the doubts about French's suitability for high command. Haig had complained to Kitchener as early as 29 September about French's conduct at Loos.[24] The King

23. G.C. Wynne, *If Germany Attacks. The Battle in Depth in the West* (London, Faber & Faber, 1940), p. 42.
24. Haig, *Private Papers*, p. 105.

and Asquith had also been given the benefit of his views on the war. On 8 December the Prime Minister asked Haig to succeed French as Commander-in-Chief..His appointment was formally announced on 16 December.

On Haig's shoulders would fall the responsibility of leading the great new volunteer armies. 'You have a great strategical mind,' his old patron Lord Haldane wrote to him. 'But now you have a great task and responsibility, a task and responsibility with which you are admirably fitted by gifts and training to deal. My best wishes are with you in this new and higher phase of one of the most brilliant military careers of modern times.'[25]

Gallipoli[26]

The Western Front was not the main theatre for British military operations in 1915. While the British Expeditionary Force in France and Flanders was learning the painful lessons of war against a major military and industrial power, another British army was attempting to hasten the defeat of Germany by striking a knock-out blow against her ally Turkey in the eastern Mediterranean.

The Gallipoli campaign remains one of the major controversies of the war, haunted still by thoughts of 'might have been'. Its conduct has attracted few defenders. Asquith believed that the blows struck against the Turkish Army were so severe as to cripple it and to make possible later British victories in Mesopotamia and Palestine. But this was not the intention of the campaign, which failed to achieve any of its proclaimed objectives, and it is difficult to see it as anything other than a major British defeat.

The concept which lay behind the campaign has suffered a kinder fate. To many, it is one of the rare examples of strategic inspiration in a war which seemed to have been inoculated against an outbreak of military genius. The prevarication and timidity of its execution are seen as unworthy of the campaign's grand design. Failure was a tragic lost opportunity of bringing the war to a speedy end and of avoiding further years of futile bloody slaughter on the Western Front.

Defence of the Gallipoli campaign on the basis of its supposed strategic genius, however, rests on the false assumption that it is proper to separate consideration of the campaign's intentions from the means available for their implementation.[27] And it ignores the very great degree of wishful thinking

25. *op. cit.*, p. 118.
26. For Gallipoli, see British Official History, *Military Operations Gallipoli* (2 vols., London, Heinemann, 1929, 1932). The volumes were compiled by Brigadier-General C.F. Aspinall-Oglander. The Australian Official History is C.E.W. Bean's *The Story of Anzac: the Official History of Australia in the War of 1914–1918* (2 vols., Sydney, Angus & Robertson, 1941). (See also C.E.W. Bean, *Gallipoli Correspondent: the Frontline Diary of C.E.W. Bean*, ed. K. Fewster (London, Allen & Unwin, 1983).) The *Dardanelles Commission*, First Report and Supplement, 1917, and Final Report and Appendices, 1919, Cmd 8490, Cmd 371, is an impressive analysis of the campaign's bungled planning and co-ordination. Secondary works include: P.H. Liddle, *Men of Gallipoli* (London, Allen Lane, 1976), A. Moorehead, *Gallipoli* (London, Hamish Hamilton, 1956) and R. Rhodes James, *Gallipoli* (London, Batsford, 1965). For Hamilton, see I.B.M. Hamilton, *The Happy Warrior: a Life of General Sir Ian Hamilton* (London, Cassell, 1966).
27. Peter Liddle has drawn attention to this important consideration. P.H. Liddle, 'The Dardanelles Gallipoli Campaign: Concept and Execution' in P.H. Liddle, ed., *Home Fires and Foreign Fields. British Social and Military Experience in the First World War* (London, Brassey's, 1985), p. 102.

which riddled the strategic concept and sowed the seeds of future disaster.

Gallipoli was spawned in the fertile imagination of Winston Churchill. His was the inspiration and the driving force behind the plan for an attack designed to knock Turkey out of the war. Frustration with the stalemate on the Western Front, a restless desire to find a use for Britain's reserves of naval power, and the Grand Duke Nicholas's request for a British 'demonstration' against Turkey to relieve pressure on Russia in the Caucasus did little more than present Churchill with an opportunity to obtain War Council sanction for a plan which had long been maturing in his mind and which opened up endless vistas of strategic opportunity without any need for an increase in British resources and at no political and military cost if the expedition was not at once successful.

Even before the war began, Churchill showed acute awareness of the potential of Turkish friendship and the dangers of Turkish hostility. He had considerable sympathy for the aims and aspirations of the Young Turks and made strenuous personal efforts to try and convince them of the advantages of a British alliance.[28] When this proved unavailing, he was anxious to prevent the spread of German influence. In the last hours of peace, he sought unsuccessfully for Cabinet permission to allow Admiral Milne to pre-empt the expiry of the ultimatum to Germany and sink the cruisers *Goeben* and *Breslau* while they were still under the guns of the British fleet. Refusal brought the first of the delays which were to be so damaging to the conduct of war against Turkey in 1915. The escape of the *Goeben* and *Breslau* into the Sea of Marmora resulted in a rapid deterioration in Anglo-Turkish relations and war was declared on 5 November. This posed a serious threat to the British position in Egypt and was pregnant with menace for the Indian Empire, heavily peopled by the Turks' co-religionists. Neither danger was lost on Lord Kitchener.

For Churchill, Turkey was not only a threat but also an opportunity. A decisive blow struck against Turkey would guarantee the security of the Suez Canal and of Egypt, stifle any possible disaffection in the Muslim community of India, demonstrate to neutral opinion the omnipotence of British power, bring Italy, Greece, Bulgaria and Romania into the war on the Allied side and effect the salvation of Serbia. Above all, it would enable western resources of food and munitions to be sent to Russia all the year round and give greater (possibly decisive) weight to the massive but ill-equipped Russian armies in their fight against Germany and Austria on the Eastern Front.

Admiral Sturdee's victory at the Falkland Islands on 8 December convinced Churchill that Britain had the naval capacity to mount an operation against Turkey without jeopardizing the security of the Grand Fleet in the North Sea. Events moved swiftly. And it was downhill all the way.

On 2 January Kitchener received the Russian request for British action against Turkey. On 5 January Churchill signalled Vice-Admiral Sir Sackville Carden, commanding the British squadron in the Aegean, with a request for his opinion on the feasibility of forcing the Dardanelles and sending a fleet into the Sea of Marmora. At the War Council meeting on 8 January Kitchener expressed himself in favour of such an attack, but declared that there were no troops

28. W.S. Churchill, *The World Crisis, 1911–1914* (London, Thornton Butterworth, 1923), pp. 479–82.

available to support it. On 13 January Churchill presented Admiral Carden's reply to the War Council. It was a decisive moment.[29]

Carden rejected any possibility of the Dardanelles being 'rushed'. But he believed that their defences could be systematically destroyed by naval gunfire and a fleet then passed safely through the Straits.[30] The plan had enormous attractions. No troops would be needed. Only old surplus ships would be used. If the bombardment failed, the operation could be broken off without adverse consequences. The War Council was floundering.[31] It wished to take action, but was unsure what action to take. There was no shortage of ideas, but Churchill was alone in having a definite plan and one which appeared to offer endless strategic possibilities in return for very minimal risks. There was widespread support for Churchill's proposal and the War Council unanimously resolved to proceed with the plan.

Even at the 13 January meeting, however, many of the ambiguities, misconceptions and tensions which were to destroy the campaign were already apparent.

Confusion of purpose was encapsulated in the War Council's instructions to the Admiralty. These were to 'prepare for a naval expedition in February to bombard and take the Gallipoli peninsula, with Constantinople as its objective'. The connection between *bombarding* the peninsula and *taking* it was unclear. The navy obviously had the capacity to bombard the peninsula, but how was it to take it without the landing of troops, which was not envisaged? In what sense was Constantinople the fleet's object? What was it to do when it arrived? Would its mere presence be sufficient to cow Turkey into submission? Or would it have to bombard the capital? If so, what would be its targets? And what would it do if the Turks did not surrender?

The fundamental assumption on which the plan rested was that the intrusion of a British fleet into the Sea of Marmora and its appearance off Constantinople was capable of effecting Turkey's withdrawal from the war by inspiring a pro-British coup – gun-boat diplomacy on the grand scale. This assumption was never submitted to rigorous scrutiny. There are reasons to doubt it.

Turkish politics were undoubtedly confused and volatile.[32] There undoubtedly existed a pro-British faction. But Turkey's alliance with Germany was more than a simple product of the coercive effect of two German cruisers. The progressive forces in Turkey saw a German alliance as the best way to achieve the modernization of their country. The Germans offered help and support without strings. British motives seemed more mixed and threatening. Military action was a clumsy instrument with which to try and remedy the disastrous pre-war decline in British influence in Turkey. Given ferocious Turkish resistance to the British invasion of Gallipoli, and in the face of the strength of Turkish national aspirations, it is hard to believe that the appearance of a British fleet off Constantinople would have had the decisive effects which were imagined for it.

29. For an account of the 13 January meeting, see the extract from Hankey's notes, reprinted in M. Gilbert, *Winston S. Churchill. Volume III Companion Part 1 Documents July 1914–April 1915* (London, Heinemann, 1972), pp. 407–11.
30. For details of the plan, see *op. cit.*, pp. 405–6.
31. See F-M Sir W.R. Robertson, *Soldiers and Statesmen 1914–1918* (2 vols., London, Cassell, 1926).
32. I should like to thank Dr M.O.H. Ursinus for helpful discussions on pre-war Ottoman politics.

Consideration of a naval attack on the Dardanelles was not new. In 1906 a joint General Staff and Admiralty committee undertook a feasibility study which rejected the proposal as militarily unsound. Their recommendation – contained in CID paper 92-B – was accepted by the Committee of Imperial Defence on 28 February 1907. Belief that this advice could be disregarded rested on untested assumptions about improvements in British naval gunnery and about the decline of Turkish morale since her defeat in the Balkan War of 1912. Not everyone was convinced by these arguments.

The unanimous resolve of the War Council on 13 January did not include the acquiescence of the professional head of the Royal Navy, Admiral Lord Fisher, whose silence at the meeting was wrongly taken for consent. Fisher was never convinced of the validity of the operation. Deeply versed in naval history, he was uncomfortably aware of Nelson's dictum that a 'ship cannot defeat a fort'. He feared a piecemeal attrition of naval resources in the eastern Mediterranean with possibly disastrous consequences for the balance of power in the North Sea. He sharpened his anxiety in lonely moments of critical reflection only to see it blunted again in the company of Churchill's overpowering optimism. But the process was wearing for the old man and in the end he snapped – with important effects on the conduct of the war and for the future of British politics.[33]

Hankey was another prominent dissenter. Although he favoured a British initiative in the Mediterranean, he harboured no illusions about the difficulties which this presented. He envisaged a large-scale *combined operation* which would require the employment of substantial military forces, detailed planning and specialist equipment.[34] In order to emphasize his doubts about a purely naval operation he twice circulated the War Council with CID paper 92-B and wrote to the Prime Minister direct, but without effect. At heart, British planning was vitiated by a fatal complacency and a disregard for Turkish powers of resistance which had strong racial undertones.

British confidence that battle could be broken off at will without detriment if the bombardment failed was also dubious. Kitchener, in particular, was deeply concerned about the repercussions of a British failure on Muslim opinion. It was impossible to keep the bombardment secret. 'The publicity of the announcement had committed us,' Kitchener realized on 24 February in the aftermath of the attack on the Outer Forts. If the navy failed, the army would have to act or Britain might 'lose the East'. Prestige became the bait in a dangerous investment trap. The lurch towards a military commitment began.

On 19 February 1915 the tangle of assumptions, hopes and prejudices which constituted the British plan was finally submitted to the test of battle. The results were disappointing.

Admiral Carden's plan was in three phases. Bombardment of the peninsula's Outer Forts would diminish the volume and effectiveness of Turkish fire and allow minesweepers to operate safely inside the Dardanelles Channel. Once the minefields had been swept clear, the fleet could close with the remaining Turkish defences, destroy them systematically at close range and pass through the Straits into the Sea of Marmora unimpeded. The plan never got beyond phase two.

33. For the May Crisis, see below, Chapter 5.
34. See Hankey's 'Boxing Day Memorandum', Lord Hankey, *The Supreme Command* (2 vols., London, Allen & Unwin, 1961), I, pp. 244–50.

Bombardment of the Outer Forts was hampered by poor visibility, inadequate supplies of ammunition and the constant threat of Turkish mines and torpedoes. Naval gunnery disappointed the expectations which rested on it. Accurate ranging was difficult from moving ships. Stationary ships made tempting targets. Spotting and fire-control were ineffective. The flat trajectory of naval guns and their armour-piercing ammunition were ill-designed for the demolition of fortifications. Bad weather imposed frustrating delays.

The bombardment was renewed on 25 February and considerable damage done to the Turkish forts. Minesweeping operations began on 26 February and failed with disastrous consequences. Bombardment of the Outer Forts had not succeeded in suppressing the fire of the Turks' mobile batteries of Krupp howitzers, whose position was skilfully varied and disguised by the use of dummy guns. These batteries were able to maintain an accuracy and volume of fire which shattered the morale of the civilian minesweeping crews in their converted North Sea trawlers. The reluctance of the crews to continue their operations until the Turkish batteries were destroyed forced Carden, on 13 March, to reverse his plan and send ships to demolish the Turkish defences *before* the minesweeping was complete. On 17 March he broke down under the strain and was replaced by Rear-Admiral John de Robeck.

On 18 March de Robeck launched his Anglo-French fleet against the Turkish defences inside the Dardanelles Channel in an attempt to force a passage. The *Irresistible*, *Inflexible* and *Ocean*, and the French ships *Bouvet* and *Gaulois*, were sunk or disabled by Turkish mines. The Turkish guns were not destroyed and the minefields were not removed. It was a clear and unmitigated defeat. Some of de Robeck's subordinates, notably the belligerent Commodore Roger Keyes, advocated an immediate renewal of the attack, but de Robeck believed there was no prospect of success at acceptable cost. He fully expected to be dismissed. He looked round for a saviour and found one in General Sir Ian Hamilton.

Kitchener's instinctive feeling that naval forces alone would not be adequate to knock Turkey out of the war soon manifested itself. As early as 9 February he promised military help if it was needed and began to collect the necessary troops. On 23 February he sent his protégé Lieutenant-General William Birdwood to reconnoitre the Dardanelles. After receiving Birdwood's report, on 10 March, Kitchener finally decided to commit military forces to the campaign. These would include the last remaining unused regular division, the 29th.

Command of the Mediterranean Expeditionary Force was given to one of England's most accomplished soldiers, Ian Hamilton. He was briefed by Kitchener on 13 March, the same day on which Carden's plan had begun to come apart. The 'twelve laconic paragraphs' of Hamilton's instructions have been compared to 'the utterances of a Delphic oracle'.[35] He was given a '1912 Handbook of the Turkish Army, a pre-war report on the Dardanelles defences and an out-of-date map. This was all the information put at his disposal. And he had neither a staff nor a detailed plan.'[36] He was, however, given sweeping powers of discretion. The date was Friday, the thirteenth.

On 21 March Admiral de Robeck learned of Hamilton's unfettered powers. It

35. The view of one of the Dardanelles Commissioners, quoted in A.J. Marder, *From the Dreadnought to Scapa Flow* (5 vols., London, Oxford University Press, 1961–70), II, p. 237.
36. Marder, *Dreadnought to Scapa Flow*, II, p. 237.

was his opportunity to shift responsibility for the continuance of the campaign from the navy to the army. This time he did not fail. On 22 March Hamilton agreed to an assault on the Gallipoli peninsula by military force. It was a fatal moment. The original plan lay in ruins. Now, in face of an embarrassing defeat, it was replaced by a reckless military gamble which violated all the fundamental principles of amphibious operations and which led to an even greater disaster.

The British, French, Australian and New Zealand soldiers who landed on Gallipoli on 25 April were given an impossible task. The possibility of strategic surprise was non-existent. The foolish Anglo-French bombardment of Gallipoli on 3 November 1914 had made the Turks sensitive to Allied intentions in the area even before the formal declaration of war. This had been more than confirmed by the naval operations in February and March. Tactical surprise was compromised by a criminal lack of secrecy. The collection, purpose and destination of the expeditionary force were common knowledge in the bazaars of Cairo and Alexandria. Intelligence of enemy strength, dispositions, intentions and morale was virtually nil. The terrain of narrow beaches, steep cliffs, deep ravines, dried river beds and bare hills was ill-suited to easy assault against determined defenders. The army had no specialist landing craft and was poorly trained in amphibious warfare. It had neither the numerical superiority nor the fire power to compensate for these profound handicaps.[37] The army's only advantage was its sense of moral and racial superiority. 'Not very long ago in 1912 the Greeks tried to do what we are going to perform and lost 15,000 [men],' Private John McCarthy of the 2nd Royal Fusiliers wrote in his diary. 'But we are British.'[38] It was not enough.

The Allied armies established little more than a toe-hold on the peninsula. At Cape Helles, the Anglo-French landing met with fierce resistance. An advance towards the key position of Achi Baba was made through bitter fighting and heavy casualties, but was halted before the village of Krithia. At Anzac Cove, the Australians and New Zealanders found themselves pinned down on a small beach, hemmed in by steep cliffs and gorse-covered ravines, which gave no respite from enemy artillery fire. This was the scene of savage hand-to-hand fighting for positions of tactical advantage, since immortalized in the national memory of Australia and New Zealand: Lone Pine, Quinn's Post, Shrapnel Gully. Offensive operations were severely handicapped by lack of ammunition and by the ineffectiveness of naval gunfire against small trench targets. Turkish resistance, inspired by Mustapha Kemal and organized by the German Liman von Sanders, was fierce, even fanatical. By June, the stalemate was total.

The final Allied bid for victory was made in August with new landings at Suvla Bay, combined with simultaneous offensives at Anzac and Cape Helles. The Suvla Bay landings took the Turks by surprise, but the vacillating caution of the local commander, General Sir Frederick Stopford, unredeemed by any effective interference from the Commander-in-Chief, saw the chances of a decisive success evaporate within hours.

Within less than a fortnight the Dardanelles Committee – as the War Council was now known – was actively considering evacuation. Sir Ian Hamilton was

37. For sound principles of amphibious operations, see J. Thompson, *No Picnic. 3 Commando Brigade in the South Atlantic: 1982* (London, Guild Publishing, 1985), pp. 31–53.
38. Manuscript diary. Photocopy in the author's possession. I should like to thank Major R.J. Snell, RA, for drawing this to my attention, and Mr M. McCarthy for allowing me to quote from his father's diary.

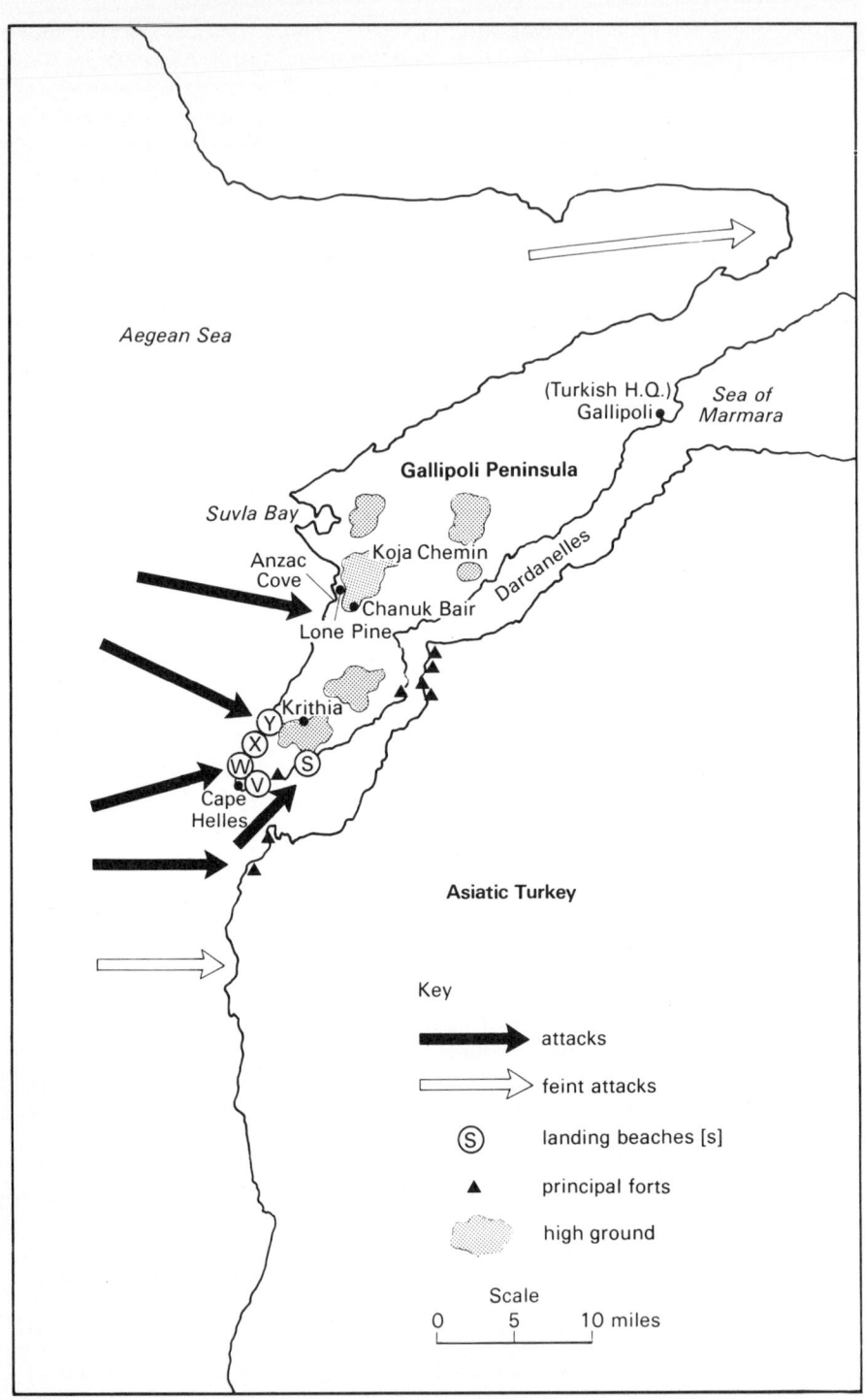

Map 3   Gallipoli, April 1915

recalled on 14 October. He was a man of great intelligence and professional distinction. Throughout his long life, and since his death, he never lacked defenders or admirers. He was undoubtedly unlucky, but he did not possess the iron will and the ruthless determination to compensate for the appalling disadvantages under which he assumed and conducted his command.

On 31 October General Monro reported on his tour of the battlefield and unhesitatingly recommended evacuation. This occasioned one of Churchill's bitterest remarks: 'He came, he saw, he capitulated.' He was also right. But it took a further six weeks before Suvla and Anzac were abandoned, six weeks in which the discomforts and casualties of the army mounted inexorably through dysentery, frostbite and heart disease. Cape Helles was evacuated on the night of 8/9 January. Only in its depressing *finale* had the conduct of the campaign shown the combination of imagination, attention to detail, thorough planning and surprise, which had been conspicuous only by their absence in April.

There remain the 'ifs'. If Fisher had given Churchill his whole-hearted support? If the naval commanders had shown greater resolution? If local British knowledge of the Turkish minefields had not been disregarded? If Kitchener had not delayed in despatching the 29th Division? If a renewed naval attack had been made after the 'Beagle' class of fast destroyer-minesweepers became available in mid-April? If Hamilton had attacked the neck of the peninsula instead of its tip? If Achi Baba had been captured in the early days of the campaign? If Stopford had not thrown away his opportunity at Suvla? If the amount of men and materials committed to the campaign by August had been made available to it from the start?

In truth, the campaign failed because the resources available for it were totally inadequate. Hankey recognized this. It was the substance of his memorandum to the War Council on 19 March, advocating a properly constituted joint operation involving substantial military forces. This received only perfunctory discussion. It may have been possible, in the early stages of the war against Turkey, to have captured Gallipoli by a *coup de main* and to have held it long enough to permit the safe passage of the fleet. But this would have required an élite commando force of trained specialists with the necessary equipment. Britain did not possess such a force in 1915. Otherwise, it should have been recognized that capture of the peninsula was a major operation of war requiring the training and equipment of a large army, the successful landing of which depended upon satisfactory intelligence, surprise and overwhelming manpower and firepower at the point of assault. Anything less invited the disaster which occurred.

The actual results of the campaign are not problematical. Churchill lost his place in the forefront of affairs and was haunted for the rest of his life by images of British dead floating in the bloody waters off Cape Helles. Advocates of an 'eastern strategy' suffered a blow from which they never really recovered. Britain's last Liberal government was replaced by an unhappy coalition under Mr Asquith. The Gallipoli experience left an indelible impression on the national consciousness of Australia and is never far below the surface of Australian Anglophobia. Bulgaria entered the war in July on the side of the Central Powers and invaded Serbia on 7 October.

Russia received no effective support.[39] The German armies occupied Warsaw,

39.   Professor Norman Stone has disputed the view, strongly held by Churchill and Lloyd George,

Ivangorod, Kovno, Novo-Georgievsk and Brest-Litovsk. Italy joined the Entente in May, but succeeded only in suffering a series of defeats on the Isonzo in July and August. A rash British advance on Baghdad had been halted by the Turks at Ctesiphon in November. General Townshend's army was forced to retreat and was now beseiged in a bend of the River Tigris at Kut. It had been a bleak year.

For the British, 1915 was a year of experiment. It had produced no clear formula for success. Hope lay with the great volunteer armies which had responded to Lord Kitchener's call to arms and which would soon be massing on the Western Front.

---

that the defeat of Turkey would have made a decisive difference to the course of the war on the Eastern Front. Russia's problem was not lack of supplies, but inability to deliver them to her armies, see Stone, *Eastern Front*, Chapters 9 and 13. For the whole question of supplies to Russia, see K. Neilson, *Strategy and Supply. The Anglo-Russian Alliance 1914–1917* (London, Allen & Unwin, 1984).

3

'The Wearing-Out Fight' 1916–1917[1]

> The war is not against the men immediately opposed to you, it
> is against the German nation. The Allied armies must press
> against the German line, and strike it hard and repeatedly:
> some day the front will waver and bend, but let me never hear
> from anyone in France any mention even of the words 'piercing
> the line'.
>
> *Lord Kitchener*[2]

> I am afraid England will have to accustom herself to far greater
> losses than those of Neuve Chapelle before we finally crush the
> German Army.
>
> *Brigadier-General John Charteris*[3]

The battles of 1915 had demonstrated the awesome resilience of the German
Army. By the end of the year neither victory nor peace was at hand. Nothing
short of a massive, sustained and co-ordinated Allied offensive on all fronts
seemed to offer hope of success. This lesson was not lost on the Entente's
military high command. 'The trouble with Allied strategy,' declared Lloyd
George, 'was that there wasn't one.'[4] The generals did not agree. At Chantilly, in
December 1915, they did their utmost to overcome the debilitating conflict of
interests which attended meetings of their political masters[5] and to find a way of
winning the war during the coming year.

The Chantilly Conference had important results. The German and Austro-
Hungarian armies were made the target of Allied strategy. Victory was
impossible until they were defeated; and they could only be defeated at those
places where the largest parts of their forces were maintained. These 'principal
fronts' were in France and Belgium, Russia, and Italy. All other fronts were
declared to be 'subsidiary' and only the minimum number of troops were to be
retained there. Co-ordinated offensives would be launched against the Central

1. For the military history of 1916, see British Official History (henceforth *OH*), *Military
   Operation France and Belgium 1916* (Vol. 1 compiled by Brigadier-General Sir J. Edmonds,
   London, Macmillan, 1932; Volume 2 complied by Captain W. Miles, London, Macmillan,
   1938).
2. Quoted in J. Charteris, *Field-Marshal Earl Haig* (London, Cassell, 1929), p. 210.
3. J. Charteris, *At GHQ* (London, Cassell, 1931), p. 85.
4. For Lloyd George's view of the importance of inter-allied co-operation and the attendant
   difficulties, see D. Lloyd George, *War Memoirs* (2 vols., London, Odhams, [1938]), I,
   pp. 211–31, 280–8, 536–76, 838–60.
5. See D. Dutton, 'The Calais Conference of December 1915', *Historical Journal*, XXI (1978),
   pp. 143–57.

Powers along the 'principal fronts' using every man and gun available. The continuing influence of Clausewitz is apparent. The whole of the Allied strategy was imbued with the concepts of mass, concentration of force and the decisive battle. The contribution of the British was to be unprecedented in its magnitude.

On the Western Front plans were agreed for a Franco-British offensive of sixty-five divisions on a forty-five mile front either side of the junction between the two armies on the River Somme. The attack was not intended as part of a long-term campaign to wear down the German Army. It was to be a *decisive* battle. Victory would not be achieved at some indeterminate date through attrition of the German national will to resist, but through a conclusive defeat of the German Army in the field in 1916. This plan was never executed. A great battle was fought on the Somme, but it was not the one intended by the Allied planners at Chantilly. 'The essence of war,' wrote Clausewitz, 'is to confront the independent will of the enemy.' And the enemy had other ideas.

General Erich von Falkenhayn was singular among German soldiers of the First World War. He alone was willing to contemplate a conclusion to the war satisfactory to Germany which did not involve achieving shattering military victories of total annihilation. His experience of the great battles in Champagne during September 1915 left him dubious about the prospects of making a breakthrough at acceptable cost. He also identified the war as a struggle for supremacy not between Germany and Russia but between Germany and England. England's principal weapon in her attempt to ruin Germany was the French Army. If the French Army could be broken England would have to accept Germany's terms. But how was the French Army to be broken? The answer was 'by attrition'. Falkenhayn would launch a massive attack against a narrow sector of the French front. The aim would not be to gain ground, but to 'bleed France white'. He thought carefully about the point of assault. It would have to be a place which the French Army would be compelled by reasons of national honour to defend to the limit of its strength. He chose Verdun.[6]

The German attack began on 21 February with an intense artillery bombardment. Fort Douaumont, the strongest part of the French defensive system which protected Verdun, was captured on 25 February. It became clear that the French Army and the French people were engaged in a battle for national survival. The effect on the preparations of the British army was immediate.

On 27 February Haig agreed to take over the front of the French Tenth Army sandwiched between the British First and Third Armies in Artois. This began a process which saw responsibility for offensive action on the Western Front in 1916 shift inexorably from the French to the British. The crisis came in May.

On the 24th Joffre wrote to Haig, requesting him to launch an offensive not later than the beginning of July. Joffre had every cause for concern. In three months of bitter fighting, which they had endured entirely alone, the French Army had lost nearly 200,000 men. Their remaining reserves were being consumed by the Verdun 'mincing machine' at an alarming rate. The need for the British to act was apparent. And not only the French needed help.

On 15 May Austrian forces, under General Conrad, had attacked the Italians in the Trentino, inflicting serious damage. On the Eastern Front, a major

6. E. von Falkenhayn, *General Headquarters 1914–1916 and its Critical Decisions* (London, Hutchinson, 1919), pp. 209–18.

Russian offensive was planned for Galicia in June. It was imperative that as much German strength as possible was pinned down in the west.

Haig understood the gravity of the situation. He was anxious to help, but he had problems of his own. His was an independent command. He was responsible to the British government and the British people for the safety and integrity of the BEF. And it was clear to him that the BEF was not ready. 'I have not got an Army in France,' he had written in his diary on 29 March, 'but a collection of divisions untrained for the field.'[7] Not until the middle of August would the BEF reach the peak of its strength and preparation. But by then it might be too late.

Haig did not take long to resolve his dilemma. On 25 May he had an important meeting with the Chief of the Imperial General Staff, Sir William Robertson. Haig's resolution was clear and unequivocal. 'I came to the conclusion that we *must* march to the support of the French,' he wrote that same evening.[8] The next day he had an amicable and emotional meeting with Joffre. Haig agreed to attack on 1 July 'or thereabouts'. The hopes of the Allied planners at Chantilly had run into the sand.

The Battle of the Somme was to be a unique experience for the British people. Never before had they attempted to wage war on such a scale. Not since have they wished to. But as far as the narrow conduct of the war was concerned the only new thing about the battle was its magnitude. The fundamental realities remained the same as they had in 1915. The British army was hostage to French need and German power. The French chose the place, the date, even the exact time of the British attack. The Germans chose the size of the French contribution. When the infantry assault began on 1 July only six French divisions could be spared, less than a seventh of those envisaged at Chantilly.

The aim of the battle also underwent a transformation. Although Haig never entirely discounted the possibility of achieving a decisive success, he thought this was improbable.[9] 'The Third and Fourth Armies will undertake offensive operations . . . with the object of relieving the pressure on the French at Verdun and inflicting loss on the enemy,' he ordered on 16 June.[10] It would be a 'wearing-out fight'.

Few doubts assailed the men of the BEF, who approached their task in a spirit of crusading ardour. To them, the impending battle would be the 'Big Push'. This was what they had come to France to take part in – to vindicate their cause, their country and their race. And they would prevail. The scale of the preparations alone seemed to ensure that.

The preparations were undoubtedly prodigious. Huge stocks of ammunition and stores were accumulated. Standard and narrow gauge railways and trench tramways were built to carry them. New roads were made and old ones improved. Causeways were thrown over the marshy valleys. Many miles of deep communications trenches were constructed and the vital telephone wires carefully buried. Three large and seven small mines were laid. A new Army, the Fourth, was created on 1 March and responsibility for detailed tactical planning

---

7. Quoted in J. Terraine, *The Smoke and the Fire. Myths and Anti-Myths of War 1861–1945* (London, Sidgwick & Jackson, 1980), p. 107.
8. F-M Earl Haig, *The Private Papers of Douglas Haig 1914–1919*, ed. R.N.W. Blake (London, Eyre & Spottiswoode, 1952), p. 144. Haig's italics.
9. Charteris, *At GHQ*, p. 143.
10. GHQ, AOD 12, 16 June 1916, see *OH 1916*, I, Appendix 13.

of the battle delegated to its commander, General Sir Henry Rawlinson. Anticipation was electric.

The shock of battle, however, was preceded by disappointment.

On the evening of 30 May 1916 the German High Seas Fleet slipped out of Wilhelmshaven and into the North Sea to dispute with the British command of the sea. The Royal Navy's chance had come.

'Today will be the day/You said so'[11]

Elements of the two great fleets had clashed before. At the Heligoland Bight on 28 August 1914 the British failed in an attempt to entice the German capital ships from the safety of Jade Bay, but succeeded in sinking three German cruisers. On 24 January 1915 a German sortie to the Dogger Bank resulted in the sinking of the battlecruiser *Blücher* and the crippling of the *Seydlitz* and *Derfflinger*. On both occasions the Germans were lucky to escape without severe losses. Neither battle provided encouragement for them to risk a major fleet engagement with the British. For the remainder of 1915 the High Seas Fleet concentrated its energies on the submarine campaign; the big ships stayed in port.

This policy was regarded with distaste by many in the German navy, including Grand Admiral von Tirpitz himself. And at the beginning of 1916 the hopes of those who wished to pursue a more aggressive naval strategy were given a significant boost, with the appointment of Vice-Admiral Reinhard Scheer to command of the High Seas Fleet.[12]

The trouble with the High Seas Fleet was that the Germans did not really know what to do with it. The Navy Act of 1898 had attempted to establish the fleet as an effective instrument for the fulfilment of national policy. This was not easy. The political dominance of the army within German society and its first claim on the resources of the state made it improbable that the navy would ever be able to challenge the British fleet on anything resembling terms of equality. If this was the case, then why build a fleet at all? Tirpitz had no doubts. He did not believe that it was necessary for the German navy to attain numerical equality with the British or even to inflict a tactical defeat on them in order to have a decisive influence on the course of the war. He favoured an all-out challenge to British naval power. If the German fleet was destroyed in the ensuing battle this was of no consequence. What mattered was that the price exacted from the Royal Navy for its tactical victory was a strategic defeat. Tirpitz believed that the destruction of a 'strong German fleet' could only be achieved at the cost of losses to the Royal Navy that would be so catastrophic as to strike a shattering blow at British national security and morale. The beguiling ruthlessness of this logic faced a major stumbling block, however: the Kaiser.

The High Seas Fleet was built principally for 'general purposes of national

11.   Jutland has been analysed in great detail, see Sir R. Bacon, *The Jutland Scandal* (London, Hutchinson, 1925); G. Bennett, *The Battle of Jutland* (London, Batsford, 1964); A.J. Marder, *From the Dreadnought to Scapa Flow. Volume III Jutland and After* (London, Oxford University Press, 1966). The Official History is Sir J.S. Corbett, *History of the Great War. Naval Operations Volume III* (London, Longmans Green, 1923), pp. 313ff. For the aftermath, see H. Newbolt, *History of the Great War. Naval Operations Volume IV* (London, Longmans Green, 1928), pp. 1–19.
12.   For Scheer's own unreliable account, see R. Scheer, *Germany's High Seas Fleet in the World War* (London, Cassell, 1920).

greatness'. It owed little to perceived military need. Conventional military opinion was hostile to the navy lobby. The Great General Staff regarded a navy as an expensive and strategically irrelevant toy. It was the Kaiser who wanted a fleet. This ambition owed much to his corrosive feelings of inferiority towards his British cousins whose sea power gave them dominion of the world. The navy would be a symbol of Germany's 'arrival' as a great power and a declaration of her intentions to remain one. The prestige which the possession of a fleet conferred, however, was a trap. The German navy was both more and less than an instrument of national policy, to be broken if necessary in the service of the state; it was an Imperial icon, whose loss was too appalling to contemplate. In this lay the fleet's weakness and the Kaiser's vacillating caution.

At the beginning of 1916 the continued existence of a powerful German fleet was an unavoidable strategic reality for both sides. The Germans faced a choice. They could remain on the defensive. Even if the High Seas Fleet never left port it posed a constant threat to Britain and limited her strategic options. This was the strategy favoured by the Kaiser, but resented by many of his professional advisers, who were becoming increasingly restless. Or they could seek a decision at sea. This was the strategy favoured by Tirpitz, but dreaded by the Kaiser. It was Admiral Scheer who broke the deadlock.

Scheer was determined upon a more aggressive use of Germany's naval power, but he was less sanguine than Tirpitz and less ambitious. The thought of facing the full might of the British Grand Fleet made little appeal. Instead, he advocated a strategy common to the weaker side throughout military history – that of ambush. He planned to trap part of the British fleet and destroy it in detail. A successful engagement of this kind would provide an important boost to morale and reduce the odds in his favour in the event of a future major fleet action. He was confident that he could achieve a victory at acceptable cost. More importantly, he also convinced the Kaiser.

Although Scheer's plan tempered aggression with caution, it soon became apparent that it would take a bold stroke to tempt the British into a trap. His reversion to the old tactic of bombarding the British coast met with little success. So, in May 1916, he made his gambler's throw. He decided to offer his battle-cruiser squadron as bait to the British battle-cruisers, based at Rosyth on the Firth of Forth. Sixteen U-boats would be sent to ambush the Grand Fleet as it raced south out of its anchorage at Scapa Flow, in the Orkneys, to join in the fray. The High Seas Fleet would wait its chance to pounce.

The plan had little chance of success. British possession of the German naval cypher and the consistent ability displayed by British naval intelligence to intercept and decode German wireless traffic denied Scheer the precious element of surprise.[13] The faith which he put in the effectiveness of his submarines was also doomed to disappointment. But this was cold comfort to the British Commander-in-Chief, Admiral Sir J.R. Jellicoe, when he received the news for which he and his men had long been waiting.

John Jellicoe is an unusual figure in British naval history.[14] He was pre-

13. For naval intelligence, see A.W. Ewing, *The Man of Room 40: the Life of Sir Alfred Ewing* (London, Hutchinson, 1939) and Sir W. James, *The Eyes of the Navy: a Biographical Study of Admiral Sir Reginald Hall* (London, Methuen, 1955).
14. The authorized biography is Sir R. Bacon, *The Life of John Rushworth, Earl Jellicoe* (London, Cassell, 1936). J. Winton, *Jellicoe* (London, Michael Joseph, 1981) is excellent. See also, *The Jellicoe Papers*, ed. A. Temple Patterson (2 vols., London, Navy Records Society, 1966–8).

eminently a technician. In a service which favoured 'character' above 'training', his rise depended upon his reputation as a gunnery expert and his superb abilities as a seaman. Posterity has not found in him a satisfactory naval hero, preferring instead his dashing subordinate David Beatty.[15]

Jellicoe was not made in the heroic mould. His strategy was cautious and prudential. His decision – at Jutland – to deploy the Grand Fleet to port (and away from the enemy) rather than to starboard (and towards them) has occasioned dark hints of cowardice. This was not how the navy was expected to behave and not how it had behaved in the past. Jellicoe's dominating characteristic was the mundane quality of conscientiousness. Even this could be a weakness. There were those who found him fussy and over-concerned with trivia, and he showed a worrying inability to delegate. Haig dismissed him as 'an old woman'. He certainly lacked the arresting glamour of his great predecessors; above all he failed to reproduce their annihilating victories. It is to his credit that he did not expect to do so.

Posterity's treatment of Jellicoe has not only been unkind but also curious and paradoxical when compared with that meted out to the 'Western' generals. While they have been castigated for their myopic failure to predict or even to understand the nature of the war, for their lack of tactical acumen and for their willingness – nevertheless – to continue sacrificing the lives of countless brave men in pursuit of an overweening optimism, Jellicoe has received little credit for his far-sighted appreciation of the likelihood of tactical stalemate in the war at sea or for the prudence which his perception dictated. For the British public, fed on a rich diet of naval victories, that which was not magnificent was not war.

Jellicoe was hand-picked by Lord Fisher for the supreme command in the greatest naval battle in history. In the second Trafalgar Jellicoe was to be the new Nelson. He did not relish the rôle. This was more than a matter of temperament; it was a matter of judgement. He understood – better even than Churchill, who coined the haunting phrase – that he was 'the only man who could lose the war in an afternoon'. The consequence of his losing command of the sea would be national catastrophe. He also understood the advantages and opportunities that would result from his achieving a smashing victory. He was doubtful, however, whether this was a realistic possibility. He had good cause.

No one understood better than Jellicoe the weaknesses and limitations of the great fleet that Fisher had built for him. He spent the first few months of the war complaining bitterly about the fleet's inadequate and almost undefended base facilities. The margin of numerical superiority over the German fleet was clear, but too small for comfort, and it could easily be eroded by dangerous adventures like the Dardanelles or by the careless or cavalier actions of his subordinates, in whom he showed a disturbing lack of confidence.[16] He was painfully conscious of the navy's lack of 'doctrine', of standard tactical and operational procedures. The Admiralty – owing to Fisher's bigoted resistance – did not even possess a proper Staff until 1912, and the Grand Fleet itself had to wait until after the war began before Jellicoe was able to institute effective staff arrangements. He had grave doubts about the quality of British

---

15. For Beatty, see W.S. Chalmers, *The Life and Letters of David, Earl Beatty* (London, Hodder & Stoughton, 1951) and A.J. Marder, *Admiral of the Fleet Earl Beatty: The Last Naval Hero: An Intimate Biography* (London, Collins, 1980).
16. For Jellicoe's view of the Dardanelles, see *Jellicoe Papers*, I, p. 187; for the rôle of the battle-cruisers, see *op. cit.*, I, p. 152.

gunnery. Most of all, he was concerned that the revolution in naval technology since 1900 had effectively ended the possibility of crushing victories of total annihilation of the Nelsonic type.[17]

Jellicoe had few precedents to guide him. Those that existed were not encouraging. Study of the naval battles of the Russo-Japanese war left him with an exaggerated fear of torpedoes and of their disruptive effects on a major fleet action. The sinking of the three British cruisers *Aboukir*, *Hogue* and *Cressy* – with fearful loss of life – by the German submarine U9 on 22 September 1914 was a shocking reminder of the power of underwater weapons. And it was contemplation of these which did much to determine Jellicoe's tactics.

His unwavering concern was that he must not lose command of the sea. There is truth in Captain Cyril Falls's judgement that Jellicoe's aim was 'to make a German victory impossible rather than to make a British victory certain'.[18] By the end of October 1914 he had refined the principles on which he was prepared to accept battle. He was careful to explain these to his superiors.[19] He would seek a decision only in line of battle, through a long-range heavy gun duel in broad daylight in the northern part of the North Sea. He considered a more traditional strategy of finding the enemy, fixing him and then annihilating him much too hazardous. His response to the chaos and uncertainty of war was to place in his own hands the entire conduct of the battle. Nothing would be left to chance. By the time of their final revision, in December 1915, his fleet 'Battle Orders' had grown to inordinate length, aiming to accommodate every eventuality which might arise in the one battle he was prepared to fight, and stifling all independence and initiative in subordinate commanders. This was apparent as soon as battle was joined.

The Battle of Jutland began at 2.28 p.m. on 31 May 1916 when HMS *Galatea*, part of the scouting forces of Vice-Admiral Beatty's battle-cruiser squadron, opened fire on the German light-cruiser *Elbing*, while both were engaged in checking the credentials of an innocent Danish steamer. It ended a little over fourteen hours later when the Admiralty gave Jellicoe the bitter news that the German fleet had escaped across his rear in the middle of the night and was back in port. The number of ships involved was enormous, but the battleships of the two main fleets clashed only briefly for about twenty minutes during the evening of 31 May. The battle mainly took the form of a complicated series of feints and manoeuvres which presented uncomfortable surprises and tantalizing opportunities to both commanders-in-chief.

Scheer's plan began well. Beatty took the bait. Once contact with the German battle-cruisers was established, he immediately manoeuvred to cut them off from their base. Some have considered this to be reckless, but Beatty had every cause for confidence. Under his command he had not only his six battle-cruisers but also Rear-Admiral H. Evan-Thomas's four Dreadnought battleships, the most powerful warships ever built. Despite this, Beatty soon found himself facing a crisis. In the running fight with the German battle-cruisers, which began at 3.48 p.m., Beatty's squadron suffered grievous losses with the dramatic

17. See C. White, 'The Navy and the Naval War Reconsidered', in P.H. Liddle, ed., *Home Fires and Foreign Fields. British Social and Military Experience in the First World War* (London, Brassey's, 1985), p. 123.

18. C. Falls, *The First World War* (London, Longman, 1960), p. 186.

19. *Jellicoe Papers*, I, pp. 75–7. See especially paragraphs 11 and 12.

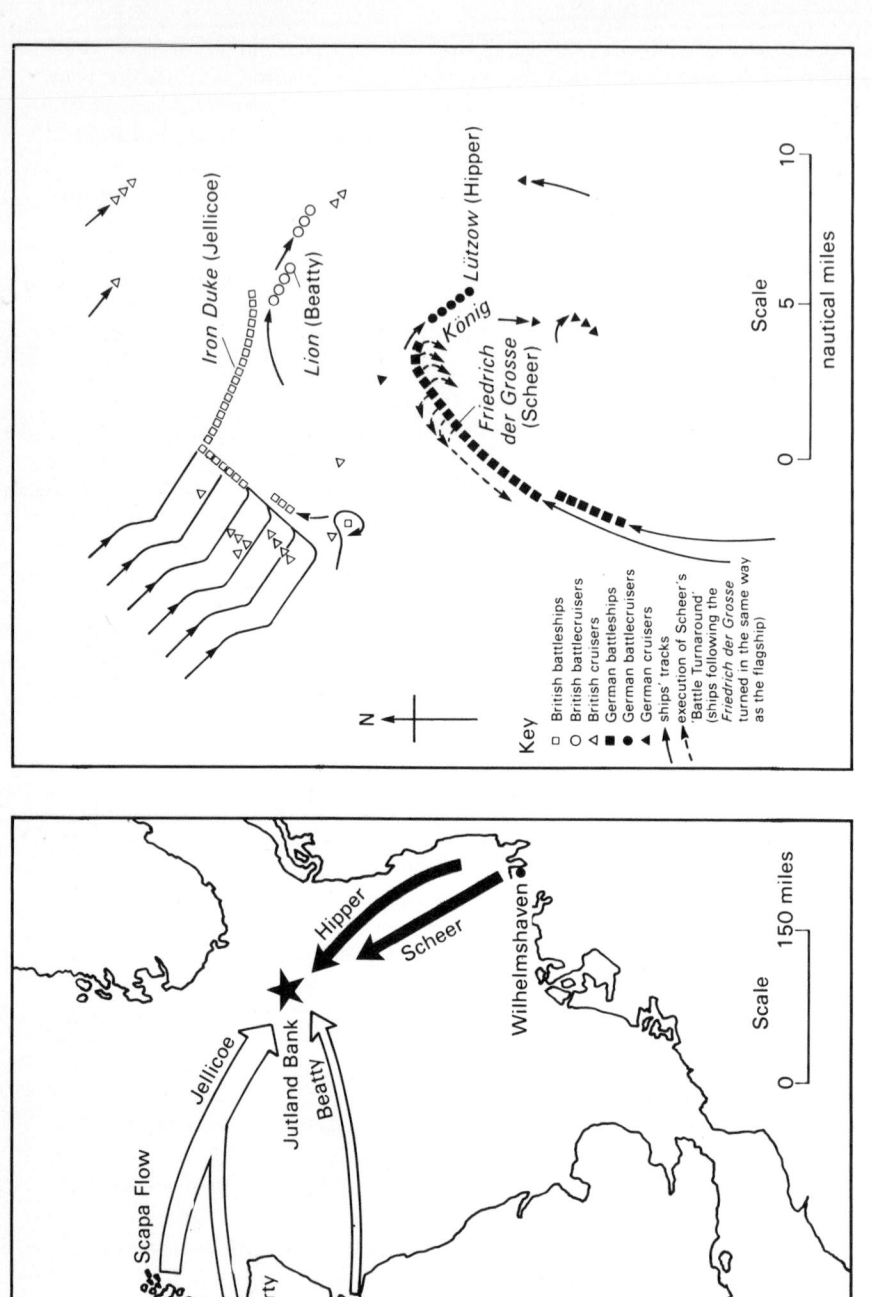

Map 4a Jutland
Map 4b Deployment of the Grand Fleet into Line of Battle and Scheer's 'Battle Turnaround'

sinking of the *Indefatigable* and *Queen Mary*. Worse was to come. At 4.33 p.m. the cruiser *Southampton* sighted the main German battle fleet. Beatty was steaming head first into a trap at 27 knots. It looked as though Scheer would get his opportunity to destroy part of the British fleet in detail. Instead, within two hours, he himself was facing disaster.

As soon as Beatty realized the danger of his position, he ordered his ships to turn. This was a manoeuvre of great hazard and was not achieved without serious losses, especially to Evan-Thomas's Fifth Battle Squadron. But it reaped a rich reward. Beatty's 'run to the North' drew the High Seas Fleet inexorably towards the deadly embrace of Jellicoe's Grand Fleet sixty miles away and closing fast.

Admiral Scheer was entirely innocent of the whereabouts of the Grand Fleet; he had no idea even that it had left port. Its imminent appearance came as a shock. Admiralty forewarning of German intentions had resulted in the British battle fleet arriving on the scene much earlier than he believed possible. And it arrived unscathed. The Grand Fleet had steamed through the sixteen German U-boats without being aware of their existence. For the Germans, their worst fears had been realized; for the Royal Navy, not only the day but also the hour had come.

The First Battle Cruiser Squadron and the Grand Fleet made visual contact at 6.01 p.m. Jellicoe's life had been a preparation for this moment. He did not fail. Within seconds[20] of establishing the course of the High Seas Fleet, Jellicoe gave the orders for the Grand Fleet to deploy in line to port. He has been heavily criticized for this decision,[21] but there can be no doubt that it was not only correct but also masterful. He gained two advantages, each important in its own right but together potentially decisive. He placed the Grand Fleet across the German Line of retreat and he crossed their 'T'.[22] Success, however, eluded him.

Faced with the prospect of defeat, Scheer displayed professionalism and courage of a high order. He acted decisively and immediately. He executed his dramatic 'battle turn-around',[23] manoeuvring first to the south and then the west. After steering west for twenty minutes he ordered another 180-degree turn, hoping to pass across the tail of the Grand Fleet as it pursued his original retreat south. He miscalculated and ran straight into the centre of the British line, which again crossed his 'T'. The German ships suffered heavy damage. Scheer had no option but to retreat. He again turned west, but this time he launched a mass torpedo attack on the British from his escorting destroyers. In conformity with the principles laid down in his memorandum of 30 October 1914,[24] Jellicoe turned away and refused battle. Posterity has found it hard to forgive him.

Scheer was still in jeopardy, however. Jellicoe lay with his entire fleet between the Germans and the safety of their bases. In the fading twilight around 8 o'clock, Scheer was again threatened with the prospect of a British broadside

20. R. Hough, *The Great War at Sea 1914–1918* (Oxford, Oxford University Press, 1983), p. 240.
21. See Churchill, *The World Crisis 1911–1918* (abridged and revised edition, London, Thornton Butterworth, 1931), pp. 609–13.
22. This was one of the main aims of naval tactics. A fleet in line cutting across the course of another fleet in column could fire all its guns in a broadside; the fleet in column could only reply with its forward firing guns and was susceptible to defeat in detail.
23. *Gefechtskehrtwendung*.
24. *Jellicoe Papers*, I, pp. 75–7.

and once more manoeuvred to the west. Darkness and the failure of successive British ships to report enemy contacts to the Grand Fleet finally allowed Scheer to escape during the night. By dawn he reached sanctuary and found himself a hero.

The Battle of Jutland was an unhappy experience for the Royal Navy. The great opportunity was missed. Many weaknesses were revealed. Some of these had been apparent beforehand and a heavy price was exacted for failure to remedy them.

The Dogger Bank had demonstrated the ineptitude of Beatty's signals officer, but he was not replaced. Poor signalling denied Beatty the support of Evan-Thomas's battleships for crucial minutes at the start of the battle-cruiser engagement, and then left them at the mercy of the whole German battle-cruiser squadron when Beatty began his 'run to the North'. Beatty himself was at fault in failing to keep Jellicoe fully informed. Only when the Grand Fleet made visual contact with Beatty's ships was Jellicoe aware of the enemy's position and able to make his deployment, and not until after the battle did he learn of the sinking of the *Queen Mary*.

There were also important material and technical inadequacies. The lack of aerial reconnaissance was a major weakness. Provision of effective illuminants for night fighting was greatly inferior to that of the Germans and this played a significant part in the escape of the High Seas Fleet. The British battle-cruisers proved extremely vulnerable to enemy fire. Three exploded during the course of the battle, and the loss of one of them – Admiral Hood's flagship *Invincible* – occurred at a moment which was certainly detrimental to prospects of a crushing British victory. The cause of the explosions was later found to be flash igniting the magazine. This danger had become apparent to the Germans after the Dogger Bank. The design of their battle-cruisers was greatly improved and at Jutland they showed an immense resilience even to the heaviest British fire, handicapped (as it was) by the poor quality of British armour-piercing ammunition. This resilience alone was a fundamental obstacle to the attainment of the kind of annihilating victory which Jellicoe was expected to achieve.

Initiative failed to repair the fleet's damaging material and technical deficiencies. From Admiral Evan-Thomas down subordinate commanders displayed a dispiriting lack of imagination. During the night of 31 May/1 June the chronic inability of junior officers to take responsibility to inform the Commander-in-Chief of the enemy's position had lamentable consequences and constituted a serious dereliction of duty. Jellicoe has been rightly criticized for the rigidity of his planning and his failure to encourage independence in his officers, but at Jutland inertia was so gross and widespread that both blame and remedy was beyond the jurisdiction of one man. Fault lay with the Navy's system and its traditions.

Jellicoe has borne the brunt of British disappointment with the Battle of Jutland. It is difficult not to sympathize with him. He was the victim of high expectations and inadequate resources and in Scheer he found a courageous and skilful opponent. Nevertheless, he fought the battle exactly as he had intended, exhibited consummate seamanship and crossed the German 'T' twice. No ship was lost through fault of his. And he remained in command of the sea. His greatest failure was the cardinal sin of all commanders. He was unlucky.

The Germans were quick to claim a victory, an impression which the pessimistic tone of the original Admiralty despatch did little to remove.[25] British losses in ships and men were significantly greater than those of Germany.[26] This was galling to British opinion, but there was no doubt who had really won. Tirpitz had been willing to purchase a strategic victory at the price of a tactical defeat. But for all the professionalism and courage of his men and their commanders and the superb engineering of their ships, they had succeeded only in winning a tactical victory at the price of a strategic defeat. 'The German fleet has assaulted its jailor,' the *New York Times* reported with cruel accuracy, 'but it is still in jail.'

Four days after the Battle of Jutland the Royal Navy and the British people suffered another blow. HMS *Hampshire* struck a mine off the Orkneys and sank. Among the dead was Lord Kitchener, who was on his way to a mission in Russia. He was destined never to witness the climactic moment of the great armies which he had recruited and inspired. Perhaps it was as well.

The Somme[27]

The Battle of the Somme lasted for 141 days.[28] Only the first day is remembered.

At 7.30 a.m. on 1 July 1916, in warm sunshine, the attacking infantry of fourteen British divisions left their assault trenches and crossed No-Man's Land towards the German wire.[29] It was the most dangerous journey on earth. By nightfall 57,000 British soldiers had become casualties. Twenty thousand of them were dead. This was more than the entire strength of the German front-line garrison at the start of the battle.[30] The day which began with such high hopes had ended in tragedy. The shock of it is still felt. 'The army recovered almost immediately,' wrote John Terraine, 'the nation never recovered.'[31]

The sense of loss was heightened by the pattern of recruitment to the Kitchener armies. Sixty per cent of the British infantry on 1 July belonged to the 'New Army'. Kitchener had agreed that those who 'joined together' should 'serve together'. And on the Somme they died together. In the industrial north of England, on Tyneside and in Ulster whole communities were plunged into mourning. The 10th West Yorks lost 22 officers and 688 men, the Accrington Pals 21 officers and 585 men, the 4th Tyneside Scottish 19 officers and 610 men,

---

25. For this, see Newbolt, *Naval Operations IV*, p. 3. It was apparently written by the First Lord, A.J. Balfour. It was not included in the collection *Battle of Jutland 30th May to 1st June 1916. Official Despatches with Appendices* (London, HMSO, n.d.) A corrective was issued on 5 June, see Newbolt, p. 6. Newbolt also prints the German despatch, pp. 4–5.
26. The Royal Navy lost 14 ships (including 3 battle-cruisers) and 6,097 men; the Germans lost 11 ships (including 1 battleship and 1 battle-cruiser) and 2,551 men.
27. For the Somme, see A.H. Farrar-Hockley, *The Somme* (London, Batsford, 1964); J. Keegan, *The Face of Battle* (London, Jonathan Cape, 1976), especially pp. 204–85; and M. Middlebrook, *The First Day on the Somme* (London, Allen Lane, 1971).
28. Purists will point out that the Somme was a campaign involving many separate battles. The naming of these was the responsibility of the post-war Battle Nomenclature Committee. They existed as discrete, comprehensible entities only in the mind of the Official Historian.
29. For the British Order of Battle on 1 July, see Middlebrook, *First Day on the Somme*, pp. 317–24.
30. G.C. Wynne, *If Germany Attacks. The Battle in Depth in the West* (London, Faber & Faber, 1940), p. 117.
31. Terraine, *Smoke and the Fire*, p. 108.

the 1st Tyneside Irish 18 officers and 602 men, the County Down Volunteers 12 officers and 577 men.[32]

Their sacrifice was to little effect. In the south the attack met with some success, but in the centre (where any breakthrough was expected) and in the north there was a clear and unmistakable defeat. The German fortified village of Beaumont Hamel, a first-day objective for Major-General H. de B. de Lisle's veteran 29th Division, was not captured until 13 November; Serre, on the 31st Division front, was never captured during the course of the battle. As L/Cpl Jack Cousins drily observed more than sixty years later, 'someone, somewhere, had miscalculated'.[33]

The principal miscalculator was General Sir Henry Rawlinson, GOC Fourth Army. He must take most of the blame for the appalling casualties of the first day. His were the crucial mistakes. Many of these were avoidable and arose from neglect of past experience and failure to implement standard tactical doctrine.

Haig, however, cannot escape censure. The initial plan for the battle suffered from a fundamental flaw. There was a critical disjunction between the view of the battle taken by the British Commander-in-Chief and that taken by his principal subordinate. As the superior officer, responsibility for this failure lies with Haig.

Haig had two aims: to capture the German trench system on a wide front in conjunction with the French; and to achieve a breakthrough which would allow his cavalry to pass into open country and 'roll up' the German line northwards. A Reserve Army of three cavalry and two infantry divisions was placed under the command of Lieutenant-General Sir Hubert Gough and made ready for this purpose.

Haig, himself, was not wholly confident of achieving a breakthrough. The success of his strategy did not depend on it. His plan allowed for contingencies which might make the attempt 'unadvisable'.[34] Rawlinson's plan, however, doomed any prospect of success from the outset.

Rawlinson's plan did not accord with that of his chief. The battle which he aimed to fight was very different. His experience of the battles of 1915 had convinced him that no breakthrough was possible and he certainly did not attempt one. The key feature of the battlefield was the Pozières Ridge, which dominated the British positions for ten miles between Montauban and the River Ancre. This was the principal objective of the Fourth Army. If Haig's hoped for breakthrough was to succeed, the ridge had to be captured quickly and this required the whole of the German trench system to be included in the opening attack. Rawlinson considered this to be a reckless gamble.[35] The battles of 1915 provided ample warnings of its dangers,[36] and since then the German defences had been greatly strengthened.[37] In places the attacker was confronted by as many as four separate trench systems and might have to cross twelve trenches

32. Middlebrook, *First Day on the Somme*, p. 330, lists all battalions suffering more than 500 casualties.
33. In an interview with N. Tester for his unpublished BA dissertation, 'A Citizen's War. The 7th Bedfords During the Great War 1914–1918' (Birmingham University, 1980).
34. GHQ, AOD 12, 16 June, *OH 1916 I*, Appendix 13, paragraph 2 (ii).
35. Sir F. Maurice, *The Life of General Lord Rawlinson of Trent* (London, Cassell, 1928), p. 155.
36. See above, p. 38.
37. Wynne, *If Germany Attacks*, pp. 100–4, provides an excellent analysis of the German position.

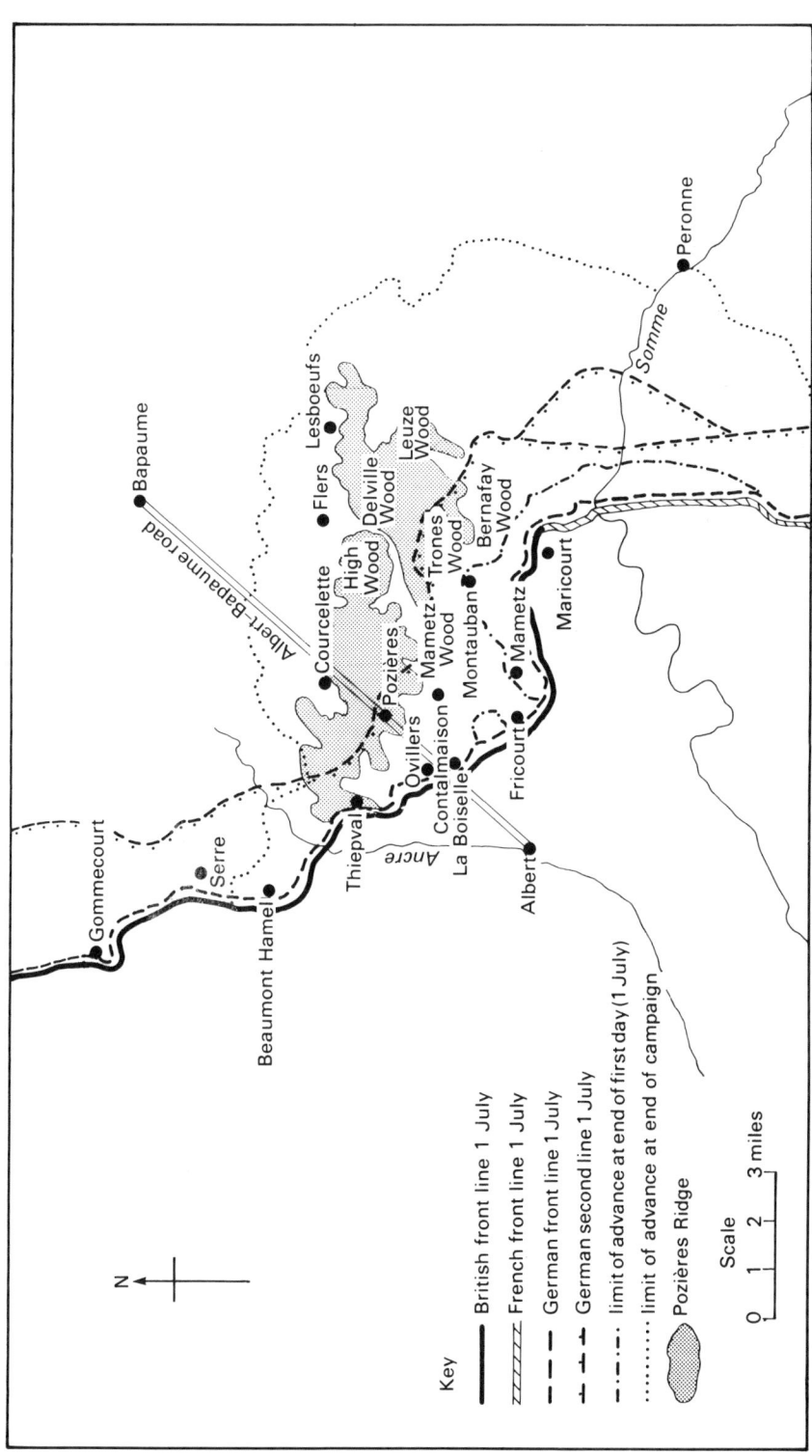

Map 5 The Somme Battlefield, 1916

Key

— British front line 1 July

///// French front line 1 July

– – – German front line 1 July

–+–+– German second line 1 July

–·–·– limit of advance at end of first day (1 July)

·········· limit of advance at end of campaign

▨ Pozières Ridge

Scale

0   1   2   3 miles

before reaching open country. Each trench system was reinforced by deep concrete dug-outs and the ground between them raked by intersecting arcs of machine-gun fire. This was known, and it dictated a cautious approach. Rawlinson had no intention of breaching the German lines. His aim was to capture them one by one. The infantry would remain always under the protective fire of their artillery and would present a solid defence against the inevitability of German counter-attack. The enemy's Second Line was deliberately excluded from the Fourth Army's first objective. All possibility of an immediate breakthrough was excluded with it.

The confusion of purpose between Haig and Rawlinson, however, does not provide an adequate explanation of the first day's losses. Nor does Rawlinson's plan. Rawlinson's concept of the battle was sound, sounder indeed than Haig's. The strategy of limited objectives was the foundation of British success in 1918. His failure lay in the execution. This owed much to the unjustifiable confidence which he placed in the power of his artillery, to the awesome rigidity of Fourth Army tactical planning and to the virtual abandonment of infantry tactics.

Artillery was vital to the success of Rawlinson's plan. Its function was to destroy the German front line defences and to kill or demoralize their inhabitants. The infantry's job was simply to occupy the conquered position and prepare themselves to resist a German counter-attack. The British artillery would move forward and the process would be repeated against the German Second and then the Third lines.

Guns and ammunition were available for this purpose in previously unimaginable quantities. There was a field-gun, howitzer or trench mortar for every seventeen yards of front to be attacked. Over two million shells were stockpiled prior to the battle and 1,508,652 of them fired during the seven-day barrage which began on 24 June. This was done according to a fire-plan of great complexity which able men worked long hours to perfect.[38]

Rarely can so much effort have been expended to such little effect. The barrage did considerable damage to the German front line, which was obliterated in places.[39] But this was not enough to permit the success of a British attack which deliberately ignored the basic principles of infantry assault tactics. Sufficient Germans survived death and demoralization. When the barrage lifted and they escaped from the shelter of their dug-outs, the German machine-gunners found inviting targets. Across large sections of the front the British infantry walked forward in orderly lines and were mown down like standing corn.[40] 'As a display of bravery it was magnificent,' wrote Sir Edward Spears, 'as an example of tactics its very memory made one shudder.'[41]

The failure of the artillery was partly due to material inadequacies.[42] Rawlinson's resources were less impressive than they seemed. Large-calibre heavy guns firing high-explosive ammunition were required to inflict effective damage on the German defences. Neither of these was available in sufficient quantities. The British had 467 heavy guns on a sixteen-mile front. Only thirty-four were above 9.2 inch calibre and half of these were provided by the French,

38. For this, see OH 1916, I, Appendices, Appendix 19.
39. Wynne, If Germany Attacks, pp. 110–11.
40. This was not universally the case, see op. cit., pp. 113–14, and Keegan, Face of Battle, pp. 241, 244.
41. E.L. Spears, Prelude to Victory (London, Jonathan Cape, 1939), p. 91.
42. Keegan, Face of Battle, pp. 243–6.

who had 900 'heavies' on their eight-mile front.[43] This serious weakness was exacerbated by problems concerning ammunition. Much of it was of shoddy American manufacture and large amounts failed to explode. Two-thirds of the shells fired were shrapnel, a devastating anti-personnel weapon but inherently defective against earthworks protected by barbed wire 'so dense that daylight could barely be seen through it'.[44] John Keegan has calculated that only 900 of the 12,000 tons of shells fired by the British heavy guns were high explosive.[45] This represented about 30 tons for every square mile of German front. Compared with the weight and density of fire achieved in later stages of the Somme battle, this figure is very low;[46] compared with the battles of 1917 and 1918, and with those of the Second World War, it seems almost trivial.[47]

Rawlinson's tactics did nothing to remedy the malign consequences of his army's material weakness. His limited number of heavy guns were further dissipated by the decision to spread them evenly along the whole length of the front. They could have been rendered much more effective if they had been grouped together and their fire concentrated against known German strongpoints. The topography of the battlefield afforded some excellent opportunities of providing supporting artillery fire from the flank. This would have allowed fire to be maintained on the German defences until the very last moment of the infantry assault, while minimizing the risk of inflicting casualties on the attacking infantry from their own guns. Gallipoli had demonstrated the absolute importance of adopting this tactic where possible. Failure to do so was one of the principal causes of the enormous British casualties on 1 July.[48] The response of Fourth Army planners to the inherent difficulties of infantry–artillery co-operation in a war without a reliable portable wireless was to restrict all tactical initiative to centralized control. The front was divided into perpendicular 'lanes', the width of which was calculated on the basis of the number of shells believed necessary to destroy a yard of trench.[49] Battery commanders were given tactical responsibility only for their own 'lane'; they were not to concern themselves with anything else. Firing proceeded according to a fixed timetable. Changes could only be made at Corps level, physically and psychologically remote from the front line and the conduct of the battle. The fire-plan developed a logic and momentum of its own. In the event this bore no relationship to the realities of the battlefield or to the needs of the infantry.

Once the artillery failed, the infantry were doomed. The role of the infantry was entirely subordinated to that of the artillery. This was based on two assumptions: that once the artillery had finished its job nothing would be required of the infantry except the occupation of a flattened and defenceless trench system; and that the infantry were so ill-trained and inexperienced that they were incapable of anything else. The first assumption was false; the second was self-fulfilling. Fourth Army 'Tactical Notes' allowed nothing to the

43. Middlebrook, *First Day on the Somme*, pp. 87, 227.
44. G. Coppard, *With a Machine Gun to Cambrai* (London, Imperial War Museum, 1980), p. 83.
45. Keegan, *Face of Battle*, p. 236.
46. Haig, *Private Papers*, p. 177, illustrates the much greater artillery densities attained at the end of the battle.
47. See Keegan, *Face of Battle*, p. 236; and Terraine, *Smoke and the Fire*, p. 127.
48. Wynne, *If Germany Attacks*, p. 113.
49. M. Van Creveld, *Command in War* (London, Harvard University Press, 1985), p. 160.

initiative and independence of the infantry.[50] The tactical possibilities of the battlefield were barely considered; infantry objectives were set by the observable range of the artillery.[51] Rawlinson sought not to confront the 'independent will of the enemy' but to pretend that it did not exist. He rejected Haig's suggestion that the infantry attack in short rushes preceded by skirmishers, and Haig failed to insist on the implementation of the standard tactical doctrine of 'fire and manoeuvre', which he himself had done much to formulate. Established tactical procedures for the capture of dug-outs and woods, which had been carefully fashioned from the painful experiences of 1915, were completely ignored at great cost in British lives. The explosion of mines under the German position minutes before the attack, instead of at the moment of assault, forewarned the Germans of the impending attack and sealed the infantry's fate.

Sir Douglas Haig was undismayed by the events of 1 July. He showed little real awareness of the tragedy that had befallen his army. His response to the casualty figures – provisionally estimated at 40,000 – was that they were to be expected.[52] He reserved his concern for the 'cowardly' performance of VIII Corps, whose total failure before Beaumont Hamel and Serre had compromised the success of the whole plan.[53] Above all, he continued the battle. He had no choice. The strategic needs of the alliance remained paramount and they could be achieved only through the exertion of constant pressure on the German line.

The experience of the first day was not repeated during the months of bitter fighting which followed. Tactical innovations were introduced. The dawn attack by XIII and XV Corps of Fourth Army on 14 July was a conspicuous success and demonstrated the advantages of flexible and imaginative infantry tactics. For a few moments a breakthrough seemed possible. Rawlinson launched a squadron of cavalry against High Wood, most of which was cleared.[54] A few British soldiers glimpsed the rolling, unbroken country in the German rear, but the momentum of the advance could not be maintained in the face of stiffening German resistance. The artillery creeping barrage was gradually perfected. This was assisted by the improved artillery observation afforded by British domination of the air. The secret and experimental 'tanks' were launched against the unsuspecting German infantry on 15 September with immediate effect.[55] The British worked their way further and further into the German position. On 27 September the important fortified village of Thiepval – another first-day objective, and a bastion of the entire German position – fell at last to the 18th (Eastern) Division. The German infantry began to develop a defensive mentality and became wedded to the security of their deep dug-outs. These yielded a constant stream of prisoners to the British.[56]

The price, however, was high. German resistance was fierce and skilful. Falkenhayn's policy of defending and regaining ground at all costs was

---

50. OH 1916, I, Appendices, Appendix 18, prints Fourth Army 'Tactical Notes' in full. They were not always strictly adhered to, see above n. 40.
51. Van Creveld, Command in War, pp. 161–2.
52. Haig, Private Papers, p. 154.
53. op. cit., p. 153. Haig believed that 'few of the VIII Corps left their trenches'. In fact, they suffered over 13,000 casualties, the highest of any corps involved.
54. For this, see T. Norman, The Hell They Called High Wood. The Somme 1916 (London, William Kimber, 1984).
55. For tanks, see below, Chapter 7.
56. E. Ludendorff, My War Memories 1914–1918 (2 vols., London, Hutchinson, n.d.), II, pp. 244–5.

2 'If you knows of a better 'ole, go to it': the classic landscape of trench warfare. The 8th Seaforths holding a front-line trench before Martinpuich on the Somme, 25 August 1916 (*The Trustees of the Imperial War Museum, London*)

abandoned by his successors, Hindenburg and Ludendorff, at the end of August in favour of a mobile defence in great depth designed to negate the weight of Allied material resources.[57] This change did much to redress the grim statistics of attrition in the Germans' favour.[58] Bad weather also conspired against British success. Predictably heavy autumn rains turned the cratered battlefield into a wilderness of evil-smelling mud. Simple movement became extraordinarily difficult and hazardous. The battle literally bogged down. The final offensive was launched across the River Ancre by General Sir Hubert Gough's Fifth Army on 13 November. The 51st (Highland) Division captured Beaumont Hamel and took a large number of Germans prisoner. The battle was officially ended five days later.

The Battle of the Somme has become an epitome of the Great War. Lloyd George described it as one of 'the most gigantic, tenacious, grim, futile and bloody fights ever waged in the history of war'.[59] The British lost over 400,000 men. And yet nowhere did they advance more than ten miles from their start line of 1 July; no enemy positions of strategic importance were captured; no breakthrough was achieved. Despite a scale of military effort unparalleled in British history, there was no 'victory' to celebrate.

Sir Douglas Haig, however, did not agree.

The Battle of the Somme was fought for compelling reasons of Allied grand strategy. Haig, himself, clearly stated the objectives of the campaign. These were: to relieve Verdun; to fix German reserves in the West; and to erode the fighting capacity of the German Army. He believed that these objectives had

---

57. Wynne, *If Germany Attacks*, pp. 128–30.
58. *op. cit.*, p. 128.
59. Lloyd George, *War Memoirs*, II, p. 1247.

been achieved as a result of his army's efforts. It is difficult not to agree with him.

British accounts of the battle have generally ignored the instantaneous effect which it had on German conduct of the war in the West. The events of 1 July were not the occasion for celebration but for alarm in the German High Command. Falkenhayn arrived at his Second Army headquarters in the late afternoon and was horrified to discover the staff making plans for the abandonment of their Second Line, which had been entered by the French west of Péronne. He countermanded the order and dismissed General Grünert, the Second Army Chief of Staff. Grünert's appointment was offered to one of the leading tacticians in the German Army, Colonel Fritz von Lossberg, who made his reputation in the great defensive battles of September 1915 in Champagne.[60]

Falkenhayn and Lossberg met at Mézières at 1 a.m. on 2 July. Lossberg quickly realized the gravity of the situation facing the German Army on the Somme. He accepted the appointment on the understanding that Falkenhayn would stop all offensive action at Verdun. Lossberg intended to conduct the battle on the principle of a mobile defence in depth. This required reserves. Unless Verdun was halted these would not be available to him. Falkenhayn gave his verbal agreement and the two men shook hands, but the promise was never kept. This had a most detrimental effect on the German defence. For Falkenhayn personally it was a crucial error of judgement. On 28 August he was dismissed. The first act of his successors was to stop all German attacks at Verdun. The first of Haig's objectives was achieved.

And so was the second. The British Expeditionary Force attracted to itself the full strength of the German field army. There were six German divisions on the Somme front when the battle began; by 17 July their number had doubled. In all, ninety-five divisions served on the Somme, 48 of them once, 43 twice and 4 three times.[61] The German Army was stretched to the limits of its strength for the first time in the war. This had serious repercussions not only for Germany but also for her allies.

In June, Russian armies under the command of General Alexei Brusilov launched a massive and sustained offensive against the Austrians in Galicia. It was one of the most important events of the war. The Austrians suffered a major defeat, instrumental in the eventual disintegration of the Habsburg Empire. Without German support it is likely that Austria would have been knocked out of the war in 1916. The Germans were compelled to send divisions which they could ill spare from the Western Front to plug the gap. The Austrian stranglehold on Italy was broken.

The cost to the Entente, however, was high. Russian casualties were colossal. Ominous signs of disaffection began to appear in the Russian Army. Russian success proved a fatal attraction to Romania, which entered the war on the Allied side in August. King Ferdinand had waited since 1914 to enter the war on the winning side at the moment of maximum opportunity for his country. He delayed too long. The Germans regarded his act as treachery. Their response was swift and terrible. Two armies, under Mackensen and Falkenhayn, invaded Romania in September and crushed all resistance. Bucharest fell on 6 December. Romania's great natural resources of wheat and oil came under German control

60. Wynne, *If Germany Attacks*, pp. 83–99.
61. *op. cit.*, p. 127.

and played a major part in enabling the German economy to sustain a further two years of war.

Haig's third aim was to erode the fighting capacity of the German Army. There can be no doubt that he did this. The Somme was as great an ordeal for the German Army as Verdun was for the French. More than half of the German Army passed through it. During the first five months of the campaign there were 146 divisional reliefs, involving 1M men in infantry alone.[62] Lossberg devoted much of his exceptional energy and ability to the proper supervision of these reliefs. To leave units in the line for too long was to invite a disastrous decline in fighting efficiency and morale. 'The strain on physical and moral strength was tremendous,' wrote Ludendorff, 'and divisions could only be kept in the line for a few days at a time. They had to be frequently relieved and sent to recuperate on quiet fronts. It was impossible to leave them behind the line – we had not enough men.'[63]

The German Army was never quite the same again after the Somme. The army's mainspring was its cadre of 100,000 professional officers and NCOs. These men were the finest soldiers in the world. The battle took a heavy toll of them, just as the battles of 1914 and 1915 had destroyed the pre-war British regular army. 'What still remained of the old first-class peace-trained German infantry had been expended on the battlefield,' wrote Crown Prince Rupprecht of Bavaria.[64] The Somme was 'the muddy field grave of the German Army'.[65]

Haig has received only grudging recognition for the strategic success achieved by his armies on the Somme. His success is rarely denied; it is merely seen as irrelevant. British perceptions of the battle have been transfixed by its human costs. These were on a scale utterly unprecedented in the British experience. They made the very concept of 'success' appear absurd and immoral. Haig won a Pyrrhic victory; the nation suffered a psychological defeat. No amount of revisionist historical scholarship, however exacting or eloquent, will ever change this verdict.

Convoy

By the end of 1916 German prospects looked bleak. The French had survived Verdun. The Russians had inflicted humiliating defeats on Austria. The British could no longer be dismissed as 'an amateur army of tennis players'; they had become a formidable enemy, millions strong, well-equipped and infinitely determined. The achievements of the German Army had been immense, but victory appeared remote, costly and increasingly uncertain. On 12 December the Central Powers made their first, vague, clumsy (but public) offer of peace.

The Peace Note was the product of conflict and compromise between the Central Powers and within the German government. Austria's need for peace was pressing. There were Germans who shared this concern and who believed that a negotiated settlement was possible. But theirs was not the dominant voice. The Note's tone of truculent intransigence and its complete failure to state terms made it apparent which side had won. The military party in Germany saw

62. *ibid.*
63. Ludendorff, *War Memories*, I, pp. 244–6.
64. Quoted in C. Messenger, *Trench Fighting* (New York, Ballantine, 1972), p. 87.
65. *OH 1916, I*, p. 494.

the Note as a tactical diversion designed to embarrass and possibly to divide the Entente. Its anticipated rejection would provide the justification for a policy of unrestricted submarine warfare on which Germany's best hope of victory appeared to rest. The Allies summarily dismissed the Note; unrestricted submarine warfare was announced on 1 February 1917.

This was a fateful decision for Germany and for the world. The consequences for Britain were very nearly fatal. Within three months British shipping losses were so severe that defeat seemed imminent. The new Prime Minister, David Lloyd George, was brought into an anguished conflict with his senior naval advisers which threatened the always delicate political balance of his government. And on the Western Front the British Commander-in-Chief, Sir Douglas Haig, found in the existence of the German U-boats' Channel bases helpful support for his long-held belief that the most advantageous place in which to attack and break the German Army was Flanders.

The Germans had toyed with the idea of unrestricted submarine warfare before. Admiral Scheer was one who regretted this. He believed that earlier half-hearted attempts had betrayed German intentions and tactics to the British and given them time to effect counter-measures; they had also alienated American opinion without achieving significant military results. This time would have to be different or Germany would lose the war. 'If we did not succeed in overcoming England's will to destroy us,' Scheer recognised, 'then the war of exhaustion must end in Germany's certain defeat.'[66]

The situation seemed not only desperate but also opportune. Technical advances offered the possibility of decisive success. In June 1916 the Germans began to launch a new generation of submarines which could operate submerged for long periods in the deep oceans as far as the eastern seaboard of the United States. Even without unrestricted warfare these vessels inflicted serious losses. As early as 9 November, the President of the Board of Trade, Walter Runciman, warned the War Committee that 'a complete breakdown in shipping would come before June 1917.'[67] By the beginning of the new year the Germans had about 150 of the new craft, of which less than half were operational at any one time. This was a small number, but once the political will to unleash them was found the effect was dramatic and instantaneous. In January 1917 Britain lost 153,666 tons of merchant shipping. In February, after German submarines were allowed to sink all merchant ships proceeding to or from Allied ports on sight and without warning, the figure rose to 313,486 tons. Worse was to come. In March 353,478 tons were lost; in April 545,282 tons. The total for world losses in April was a catastrophic 881,027 tons.[68] The Royal Navy and the British people faced one of the supreme crises in their history. Once more the burden fell on Admiral Jellicoe. This time he failed.

Jellicoe surrendered command of the Grand Fleet to Sir David Beatty in December 1916 and took office as First Sea Lord, professional head of the Royal Navy. He was the obvious choice, perhaps the only choice, but it soon became apparent that he was the wrong choice. Jellicoe's besetting weaknesses were his inability to delegate and his inflexibility. These had already limited his claims to

66. Scheer, *High Seas Fleet*, p. 49.
67. Lloyd George, *War Memoirs*, I, p. 670.
68. C.E. Fayle, *History of the Great War. Seaborne Trade Volume III* (London, John Murray, 1924), Table 1 (a), p. 465.

greatness as a fleet commander. In an administrator and planner, at a time of grave national crisis, they were crippling. Admiralty bureaucracy suffocated him. Activity became a substitute for action. His perennial caution hardened into pessimism and, perhaps, into defeatism. As he stonily worked his way through mountains of paper, he began to lose his energy, his health, his self-confidence and the confidence of his prime minister. It was the prelude to a personal tragedy.

Jellicoe liked 'facts'. By the end of April the 'facts' were clear. Britain was losing the war. 'Is there no solution for the problem?' asked Admiral Sims of the United States Navy. 'Absolutely none that we can see now,' Jellicoe replied.[69] These twin perceptions, that something must be done and nothing could be done, began to exercise a corrosive influence on Jellicoe's personality and on the conduct of the war.

Jellicoe's sense of powerlessness did not extend to his prime minister. Lloyd George was full of ideas. Something *would* be done. An emergency shipbuilding programme was begun, greater efficiency in ship-space and port-usage was sought; the arming of merchantmen was speeded up; non-essential imports were reduced; home production of food, timber and minerals was encouraged and consumption restricted.[70] These were matters outside the jurisdiction of the Admiralty. They were attempts to limit the consequences of the 'submarine peril'. They did nothing to prevent it. Only the Royal Navy could do that. Lloyd George became quickly convinced that the only way in which they could do it was through the convoy system. But for the system to be implemented the Admiralty had to agree, and the Admiralty was not easy to persuade.

Jellicoe was a major stumbling block. His command of the 'facts' destroyed his sense of perspective. The 'facts' were not encouraging. Collecting ships into convoy wasted valuable time; keeping them in convoy wasted even more, as the speed of the convoy was determined by that of the slowest ship; convoys would cause congestion at ports of destination; merchant ships lacked the necessary means for effective blackout at night; merchant skippers lacked the necessary skills or equipment enabling them to keep the close station essential to convoy protection; the Royal Navy had insufficient cruisers to spare for commerce duties; inability to use United States territory massively complicated the assembly of eastbound convoys; the navigation of convoys through minefields in pilotage waters would be hazardous; convoys were very vulnerable to enemy surface raiders.[71]

These objections were neither as fallacious nor as absurd as Lloyd George believed. Neither were they fundamental. They were indications of some of the difficulties which would attend the immediate implementation of a convoy system, not an argument that it should not be introduced. This was a distinction which Jellicoe himself drew in his post-war *apologia*, *The Submarine Peril* (1934), but it was too fine for Lloyd George. He saw Admiralty opposition as 'amazing and incomprehensible', the product of 'blind obstinacy'. His professional advisers at the Admiralty and the War Office were 'stunned by pessimism'. They were hidebound and unimaginative. His faith in them (already badly shaken by the Somme) was further eroded; the search for alternative strategies was pursued with fresh intensity.[71]

69. W.S. Sims, *The Victory at Sea* (London, John Murray, 1920), pp. 6–7.
70. See below, Chapter 8.
71. Admiral Lord Jellicoe, *The Submarine Peril* (London, Cassell, 1934), pp. 96–103.

On 27 April, with the help of prominent professional dissenters like Richmond[72] and Hamilton,[73] Lloyd George at last succeeded in persuading the Admiralty to accept the convoy system. Its introduction was as arduous, complicated and uncertain as Jellicoe predicted, but it worked. The entry of the United States into the war on 6 April eased many difficulties. Shipping losses were kept at manageable levels. 'Out of 800 vessels convoyed in July and August 1917, only five were lost.'[74] In September, for the first time, U-boat losses exceeded new launchings. But the system was not a panacea. The loss of merchant shipping remained high. Not until August 1918 were British losses reduced to below the level experienced immediately before the declaration of unrestricted submarine warfare.[75]

The Admiralty's senior figures paid the price of their resistance. Sir Edward Carson, the First Lord of the Admiralty, was removed at the end of July. Carson had been one of the key figures in the overthrow of the Asquith Coalition. Lloyd George was beholden to him, and his removal was fraught with dangers, but he went surprisingly quietly.[76] His replacement was the former railway manager and logistics expert Sir Eric Geddes, an inspired choice suggested originally by Sir Douglas Haig. Jellicoe survived until the end of the year. Geddes sacked him unceremoniously on Christmas Eve. 'One obstacle to a successful war is now out of the way,' commented Herbert Richmond by way of farewell.[77] It was a sad end to a great career.

Flanders Fields[78]

On 15 and 16 November 1916 the commanders-in-chief of the Allied armies met once more at Chantilly. Their discussions were uneventful.[79] The pledge of mutual support made the previous year was renewed. The importance of maintaining pressure on the Central Powers was recognized, and it was agreed that 'general offensive action' should be undertaken 'with all the means at their disposal' from the first fortnight in February, but no detailed plans were laid. This was as well, for in the next few weeks the political and military direction of the Entente underwent major transformation.

On 7 December Lloyd George succeeded Asquith as Prime Minister.[80] This

---

72. Sir Herbert Richmond, then a Captain. See A.J. Marder, ed., *Portrait of an Admiral: the Life and Papers of Sir Herbert Richmond* (London, Jonathan Cape, 1952).
73. Admiral Sir Frederick Hamilton, Commander-in-Chief Rosyth.
74. Hough, *Great War at Sea*, p. 309.
75. *op. cit.*, p. 158.
76. For Carson, see below, pp. 119, 123–5.
77. Quoted in Hough, *Great War at Sea*, p. 312. See also, S.W. Roskill, 'The Dismissal of Jellicoe', *Journal of Contemporary History*, I (1966), pp. 69–93.
78. For the military history of 1917, see *Military Operations France and Belgium 1917* (Volume 1 compiled by Captain C. Falls, London, Macmillan, 1932; Volume 2 compiled by Sir J. Edmonds, London, HMSO, 1948). Volume 1 deals with the Retreat to the Hindenburg Line and the Battle of Arras; Volume 2 with Messines and Third Ypres. Volume 2 is controversial. Captain Wilfred Miles objected to its conclusions and had his name removed from the title page. Liddell Hart accused Edmonds of falsifying the German casualty figures. See also L. Wolff, *In Flanders Fields* (London, Longmans Green, 1959); L. MacDonald, *They Called it Passchendaele* (London, Michael Joseph, 1979); and P. Warner, *Passchendaele* (London, Sidgwick & Jackson, 1987).
79. For the resolutions of this conference, see *OH 1917, I, Appendics*, Appendix 1.
80. See below, pp. 119–27.

was an ominous development for Haig and his most faithful supporter, General Sir William Robertson, Chief of the Imperial General Staff. Lloyd George was appalled by the casualties on the Somme and by the apparent absence of achievement. He had no wish for a repetition. He had long favoured a strategy designed to destroy Germany's allies, especially Turkey and Bulgaria, but he was not averse to striking a knockout blow against Germany in the West so long as British casualties were minimized. Changes in the French High Command soon convinced him that this could be the case.

The principal casualty of the Battle of Verdun was General Joffre. In December he was eased into retirement with the title 'Marshal of France'. His great achievements on the Marne had become a distant memory. After two years of savage 'attrition' the French Army appeared to be no closer to victory. The French needed renewed hope of quick and decisive success. They found it in General Robert Nivelle.

Nivelle was a gunner. He made his reputation at Verdun with the recapture of Fort Douaumont on 2 November. He was charming, accessible, untouched by failure, politically safe and utterly self-confident. Above all, he promised an end to the wasteful battles of 1915 and 1916. He envisaged a crushing artillery bombardment which would break the German line within forty-eight hours and lead to a victorious pursuit of the German Army. If no breakthrough was achieved within that time the battle would be stopped. The French Army had endured its martyrdom. There would be no return to Calvary. There would be no more attrition.[81]

Lloyd George was among those who were happy to be convinced. At the notorious Calais Conference on 26–27 February 1917, he committed the British Expeditionary Force to full co-operation in the Nivelle Offensive and placed the British Commander-in-Chief under Nivelle's command for the duration of the battle.[82] This had serious consequences for Haig's plans for 1917.

Haig was acutely conscious that the British had never at any time during the war been able to choose their own battlefield. These had always been chosen for them either by the French or by the Germans. He was anxious that this should change. He believed that the strength of his armies and the scale of their endeavours in 1916 had established his right to greater strategic independence. He had no doubts where he wanted to fight. It was Flanders. His reluctant acquiescence in the Calais Agreement was obtained only on the understanding that after the conclusion of the Nivelle Offensive the British army would be able to launch its own attack there. But the delays which this imposed were ultimately very damaging to the British Expeditionary Force's chances of success.

The British contribution to the Nivelle Offensive is known to history as the Battle of Arras. It began in a snowstorm on 9 April and is chiefly remembered for the capture of the German stronghold of Vimy Ridge by Byng's Canadian Corps.[83] The early stages of the battle, with the exception of Gough's bungled attack at Bullecourt, were notably successful. This owed much to the

81. E.L. Spears, *Prelude to Victory* (London, Jonathan Cape, 1939) is a vivid and brilliant account of the genesis, planning and execution of the Nivelle Offensive.
82. See below, pp. 150–1.
83. See H.F. Wood, *Vimy!* (London, MacDonald, 1967) and J. Williams, *Byng of Vimy: General and Governor-General* (London, Leo Cooper at Secker & Warburg, 1983), pp. 143–67.

augmented firepower of the British artillery. Impressive concentrations were achieved. The Canadian Corps alone was supported by more than a thousand guns. Ammunition was much improved. The new '106' fuse detonated high explosive shell instantaneously on impact. This gave it much greater concussive effect, made it much more destructive of barbed wire, but kept the ground from becoming too badly cratered. Gas shells and the Livens gas projector were other important additions to the British arsenal. Success, however, was not to last.

On 16 April Nivelle launched his offensive on the Aisne. It was almost doomed to failure. The German 'retreat to the Hindenburg Line' between 25 February and 5 April rendered much of the offensive's strategic purpose nugatory. Nivelle's intentions were an open secret. What shreds of confidentiality remained were hopelessly compromised by the German capture of the detailed plans of the French Fifth Army on 6 April. Nivelle's opening bombardment was not a complete failure, but it came nowhere near to fulfilling the grandiose promises which had sustained French spirit through a bitter winter and a cruel spring. The result was mutiny.[84]

The repercussions for Sir Douglas Haig were enormous. The crumbling of the French offensive compelled him to extend the fighting at Arras. This proved costly. The battle was successful only as long as it was pursued within a framework of strictly limited objectives as a feint for the major attack to the south. The abandonment of a methodical advance in favour of a breakthrough suited the German defensive strategy and British casualties rose calamitously. Daily losses between 9 April and 17 May were 4,070. These were exceeded during the course of the war only in the German Spring Offensive of 1918.[85] Equally serious, the extension of the fighting at Arras imposed a crucial eight-week delay in the opening of the long-awaited Flanders Campaign.

This began with a very big bang on 7 June. At 3.10 a.m. nineteen huge mines, containing nearly a million pounds of ammonal, were exploded under the German front line along the Messines Ridge, south-west of Ypres. Infantry of the British Second Army, supported by 72 new Mark IV tanks and by a creeping barrage of crushing intensity, swept over the devastated German positions and captured all their objectives.

The purpose of the Battle of Messines was to capture the eight-mile long, 200 feet high Messines–Wytschaete Ridge, which enfiladed the British position at Ypres. Its capture was the essential preliminary to the development of any major British offensive in Flanders. The battle's stunning success owed much to the careful planning of the Second Army and its commanding officer, General Sir Herbert Plumer.

Plumer was one of the great British soldiers of the First World War. He did not look like a great soldier. He was blessed with a face which gave every appearance of irredeemable stupidity. He inspired affection rather than terror. He was universally known to his troops as 'Daddy', though a few irreverent junior officers refered to him as 'Drip', a tribute to his permanently runny nose.[86] Plumer brought immense advantages to his task. He had been in command in

84. For the French Army mutinies, see G. Pedroncini, *Les Mutineries de 1917* (Paris, Presses Universitaires de France, 1967). For French morale in general, see J-J. Becker, *The Great War and the French People* trans. A. Pomerans (Leamington Spa, Berg, 1985), pp. 197–249. See also, D. Englander, 'The French Soldier, 1914–1918', *French History*, I (1987), pp. 49–67.
85. Terraine, *Smoke and the Fire*, p. 46.
86. I owe this information to the 6th Earl of Harrowby.

the Ypres Salient since succeeding Smith-Dorrien in the spring of 1915. He knew the area intimately. This was more than usually important on a battlefield where disregard of the imperatives of topography was pregnant with disaster. Plumer's cherubic appearance hid a prudent professional mind, deeply imbued by experience with the importance of thorough planning and preparation. In June 1916, he was joined by an outstanding Chief of Staff, Major-General Charles 'Tim' Harington, who shared Plumer's view of war and with whom he developed a close and effective collaboration.[87]

Plumer left nothing to chance. He was a firm believer in the strategy of limited objectives, which Rawlinson had instigated on the Somme. The peculiar difficulties of fighting in a salient made this an almost necessary approach, but Plumer brought to it his own genius for painstaking planning and administration. Nowhere was this more apparent than in relation to artillery.

The foundation of the Second Army's successes throughout 1917 was the power of its artillery. At Messines, Plumer amassed 2,500 guns of all types for a 9-mile front, the greatest concentration attained in the war so far. The preliminary bombardment, which began on 30 May, aimed principally at disrupting the Germans' ability to organize and co-ordinate their defence. Special attention was given to German rear areas: communications trenches, command posts, supply dumps, rest camps. In the later stages of the bombardment, gas shells were used in counter-battery fire against the German gunners. The effectiveness of the bombardment was greatly assisted by the Royal Flying Corps' achievement of air supremacy over the battlefield. This allowed good observation and permitted some ground support attacks.

Nor was the infantry neglected. All three corps involved in the attack constructed facsimile objectives against which they repeatedly practised assaults. Detailed briefings were given to all ranks and no one was left in doubt as to his task. The evident scale, imagination and thoroughness of the preparations also lifted morale and encouraged the anticipation of success.

The Battle of Messines was a vindication of careful planning, overwhelming concentration of artillery, limited objectives and methodical advance. During the great Flanders battles in the second half of 1917, whenever these principles were adopted, severe damage was inflicted on the moral and material strength of the German Army. Unhappily, this was not always the case.

Haig's plan for the 'Battle of Flanders' involved three stages. His first objective was to capture the Passchendaele–Staden Ridge and to break out of the Ypres Salient into the watery plain beyond. His second objective was to cut the key German strategic railway which ran north from Menin to Ostend through Roulers and Thourout. His ultimate objective was Bruges, 30 miles north-east of Ypres. The capture of Bruges would threaten the whole of the German position in Belgium and compel a withdrawal from the vital Channel coast. The plan never proceeded beyond stage one.

Responsibility for the capture of the Passchendaele Ridge was given to Haig's youngest Army Commander, the 45-year old General Sir Hubert Gough. Gough was new to Flanders and was unacquainted with the special difficulties

87. For an affectionate portrait, see P. Gibbs, *Realities of War* (London, Heinemann, 1920), pp. 47–50. Gibbs erroneously calls Harington 'Sir John Harrington'. See also, C.H. Harington, *Plumer of Messines* (London, John Murray, 1935) and *'Tim' Harington Looks Back* (London, John Murray, 1940).

of fighting there. This became apparent even before the opening attack was launched on 31 July.

In his original instructions from GHQ, Gough was strongly advised to preface his attempt to capture the Passchendaele Ridge with a separate, preliminary attack designed to take the high ground on his right flank near Gheluvelt.[88] This would ensure that the Germans could not enfilade his main assault. Gough rejected the advice. He preferred instead to take the Gheluvelt Plateau *at the same time* as he attacked the Passchendaele Ridge. He put his objections to Haig at a meeting in Cassel on 28 June. He argued that 'a partial attack, even if successful, would only throw the troops employed into a very pronounced salient, and expose them to the concentrated fury of all the German artillery'.[89] Rather surprisingly, Gough was supported in his views by Plumer and Haig agreed to the change.[90] As on the Somme, Haig deferred to the opinions of 'the man on the spot' and failed to insist on the execution of his own better judgement. It was a tragic error.

Gough's attack went badly and was almost immediately interrupted by the appalling weather that was to characterize the campaign and to give it its sinister reputation. All attempts to capture the Gheluvelt Plateau failed. This had fatal consequences. The enemy was able to observe the whole of the British attack and to inflict serious losses with his artillery. By the end of August British casualties were approaching 70,000 men. Haig decided that the battle was leading nowhere. He took immediate and decisive action. Tactical responsibility was given back to the Second Army. Plumer was ordered to take the Gheluvelt Plateau and the ridge beyond. Haig was insistent that the offensive should be conducted on the 'principle of advancing step by step with limited objectives and overwhelming artillery power'.[91] This was congenial advice.

The 'second phase' of the battle began on 28 August and lasted for five weeks. Plumer's preparations were reminiscent of those for Messines. At the Battle of the Menin Road Ridge on 20 September, he assembled an artillery piece for every 5.2 yards of front. Two hundred and forty machine-guns were used to lay down harassing fire.[92] Over 12,000 men of the Labour Corps were employed in the task of road and track construction.[93] This freed the assaulting infantry from unnecessary fatigue. Four divisions (two British and two Australian) were deployed for the capture of 1,500 yards of ground. Altogether, double the force for half the length of front was used compared with Gough's attack on 31 July. This pattern was repeated at the Battle of Polygon Wood on 26 September and at the Battle of Broodseinde on 4 October. Then the rain intervened again. The battlefield, with its high water-table, was turned into a swamp of liquid mud, often waist-deep. Parts of it have still fully to recover. Despite the appalling conditions, of which he was certainly aware,[94] Haig continued the battle until the ridge was captured. The Canadians took the ruined village of Passchendaele on 6 November. The battle was broken off four days later.

88. *OH 1917, II*, Appendix 15.
89. Sir H. Gough, *The Fifth Army* (London, Hodder & Stoughton, 1931), p. 195.
90. Sir J. Davidson, *Haig, Master of the Field* (London, Peter Nevill, 1953), p. 31. Davidson was Haig's Director of Operations.
91. Davidson, *Haig*, p. 40.
92. J. Terraine, 'Passchendaele and Amiens I', *Journal of the Royal United Services Institution*, CIV (1959), p. 180.
93. Davidson, *Haig*, p. 45.
94. See Haig's *Private Papers*, p. 260.

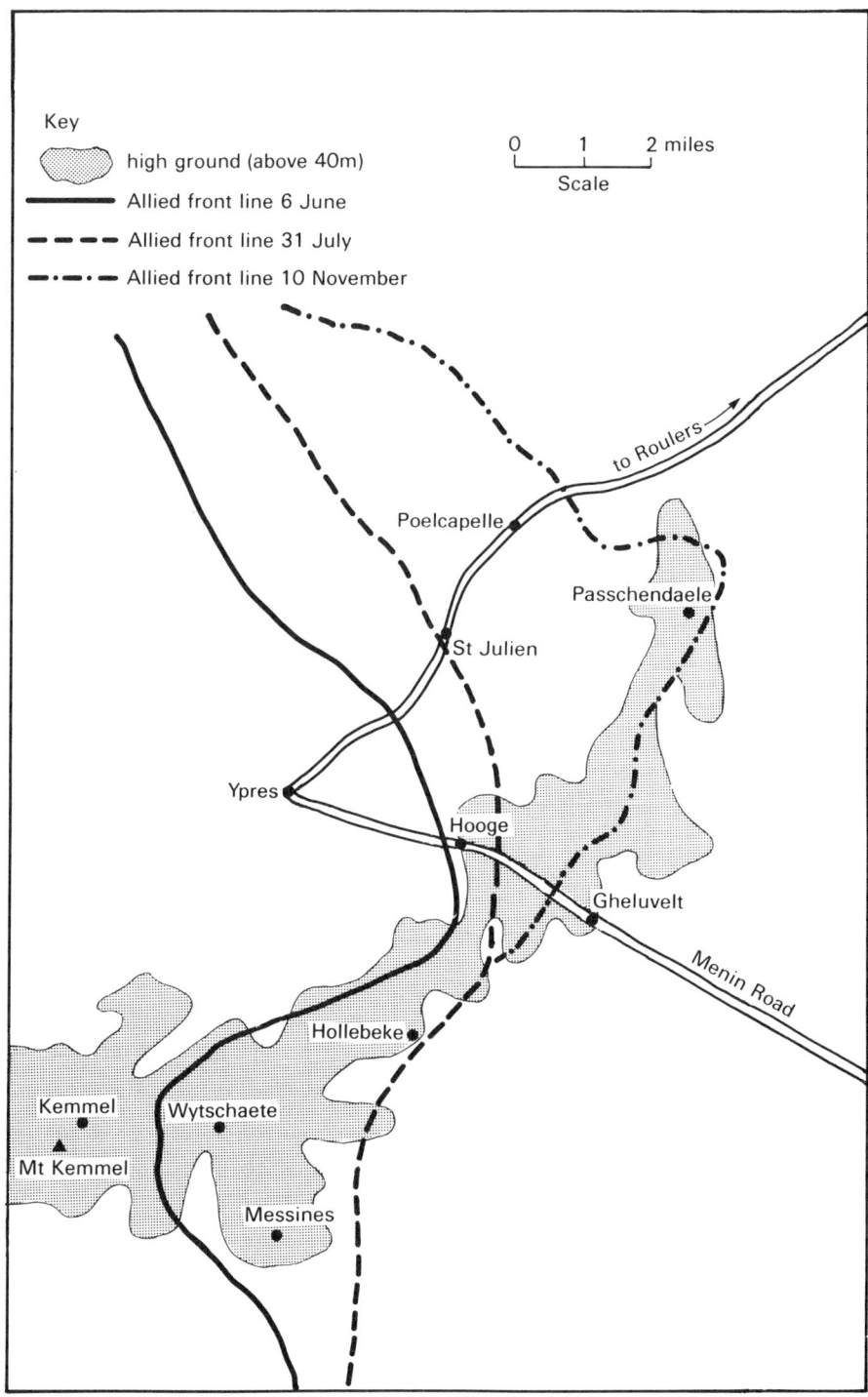

Map 6   The Flanders Campaign ('Passchendaele'), 1917

3 Flanders Fields: British troops crossing shell-torn ground near Pilckem, Battle of Langemarck, 16 August 1917 (*The Trustees of the Imperial War Museum, London*)

'Passchendaele' is the source of some of the bitterest criticism of Haig's generalship.[95] Few aspects of the campaign have escaped censure: the choice of battlefield, strategy, tactics, the employment of Gough's Fifth Army for the key assault, the relative casualties of the two sides all remain contentious issues.

Some, however, are less contentious than others. It is difficult to regard the choice of battlefield as fundamentally flawed by considerations of weather and terrain. Great battles were fought in Flanders deep into the autumn of 1914 without the malign interference of the weather. Haig was a major protagonist in those battles and the experience had a great influence on him. The autumn of 1917 was quite exceptionally wet,[96] the culmination of a dreadful year in which a long cold winter was succeeded by a late spring, a short summer and a sodden autumn. The effects of the weather were intensified by the late start to the campaign. This was not Haig's fault, but arose once more out of the obligations of the alliance with France and the military needs of the French Army. The low-lying, marshy nature of the Flanders terrain and Plumer's propensity for intense artillery bombardments on narrow fronts contributed to the peculiar awfulness of the Passchendaele mud and made the effective use of tanks impossible, but this was a difference of degree not of kind. Wherever the British might have fought on the Western Front in 1917 mud would have been a problem, just as it was on the Somme in 1916.

95. See, in particular, Lloyd George, *War Memoirs*, II, pp. 1247–1334. See also, Wolff, *In Flanders Fields*, *passim*.
96. J. Terraine, *Douglas Haig, The Educated Soldier* (London, Hutchinson, 1963), pp. 348–9. See also, *OH 1917 II*, pp. 211–12.

Little can be said in defence of Haig's choice of Gough as battlefield commander. Gough's record on the Somme was good. He had achieved the greatest gains at the least cost, but his handling of the Fifth Army in the spring of 1917 revealed important weaknesses of planning and control. In Plumer, Haig possessed a reliable subordinate who was an acknowledged expert on the area, and whose Army had already won a dramatic victory. The choice is also difficult to reconcile with Haig's own preference for a deliberate advance, expressed as early as 3 May.[97] Haig, himself, seems to have recognized the error, but his transfer of responsibility back to Plumer at the end of August came after the crucial mistakes had already been made.

Elsewhere, the truth is less easy to discern. Haig's motives for initiating the Flanders Campaign are far from obvious. Some things are clear. Flanders had always been Haig's favoured battleground. He believed that the area was vital to both the British and German positions on the Western Front and the one which presented the greatest strategic opportunities. It was close to the BEF's Channel bases. The loss of these would be disastrous. A successful advance in Flanders would do much to increase their security. Such an advance was, in turn, facilitated by the short lines of communication and supply offered by the proximity of the Channel ports. The defending German Army had little room for manoeuvre. Its lateral rail communications, essential to the effective movement of reserves, were in places only ten miles behind the front line. In Flanders, unlike on the Somme, the Germans would have to stand and fight and be killed in large numbers or yield positions of strategic importance, the loss of which would necessitate a withdrawal of the whole of the German line in the West. Haig believed absolutely that the war could only be won on the Western Front through unremitting pressure on the German Army. He considered that this pressure could best be applied in Flanders. That is why he chose to fight there. The clarity of these perceptions has been obscured by the 'submarine peril' and the state of the French Army in the wake of the Nivelle Offensive.

Haig's plans for 1917 were not primarily motivated by a concern for the threat of German submarines. The main purpose of the Flanders Campaign was not to capture Ostend and Zeebrugge, though German evacuation of those places would have been a likely outcome of a successful British advance. Proposals for a project to capture the German U-boat bases, including an amphibious landing on the Channel coast, were considered at the beginning of December 1916.[98] Haig discussed plans with Admiral Bacon,[99] but the idea was quietly dropped. Haig's interest in the fate of the bases remained, but it was political rather than military. Haig was aware of the nervousness with which prospects of a renewed offensive were regarded in political circles. He had no doubts in his own mind that an offensive must be undertaken or that Flanders was the best place to undertake it. There were great political advantages in presenting the campaign as a contribution to the struggle against the U-boats. This had been signalled to him as early as 21 November when Asquith wrote to Sir William Robertson with a frank explanation of the Admiralty's difficulties.[100] Throughout 1917, whenever the campaign seemed threatened by the hostility of the Prime

97. Haig, *Private Papers*, p. 226. *OH 1917* II, Appendix I, pp. 396–9.
98. Haig, *op. cit.*, p. 184.
99. Admiral Sir R.H. Bacon, commander Dover Patrol, 1915–17.
100. Quoted in Lloyd George, *War Memoirs*, II, p. 1252.

Minister, Haig played this card with great success. The 'need' to capture Ostend and Zeebrugge was a convenient one for Haig and one which he used skilfully to outflank his political opponents.[101]

Haig did not fight Third Ypres[102] for the sake of the French, except in general terms. Fear of French exhaustion and defeatism was an ever-present concern from the summer of 1916. The French Army mutinies at the end of May 1917 only strengthened his view. Precisely how much Haig was told about the mutinies remains a matter for debate. It seems probable that the situation in the French Army was so serious that its new Commander-in-Chief, General Philippe Pétain, was forced to be candid with Haig and to subject him to intense and secret pressure to distract German attention from French sectors of the front.[103] This crisis, however, was short-lived. It cannot provide adequate explanation for Haig's remorseless pursuit of his offensive into October and November. The French Army staged a remarkable recovery. Offensive activity was renewed at Verdun as early as 20 August and on 23 October a successful attack was made against the Chemin des Dames. More significant perhaps than Haig's knowledge of the French mutinies was his failure to inform the British government of the demands for British support which they caused. The suspicion is that knowledge of French weakness would have undermined the confidence of his political masters – especially the Prime Minister – in the ability of the BEF to 'go it alone' in Flanders. Haig's determination to attack was not the result of either French mutinies or German submarines, though both reinforced his belief and helped him to justify it to others. It arose out of his general understanding of the war. Haig feared that British failure to press the German Army to the utmost of its strength would result in the defeat of the Entente in the West and seal the fate of Russia in the East. Haig fought in Flanders because he wanted to, because without the Flanders Campaign there was the prospect of an Allied defeat and no prospect of an Allied victory. This belief sustained him throughout 1917 and was the driving force behind 'Passchendaele'.

The Flanders Campaign was a bitter disappointment. No strategic objectives were achieved. The German strategic railways were not cut. The Belgian coast was not cleared. Aspects of the battle had been badly handled. The systematic application of overwhelming firepower in pursuit of limited objectives had been an undoubted success. During the 'second phase' of operations between 20 September and 4 October great damage was done to German moral and material strength. All the German sources agree on this.[104] But overall, the battle was costly to the British, both in manpower and morale.[105] It was still not apparent that victory was possible in the foreseeable future.

101. Haig's *Private Papers*, pp. 226–36, 38, confirm that the U-boat menace was a subsidiary element in Haig's thinking, but during the key meetings of the War Cabinet in London in June, which finally sanctioned the Flanders Campaign, the whole question of the Navy's difficulties became paramount, see pp. 240–2.
102. This is the official title for the battle popularly known as 'Passchendaele'.
103. For Haig's knowledge of the French crisis, see *Private Papers*, pp. 234–5, 236, 239, 242, 252, 255.
104. These include the German Official History and the accounts of Lieutenant-General von Kuhl, Crown Prince Rupprecht's Chief of Staff, and Hindenburg, as well as that of Ludendorff, which on its own is unreliable, see J. Terraine, *The Road to Passchendaele. The Flanders Offensive of 1917: a Study in Inevitability* (London, Leo Cooper in Association with Secker & Warburg, 1984), pp. 332–5.
105. For a discussion of the casualties, see Terraine, *Road to Passchendaele*, pp. 343–7.

Events on the Western Front in late November, however, provided a glimmer of hope.

The Way Ahead[106]

The capture of Passchendaele did not bring to an end all British offensive activity on the Western Front in 1917. At 6.20 a.m. on 20 November, the British Army under the command of General Sir Julian Byng launched a mass tank attack against the German line near Cambrai. The attack met with immediate success along almost the whole of the 13,000 yard front. The Germans retreated in panic before the tanks. The British captured 7,500 prisoners and 120 guns and penetrated the German front to a maximum depth of 7,000 yards.[107] It was a stunning success. Church bells were rung to celebrate the 'victory'.

Celebrations, however, were premature. The momentum of attack was not maintained. The drain of the Flanders Campaign and the diversion of five British divisions to Italy[108] left Haig without a reserve of infantry. Cavalry was available to exploit the breakthrough, but unaccountably failed to act. German resistance stiffened round the strongpoint of Bourlon Wood. On 30 November the Germans counter-attacked and recaptured more ground than they had lost. The British line was stabilized only with difficulty and amid mounting recrimination. The fighting petered out a few days later.

The brilliant opening of the Battle of Cambrai taught important lessons for the future. The battle put surprise back on to the tactical agenda, from which it had been generally absent since Neuve Chapelle in the spring of 1915. The initial attack was made without a preliminary artillery bombardment. The British guns were ranged by the 'silent' method.[109] Great care was taken to camouflage the 381 tanks and to disguise the noise of their assembly with the sound of aircraft engines. The infantry assault was protected by a creeping barrage and a smoke-screen. Effective use was made of 'dummy smokescreens' to confuse the Germans as to the actual point of assault. The importance of direct firepower was recognized and the infantry liberally supplied with Lewis guns, mortars and hand grenades.

The lessons of failure were equally salutary. The most important concerned tanks. The inability of the 51st (Highland) Division to capture the dominating heights of the Flesquières Ridge during the opening assault had grave consequences for the development of the whole British attack. This failure was due principally to Major-General Harper's misuse of his tanks. These were ordered to press on ahead of the infantry in order to achieve a maximum degree of initial penetration. This repeated Gough's mistake at Bullecourt in April. Tanks and infantry were denied mutual support. The tanks suffered heavy losses to German artillery and the infantry became pinned down by machine-guns. The proper use of tanks was thus cruelly demonstrated. They had no effective independent role. They were essentially infantry support weapons. Their ability to crush barbed wire entanglements and to suppress machine-gun fire permitted

106. For Cambrai, see *Military Operations France and Belgium 1917* (Volume III, compiled by Captain W. Miles, London, HMSO, 1948).
107. C.R.M.F. Cruttwell, *A History of the Great War 1914–1918* (2nd edn, Oxford, Clarendon Press, 1936), p. 474.
108. See below, p. 80.
109. That is, without preliminary firing.

the infantry to cross the fire-swept zone in relative safety. But without close infantry support the tanks themselves became extremely vulnerable to artillery fire, which only the infantry could suppress.

The battle also demonstrated once more the dangers of tactical over-ambition. The dramatic opening success and subsequent German resistance exposed crucial divisions of purpose between Haig and the tank experts and General Byng. The origins of the attack may be found in Colonel J.F.C. Fuller's paper 'Tank Raids', which was distributed throughout the BEF in the summer of 1917. Fuller envisaged a large-scale raid on the German lines designed to capture prisoners and inflict damage, but not to capture ground. The raid was to be of strictly limited duration and for strictly limited objectives. Haig wished to win a significant local victory by pivoting on Cambrai and rolling up the German line between Bourlon and the River Sensée.[110] Byng's ambitions were much more grandiose. He aspired to achieving a major breakthrough deep into the German position, threatening their lines of communication and effecting a wholesale withdrawal. The course of the battle proved this to be hopelessly optimistic, even with the massed use of tanks.[111] The importance of limited objectives and a methodical advance were reasserted.

These lessons were not forgotten in 1918.

It was commonplace even at the time to see the great battles of 1916 as barren of achievement. They were not, however, barren of consequences. This became apparent during 1917. The Germans' desire to avoid battle encouraged them to seek salvation in unrestricted submarine warfare. This provided powerful arguments with which President Woodrow Wilson sought to justify an American declaration of war. The strains of war at last proved too much for Tsarist autocracy. Revolution broke out in Petrograd in March and a liberal government was established. This did much to ease the conscience of the United States Congress, which declared war on Germany on 6 April. Verdun brought the French Army to the point of exhaustion; the Nivelle Offensive brought it to the point of defeat. German pressure on Russia remained remorseless. The capture of Riga shattered the flimsy authority of the Kerensky government and paved the way for the Bolshevik Revolution in November. The Germans had won the war in the East. And in October they threatened victory elsewhere. Ludendorff transfered his strategic reserve of seven divisions to the Italian front where they were instrumental in the rout of the Italian Army at Caporetto. Complete disaster was averted only by the despatch of British and French reinforcements. Only in Mesopotamia and Palestine could the British report good news.[112] 'This may well prove to be the darkest year of the war,' wrote Sir William Robertson on 29 December.

He was right.

---

110.   F-M Earl Haig, *Sir Douglas Haig's Despatches December 1915–April 1919*, ed. Lt. Col. J.H. Boraston (London, Dent, 1919), p. 151.
111.   For a contrary view, see Wiliams, *Byng*, p. 182.
112.   See below, pp. 92–7.

4

'The Decisive Blow' 1918[1]

The offensive is the most effective means of making war; it
alone is decisive. Military history proves it on every page.

General Erich Ludendorff[2]

We cannot hope to win until we have defeated the German
Army.

Field-Marshal Sir Douglas Haig[3]

During the winter of 1917 Ludendorff convinced himself that Germany must
return to the offensive in the West. He had no difficulty in finding arguments to
sustain his belief.[4] He described them fully in his memoirs.

The condition of Germany's allies called for offensive action. The Quadruple
Alliance was held together principally by the hope of a German victory.
Austria-Hungary had suffered enormous losses and was nearing the end of its
strength. The collapse of Russia was a mixed blessing. It removed a major
military burden from Austria, but it also encouraged Austrian desire for a
general settlement or – worse – a separate peace. Bulgaria had achieved most
of its territorial ambitions. Its interests were now also best served by negotiations. It could be relied upon only as a fair-weather friend. Turkey was
different. It would remain faithful even unto death, but this did not seem far
away. The Turkish Army was on the point of collapse and was certain to come
under renewed British pressure in Palestine in 1918. The dissolution of the
Ottoman Empire would have profound political consequences over a wide area.
These were unlikely to be favourable to Germany and must at all costs be
prevented.

1. For the military history of 1918, see British Official History (henceforth *OH*), *Military Operations France and Belgium* (4 vols. Vols. 1–3 compiled by Sir J. Edmonds, London, Macmillan, 1935–39; Vol. 4 compiled by Lt. Col. R. Maxwell-Hyslop, London, HMSO, 1947). See also, H. Essame, *The Battle for Europe 1918* (London, Batsford, 1972); M. Middlebrook, *The Kaiser's Battle. 21 March 1918: The First Day of the German Spring Offensive* (London, Allen Lane, 1978); J. Terraine, *To Win a War. 1918, the Year of Victory* (London, Sidgwick & Jackson, 1978); and J. Toland, *No Man's Land* (London, Eyre Methuen, 1980).
2. E. Ludendorff, *My War Memories 1914–1918* (2 vols., London, Hutchinson, n.d.), II, p. 543.
3. Quoted in J. Terraine, *The Road to Passchendaele. The Flanders Offensive of 1917: a Study in Inevitability* (London, Leo Cooper in Association with Secker & Warburg, 1984), p. 290.
4. The following account of Ludendorff's reasoning is based on his *War Memories*, II, pp. 537–43. For Ludendorff in general, see C. Barnett, *The Swordbearers. Studies in Supreme Command in the First World War* (Harmondsworth, Penguin, 1966), pp. 297–395, and N. Stone, 'Ludendorff', in M. Carver, *The War Lords* (London, Weidenfeld & Nicolson, 1976).

The condition of Germany itself gave cause for concern. Ludendorff became aware of a decline in civilian morale as early as July 1917. He had unsuccessfully urged the political authorities to institute a programme of 'patriotic enlightenment'. The Army was not immune to the spirit of disaffection. The Flanders fighting took a heavy toll of confidence in ultimate victory. Desertions were running at record levels. Thousands of German soldiers sought sanctuary in neutral Holland. Further defensive battles offered the prospect only of eventual submission to the Entente's superior material resources.

It was unlikely that the German Navy could do anything to prevent this. Ludendorff recognized the prodigious achievements of the U-boat crews, but the British and their new American allies showed no signs of being ready to succumb. The Navy was optimistic that it could impede the arrival in France of the American army. Ludendorff was dubious. He expected it to be in the field in strength by the summer of 1918. It would, however, be a poor substitute for the loss to the Allies of the Russian Army. Amid the darkening dangers and uncertainties which beset the German High Command at the end of 1917 the disintegration of Russia lit a beacon which showed the way ahead.

Ludendorff drew his inevitable conclusions. The condition of Germany's allies and of the German Army called for an offensive that would bring a swift decision. The collapse of Russia made this opportune. The need was great. The time was ripe. Germany must attack, and it must attack soon.

It is difficult to accept Ludendorff's argument as a reasoned analysis of objective facts. His war memoirs were written in the immediate aftermath of German defeat. This had been precipitated by the collapse of his Spring Offensive. He had good cause for portraying the decision to attack as unavoidable. But it is doubtful whether this was really the case. Ludendorff did not attack because he had to. He attacked because he wanted to. Alternative strategies were available. These were dismissed not because they were unfeasible, but because they were unpalatable to German military opinion. This was deeply imbued with the spirit of the offensive. German instinct was for rapid and decisive success. This had been the aim of the Schlieffen Plan in 1914. The purpose of war was to advance the interests of the State. The successful pursuit of these interests could only be achieved through victory, and victory required the comprehensive defeat of the enemy's military forces. It was beyond the power of even the most resolute and skilful defence to effect this. The German conduct of the war in the West in 1916 and 1917 was an aberration. In 1918 the German High Command simply reverted to type.

The success of a German offensive required solutions to be found for three fundamental problems. The first of these was manpower. Germany would have to depend on its own forces. These were greatly inferior in number to those available to the Entente. This helped to dictate the choice of strategy. There were too few men available to make simultaneous attacks on different fronts. A single-front attack on a grand scale was the only one that was feasible. This would necessitate maximum economy of force. Every man and gun would have to be concentrated on the decisive front. This could only be done if the High Command was free to dispose of the German Army on the Eastern Front. Peace with Russia was essential.

The Bolshevik Revolution effectively took Russia out of the war. An armistice was signed, but peace negotiations made no progress. Trotsky skilfully delayed proceedings in the hope that revolution would spread to Germany and Austria. The German position was desperate and time was running out. Ludendorff had no wish for further fighting in the East. He could no longer afford a two-front war. The renewal of hostilities would be regarded with alarm in Austria. But he had no choice. On 13 February after a meeting at Homburg it was decided to repudiate the armistice. German forces attacked along the whole of the Russian front on 18 February and met with no resistance. The German action injected a dose of realism into Bolshevik diplomacy. Peace negotiations began in earnest. Terms were agreed at Brest-Litovsk on 3 March. German anxiety for a settlement did not soften their demands. The treaty was punitive. Russia surrendered Poland, the Baltic provinces, the Ukraine, Finland and the Caucasus to the Reich. This gave Germany and Austria access to much-needed supplies of food, but the annexations required the superintendence of nearly half a million (mostly second line) German troops. Thirty-four divisions were freed for offensive action elsewhere.

This was barely enough. Germany had 150 divisions on the Western Front. There were another eight in Italy. The shattering Italian defeat at Caporetto meant that these could probably be spared. Together with the forces from the Russian front, this gave Germany a total of 192 divisions, no more than numerical equality with the combined French and British armies in the West. The Germans themselves had survived against a numerical superiority of more than 3 to 2 throughout 1917. The choice of place of attack and method of assault would be crucial.

The choice of the point of attack was the second fundamental problem. Part of the solution was straightforward. Ludendorff was convinced that the only place where the German Army could win a decisive victory was on the Western Front against the main forces of the enemy. He quickly dismissed the possibility of attacks in Macedonia or Italy. The exact point of assault in the West, however, was more contentious. Flanders offered the most inviting strategic targets and defending forces had little room for manoeuvre, but the position was heavily entrenched and fierce resistance was likely. Prospects of effecting a breakthrough were slim. Unless a breakthrough was possible no victory could be achieved. The attack would have to be against the most vulnerable part of the Allied line. Judgement suggested that this point lay at the junction of the British and French armies. This was reinforced by evidence that the British line was being extended southwards and was held by weak forces recuperating after the Flanders fighting. The German attack would be between the Rivers Oise and Scarpe along the axis Arras–La Fère. Its target would be the British Fifth and Third Armies.

The third fundamental problem was to find an effective method of assault. Ludendorff was aware that he was attempting the most difficult operation in military history. The comforting illusions which sustained the Schlieffen Plan had long been shattered. Since the trench lines had become established successive armies, British, German and French, had failed to break the stalemate. The most impressive attempt was by the British at Cambrai, but this was achieved principally by the use of tanks and these were not available to the Germans in quantity. Ludendorff concluded that tanks were only effective *en masse*. He had too few to use in this way. Tanks would not provide the foundation of German salvation. Nor would cavalry. Ludendorff foresaw no rôle for them and made no provision for the use of a mounted arm. He would have to rely on infantry and artillery. But his use of both would be exceptional in its subtlety and ferocity.

Ludendorff's attempt to succeed where all others had failed was based upon changes in attitude, organization and equipment. His first aim was to re-establish the 'offensive spirit' among his troops after more than a year in which German tactical doctrine had been based on the 'defence in depth'. Divisions were removed from the line for special training.[5] This stressed the vital importance of momentum. Attacks must be made on narrow fronts, constantly reinforced from behind. Assault troops must seek the line of least resistance, leaving enemy strongpoints to be 'mopped up' by the forces following on. These 'infiltration' tactics had already been used with conspicuous success at Riga and in the counter-attack at Cambrai. The normal practice of relieving attacking divisions after three days was abandoned. Attacks would have to be sustained for longer periods. The aim was deep penetration into the enemy's position designed to destroy his equilibrium and threaten his communications and line of retreat.

Momentum could not rely on weight of numbers. Germany's numerical advantage was too slight, even at the point of assault.[6] Firepower would have to be substituted for manpower. The quantity of firepower directly available to the assaulting infantry was increased. Light machine-guns, rifle grenades and trench mortars became the staple weapons of the assault troops and their training laid emphasis on individual initiative and personal discipline. Ludendorff was one of the first modern commanders to recognize that the infantryman must also be a specialist, like the signaller or sapper, and not just an unskilled rifle carrier. On the courage, endurance and tactical acumen of the infantry rested Germany's fate.

The epic battles of 1916 and 1917 clearly demonstrated that concentrated preparation by massed artillery was essential to secure an infantry advance. No one understood this better than Ludendorff. Six thousand five hundred guns and 3,500 mortars were assembled for the attack. The need for surprise dictated the abandonment of a preliminary bombardment and of ranging by firing. Ludendorff wished to avoid an artillery duel which would reveal his disposi-tions and intentions and imperil his precious reserves of ammunition. The 'silent' method of ranging used by the British at Cambrai was adopted and sophisti-cated techniques of target acquisition – sound ranging, flash spotting and aerial photography – were used. Care was taken to mask the assembly of the guns from air and ground observation. The guns were brought as close as possible to the front in order to engage targets deep in the enemy's rear and to ensure forward mobility once the battle began. Squadrons of aircraft were specially prepared and given key tactical roles in support of the infantry and artillery. Vast quantities of engineering materials were provided so that supplies could be quickly brought forward to the attacking troops and their guns. An extensive use of motor transport was anticipated.

Tactical employment of the artillery was heavily influenced by the ideas of

5. Maj. Gen. H. Rowan-Robinson, *Belated Comments on a Great Event* (London, Williams & Norgate, 1932), p. 26, states that 52 out of 66 divisions were 'shock' troops. I am indebted to Mr R.E.J. Dunk for a copy of this book.
6. Rowan-Robinson, *Belated Comments*, p. 77.

Colonel Georg Bruchmüller, artillery commander of von Hutier's Eighteenth Army, spearhead of the German attack. Bruchmüller favoured a short bombardment of violent intensity opening without warning. Its principal aim would be to paralyse British communications. Gun positions, command posts, telephone exchanges, billets and bivouacs were the main targets. Mixed gas, lethal and lachrymatory, would be used extensively, forcing defending troops to adopt uncomfortable protective measures or risk death or disablement. The advance of the infantry would be preceded by a deep creeping barrage to which the German soldiers were ordered to adhere even at the risk of suffering casualties from their own guns.

The signing of the Treaty of Brest-Litovsk on 3 March removed the last obstacle to Ludendorff's intentions. 'The Day' was fixed for 21 March, the first day of spring. Ludendorff's hopes rested on the ability of his infantry to break through the British line and to roll it up northwards. Their task was a formidable one. They lacked overall numerical superiority. They could advance only at the pace at which a man could walk. And time was not on their side. But they also had advantages: of choosing the point of assault, of unity of command, of interior lines of communication, and of a superb strategic railway system. Most of all, they faced an enemy who was in considerable disarray.

'The Kaiser's Battle'

The German Spring Offensive began with a sudden and violent bombardment at 4.40 a.m. on 21 March 1918. The infantry attack followed five hours later in thick mist. The main blow fell on the extended front of General Gough's Fifth Army. Communications were immediately reduced to a shambles. The front broke in two places. Plans for repairing the breach in co-operation with the French collapsed. The French Third Army, in reserve behind the Fifth Army's right, was expected to reinforce the British line in case of need, but when General Humbert visited Gough at 1 p.m. he quickly made it clear that the only aid he brought was the pennant on his motor-car.[7] Attempts to maintain a continuous line precipitated a rapid retreat as successive formations found their flanks exposed. The German advance was dramatic. Ham, Bapaume, Péronne, Nesle, Noyon and Albert fell in less than a week. By 27 March the British had been pushed back beyond the position from which they started in 1916. The German Army was within twelve miles of the key rail centre of Amiens. The Fifth Army continued to retreat in an increasing state of disintegration.

The Entente was plunged into crisis. On the third day of the battle Clemenceau advised President Poincaré to withdraw the French government to Bordeaux. Hurried plans were drawn up for the evacuation of the remainder of the BEF from the Channel ports. The peril threatened by German submarines in April 1917 had been known only to a few; now, even ordinary British people began to recognize the awful possibility that Britain might lose the war.[8] There was a desperate anxiety for news. British national newspapers were published for the first time ever on Good Friday (29 March), something which did not recur until the rather different circumstances of the appearance of Mr Eddie Shah's *Today* in 1986. It was apparent that the war had reached a profound moment of decision.

7. Sir H. Gough, *The Fifth Army* (London, Hodder & Stoughton, 1931), p. 266.
8. See V. Brittain, *Testament of Youth* (London, Victor Gollancz, 1933), p. 412.

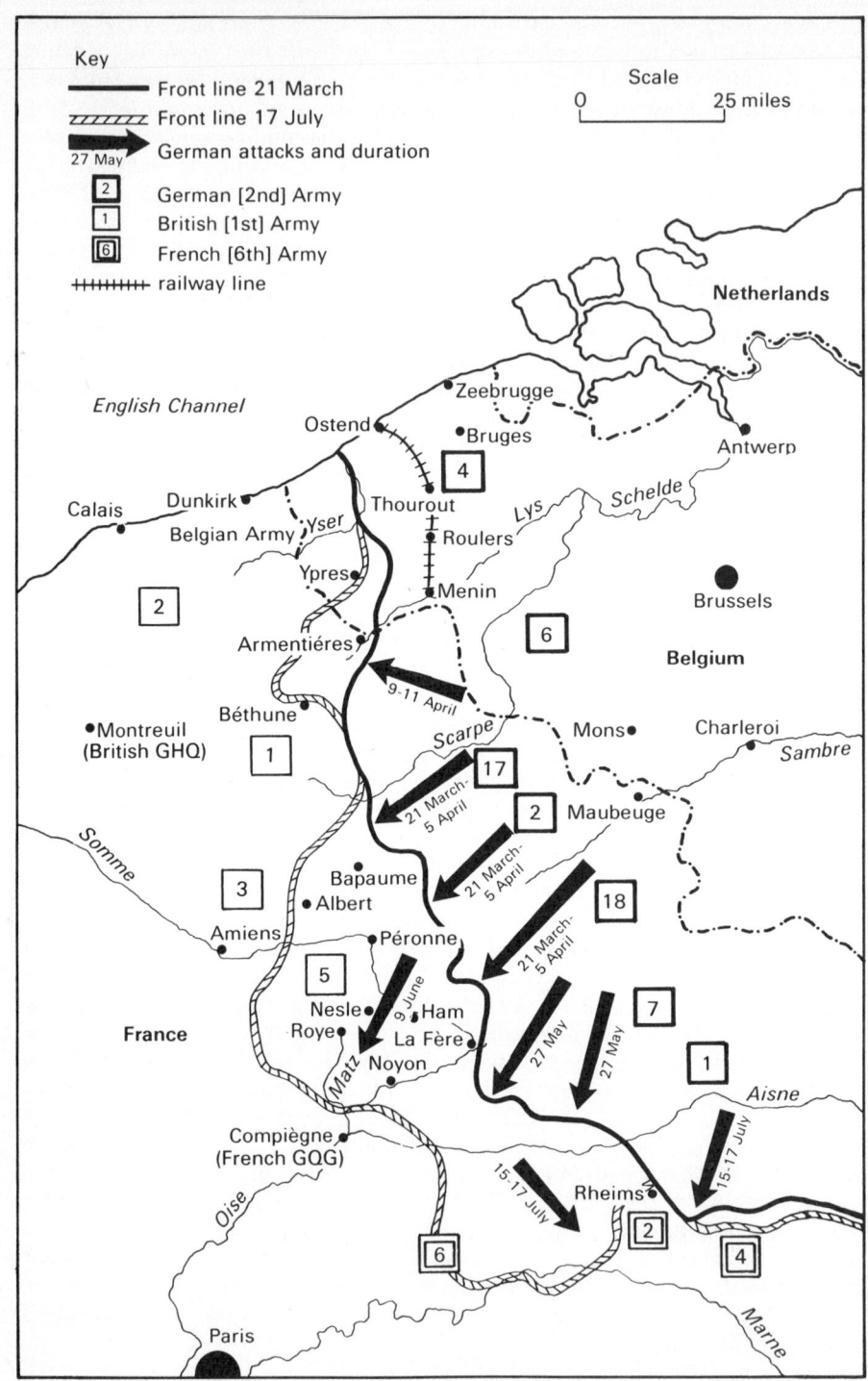

Map 7   The German Offensives 21 March–17 July 1918

The most important decision was taken by Field-Marshal Haig. On 25 March he abandoned his long-standing opposition to the appointment of an Allied supreme commander.[9] The following day, when Allied political and military leaders met at Doullens, Haig's recommendation that Foch should be appointed to 'co-ordinate the action of all the Allied Armies on the Western front' was accepted.[10] The defence of Amiens was made an absolute priority. Two days later General Gough was dismissed. The Fifth Army disappeared from the British line and was replaced by a reconstituted Fourth Army under the command of Sir Henry Rawlinson. Reinforcements poured into the Amiens sector. The last German attempt to capture the town was made on 4–5 April and was repulsed with heavy losses.

Thus denied, Ludendorff turned his attention to the north. This was what Haig feared most. He was determined to defend the Channel ports at all costs. Flanders was held in greater strength than any other part of the British line. Haig was reluctant to alter the distribution of his forces, but the defeat of the Fifth Army left him no choice. He was compelled to use 46 of his 58 divisions in the battle for Amiens. The Flanders front was necessarily weakened. The German attack was anticipated. Plans were made to shorten the line by evacuating the Passchendaele salient won at such cost only a few months before. Steps were also taken to relieve Portuguese troops to the south of Ypres.[11] But the Germans struck first.

On 9 and 10 April Ludendorff launched a massive two-pronged assault against the battle-scarred Ypres Salient. General Horne's First Army was the first to suffer. On 9 April the German Sixth Army burst through the Portuguese sector for a distance of 3½ miles to the River Lys. This was fortunate. The section of front held by the weakened and tired Portuguese divisions was the only one in which ground could be yielded without fatal consequences. More important than the Portuguese defeat was the resistance of Major-General Jeudwine's 55th (West Lancashire) Division on their right flank. This prevented a major catastrophe.[12] Plumer's Second Army was attacked the following day by the German Fourth Army and forced to retreat between Armentières and Hollebeke. The German armies pressed their advantage on both fronts. The River Lys was crossed in the south. The Messines Ridge, Laventie and Ploegsteert were carried in the north. Armentières was outflanked and abandoned. The gravity of the situation was reflected in Haig's famous 'backs to the wall' Order of the Day on 11 April.[13] The Passchendaele Ridge was evacuated on 15 April. The French failed to hold Kemmel Hill, with its commanding view of Ypres, which was now dominated from both Kemmel and Messines. A further shortening of the line was ordered on 26–27 April. This was

---

9. F-M Earl Haig, *The Private Papers of Douglas Haig 1914–1919* (London, Eyre & Spottiswoode, 1952), p. 297.

10. Haig, *Private Papers*, p. 298. Haig's italics. Foch was formally appointed Generalissimo on 14 April.

11. Germany declared war on Portugal on 9 March 1916 after the Portuguese goverment seized German merchant ships which had taken refuge in the Tagus.

12. See F-M Earl Haig, *The Despatches of Sir Douglas Haig, December 1915–April 1919*, ed. Lt. Col. J.H. Boraston (London, Dent, 1919), p. 151, for the importance of this action.

13. The full text is given in J. Charteris, *Field-Marshal Earl Haig* (London, Cassell, 1929), pp. 333–4. It is fashionable to represent the response to this Order as cynical. This was not always the case, see Brittain, *Testament of Youth*, pp. 419–20.

4 Full Circle: Stragglers from the 31st Division line the railway at Merris, near Hazebrouck, 12 April 1918 with not a trench in sight (*The Trustees of the Imperial War Museum, London*)

the last backward step taken by the British Expeditionary Force as an organized entity during the Great War. The Germans made a final bid for the Channel ports on 29 April and were repulsed with sanguinary losses by the artillery of the British 21st, 49th and 25th Divisions.

By the end of April Ludendorff had failed to reach his objectives on either the Somme or the Flanders fronts. American troops were arriving in France at the rate of 150,000 a month. The German position was becoming desperate, but Ludendorff was not finished. On 27 May he launched three armies across the Aisne towards Paris. He achieved complete strategic surprise. The Aisne front was considered to be impregnable. Worn-out British and French divisions had been sent there to recuperate because of its very strength. The French learned of the impending attack only the day before, too late to avert disaster. The Germans enjoyed a numerical superiority of 6 to 1. They advanced 12 miles in three days, sweeping over the Chemin des Dames and crossing the Aisne on an 18-mile front as far as the River Vesle. Soissons fell on 29 May. And two days later a German army looked once more upon the Marne at Château-Thierry. They were less than 40 miles from Paris.

The Marne was a river of ill-omen for the German Army in 1914. It became so again in 1918. French and American counter-attacks blocked the Germans' path at Villers-Cotterets and Château-Thierry. An attempt to link the two great salients on the Marne and at Amiens and to capture Rheims failed. Ludendorff made his last great Herculean effort to break through the Allied line on a 50-mile front either side of Rheims on 15 July. His left flank was bloodily repulsed by the French Fourth Army which had reluctantly adopted the concept of 'elastic defence' with a lightly held forward zone where destructive use was made of land-mines and mustard gas. Foch counter-attacked three days later supported by hundreds of small 'whippet' tanks. By 20 July the Germans lost 20,000 prisoners and 450 guns. It was the first in an unending succession of German defeats.

Ludendorff had staked all on winning a victory of total annihilation in the West. He had lost.

The daring of Ludendorff's plan was worthy of Rommel. He failed essentially because he lacked Rommel's mobility. The speed of advance of the German infantry was unparalleled in the history of trench warfare: 40 miles from St Quentin to Amiens between 21 March and 5 April; 35 miles from the Aisne to the Marne between 27 and 31 May. But the cruel fact was that this pace was too slow to inflict the kind of psychological paralysis achieved by the German *panzers* in 1940. Once initial penetrations had been made the advance spread out like a fan and lost force through dispersion. This was aggravated by Ludendorff's unwillingness to reinforce success. He has often been accused of mistakenly subordinating strategy to tactics. He faced a dilemma. On the Western Front what was strategically desirable was usually tactically impossible. The success of the attack against the Fifth Army and its relative failure against much more strongly held and heavily entrenched sectors of the British front vindicates Ludendorff's decision to give precedence to what was tactically possible. His real failure was in departing from the logic of his analysis. Success in the opening assault came principally on the front of the Eighteenth Army south of the River Somme, but this appeared less threatening to the British position than the advance on Amiens further north. This was continually reinforced even after it was apparent that the attack had stalled and was being met with stiffening resistance. Logistical difficulties also contributed to the loss of momentum. The Germans were weak in transport; Ludendorff's faith in motor lorries proved illusory. German troops continually outdistanced their supplies, which had to be brought forward over the shattered Somme battlefields. The capture of British dumps eased some of their problems, but it also led to looting, drunkenness and demoralization by the lavish scale of Allied material provision. The Allies were saved by no great acts of generalship. German attacks simply petered out. What Ludendorff had attempted was beyond his country's resources.

The collapse of the Fifth Army was the worst defeat suffered by the British Expeditionary Force during the Great War: 160,000 men and 1,000 guns were lost. No one had the least excuse for surprise.

By the middle of February the imminence of a German attack was certain. 'The enemy will attack. He will attack soon. He will attack on the Western Front,' declared Haig's brilliant new intelligence chief, Brigadier-General Edgar Cox, at a conference in the *mairie* at Doullens on 16 February.[14] The collapse of Russia had made this probable for some time[15] and the scale of German preparations was far too extensive to remain hidden. The British, however, were very far from ready.

During the final winter of the war the British Expeditionary Force reached a manpower crisis. The Flanders fighting severely depleted the strength of the infantry;[16] five divisions were lost to the Italian front; and later the needs of the war economy required large numbers of Category A men to be returned to civilian employment. Haig calculated that unless remedial action was taken he would be 248,226 men short by 31 March 1918.[17] It soon became apparent that remedial action would not be taken and that he would receive no reinforcements.[18] He proposed to disband 15 divisions. Permission was refused. He was compelled to reorganize the army – except for Dominion troops – into divisions of 9 instead of 12 infantry battalions. This caused considerable dislocation. On the Fifth Army front arrangements were not completed until 25 February, less than a month before the German attack.

This reduced force found itself with greater responsibilities. The French insisted that the BEF take over more of the line. They had a good case: with only 25 per cent more men they were holding a line over three times longer than the British. A 28 mile extension of the British line was agreed in principle at a

14. *OH 1918*, I, p. 104.

15. See GHQ Intelligence Appreciation of German Intentions in 1918, in J. Charteris, *At GHQ* (London, Cassell, 1931), pp. 321–6.

16. Official British casualties on the Flanders Front, 31 July–12 November 1917 (including 'normal wastage') were 244, 897, see *OH 1917, II*, pp. 360–1. Some put the figure higher, see above, p. 78, n. 105.

17. Letter from Sir Douglas Haig to the War Office, 24 November 1917, *OH 1918, I, Appendices*, Appendix 4, pp. 17–19.

18. It is now clear that Lloyd George, with War Cabinet approval, attempted to control Haig's actions by restricting the 'flow of men from civil life to the army'. He did not, however, hoard men who were already in uniform. See D.R. Woodward, 'Did Lloyd George starve the British army of men prior to the German offensive of 21 March 1918?' *Historical Journal*, XXVII (1984), pp. 241–52. (It is argued below that the British defeat owed less to the lack of men than to their faulty deployment and to the inadequacy of their defences. The Germans maintained a coherent defence throughout 1917 despite facing a numerical inferiority similar to that of Fifth Army in 1918.)

meeting between Robertson and Lloyd George in September. Haig prevaricated. But towards the end of October he met Pétain and arranged to comply with French wishes. The Fifth Army again suffered most. Gough's troops entered the line between Gouzeaucourt and the River Omignon on 10 December. One month later they began to extend their front a further 17 miles south to the junction with the French at Barisis, south of the River Oise. This process was not completed until 3 February. By 21 March the Fifth Army was holding a massive 42-mile front with only 11 divisions in line and 4 in reserve, 3 of which were cavalry.[19]

Defence of the Fifth Army front was to be 'in depth'. This was the urgent recommendation of the Committee of Inquiry established following the Cambrai *débâcle*. The aim was to create a lightly held Forward Zone, 600 yards to 2½ miles deep, consisting principally of an almost continuous line of outposts behind which was a row of strong-points designed to dislocate and disorganize an enemy attack. The main line of resistance would be in the Battle Zone, 1 to 2 miles deep, heavily entrenched and with dense belts of barbed wire intended to channel attacking infantry on to carefully sited machine-guns. Here would be the bulk of the protective artillery, placed in specially reconnoitred positions and prepared to respond with detailed fire-plans for harassing, infantry support and counter-battery fire. Finally, there would be a Rear Zone, out of range of enemy artillery, where reserves would be kept. Defensive positions in all three zones would be constructed so as to make the best use of tactical cover. The infantry would be provided with deep dug-outs and fortified observation posts. 'Elastic defence' would be permitted only in the Forward Zone; the Battle Zone must be held at all costs.

This was the ideal. It bore no relationship to the reality. The position which Gough's troops inherited from the French had received no preparation for defence in depth. Fifth Army was left with only six weeks in which to construct such a position. By the time the Germans attacked, the Rear Zone existed in places as little more than a line of cut turf. The labour of building the position added considerably to the burdens of already tired troops and prevented them from training in the new methods of defence. The intention of the planners was that the Forward Zone would be lightly held, but the enormous length of the Fifth Army front encouraged an obsession with linear defence and resulted in three-fifths of the infantry being deployed in the Forward Zone where it was exposed to the full violence of the German bombardment. Eighteen complete battalions were lost, equivalent to the infantry of two divisions.

Gough was aware of the weakness of the Fifth Army's position.[20] And so was Haig. The Commander-in-Chief's orders to Fifth Army were very curious. They seemed to envisage a battle in retreat.[21] Gough was not enjoined to fight in the Battle Zone (as the 'defence in depth' required), but to defend Péronne and the River Somme to the south of it at all costs. Neither the ground covered by the Forward and Battle Zones nor the communications leading to them were considered important enough to warrant reinforcement. In these circumstances it is to be wondered why it was not decided to anticipate the German attack and withdraw to the line Péronne-Somme. In practice Haig did nothing to

19. Sir J. Davidson, *Haig, Master of the Field* (London, Peter Nevill, 1953), p. 82.
20. See the letter from General Sir H.P. Gough to GHQ, 1 February 1918, *OH 1918, I, Appendices*, Appendix 11, pp. 45–7.
21. The order is given in Rowan-Robinson, *Belated Comments*, pp. 70–1.

discourage a deployment of Gough's troops which accorded neither with the concept of 'defence in depth' nor with his injunction to defend the line Péronne-Somme at all costs. This was not the only aspect of Haig's conduct that was culpable. It is difficult to be convinced that his concern for the fate of Gough's army was entirely prudent. Gough was never Haig's priority. That was the defence of the Channel ports. Haig did not believe that the war could be won or lost between the Oise and the Scarpe. It is significant that he chose to make his rallying call[22] at the height of the fighting in Flanders rather than on the Somme. The arrangements which he made with Pétain for French support for Fifth Army proved to be extraordinarily flimsy.[23] This was predictable. Certainly the Germans predicted it. Their belief that the French would not hurry to the aid of the British was instrumental in them choosing the Fifth Army front for attack.[24] During the course of the battle Haig visited Gough only once – on 23 March – when he announced himself 'surprised' to find the Fifth Army already behind the River Somme.[25] Apart from this Gough received precious little advice, encouragement or material support from his Commander-in-Chief. He was left to fight the battle alone.

Gough's conduct of the battle has been the subject of extravagant praise and bitter criticism. He deserves neither. His claim[26] to have brought his operations to a successful conclusion before falling to the scandalous injustice of political necessity cannot be substantiated. 'All that can reasonably be admitted,' wrote Major-General Rowan-Robinson, 'is that in spite of serious handicaps imposed on him by higher authority and in spite of devastating losses, he eventually succeeded, with the exiguous assistance afforded him, in avoiding irreparable disaster.'[27]

Gough was left to look to posterity for his justification. It is ironic that his dismissal resurrected the career of the architect of the earlier Somme disaster, Sir Henry Rawlinson, upon whose Fourth Army fell the mantle of victory in the months ahead.

The Defeat of Turkey[28]

In 1918 the war against Britain's tough secondary enemy – Turkey – came also to its climax. This had taken a long time. The Turks proved themselves a formidable enemy, especially in defence. The campaigns on Gallipoli and in Mesopotamia and Palestine absorbed vast numbers of British, Dominion and Indian troops, but until the end of 1916 there was little to show for their efforts other than failure and humiliation. British conduct of the war was reminiscent

22. See above, p. 87.
23. Rowan-Robinson, *Belated Comments*, pp. 38–57.
24. Gough, *Fifth Army*, pp. 265–6, quoting the Chief of Staff, German Second Army.
25. Haig, *Private Papers*, p. 296.
26. Gough, *Fifth Army*, pp. 321–5.
27. Rowan-Robinson, *Belated Comments*, p. 10.
28. For Mesopotamia, see British Official History, *The Campaign in Mesopotomia* (4 vols., compiled by Brigadier-General F.J. Moberly, London, HMSO, 1923–27). See also A.J. Barker, *The Neglected War: Mesopotamia 1914–1918* (London, Faber & Faber, 1967). For Palestine, see British Official History, *Military Operations Egypt and Palestine* (3 vols., compiled by Captain C. Falls, London, HMSO, 1930). See also, C. Falls, *Armageddon, 1918* (London, Weidenfeld & Nicolson, 1964) and A.P. Wavell, *The Palestine Campaign* (London, Constable, 1931).

of the Crimea in its muddle, incompetence and arrogant complacency.[29] The change in British fortunes owed much to the appointment of new military leaders and to the increasing influence exercised on the making of policy by David Lloyd George, first as Secretary of State for War and then as Prime Minister.

The key to the British position in the Middle East was Egypt, nominally a province of the Ottoman Empire but in reality a British protectorate. Defence of the Suez Canal was one of the fundamental aims of Imperial strategy. The need to safeguard this vital lifeline led ultimately to the Palestine campaign, the success of which had far-reaching consequences in the history of the modern world. Britain's other major concern was with Mesopotamia.[30] Its position at the head of the Persian Gulf and the common frontiers which it enjoyed with Persia, Russia and Turkey made it an area which the Government of India could not afford to ignore. The interest of the Home Government was stimulated by the discovery of oil. The conversion of the Royal Navy to oil-burning ships made this a commodity of growing strategic importance. The refinery at Abadan served the oilfields of the Anglo-Persian Oil Company, which was 51 per cent owned by the British government. Defence of these oilfields led to British military action immediately after the declaration of war on Turkey in November 1914. Mesopotamia became the scene of the worst humiliation and the first real success to attend British arms during the Great War.

On 6 November 1914 the 6th Indian Division landed on Abadan Island to protect its oil installations. The decision was taken by the Government of India under pressure from the British Admiralty. The Government of India had no interest in oil.[31] Its own motives for intervention were resolutely Imperialist in their reasoning. The outbreak of war with Turkey presented immense difficulties and dangers for the Raj, with its millions of Muslim subjects. It also presented opportunities. One of these was the possibility of forestalling the growth of Turkish or German or (worst of all) Russian influence in Mesopotamia. This could not be achieved by the mere defensive occupation of Abadan. It required an advance deep inland. Permission for this was granted by the British government. The easy success which it enjoyed led to a fatal over-ambition and ended in disaster.

The port of Basra was captured on 22 November and Qurna (near the junction of the Tigris and Euphrates rivers) on 9 December. In April 1915 the expeditionary force was raised to Corps strength and placed under the command of General Sir John Nixon. Nixon was confident of success. He ordered advances to be made up both rivers. The Tigris expedition was entrusted to Major-General C.V.F. Townshend. The achievements of his small, ill-equipped force were remarkable.[32] On 3 June he captured Amara. Liddell Hart described this as a 'brilliant little victory'.[33] It was followed on 28 September by

29. This point is much better made in Brian Porter's excellent article, 'Britain and the Middle East in the Great War', in P.H. Liddle, ed., Home Fires and Foreign Fields. British Social and Military Experience in the Great War (London, Brassey's, 1985), pp. 175–93.
30. The name given to the Turkish provinces of Mosul, Baghdad and Basra. Now the state of Iraq.
31. See M. Kent, Oil and Empire (London, Macmillan, 1976), pp. 118–19.
32. For Townshend's own account, see C.V.F. Townshend, My Campaign in Mesopotamia (London, Thornton Butterworth, 1920). See also A.J. Barker, Townshend of Kut (London, Cassell, 1967).
33. B.H. Liddell Hart, History of the First World War (London, Pan, 1972), p. 154.

the capture of Kut al Amara after heavy fighting. Townshend was short of shallow-draft river transport, doctors and medical supplies. His Anglo-Indian troops suffered remorseless attrition from disease in an unremittingly hostile environment, but they were less than 100 miles from Baghdad. The British government was at first wary of continuing, but it soon succumbed to temptation and to the unflagging optimism of the Commander-in-Chief. On 23 October the Cabinet ordered an advance on Baghdad, after first ensuring that responsibility for any failure would fall on Nixon. Townshend's response was gallant, but on 25 November his attempt to capture Baghdad was finally checked amid the ancient ruins of Ctesiphon. Superior Turkish numbers compelled a cruel retreat. On 3 December Townshend's depleted force reached Kut where it was encircled and besieged. All attempts to relieve it failed and on 29 April 1916 the starving garrison surrendered. Townshend was treated with lavish respect by his captors and imprisoned in some comfort, but he secured better treatment for his dog than his men, who were subjected to every kind of indignity including torture and homosexual rape. Two-thirds of them failed to survive their captivity.

On 16 February 1916 the British War Office assumed responsibility for the conduct of the war in Mesopotamia from the Government of India. The Chief of the Imperial General Staff, Sir William Robertson, was unsympathetic to the continuance of offensive operations. He fully supported the Allied agreement, reached at Chantilly in December 1915, to wind down activity on 'subsidiary' fronts and to concentrate resources for the decisive battle anticipated on the Somme. The catastrophe which befell Townshend's army reinforced this belief. In the aftermath of the surrender he personally chose a new Commander-in-Chief, Lieutenant-General Sir F.S. Maude, with instructions to maintain a defensive posture concerned only with the protection of the Persian oilfields.

Sir Stanley Maude has won the reputation of 'a truly great soldier'.[34] His motto was 'slow but sure'. He recognized the importance of what his fellow Etonian, Plumer, called 'the back arrangements'. Maude devoted himself to their detailed supervision. The welfare of his troops was ameliorated, their morale and training improved, their supplies of food, equipment and ammunition augmented, their lines of communication rendered secure and effective. In Mesopotamia this attention to logistical imperatives was more than enough to constitute greatness. On it, all Maude's success was based.[35]

Maude soon became convinced that Robertson's defensive strategy was neither prudent nor appropriate. More importantly, he persuaded Robertson. Offensive operations began, almost imperceptibly, on 12 December, with small-scale, methodical attacks on Turkish positions on the west bank of the Tigris, which was cleared by 22 February 1917. Maude's advance was deliberate and economical. This was not only the result of his style of command but also because of his fear of Robertson's response to any setback. None came. The advance was measured but relentless. Kut was captured on 25 February. The disintegrating remnants of the Turkish Army retreated to Baghdad, which Maude entered in triumph on 11 March. Baghdad was a disappointment to men brought up on *The Arabian Nights*. They found not 'the fabled city of the

---

34. C.R.M.F. Cruttwell, *A History of the Great War 1914–1918* (2nd edn, Oxford, Clarendon Press, 1936), p. 606.
35. For Maude, see C.E. Callwell, *The Life of Sir Stanley Maude* (London, Constable, 1920).

Caliphs' but 'a fetid and insanitary slum' which contributed to Maude's death from cholera in November at the age of 53.

Maude's methods and his success were perpetuated by his replacement, Sir William Marshall. British forces continued their advance up the Tigris to Mosul, where they received the Turkish surrender on 1 November 1918. Mosul's important oilfields were occupied two days later.

The capture of Baghdad was the first tangible success of Lloyd George's prime ministership. It concentrated his attention more than ever on the Middle East and especially upon Palestine.

The Suez Canal had been the first object of Turkish ambition once war was declared, but their attacks early in 1915 were comfortably repelled. The beginning of the Allied landing on Gallipoli in April distracted Turkish attention from the Suez front and turned Egypt into an armed camp. The subsequent evacuation of Gallipoli in January 1916 freed large reserves of manpower for offensive action elsewhere against the Ottoman Empire. As far as Palestine was concerned, the results were disappointing. The most notable event of 1916 was British encouragement of the Arab Revolt, proclaimed by Sherif Hussein at Mecca on 10 June. Arab guerrillas, organized by the 29-year-old Colonel T.E. Lawrence, harassed Turkish rail communications across the Hejaz and diverted Turkish troops from the Palestine front,[36] but little was done to take advantage of this. Elaborate and extensive fortifications were completed east of the Canal, and with the security which these afforded General Murray, French's former Chief of Staff, made a cautious advance into the Sinai, capturing El Arish on 21 December. This was not enough to satisfy the new Prime Minister. Lloyd George wished to strike a knock-out blow against Turkey, and he believed the time was ripe.

General Sir Archibald Murray was not the man for knock-out blows. His inconclusive attacks on Gaza in March and April 1917 infuriated Lloyd George, who ordered his replacement in June. Murray's successor was General Sir Edmund Allenby, a veteran of the Western Front, where he had risen to the command of the Third Army. His instructions were clear: take Jerusalem by Christmas. Allenby was more impatient even than his Prime Minister. He entered Jerusalem on foot on 9 December.

Allenby began the war as commander of the Cavalry Division in the original BEF. He ended it as the first Christian conqueror of the Holy Land since the Crusades. His success, like that of Maude, was based upon thorough preparation and efficient communications in a terrain which did not forgive mistakes. He had a strong personality and a violent temper. The army immediately felt the reality of his leadership. This was important in a polyglot force. His strategy, however, belied his nickname – 'The Bull'. He believed in the importance of surprise and made effective use of ruses to mystify and mislead his enemy. His mass employment of mounted troops marked him out as not only one of the last but also one of the greatest cavalry generals.[37]

The capture of Jerusalem was to be the prelude to the destruction of Turkish

36. For Lawrence's own account, see T.E. Lawrence, *Seven Pillars of Wisdom* (London, Jonathan Cape, 1935). The best biography is J.E. Mack, *A Prince of our Disorder: the Life of T.E. Lawrence* (London, Weidenfeld & Nicolson, 1976).

37. There is no satisfactory study of Allenby. The best is still A.P. Wavell, *Allenby: a Study in Greatness* (London, Harrap, 1940). See also, B. Gardner, *Allenby* (London, Cassell, 1965).

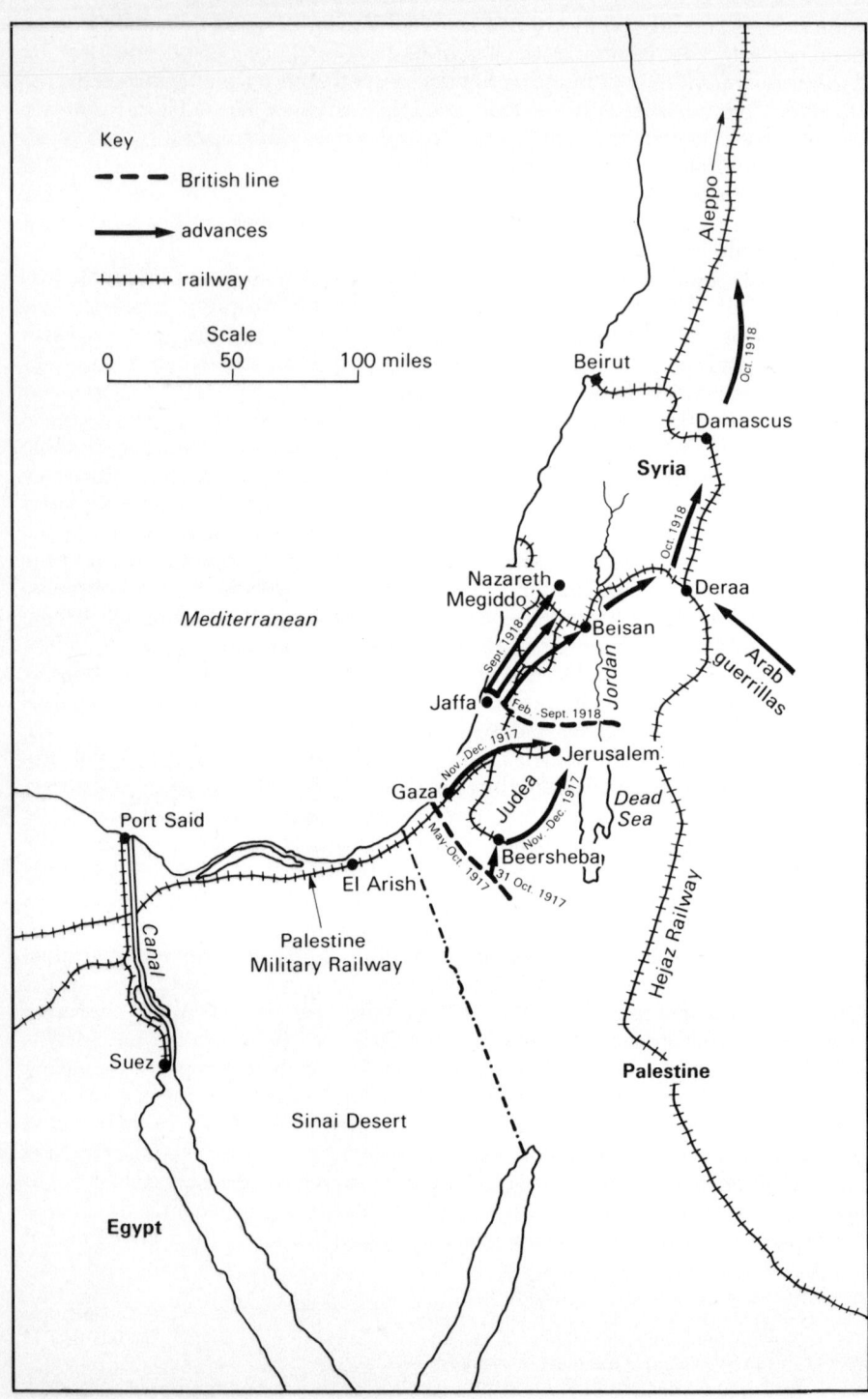

Map 8   The Defeat of Turkey 1917–1918

power in Palestine and Syria, but the Germans interrupted Allenby's preparations. The Spring Offensive resulted in his losing 60,000 men to the fighting in France, including all his British infantry. The signing of a peace treaty between Turkey and Russia in March also threatened to release Turkish forces for use on the Palestine front. Allenby was undismayed. The careful superintendence of Sir Charles Monro permitted his reinforcement by troops from India. Unusually for a British soldier, he sat down to plan a victory of total annihilation. He was confident of success. He enjoyed a great disparity of strength: a numerical superiority of 2 to 1; an even greater superiority of firepower; overwhelming air superiority; superior morale; and greater mobility. The last was crucial. The Turkish commander was once more the German Liman von Sanders, hero of Gallipoli. He believed that the Turks fought best from entrenched defensive positions. But Allenby had no intentions of allowing them the luxury of this. He envisaged a campaign of feint and manoeuvre. His target was not the Turkish Army, but its communications. His plan was to paralyse the Turkish High Command. It succeeded brilliantly.

Allenby's offensive began on 19 September. Arab guerrillas disrupted Turkish communications. The important rail link with Damascus was severed on 17 September, north of Deraa. British aircraft prevented enemy aerial reconnaissance and systematically bombed telephone and telegraph exchanges. An elaborate deception plan (including the use of 15,000 dummy canvas horses) concentrated Turkish attention on Trans-Jordan. Allenby's infantry, accompanied by a hurricane bombardment, immediately broke through the Turkish positions in the Judaean Hills. Fifteen thousand cavalry rode through the gap to seize the railway running through the valley of Jezreel between El Affule and Beisan. Liman, himself, was almost captured in bed at Nazareth. By 21 September the two Turkish armies west of the Jordan ceased to exist as effective fighting forces. The battle became known as 'Megiddo', the modern name of the Hebrew Armageddon. The rest was straightforward. Chauvel's Australian Desert Mounted Corps took Damascus on 1 October. The 5th Cavalry Division raced 200 miles to Aleppo, which was captured on 23 October. Turkey capitulated eight days later.

Götterdämmerung

By the end of July 1918 Germany had lost the war. The Allies, however, had still to win it. The precondition for victory was the defeat of the German Army in the field. Haig was the first of the Allies' political or military leaders to recognize that this could be accomplished in 1918. Between 8 August and 11 November, in a series of forgotten battles, Haig's 59 divisions outfought and defeated 99 German divisions, capturing one and a half million prisoners and nearly 2,300 guns. Lloyd George attributed this triumph of British arms to the guiding 'strategic genius' of Marshal Foch.[38] He was wrong. The principal achievement was Haig's. 'In the last hundred days of the war,' wrote C.R.M.F. Cruttwell, 'he showed a vision and a calculated resolution in taking chances worthy of a great captain.'[39] Haig's success came not through the discovery of a magical tactical

---

38. D. Lloyd George, *War Memoirs* (2 vols., London, Odhams, [1938]), II, p. 1876.
39. C.R.M.F. Cruttwell, *The Role of British Strategy in the Great War* (Cambridge, Cambridge University Press, 1936), p. 90.

formula or through the power of a secret weapon or through the guidance of a strategic genius, but through the systematic application by seasoned troops of the lessons distilled from the harsh experience of four years of war. His conduct of the sustained offensive which began on 8 August showed that he had, at the last, learned these lessons better than Foch or Lloyd George or Ludendorff.

None of the tactics adopted during the Battle of the Hundred Days was new. The novelty lay in a deeper understanding of their proper combination and in a more ruthless pursuit of their logic. All planning and preparation was suffused with a dedication to secrecy and surprise. Tanks and infantry underwent intensive training in the tactics of mutual co-operation. The role of the tank was entirely subordinated to the infantry's need for accurate close fire-support against enemy machine-gun nests and artillery positions which the indirect fire of the artillery was unable to supply. Preliminary bombardments were completely abandoned. *All* guns were laid and targeted silently, something which had not been attempted even at Cambrai. Tanks and infantry were pushed closer to the creeping barrage than many thought possible or prudent. A contemporary cartoon showed a soldier with his arm in a sling. 'What happened to you, Tommy?' the caption enquired. 'I was leaning on the barrage when it suddenly moved on, and I fell over and broke me arm,' Tommy replied.[40] Artillery command structures were simplified in order to encourage greater initiative, mobility and aggression, particularly at the small-unit level.[41] Major-General H.C.C. Uniacke played a key part in combining the scientific gunnery of the heavy artillery with the quick-firing, close-support traditions of the pre-war field and horse artillery.[42] Firepower was further augmented by the mass deployment of aircraft in a ground support role, harassing enemy troop concentrations, interdicting their lines of supply and disrupting their communications.[43]

Credit for the effective orchestration of available tactical resources belongs to no one man. Much has been claimed for the contribution made by the Australian Corps commander, Lieutenant-General Sir John Monash. His minor operation at Le Hamel on 4 July 1918 certainly pioneered the tactics which were used until the end of the war, but Monash did not invent them. He was part of the British army's learning process, not the cause of it.[44] The completion of this process required more than the discovery of an effective tactical combination. A strategy had to be found to fit the tactics. The man who found it was Sir Douglas Haig.

The Great Advance was the result of a skilfully conducted strategy of attrition. The concept of attrition is much misunderstood. It is generally regarded as a synonym for pointless slaughter, a crude substitute for real strategy on the part of ruthless generals whose inhumanity was matched only by

40. I owe this information to the 6th Earl of Harrowby (late Royal Field Artillery).
41. See below, Chapter 7.
42. For Uniacke, see S. Bidwell, *Gunners at War. A Tactical Study of the Royal Artillery in the Twentieth Century* (London, Arms and Armour Press, 1970), pp. 41–5.
43. For the tactical employment of aircraft, see below, Chapter 7.
44. For Monash, see A.G. Serle, *John Monash: a Biography* (Melbourne, Melbourne University Press, 1982). Monash's own account is in J. Monash, *The Australian Victories in France in 1918* (London, Hutchinson, 1920). P.A. Pedersen, 'General Sir John Monash: Corps Commander on the Western Front', in D.M. Horner, ed., *The Commanders. Australian Military Leadership in the Twentieth Century* (Sydney, Allen & Unwin, 1984), pp. 85–125, is a very fair-minded summary of Monash's importance and achievements.

their lack of imagination. 'He just mumbled about "attrition",' Lloyd George complained of Robertson's reply to his pointed question whether the army had a plan to win the war.[45] The hard fact was that the German Army could only be beaten by attrition – the remorseless erosion of its will to resist. Both the Army and the nation which sustained it were too strong for anything less. Their defeat required the mobilization and sustained application of the whole of the Entente's superior economic, industrial, diplomatic, psychological and moral resources as well as its military power.

Kitchener quickly realized this. He counselled against the dangerous belief that the war could be won simply by 'piercing' the German line in France.[46] Haig came to the understanding more slowly and at great cost in British lives. During 1916 and 1917 it was often difficult to tell whether Haig was waging a war of attrition by wearing the enemy out or attempting to strike a knock-out blow by breaking through the German line and destroying the German Army in the field or aiming at a breakthrough solely as the most effective means of attrition. Some of his closest advisers were unsure.[47] But by the second half of 1918 there was no confusion. There was no more talk of a 'breakthrough'. The failure of Ludendorff's magnificent infantry proved conclusively that the war could not be won in this way. The German line would be repeatedly struck, and struck hard, but the unwavering pursuit of limited objectives on small fronts (as at Passchendaele) was abandoned. The front of attack would be continually switched; attacks would be broken off once resistance stiffened. This would require logistical arrangements and staff work of a high order,[48] but it would sap the enemy's reserves and render ineffective the kind of 'elastic defence' which had terminated previous British offensives in costly exhaustion. Haig came to this determination alone and maintained it in the face of opposition from his political and military superiors and doubts from his subordinates. In it lies one of his principal claims to greatness as a soldier.

On 8 August 1918 Fourth Army launched the British contribution to Foch's great Allied offensive. Rawlinson assembled 2,070 guns, 534 tanks and more than 800 aircraft for the attack at Amiens. Success was dramatic. An advance of three miles was made in the first day. German demoralization was apparent. Mass surrenders took place. Even so, the attack soon stalled. Tank losses were enormous: only 145 were still in the field after one day's fighting.[49] Foch urged Haig to continue the attack;[50] Lloyd George bitterly criticized him later for his failure to do so.[51] But Haig refused.[52] The attack was broken off and switched to the front of Byng's Third Army between Beaucourt-sur-Ancre and Moyenneville. The assault was made on 21 August and achieved 'complete surprise'.

Haig scented victory. The following day he despatched a telegram to all his Army Commanders urging the 'most resolute offensive'. The principle of a step-by-step linear advance was abandoned. Divisions were given distant objectives

45. Lloyd George, *War Memoirs*, I, p. 536.
46. Charteris, *Haig*, p. 210.
47. Charteris, *At GHQ*, p. 143.
48. See Essame, *Battle for Europe*, pp. 17–28.
49. C. Messenger, *Trench Fighting 1914–1918* (London, Pan Books, 1973), p. 152.
50. Haig, *Private Papers*, p. 323.
51. Lloyd George, *War Memoirs*, II, pp. 1869–70.
52. Haig, *Private Papers*, pp. 323–4.

which they were to gain independent of their neighbours and without regard for their flanks. Reinforcements would be sent only where ground was being gained, not where resistance imposed a check. Forward momentum was to be maintained regardless of risk.[53]

The Battle of Amiens demonstrated to Ludendorff the catastrophic decline in the fighting power of the German Army.[54] The only course realistically open to him was a 'strategic retirement'. He had disconcerted Nivelle's offensive in 1917 with the sudden withdrawal to the Hindenburg Line, but this time he did not escape without injury. Third and Fourth Armies pressed him all the way. Bapaume fell on 30 August. Péronne was brilliantly captured by the Australians on 1 September. Between 12 and 14 September the United States Army, supported by the French II Colonial Corps, wiped out the great German salient at St Mihiel, taking 15,000 prisoners. The 207 divisions which Ludendorff once had under his command were reduced to 185; only 21 were left in reserve. His last serious chance of avoiding defeat rested on the defences of the Hindenburg Line, but on 27 September Haig's armies struck what Foch declared to be the blow from which there could be no recovery. First and Third Armies seized the crossings of the Canal du Nord. This prepared the way for the main attack on the Hindenburg defences by Fourth Army two days later. The honour of 'breaking the Hindenburg Line' fell to the veteran 46th (North Midland) Division, the first Territorial Division to take the field in France.[55] The 137th (Staffordshire) Brigade, men from Burton-on-Trent and Hanley, Wolverhampton and Cannock, stormed the awesome-looking German position along the St Quentin Canal at Bellenglise using collapsible boats and life-belts. By 9 October the German Army had suffered a shattering defeat, losing 36,000 prisoners and 380 guns.

The end came quickly. Disaster was everywhere. On 15 September General Franchet d'Esperey's Anglo-French army at last broke out of the Salonika 'bird cage' and swept north towards the Danube.[56] Bulgaria collapsed and signed an armistice on 30 September. Ludendorff concluded that he must seek an end to the war. The German government resigned the same day. The liberation of the Belgian coast began on 28 September. Initial German resistance weakened after 1 October and was followed by a general retirement. King Albert entered Bruges in state on 25 October. On the night of 23–24 October three Italian armies, spear-headed by the Tenth (under the command of a British general, the Earl of Cavan), crossed the Piave and smashed through the Austrians at Vittorio Veneto.[57] Ludendorff resigned on 27 October. Turkey capitulated on 1 November. The German High Seas Fleet mutinied at Kiel on 3 November, and Austria-Hungary signed an armistice. Revolution broke out in Munich on 7 November. The German military High Command could not bring itself to

53. See the telegram from Haig to his Army Commanders and the GOC Cavalry Corps, 22 August 1918, OH 1918, IV, Appendix 20.
54. Ludendorff, War Memories, II, p. 683.
55. See R.E. Priestley, Breaking the Hindenburg Line. The Story of the 46th (North Midland) Division (London, T. Fisher Unwin, 1919).
56. For Salonika, see below, p. 149.
57. For Italy, see British Official History, Military Operations Italy 1915–1919 (compiled by Sir J. Edmonds and Maj. Gen. H.R. Davies, London, HMSO, 1949). For the worm's eye view, see H. Dalton, With British Guns in Italy (London, Methuen, 1919) and N. Gladden, Across the Piave: a Personal Account of the British Forces in Italy 1915–1919 (London, HMSO, 1971).

5 The Way Ahead: British Mark V tanks and infantry advance in mutual support. Battle of the St Quentin Canal, Bellicourt, 29 September 1918 (*The Trustess of the Imperial War Museum, London*)

accept responsibility for defeat. Negotiations for the surrender were left to junior officers and civilians. Plenipotentiaries, led by the Centre politician Matthias Erzberger, were received by Marshal Foch in a railway carriage in the Forest of Compiègne on 8 November. The Kaiser abdicated the following day and fled to exile in Holland; the German Republic was proclaimed in Berlin. An armistice between Germany and the Entente was signed on 11 November. Hostilities on the Western Front ceased at 11.00 a.m. News of this was greeted with an orgy of celebration and rejoicing in Britain. The troops in the front line remained calm and sober. It was over. That was enough.

PART II

High Command

5

Politicians at War[1]

In the world of politics remarkable transformations were to
take place. Some men were to climb the glittering peaks of
prosperity and fame, others were to recede into the darkness of
failure and obscurity. The old party divisions were to blur and
fade. New alignments were to arise, new allegiances, new
enmities. In this strange and unmapped political territory every
step was fraught with difficulty and peril. The old landmarks
had vanished, the familiar scene had disappeared. In its place
was a new and unknown landscape full of false tracks for the
imprudent and snares for the unwary.

Lord Blake[2]

. . . under such a constitution as ours the control of a political
machine, even from the point of view of the conduct of the war,
was as essential as the preparation of big armies . . .

Andrew Bonar Law[3]

The British government entered upon the Great War full of apprehension.
Traditional Liberal distaste for war as an instrument of international relations
was only partly responsible. More important was fear of the war's domestic
consequences. The retention at home of two of the British Expeditionary Force's
six infantry divisions reflected deep concern with the possibility of civil war in
Ireland and of civil unrest elsewhere. This was understandable.

British politics had been in a state of turmoil since the 'People's Budget' of
1909. Lloyd George's attack on property and privilege ushered in a period
of frenzied political partisanship, culminating in the Constitutional Crisis of
1911 and the truncation of the power of the House of Lords. After the general
election of December 1910 the Liberal party became dependent upon the votes
of the Irish Nationalists for its parliamentary majority. Outside parliament

1. The best general account of wartime politics is in A.J.P. Taylor's *English History 1914–1945*
    (Oxford, Clarendon Press, 1965; Harmondsworth, Penguin, 1970). Lord Beaverbrook's
    Politicians and the War 1914–1916 (2 vols., London, Thornton Butterworth, 1928–32; 1 vol.
    edn., London, Oldbourne, 1960) is indispensable. C. Hazlehurst, *Politicians at War, July
    1914 to May 1915. A Prologue to the Triumph of Lloyd George* (London, Jonathan Cape,
    1971) and T. Wilson, *The Downfall of the Liberal Party 1914–1935* (London, Pan, 1968) are
    both outstanding as well as important.
2. R.N.W. Blake, *The Unknown Prime Minister. The Life and Times of Andrew Bonar Law
    1858–1923* (London, Eyre & Spottiswoode, 1955), p. 225.
3. From a memorandum dated 30 December 1916, quoted in Blake, *Bonar Law*, p. 304.

disaffection was rife. A rising tide of working-class militancy expressed itself in a wave of bitter industrial disputes in the mines, on the railways and at the docks. The campaign for female suffrage became increasingly strident and embraced extreme forms of 'direct action'. The introduction of a third Home Rule Bill for Ireland in 1912 aroused great opposition among Ulster Protestants and their supporters. An Ulster Volunteer Force was raised under the leadership of Sir Edward Carson and began to arm. The willingness of all these disparate groups to use violence to attain their ends disturbed comforting notions of consensus and seemed to some a portent of revolutionary change.[4]

The events of August 1914, however, proved these fears to be unfounded. The British declaration of war met with an impressive display of national unity. Trades unionists responded to Lord Kitchener's call to arms in overwhelming numbers. Battalions were formed consisting almost entirely of miners or railwaymen or dockers. Mrs Pankhurst ended the militant suffrage campaign of the Women's Social and Political Union. Both the WSPU and the more moderate National Union of Women's Suffrage Societies were soon involved in the recruitment drive. Participation in the war effort replaced the Vote as the focus of suppressed female energy and ambition. Nursing, in particular, became *chic*.[5] Ireland subsided into quiescence. Redmond pledged the support of Irish Nationalists in the struggle against Germany. The Ulster Volunteer Force was transformed into the 36th (Ulster) Division. The Home Rule Bill was placed on the Statute Book in September, but its implementation was postponed until the end of the war.

Even the 'rage of politics' was stilled. Nowhere was the mood of national unity more apparent than in parliament itself. The rancorous party strife of the previous five years ceased. Bonar Law committed the Unionists to a régime of 'patriotic opposition'. An 'electoral truce' was agreed between the Liberal and Unionist chief whips: in the event of a by-election whichever party formerly held the seat would not be opposed by the other. Party political activity in the constituencies was suspended. Liberal and Unionist MPs appeared side-by-side on recruiting platforms. Parliament showed no desire to exercise its responsibilities as the 'great Council of State'. Rather, it wished to abdicate them and leave the war to the government and the army. The pace of parliamentary life slackened. Parliament adjourned on 10 August and apart from a short unhappy session between 25 August and 17 September – solely to deal with Irish Home Rule – did not meet again until 11 November. By January 1915 184 MPs, 139 of them Unionists, were usually absent serving with the armed forces. During nine months of Liberal wartime government the Prime Minister gave only one parliamentary account of the progress of the war – on 1 March 1915 – and this was not debated.[6] The first division of the war did not take place until 5 July 1915.[7]

Few MPs thought the declaration of war was wrong. One who did was Ramsay MacDonald. On 5 August 1914 he found himself unsupported by any of his colleagues in opposing a war credit and resigned as Chairman of the

4. See G. Dangerfield, *The Strange Death of Liberal England* (London, Constable, 1936).
5. See the comment in I. Hay, *The First Hundred Thousand. Being the Unofficial Chronicle of a Unit of 'K (1)'* (Edinburgh & London, Blackwood, 1915), p. 113. This is typical of the misogyny of much wartime writing.
6. A.J.P. Taylor, 'Politics in the First World War', *Proceedings of the British Academy*, XLV (1959), p. 69.
7. Taylor, 'Politics in the First World War', p. 78.

Parliamentary Labour Party. He spent the remainder of the war as the target for much vitriolic abuse, not least from the country's trades unionists, but his courage in the face of this helped later to establish a reputation for integrity of purpose and nobility of character which brought him to national leadership within a decade.[8] Labour was thus the first party to feel the dissolving and transforming power of war. It was not the last.

The stop put to the long period of parliamentary bitterness by the declaration of war was only temporary. The war was not over by Christmas. The stalemate on the Western Front, the mounting casualty lists and the limitations of sea-power began to open the fundamental conflict which underlay all the shady intrigues, personal ambition and disinterested patriotism of wartime politics – that between those who believed the war could be won by 'traditional' means and those who became increasingly convinced that only the wholesale reorganization of society for 'total war' would bring victory.[9] The conflict crossed party lines, but it had inevitable consequences for all the parties, their leaders and the country itself.

The May Crisis, 1915[10]

The last Liberal government in British history fell with quite extraordinary suddenness. On 12 May 1915 Asquith told the House of Commons that a Coalition was 'not in contemplation'. One week later he and Bonar Law announced that a Coalition had been formed. Negotiations preceding the announcement took place in secret while parliament was in recess and concerned very few people. Neither the Prime Minister nor the Leader of the Opposition made much pretence at consulting their senior colleagues and none at all at consulting their parliamentary supporters. Arrangements for the new government were completed before MPs returned from their Whitsun break and were presented to them as a *fait accompli*.

The sequence of events associated with the formation of the Coalition is reasonably clear. 1915 brought an increased restlessness to the Unionist back-benches. In February an innocent-sounding Unionist Business Committee was formed. Its principal inspirer was the veteran Imperial propagandist W.A.S. Hewins.[11] Its purpose was to agitate for a more ruthless prosecution of the war. After the Battle of Neuve Chapelle, in March,[12] the British Commander-in-Chief, Field-Marshal Sir John French, sent emissaries to London to draw attention in political circles to his army's serious lack of material resources, especially high-explosive shell.[13] A 'mild and inconclusive' parliamentary debate followed on 21 April. Hewins was one of the speakers. Concern remained. On 7 May John Redmond, leader of the Irish National Party, moved

8. For MacDonald, see D. Marquand, *Ramsay MacDonald* (London, Jonathan Cape, 1977).
9. Taylor, 'Politics in the First World War', p. 76. The 'traditional' view was perhaps more important in relation to strategy than it was to politics and economics, see below, pp. 133–5.
10. See, in particular, S.E. Koss, 'The destruction of Britain's last Liberal government', *Journal of Modern History*, XL (1968), pp. 257–77, and M.D. Pugh, 'Asquith, Bonar Law and the First Coalition', *Historical Journal*, XVII (1974), pp. 813–36.
11. For Hewins, see W.A.S. Hewins, *The Apologia of an Imperialist* (2 vols., London, Constable, 1929).
12. See above, pp. 36–9.
13. F-M Viscount French, *1914* (London, Constable, 1919), pp. 357–60.

the adjournment of the House, ostensibly in opposition to State control of the liquor trade but actually in protest against the government's failure to give proper attention to the munitions question. This encouraged the Unionist Business Committee, which threatened to introduce an open motion on the subject.[14] On 9 May the British Expeditionary Force was bloodily repulsed on the slopes of Aubers Ridge.[15] Sir John French sought to deflect criticism from the failure by drawing renewed attention to the 'shells scandal'. He did this by leaking official information to the military correspondent of *The Times*, Colonel Repington.[16] On 13 May Bonar Law succeeded in restraining the Unionist Business Committee from proceeding with its motion. Asquith received unwelcome personal news the same day. His 26-year-old confidante, Venetia Stanley, informed him that she had accepted a proposal of marriage from the Liberal politician Edwin Montagu.[17] On 14 May *The Times* published Repington's despatch and accompanied it with a leading article, 'Shells and the Great Battle', which included the sentence 'The shortage of high explosive was a fatal bar to our military success'. On 15 May Admiral Lord Fisher resigned in protest against Churchill's conduct of the Dardanelles expedition. Bonar Law received an envelope addressed to him in Fisher's singular handwriting. It contained nothing except a cutting from the *Pall Mall Gazette* stating that Fisher had had an audience with the King lasting half an hour. Bonar Law concluded that Fisher wished him to know of his resignation.[18] On 16 May – a Sunday – Churchill visited Asquith at his country home, the Wharf, at Sutton Courtenay in Berkshire and offered also to resign. The offer was refused.[19] On 17 May Hewins warned Bonar Law that he would force a debate on munitions once the House resumed.[20] Bonar Law received a manic letter from Fisher urging him not to 'be cajoled privately by the P[rime] M[inister] to keep silence' and describing Churchill as 'a real danger' to the country.[21] Armed with this, Bonar Law sought Lloyd George's advice at the Treasury. They discussed the political situation in the light of Fisher's resignation, the fact of which Lloyd George confirmed.[22] Both agreed that it made a Coalition necessary.[23] Lloyd George immediately went to see Asquith at 10 Downing Street, leaving Bonar Law at the Chancellor of the Exchequer's residence next door. Lloyd George put the proposal for a Coalition to Asquith, who speedily agreed. Bonar Law was summoned and the matter was settled 'in less than a quarter of an hour'.[24]

Asquith's ready acquiescence surprised many, then and since. 'Why the fact

14. Taylor, 'Politics in the First World War', p. 74.
15. See above, pp. 36–9.
16. For this episode, see D. French, 'The military background to the "shell crisis" of May 1915', *Journal of Strategic Studies*, II (1979), pp. 192–205. Stephen Koss argued in 'Britain's last Liberal government' that the 'shell scandal' was part of a conspiracy by Churchill, Balfour and Lloyd George to depose Kitchener, but this thesis has been demolished by Hazlehurst in *Politicians at War*, Part III. See also, M. Gilbert, *Winston S. Churchill, Volume III, 1914–1916* (London, Heinemann, 1971), p. 460.
17. R. Jenkins, *Asquith* (London, Collins, 1964), pp. 363–6.
18. Blake, *Bonar Law*, p. 243.
19. Gilbert, *Churchill III*, p. 444.
20. Taylor, 'Politics in the First World War', p. 74.
21. M. Gilbert, *Winston S. Churchill, III, Companion Volume, Part II* (London, Heinemann, 1972), pp. 914–15.
22. Blake, *Bonar Law*, p. 243.
23. *ibid.*
24. D. Lloyd George, *War Memoirs* (2 vols., London, Odhams, [1938]), I, p. 136.

that Winston quarrelled with Fisher should mean your giving up the L[ocal] G[overnment] B[oard] is a *non-sequitur* which today and tomorrow will find it hard to understand,' Charles Masterman wrote to Herbert Samuel a week after the Coalition was announced.[25] Because Asquith's conduct seemed inexplicable on the basis of the known facts it was easy to assume that not all the facts were known. Rumour and recrimination fed allegations of a conspiracy. In retrospect Asquith's decision to accept a Coalition seemed instrumental not only in ending the life of a great reforming administration which had presided impressively over a troubled decade but also in taking the first tragic step along the road which led to the destruction of the Liberal party and the ruin of the philosophy which sustained it.[26] This confirmed the impression of Asquith as the victim of a calculated return to party strife in which Unionism had been the winner and Liberalism the loser. Liberal apologists have been crying 'foul' ever since.

Asquith himself never accepted this view. He always stressed his own responsibility for the formation of the Coalition.[27] The clue to Asquith's motives lies in the speed with which he agreed to the Lloyd George–Bonar Law proposal. There are four possible explanations for his haste.

The first is that once it became evident that Lloyd George and Bonar Law were agreed upon the necessity of a Coalition Asquith immediately recognized that he was faced with a political combination so powerful as to leave him no alternative to acceptance of their proposal other than resignation and that he took the preferable way out while he still had the chance. This is an unsatisfactory explanation.

Neither Lloyd George nor Bonar Law was able to dictate to Asquith. The Prime Minister was in a very strong position. The absence of so many Unionist members in the armed forces made him unusually secure in his parliamentary majority. He retained the overwhelming support of both his Cabinet colleagues and his backbenchers, most of whom were hostile to the idea of a Coalition. Far from being quick to sense a threat to his authority from the alliance of Lloyd George and Bonar Law, Asquith was slow to recognize it even from the much more vulnerable position in which he found himself in December 1916, when the coming together of Lloyd George and Bonar Law *was* instrumental in the collapse of the government.[28]

The second explanation is that Asquith's peremptory 'surrender' to Lloyd George and Bonar Law's 'ultimatum' was caused by a temporary paralysis of will arising out of the emotional distress of his 'rejection' by Venetia Stanley.[29] This is difficult to accept.

There is no doubt that Asquith took Miss Stanley's news badly, but there is little evidence that it affected his judgement. Rejection is a particularly wounding experience, but Asquith was not a love-lorn adolescent or a middle-aged suburban clerk with a crush on the office typist. He was the leader of a great party who had already steered his country successfully through seven turbulent

25. Quoted in Pugh, 'Asquith, Bonar Law and the First Coalition', p. 817. The authorities disagree about Masterman's meaning, see Hazlehurst, *Politicians at War*, p. 237. I follow Pugh.
26. Wilson, *Downfall of the Liberal Party*, pp. 40–4, 67–8, 69–97.
27. H.H. Asquith, *Memories and Reflections 1852–1897* (2 vols., London, Cassell, 1928), II, p. 95.
28. See below, pp. 119–27.
29. See Gilbert, *Churchill III*, pp. 446–7.

years, during which his emotional resources had been tested to the full. Asquith possessed to an unusual degree the ability to control his personal feelings. This was one of his greatest strengths; it regularly confounded his opponents. His bland and conciliating manner disguised an ambitious, resilient and resourceful politician. In May 1915 he remained fully self-possessed and convinced of his indispensable importance to the management of the nation's affairs. He was not a man to give up easily, as his conduct in December 1916 was later to confirm.

The third explanation is that Admiral Fisher's resignation transformed the political situation so fundamentally that neither Asquith nor Lloyd George nor Bonar Law had any alternative to immediate acquiescence in its inevitable consequences. This is also unsatisfactory.

Fisher's resignation was bound to cause problems. It was certain to bring once more into sharp focus the character and conduct of the First Lord of the Admiralty, Winston Churchill, a man who evoked distrust in both the Liberal and Unionist parties. It would also provide impetus to the mounting Unionist-backbench and press hostility towards Asquith's government, already under pressure because of the 'shells scandal'. The formation of a Coalition, however, was not the only option available to Asquith in seeking to resolve these difficulties.

The simplest solution was to dismiss Churchill and reconstruct the Admiralty – with or without Fisher. This would have met with approbation in many quarters, not least the Parliamentary Liberal Party.[30] Churchill was a dangerous man to have roaming round the backbenches without proper occupation, but he had no power base from which to cause real trouble. Asquith had an opportunity to take this way out, on 16 May, when Churchill offered him his resignation. He chose not to take it. There seemed no need. Churchill had already demonstrated his own ability to reconstruct the Admiralty (with Sir Arthur Wilson as First Sea Lord) and that he was prepared to defend government policy with the full support of his new professional naval advisers. There was no reason to believe that the government would lose a debate on the issue of Fisher's resignation.

Fisher's conduct itself put Asquith and Churchill at an advantage. Fisher's 'resignation' took the form of a curt note to Churchill.[31] The grounds for his going were poorly expressed and difficult to defend, for, as Lord Stamfordham explained to the King, Fisher had 'concurred in every order . . . issued by the Admiralty . . . and entirely approved of the first bombardment of the Dardanelles'.[32] The manner of Fisher's going was even more indefensible.[33] The King was shocked when he learned of it. Following his letter to Churchill, Fisher virtually abandoned his post. He deliberately laid a false trail – suggesting he had gone to Scotland – while actually taking refuge in a private room at the Charing Cross Hotel. Asquith had to send a special messenger to track him down and order him to return to his duties until his resignation was accepted. Fisher resisted impassioned attempts by Churchill,

30. Koss, 'Britain's last Liberal government', p. 274.
31. Gilbert, *Churchill III, Companion II*, p. 887.
32. Lord Stamfordham to King George V, 19 May 1915, in *op. cit.*, pp. 911–12.
33. This extraordinary episode is best followed from the contemporary exchanges of correspondence printed in *op. cit.*, pp. 887–916, especially Fisher's letter to Asquith of 19 May, pp. 906–7.

Lloyd George, Asquith and Reginald McKenna[34] to dissuade him from his chosen course. He gave the impression that his decision was irrevocable and that he was an old man who had had enough. But Fisher's correspondence with Bonar Law suggests that he wished his resignation to provoke a political crisis and a reconstruction of the government from which he would emerge with Kitchener-like powers over naval affairs. Once he sensed the opportunity to overthrow the government to his own advantage, Fisher became intolerable. His astonishing letter to Asquith on 19 May revealed the true extent of his megalomania and placed him firmly beyond the pale of political credibility. 'Even in wartime,' wrote Martin Pugh, 'departing Admirals do not easily bring down Governments, especially when their manner of departing is so extraordinary and difficult to defend as that of Fisher.'[35]

Fisher's resignation, however, was not without significance in the formation of the Coalition. It was what brought Bonar Law and Lloyd George together and what allowed Bonar Law – through Lloyd George – to suggest the proposal for a Coalition to Asquith.

Coalition had twice been seriously mooted during the course of the war, in August 1914 and March 1915. Bonar Law was against it on both occasions. His change of mind in May 1915 was not simply the product of Fisher's resignation. Bonar Law was converted because he no longer believed that he could confine his parliamentary supporters to their imposed role of 'patriotic opposition'. Fisher's resignation was only an element in this perception and not the most important one. Evidence of backbench Unionist discontent had been mounting for some time. The 'electoral truce' expired in January 1915. It *was* renewed, but after March only on a monthly basis. 'Patriotic opposition' was on probation. The activities of the Unionist Business Committee were even more ominous. Hewins's determination to force a debate on the munitions question was in itself a repudiation – however slight – of Bonar Law's leadership. But if the debate took place and was pressed to a division and the division revealed significant Unionist support for what would be, in effect, a motion of 'no confidence' in the Liberal government then the consequences would be grave. Bonar Law would no longer be able to act the part of leader of a 'patriotic opposition'. He would have two choices: to resign or to reassert his leadership by aligning himself with the views of his 'followers' and attacking the government from the Opposition front bench. Neither choice was appealing. The former would serve no purpose and would constitute a dereliction of duty. The latter might bring down the government. This is the last thing Bonar Law wanted. He was appalled by the thought of a wartime general election. It was bound to be divisive. It would sow confusion among Britain's friends and give aid and comfort to her enemies. Worse still, the Unionists stood every chance of winning. Bonar Law saw no advantage in this either for his party or for the country. The responsibilities of office would exacerbate ideological divisions – evident even in the Unionist party – between advocates of 'organization' and defenders of 'freedom'. This would make it doubly difficult to implement controversial policies – such as conscription – essential if the war was to be won.[36] The Unionist party would be

34. McKenna, who had served as First Lord of the Admiralty from 1908 to 1911 and who had done much to forward the Dreadnought building programme, was greatly respected by Fisher.
35. Pugh, 'Asquith, Bonar Law and the First Coalition', pp. 826–7.
36. Koss, 'Britain's last Liberal government', p. 269.

exposed to the full fury of working-class and Irish grievances, which an 'unpatriotic' Liberal Opposition would be free to exploit to its own advantage and the nation's detriment.[37] A Coalition was a convenient way out of this dilemma, simultaneously frustrating the threat of a Unionist rebellion and removing the possibility of a general election.

It is difficult to see how Bonar Law could have initiated the formation of a Coalition without the resignation of Lord Fisher. He could hardly go to Asquith and say 'I am in a dilemma. I can no longer control my supporters. I must either resign or bring down the government. The only way out is for me to join you in a Coalition.' Fisher's resignation was a Godsend. Bonar Law could now go to Asquith and say 'Lord Fisher has resigned. This is bound to cause controversy. Difficult questions will be asked. National unity will be compromised. This must be prevented at all costs. Let us form a Coalition.' This line of argument was altogether more acceptable. Certainly Asquith accepted it, but he accepted it initially not from Bonar Law but from Lloyd George.

The nature of Bonar Law's motives in first approaching Lloyd George must remain a matter for speculation. His relations with Asquith were cool and remote. He may have felt constrained by personal reasons from going to the Prime Minister direct. He knew Lloyd George much better and found him easier to get on with. But he also knew that Lloyd George was sympathetic to the idea of Coalition. This was no secret. 'Mr Lloyd George . . . always stood to attention when the word "Coalition" was uttered,' wrote Asquith's biographer, J.A. Spender.[38] Lloyd George would be easier to convince and his agreement would make him a valuable ally. If Bonar Law could not convince Lloyd George it would be impossible to persuade Asquith and probably better not to try.

Lloyd George had his own reasons for favouring a Coalition. These had nothing to do with Fisher's resignation. He was growing increasingly disenchanted with the conduct of the war, not least with what he regarded as the obstructionism and incompetence of the Kitchener-régime at the War Office. A Coalition would provide splendid cover for a reduction in the power of Lord Kitchener or even his complete removal from office. This would give greater scope for Lloyd George to take a more central rôle in the direction of the war, especially in the production of munitions.

Fisher's resignation was thus the occasion and not the cause of the Coalition's formation.

The fourth explanation for Asquith's haste is that he himself was already convinced of the necessity of a Coalition and was merely waiting the opportunity to conclude one. This comes closest to Asquith's own explanation.[39] It is the most convincing.

Asquith had none of Lloyd George's instinctive sympathy for coalitions. He was pre-eminently a party man. He had no confidence in the wisdom of the Unionist party or its leaders. He would have preferred to go on alone. But, by May 1915, the dangers of doing this were apparent. There was no real fear that the government would fall as a result of the 'shells scandal' or Fisher's resignation. Hewins's activities were an immediate threat to Bonar Law rather than to Asquith. The fundamental problem was the government's lack of military

37. Taylor, 'Politics in the First World War', p. 74.
38. J.A. Spender and C. Asquith, *The Life of Lord Oxford and Asquith* (2 vols., London, Hutchinson, 1932), II, p. 166.
39. See Hazlehurst, *Politicians at War*, p. 261.

success. This would not go away and would continue to provide inspiration for the government's detractors in the Unionist party and the press. There seemed little prospect of a major change in fortunes before the Kitchener armies were ready for battle in the summer or 1916. Before then, parliament would come to the end of its statutory five-year term and the government would have to face the general election which Bonar Law feared might come even earlier. Bonar Law and Asquith were both agreed in taking a dim view of the Liberal party's chances of winning.[40]

In these circumstances, a Coalition had many attractions for Asquith. At the very least, it would extend the 'electoral truce'.[41] More importantly, it would almost certainly avoid the need for a general election.[42] The formation of a 'National government – complete with Unionist ministers taking shared responsibility for policy decisions – would also mitigate the viciousness of press attacks and provide a breathing space in which Liberalism might yet win the war.

Asquith's real problem was not whether to form a Coalition but how to. There was no consensus in the Liberal party on the need for a Coalition. Creating one would be difficult and dangerous. As so often in his political career, Asquith waited for events to determine the decision which he himself was unable or unwilling to impose. Bonar Law's difficulties with the Unionist Business Committee and Fisher's resignation gave him his opportunity.

After their meeting on 17 May, Bonar Law wrote Asquith a letter.[43] 'There was no mistaking the nature of Mr Bonar Law's communication,' wrote J.A. Spender. 'It was a pistol at Asquith's head.'[44] This is nonsense. Bonar Law had no need to point a pistol at Asquith's head. Asquith had already agreed to the formation of a Coalition. The letter was written at Asquith's insistence and with his connivance.[45] Its purpose was to allow Asquith to say to his colleagues – especially those in the Cabinet – 'Lord Fisher resigned. Bonar Law put a pistol to my head. I could do no other than agree to a Coalition.'

The letter showed equal deviousness on the part of Bonar Law and his advisers.[46] It was careful never to mention the word 'coalition'. It confined itself to the suggestion that 'some change in the constitution of the Government' seemed 'inevitable'. The precise nature of the 'change' it was left to Asquith to appear to decide.

The letter gave both sides what they wanted: the appearance that their actions had been determined and constrained by the other's.[47] But, in reality, the formation of the Coalition was the result of collusion rather than conflict between the party leaders. The only conspiracy was by elements of the two front benches against growing parliamentary dissent caused by frustration with a war which no one appeared to know how to win.

40. Pugh, 'Asquith, Bonar Law and the First Coalition', pp. 815–17.
41. The 'truce' was immediately extended for three months, see B. McGill, 'Asquith's predicament, 1914–1918', *Journal of Modern History*, XXXIX (1967), p. 287.
42. The life of parliament was extended in December 1915 from January 1916 to 30 September 1916, avoiding a general election, McGill, 'Asquith's predicament', p. 287.
43. Blake, *Bonar Law*, pp. 246–7.
44. Spender and Asquith, *Asquith*, II, p. 165.
45. Blake, *Bonar Law*, p. 247; Lloyd George, *War Memoirs*, I, p. 136.
46. He consulted Lord Lansdowne and Austen Chamberlain.
47. Pugh, 'Asquith, Bonar Law and the First Coalition', pp. 813, 835–6, stresses the element of collusion.

Liberalism at Bay

The Asquith Coalition lasted for nineteen months. It left an unenviable reputation for chaos and confusion. Churchill described its formation as 'one of the greatest disasters which happened in the whole of the war'.[48] He himself had good cause to mourn, for he was its principal victim.

Fisher's behaviour, however bizarre, damned Churchill.[49] The Unionists were determined to exclude him from the Admiralty. Churchill did not go gladly. He made impassioned and demeaning attempts to keep his job;[50] his wife made restrained and dignified attempts on his behalf.[51] But Bonar Law would not be moved.[52]

Balfour – almost an 'anti-Churchill' in style and personality – became First Lord of the Admiralty. Churchill retained a seat on the War Council, but only as Chancellor of the Duchy of Lancaster. 'It was indeed a melancholy decline,' wrote Lord Blake. 'He, who had moved fleets from ocean to ocean, and surveyed with an all-embracing eye the entire strategy of the war, found himself in an office whose routine business consisted of such grave matters as the appointment of a new Commission of the Peace in Bootle.'[53]

Churchill was still only 41, but his career seemed to have reached the premature end which some of his many detractors had predicted for it. He found few public sympathizers. One was J.L. Garvin, editor of the *Observer*. 'He is young,' Garvin wrote on 23 May. 'He has lion-hearted courage. No number of enemies can fight down his ability and force. His hour of triumph will come.' But it took another, graver, crisis in another, far-distant, May before Churchill was able to renew his tryst with destiny. The immediate future lay with Lloyd George.

If Churchill was the principal victim of the formation of the Coalition, Lloyd George was its principal beneficiary, and the Ministry of Munitions its principal achievement.

The creation of the Ministry of Munitions was the result of compromise. The publication of Repington's despatch in *The Times* made it imperative that something should be done to increase the production of munitions. Responsibility for munitions production lay with the Master-General of the Ordnance, Major-General Sir Stanley von Donop,[54] under the ultimate authority of the Secretary of State for War, Lord Kitchener. The 'shells scandal' was an implicit condemnation of the conduct of the War Office. The obvious solution was to replace Kitchener with a Secretary of State more capable of galvanizing the nation's industrial resources. Lloyd George hoped that the formation of the Coalition would provide such an oppotunity. He was disappointed. The 'shells scandal' also demonstrated Kitchener's awesome popularity. When Lord Northcliffe attacked Kitchener openly on 21 May in a *Daily Mail* article entitled 'The Shells Scandal: Lord Kitchener's Tragic Blunder' he became instantly reviled.

48. W.S. Churchill, *The World Crisis* (6 vols., London Thornton Butterworth, 1923–31), II, pp. 804ff.
49. Blake, *Bonar Law*, p. 245.
50. Gilbert, *Churchill, III*, pp. 458–65.
51. *op. cit.*, p. 459.
52. Blake, *Bonar Law*, p. 252.
53. *op. cit.*, p. 253.
54. The survival of a man with such a German-sounding name and plenty of enemies through the anti-German hysteria of 1915 is one of the war's minor mysteries.

The Times and the *Daily Mail* were banned from West End clubs; copies were burned on the Stock Exchange; the circulation of the *Daily Mail* alone fell by 200,000.[55] Kitchener could not be replaced. The experiment of establishing non-executive *ad hoc* committees to assist the War Office in the production of munitions had already failed.[56] The only alternative was to remove responsibility for munitions from the War Office and give it to an entirely new Department of State with complete executive authority. This is what happened.

Lloyd George was determined to secure the position for himself. His accession to the office was far from automatic. He had to fight for it. Bonar Law had strong claims, especially after Asquith refused to appoint him to the Exchequer on the grounds that it was improper to have a Tariff Reformer as Chancellor in a parliament with a Free Trade majority. Law's Unionist colleagues urged him to insist on Munitions.[57] He seemed set to agree, but Asquith sent him to discuss the matter with Lloyd George, who overwhelmed him with a flood of Celtic eloquence and an appeal to the national interest.[58] Law settled instead for the relatively minor post of Colonial Secretary.

Lloyd George's appointment as Minister of Munitions has often been represented as a calculated step in his rise to supreme power. This underestimates the very great degree of political risk which acceptance of the post involved. From a personal political point of view, there was much to be said for Lloyd George's remaining at the Exchequer and biding his time. Asquith was 62, ten years older than Lloyd George. Although he showed no signs of losing his appetite for power, he was entering his eighth year as Prime Minister, the longest continuous period of prime ministerial office since that of Lord Liverpool. Perhaps Lloyd George's wait would not be too long. Meanwhile, the Chancellorship would maintain his status as Asquith's heir-apparent, but keep him out of the direct line of recrimination in the event of further military failures. Lloyd George's 'rise' would not depend simply on his being at the Ministry of Munitions; it would depend on his success there. This was not guaranteed. There was ample room for failure. The Ministry was a cuckoo in the civil service nest; it had no staff; its powers were ill-defined; it was bound to attract opposition from vested interests inside and outside government. And if he succeeded there was always the risk that his success would tend to strengthen Asquith's position rather than to weaken it. If Lloyd George's actions were calculated and self-interested, they were also courageous. It was on this indispensable quality, rather than on any administrative abilities, that his claims to statesmanship would ultimately rest.

The history of the Asquith Coalition is essentially that of Asquith's attempt to win the war while preserving as much as possible of the pre-war order in politics and strategy. It is also the story of his failure.

It is commonplace to regard Asquith as temperamentally unsuited to the exigencies of war leadership, a good man fatally flawed by a lack of personal dynamism.[59] Harsher critics have accused him of moral cowardice in refusing to

55. G.H. Cassar, *Kitchener. Architect of Victory* (London, William Kimber, 1977), p. 356.
56. R.J.Q. Adams, *Arms and the Wizard. Lloyd George and the Ministry of Munitions 1915–1916* (London, Cassell, 1978), pp. 35–6.
57. Blake, *Bonar Law*, p. 250.
58. *op. cit.*, pp. 250–1.
59. For example, E.S. Turner, *Dear Old Blighty* (London, Michael Joseph, 1980), p. 12.

adopt measures which he knew were essential to winning the war but whose political consequences he feared.[60] These criticisms are misleading.

Asquith did not fail because of faults in his character. He failed because what he was trying to achieve was ultimately impossible. He did not believe in winning the war at all costs, especially if those costs involved the destruction of the delicate national consensus which he had saved from the bitterness of pre-war politics and of which he saw the Liberal party under his leadership as the only guarantee. This was a legitimate fear which went beyond considerations of personal ambition and party advantage. Still less was he willing to contemplate a military defeat, the consequences of which would have been even more disastrous for the values to which he aspired. He was therefore driven into a policy of 'enough, but not too much'.[61] 'Enough' to try and ensure a military victory, 'but not too much' to compromise the survival of the national consensus on which all future social and political progress depended. He looked to a decisive military success to deliver him from his self-imposed dilemma, but the Battle of the Somme doomed his hopes. That he was able to govern for so long in the face of the growing contradictions between his aims is a tribute to the remarkable virtuosity of his political skills.

Asquith's intentions were apparent from the outset. The formation of the Coalition involved minimal changes in personnel. Twelve of the new Cabinet's 22 members were Liberals.[62] Only one of the key offices – the Admiralty – was held by a Unionist,[63] and Balfour had been in a virtual one-man-coalition with the Liberals on defence matters since before the war.[64] Asquith's determination to exclude Bonar Law from a major post was clear.[65] (Bonar Law's contentment with the Colonial Office is usually attributed to his modesty and patriotism, but there were also party and personal advantages in his maintaining a discreet distance from the central direction of the war.) The appointment of staunch economic liberals like McKenna to the Exchequer and Runciman to the Board of Trade was confirmation that Asquith intended policy changes no more consequential than his 'hastily improvised shuffle of personalities'[66] implied.

One of the first acts of the Coalition government was to establish a body known as the Dardanelles Committee. This had the official status of a Cabinet Sub-Committee, but was in reality an 'inner Cabinet' concerned with the formulation and implementation of military strategy. It was the second of three bodies successively charged with the central military direction of the war during Asquith's wartime prime ministership. Each of them represented a fresh

60. S.W. Roskill, *Hankey, Man of Secrets* (3 vols., London, Collins, 1970–74), I, p. 207.
61. This phrase has been used by George C. Herring in *America's Longest War: The United States and Vietnam 1950–1975* (New York, John Wiley, 1979), p. 108, to explain President Lyndon B. Johnson's policy towards Vietnam. There are many parallels between Johnson's predicament and Asquith's.
62. The Liberal members of the Cabinet were Asquith, Buckmaster, Crewe, McKenna, Simon, Grey, M'Kinnon Wood, Birrell, Churchill, Runciman, Harcourt and Lloyd George; the Unionist members were Bonar Law, Curzon, Austen Chamberlain, Balfour, Long, Selborne, Lansdowne and Carson. Henderson and Kitchener completed the team.
63. The other 'key' posts were Prime Minister (Asquith), Exchequer (McKenna), Foreign Office (Grey), War Office (Kitchener) and Munitions (Lloyd George).
64. Balfour had regularly attended meetings of the Committee of Imperial Defence before the war; he joined the War Council when it was formed in November 1914.
65. Blake, *Bonar Law*, p. 251.
66. Hazlehurst, *Politicians at War*, p. 285.

rearguard attempt by Asquith to maintain what Hankey called 'the old Cabinet system' in the face of the challenge of war.

The essence of the 'old Cabinet system' was its informality. The absence of either agenda or minutes put a premium on prime ministerial power and provided maximum opportunities for political manipulation. Asquith's political dominance was founded on his mastery of this system. His style of leadership was eminently suited to it. He portrayed himself as a mediator, manufacturing acceptable compromises out of political discord. The Cabinet provided the forum in which he was best able to do this. It was a large body. Its size encouraged prolonged discussion. Circumlocution led to confusion of purpose among its members and made it difficult for 'extreme' views to prevail. Asquith was happy with this state of affairs. Once the Cabinet lost its way, he was able to come to the rescue as 'honest broker' skilfully and persuasively summarizing the 'consensus' which had 'emerged' after exhaustive 'debate'.

It was thus in Asquith's interests to maintain the size and informality of Cabinet government. His problem was that the successful prosecution of the war seemed increasingly to require the abandonment of both these convenient arrangements. This led to a series of characteristic expedients. The first of these was the War Council.

Until November 1914 Asquith openly maintained the control of the full Cabinet over the British war effort without undue difficulty. After November 1914 he was compelled to maintain it more covertly and at a price in administrative confusion which a diminishing number of his senior colleagues were willing to pay.

When the war began the only existing alternative to traditional Cabinet government was offered by the Committee of Imperial Defence, principal instrument of British pre-war strategic planning.[67] Asquith ignored its possibilities. This was easy for him to do. Despite accomplishing much valuable work,[68] the CID had not succeeded in achieving complete constitutional respectability. Its rôle remained limited, specific and advisory.[69] It lacked the political weight to compete with the established authority of the Admiralty and the War Office when this was exercised by powerful ministers like Churchill and Kitchener. Without prime ministerial patronage, the CID was doomed to languish, retaining influence only through the continuing utility of its secretary, Maurice Hankey.

The first serious challenge came from outside the government and was beyond Asquith's control. By the middle of November the 1st Battle of Ypres produced a clear stalemate on the Western Front and confirmed that the war would be long and bitter. The capital stock of strategic ideas with which Britain entered the war was exhausted. It was time to reassess.

Asquith recognized that the work of reassessment would have to be delegated to a body smaller than the Cabinet and consisting only of men with relevant strategic expertise and responsibility. The War Council formed for this purpose on 25 November represented a minimum adjustment to 'the old Cabinet

67. For the CID, see N. D'Ombrain, *War Machinery and High Policy. Defence Administration in Peacetime Britain 1902–1914* (London, Oxford University Press, 1973).
68. See above, pp. 14, 15, 16.
69. See J.P. Mackintosh, 'The role of the Committee of Imperial Defence before 1914', *English Historical Review*, LXXVII (1962), pp. 490–503.

system'. The Council was certainly smaller than the Cabinet, with eight members, including the professional heads of the army and the Royal Navy.[70] The presence of Hankey as Secretary ensured that a degree of formality would attend its proceedings. But neither of these was a fundamental change. The War Council's powers were never clearly defined and its relations with the Cabinet and the great departments of state left ambiguous. This was deliberate. The War Council was never intended to replace the Cabinet, which retained ultimate executive authority and the right to subject War Council 'decisions' to further scrutiny and debate. Asquith's purpose was not to change the traditional conduct of the 'supreme command' but to preserve it under the appearance of change. He succeeded in this, under mounting difficulties, for another two years.

The War Council did not survive the formation of the Coalition. It was replaced on 7 June 1915 by the Dardanelles Committee. This involved little more than a change of name. Even from the outset, its size was bigger than that of the War Council and its numbers soon grew to fourteen. It enjoyed no more executive authority than the War Council and remained equally subordinate to the full Cabinet.

The administrative disadvantages of this two-tier system were readily apparent even to Asquith's friends.[71] Successive British failures on the Western Front in 1915[72] and the growing conviction that the Gallipoli campaign would end in disaster provoked widespread demands for an end to the useless duplication of debate and the establishment of a small 'War Cabinet' with complete executive authority. This, Asquith deployed his formidable array of political skills to prevent.

The announcement of the formation of a 'War Committee' on 2 November was the third, and last, of Asquith's institutional expedients. As was usual with him, it was a device which served more than one purpose. Its immediate aim was to effect a reorganization of the government which would render it more sympathetic to the evacuation of the Gallipoli peninsula. Churchill and Curzon, both opponents of evacuation, were omitted from the new body. Churchill resigned from the government in consequence and joined the 6th Royal Scots Fusiliers on the Western Front with the rank of Major.

The formation of the War Committee was also a blow consciously struck at the authority of Lord Kitchener, who was absent on a tour of inspection of Gallipoli at the time. Kitchener's trip convinced him of the need for evacuation, but Asquith's reorganization was indicative of his willingness to force through such a decision even against Kitchener's opposition. The appointment of a new, strong-minded Chief of the Imperial General Staff – Sir William Robertson – in December provided further proof of Asquith's determination to restrain the influence of a man whom it was still impossible to replace.[73]

In these ambitions the formation of the War Committee may be accounted a success, but in its wider aim of deflecting criticism from the conduct of the war by appearing to acquiesce in the demand for a small, streamlined authority

70. Jenkins, *Asquith*, p. 345.
71. See the letter from Edwin Montagu to Maurice Hankey, 22 March 1915, quoted in Roskill, *Hankey*, I, p. 172.
72. See above, pp. 36–8.
73. See below, pp. 145–8.

capable of ruthless and decisive action it suffered an important failure. It did nothing to satisfy Asquith's most formidable critic, Sir Edward Carson. This had consequences which were ultimately fatal to the Prime Minister's government.

Carson's frustration with the Coalition did not take long to surface. He resigned as Attorney-General within five months of its formation, on 12 October 1915. In his resignation speech – made the same day as Asquith's announcement of the War Committee – Carson voiced his dissatisfaction with the machinery of government. This he regarded as fundamentally defective and at the root of British failures in the eastern Mediterranean. He saw no use in having an 'inner Cabinet', however small, unless it had power to control all the actions of government, unless it was *the* Cabinet.

Asquith's reorganization clearly failed to meet this criterion. The new body was apparently to enjoy greater executive authority than that allowed to either the War Council or the Dardanelles Committee, but the obligation to report to the full Cabinet remained. The size of the War Committee was originally given as 'from three to five', but when the names of its members were announced, on 11 November, the number had already risen to six. Its real membership was usually nine and this grew to eleven in 1916. The Ministers involved were not freed from departmental responsibilities.

Carson's continuing dissatisfaction led him to a radical conclusion. He decided that the real problem was not the machinery of government, but Asquith's control of it. The clarity of this perception guided his actions throughout 1916, when he became *de facto* Leader of the Opposition. In the December crisis Carson's conviction that the only cure for the ills of British government lay not in further revision and redefinition of the duties of the War Cabinet but in Asquith's replacement as Prime Minister made a crucial contribution to the events which brought Lloyd George to supreme power.

The Fall of Asquith

Asquith's replacement as Prime Minister against his will was no easy matter. Realistically, he had only two potential successors – Lloyd George and Bonar Law. Neither was strong enough to mount a successful individual challenge to Asquith's leadership. The succession of either would require the collaboration of both. Unless and until Lloyd George and Bonar Law were resolved that Asquith must go and were agreed upon which of them was to succeed him, the Prime Minister's position was secure.[74] At the end of 1915 the possibilities of such a collaboration seemed remote.

Lloyd George's reservations about the conduct of the war had been directed towards Lord Kitchener. The creation of the Ministry of Munitions had done much to allay his concerns. Whatever doubts Lloyd George may have harboured about Asquith's leadership, he clearly thought more highly of him than he did of Bonar Law.[75] His relationship with Asquith remained relatively warm. His career had been built on the firm foundations of prime ministerial support. He continued to see himself as Asquith's loyal lieutenant. He had little

74. Blake, *Bonar Law*, p. 281.
75. Lord Riddell, *Lord Riddell's War Diary 1914–1918* (London, Ivor Nicolson & Watson, n.d.), p. 165.

alternative. Lloyd George was respected, even admired, in the Liberal party, but he was also feared and distrusted. He could draw on none of Asquith's reserves of parliamentary affection and esteem. He had limited access to the kind of patronage with which prime ministers were able to build a political clientèle and he did little to remedy this by cultivating the Liberal backbenches. Most of his friendships were made outside parliament among his entourage of political advisers and press cronies. Even among his Cabinet colleagues, only Churchill appears to have called him by his Christian name.[76] Had Lloyd George been foolish enough to challenge Asquith openly for the leadership of the Liberal party, he would certainly have lost.

Bonar Law's status as a challenger was even less impressive. The bald fact was that he was the leader of a parliamentary minority. It was difficult to conceive of a situation in which he might become Prime Minister, except that in which he was returned as the leader of a Unionist parliamentary majority after a general election. As we have seen, this was a prospect which filled him with repugnance and dismay and one which he absolutely refused to countenance.[77] For him to become Prime Minister without a general election would require the support of Liberal votes in the House of Commons. This was a possibility which belonged to the realms of fantasy. Bonar Law's vicious opposition to Liberal policies before the war was not forgotten. He was neither liked nor respected on the Liberal benches. Although Bonar Law felt disquiet about Asquith's leadership, he was no uninhibited admirer of Lloyd George and he was less than enthusiastic about the idea of putting 'the little man' into 10 Downing Street.

The events of 1916, however, transformed these realities.

Asquith was a shrewd politician. His technique was tried and trusted. 'One thing I cannot help marvelling at is the way in which the old PM has kept his Cabinet together during all this difficult time,' Lloyd George's mistress, Frances Stevenson, wrote in her diary on 16 November 1915. 'He has done it by pure craft and cunning, propitiating here, or pretending to propitiate, making concessions there, or pretending to make them; giving promises which he never intended to keep, but which were just sufficient to keep the person concerned dangling. . . . Always wait & see! And the extraordinary thing is that this policy seems to work so extraordinar[il]y well, even in wartime, from the PM's point of view.'[78]

In 1916, however, it stopped working 'so extraordinarily well' from anyone's point of view. Asquith lost none of his skill. His will to govern was undiminished. No one could have done more to try and maintain a national political consensus. It was simply that maintaining a national political consensus on Asquith's terms became impossible. The year was barren in military achievement. The final evacuation of Gallipoli was followed by humiliating surrender at Kut[79] and the profound disappointment of Jutland.[80] Compromise went out of fashion. The circle of Asquith's critics in the press,[81] in

76. J. Ehrman, 'Lloyd George and Churchill as War Ministers', Transactions of the Royal Historical Society, 5th sers., II (1961), p. 102.
77. See above, p. 111.
78. F. Stevenson, Lloyd George. A Diary ed. A.J.P. Taylor (London, Hutchinson, 1971), p. 75.
79. See above, p. 94.
80. See above, pp. 55–9.
81. For the Derby Scheme, see R.J.Q. Adams and P.P. Poirier, The Conscription Controversy in Great Britain, 1900–1918 (London, Macmillan, 1987), pp. 119–43.

parliament and in the government itself widened. The call was for an end to vacillation and indecision. It was a call which Asquith was unwilling to answer and unable to resist. The failure of the 'Big Push' to deliver a decisive victory on the Western Front was the last straw. In the end Asquith ran out of time – and of luck.

The issue which began the unravelling of the Prime Minister's authority was that of conscription. It encapsulated the dilemma in which Asquith found himself during the war. Conscription was inherently contentious, especially for Liberals, thirty of whom voted against the establishment of a National Register of manpower in the first parliamentary division of the war on 5 July 1915. But from the middle of 1915 onwards it was increasingly apparent that some form of compulsion was unavoidable if the needs of the army and the economy were to be effectively and fairly determined.

Asquith's usual method with contentious issues was to draw them out, either in the hope that they would go away altogether or that the process of debate and discussion would produce a satisfactory compromise or that circumstances would arise in which the need for action would be recognized by all and the danger of provoking irreconcilable divisions avoided. In the case of the proposed introduction of conscription, delay was once more his favoured tactic. His principal instrument was the 'Derby Scheme' of October 1915.[81]

The scheme took its name from that of the man responsible for its establishment and implementation, the Earl of Derby, Director of Recruiting, but it bore the unmistakable imprint of Asquith. The aim of the scheme was to create the basis for a system of conscription – by dividing the adult male population into groups and classes according to age, marital status and occupation – but without the mechanism of compulsion. Instead, men were invited voluntarily to 'attest' their willingness to serve if called upon to do so. Married men who attested were assured that none of them would be called upon until all eligible bachelors had joined the colours.

Arthur Marwick described the scheme as a 'shot-gun wedding between the fair maid of Liberal idealism and the ogre of Tory militarism'.[82] Politically, it was very astute. It has been argued that the scheme 'was no last effort to save voluntaryism, but a token effort designed rather to break the idea of conscription gently to the population by proving the inadequacy of the old methods'.[83] This is to misrepresent Asquith's motives. Asquith understood the administrative advantages of conscription. He was not wedded to a pure and dogmatic Classical Liberalism. As Chancellor of the Exchequer and as Prime Minister before the war he had been a key figure in the promulgation of social reforms which involved an unprecedented degree of state intervention. But he did not *want* conscription. The scheme was not intended to fail, but to fail safe. As a political gambler Asquith favoured the each-way bet. He would have preferred not to have conscription, but if he had to accept it he wished to do so on his own terms.[84] Fundamental to these was the preservation of consensus. Whatever happened, it did not seem that he could lose. But he lost, all the same.

The scheme did not work. In January 1916 Lord Derby announced that only

---

82. A. Marwick, *The Deluge. British Society and the First World War* (Harmondsworth, Penguin, 1967), p. 80.
83. C. Hughes, 'Army recruitment in Gwynedd, 1914–1916', unpublished MA thesis, University of Wales, 1983, p. 318.
84. Adams and Poirier, *Conscription Controversy*, pp. 121–2.

1,150,000 of the 2,179,231 single men shown by the National Register of manpower to be of military age had attested.[85] It would clearly be impossible to hold married men to their attestation until some other method of bringing the eligible single men to the colours had been found. Steps were immediately taken to introduce conscription for single men.

This arrangement was widely regarded as unsatisfactory and it intensified demands for general conscription. Asquith continued to resist them. By the middle of April his inability to find an acceptable compromise threatened the survival of his government. He badly needed a diversion. He found one in events in Ireland.

On 25 April 1916 – Easter Monday – Dublin broke into open revolt following the seizure of the Post Office by a group of Irish patriots led by P.H. Pearse. This fundamentally changed the mood of the House of Commons towards conscription. It created a consensus for ruthless action. Universal military service was carried; the government did not fall.

'This was a triumph of tactics,' wrote A.J.P. Taylor, 'however undeserved. But it was disastrous for Asquith's prestige.'[86] He had carried conscription; he had preserved his government; but he had not done so on his own terms, and this was apparent to all. Worse was to come. His handling of the Irish crisis resulted in a dramatic decline in Asquith's authority and saw Lloyd George emerge as a serious alternative as national leader.

Asquith determined to repair the damage to his authority by 'solving' the Irish problem. He failed. Asquith knew what needed to be done. It was imperative to concede a measure of Home Rule if the extremists of Sinn Féin were not to seize the mantle of Irish nationalism from Asquith's supporters in the Irish National Party. But he himself was unable to secure the necessary agreement. It was left to Lloyd George's skill as a negotiator – honed in his days as President of the Board of Trade on militant trades unionists and their intransigent employers – to get Redmond and Carson to reach a settlement.

The settlement was a triumph. It did much to restore the Liberal party's battered unity and self-confidence. But within days the agreement collapsed. The cause was Unionist discontent. Bonar Law was willing to acquiesce in a settlement which was acceptable to the leaders of Ulster. He made statesmanlike attempts to persuade his supporters to do the same, but without success. A group of Tory diehards, led by Lord Lansdowne and Walter Long, launched a fierce and open attack on what they regarded as a dangerous concession, extorted by rebellion in time of war. This put Asquith into a difficult position. If he had insisted that the Unionist members of the Cabinet stand by their approval of the settlement he might have 'broken' the Unionist party. But there was a risk. If a Unionist parliamentary revolt attracted sufficient support, the Unionist members of the government would have to resign. The Coalition would fall and a general election would almost certainly ensue. This was a risk that Asquith was not prepared to take. He surrendered ignominiously to Unionist opposition. His links with the Irish National party were shattered. He was no longer master of the Coalition. He was its prisoner.

Asquith's humiliation over Ireland was symptomatic of one of his fundamental political problems, the inability of Bonar Law to control the Unionist

85. Marwick, *Deluge*, p. 82.
86. Taylor, 'Politics in the First World War', p. 80.

party in the interests of the national and political consensus which the Coalition was designed to represent. During the second half of 1916 this problem came to a head and was instrumental in the destruction of Asquith's government.

Bonar Law's problem was Carson. On 7 January 1916 Carson demonstrated his willingness to act as a focus for Unionist discontent by accepting the Chairmanship of the Unionist War Committee. It was the activities of this Committee which did most to compromise Bonar Law's leadership and to force him into supporting the reconstruction of the Coalition under a prime minister other than Asquith. Bonar Law's personal crisis came in November. The circumstances were bizarre.

On 8 November Carson initiated a debate on the subject of the confiscation of enemy businesses in Nigeria. These were mainly firms which dealt in the export of palm kernels. But the real issue was Bonar Law's authority as leader of the Unionist party. There was no doubt that the government would win the vote. The important question was how many Unionists voted for Carson's motion. Bonar Law had made it clear that he would not remain a member of the government if he did not enjoy the confidence of his own party. This was now seriously threatened. If Carson attracted more Unionist votes than the government, Bonar Law would resign. The debate was extraordinarily bitter. When the House divided 65 Unionists supported Carson. These included all the officers of the Unionist War Committee. Seventy-three supported Bonar Law. Law had won, but the result was too close for comfort. It was only a matter of time before Carson's attacks met with greater success. Bonar Law was in a perilous position. His resignation seemed imminent. The consequences of this – the fall of the Coalition, a return to party strife and a general election – were abhorrent to him. It appeared that he had nowhere to go. He was rescued by Sir Max Aitken, the future Lord Beaverbrook.[87]

Aitken, like Carson, was convinced that the war could not be won with Asquith as Prime Minister. He was also convinced that Bonar Law, Carson and Lloyd George acting in concert could effect Asquith's removal without the need for a general election, or at the very least force changes in the constitution of Cabinet government which would reduce Asquith to the level of a mere non-executive chairman and permit Lloyd George to direct the war with the required ruthlessness. More important, he convinced Bonar Law. The attitude of Lloyd George was crucial.

If Lloyd George was to succeed in ousting Asquith as Prime Minister he had to be sure that he could command the necessary support in the parliamentary Liberal party. The events of 1916 provided this. In January a Liberal War Committee was formed. It consisted of about 40 MPs dedicated to a more vigorous prosecution of the war. Their numbers, although small, were significant. They compared with the 35 Liberals who voted against the conscription of single men in January and the 41 who voted against general conscription in May. As the most outspoken champion of conscription in the Liberal hierarchy, Lloyd George was the natural leader of the War Committee's membership. But their support was won at a cost in Lloyd George's popularity with his traditional radical constituency. His success in Ireland, however, repaired the breach. It also had other important consequences, not least of which was his physical survival.

87. See Beaverbrook, *Politicians and the War*, 1960 edn, especially pp. 328–40.

Lloyd George's intervention in Irish affairs prevented him from accompanying Lord Kitchener on his mission to Russia. It also prevented him from sharing Kitchener's fate. Kitchener's death vacated the key post of Secretary of State for War. Lloyd George once more succeeded in repelling Bonar Law's claims to the office, which he assumed in July. The significance of Lloyd George's succession was not lost on Asquith's wife, Margot. 'We are out,' she wrote in her diary on 6 July, 'it is only a matter of time when we shall have to leave Downing Street.' Lloyd George's tenure of the War Office brought him into direct responsibility for the military conduct of the war, shattered his faith in Asquith's leadership and convinced him of the necessity of fundamental changes in attitude and personnel if the war was to be won.

The 'Triumvirate' of Bonar Law, Carson and Lloyd George, which Aitken had brought together, met for the first time on 25 November. They agreed that a reconstruction of the Cabinet was imperative. This would involve delegation of full executive authority for prosecution of the war to a small War Council of three or four members, freed from departmental responsibilities, under the Chairmanship of Lloyd George.[88] Bonar Law submitted the proposal to Asquith at 10 Downing Street on 26 November. It was met with a 'polite but absolute refusal'.[89] This was not a promising start.

On 30 November Bonar Law informed his Unionist ministerial colleagues of the proposal. It was received with strong disapproval. This was a shock. The 'Triumvirate's' chances of success suddenly looked remote. Bonar Law's nerve began to falter. It took a long meeting with Lloyd George, which Aitken once more arranged, to steady him again.[90]

As part of the steadying process, Lloyd George promised Bonar Law that he would speak to Asquith. They met on 1 December. Lloyd George took the opportunity to confront Asquith with a set of proposals of his own. They differed significantly from those presented by Bonar Law five days earlier.

The 'Triumvirate's' proposals envisaged Asquith as 'President' of a 'Civilian General Staff'. Lloyd George would act as 'Chairman', but would only preside at meetings which the Prime Minister was unable to attend owing to 'pressure of other duties'. Lloyd George's proposals categorically excluded Asquith from membership of the new body.[91]

The meeting was amicable. Asquith raised no immediate objections. But later the same day he wrote to Lloyd George with what amounted to a complete rejection of his proposals.[92] He admitted some of the defects of the War Committee. He agreed to changes which would 'more clearly define and more effectively assert' its authority over the departments of state, but he continued to insist that the 'Cabinet would in all cases have ultimate authority'. For Asquith, this principle was absolute and fundamental.

Lloyd George sent a copy of Asquith's reply to Bonar Law, together with a covering note in which he informed the Unionist leader that 'The life of the country depends on resolute action by you now'.[93]

88. P.J. Grigg, *Lloyd George. From Peace to War 1912–1916* (London, Methuen, 1985), p. 448.
89. Blake, *Bonar Law*, p. 308.
90. Beaverbrook, *Politicians and the War*, pp. 362–84, 385–95.
91. Grigg, *Lloyd George*, p. 450, argues that these proposals had advantages for Asquith. See also, Churchill, *World Crisis*, III, pp. 249–50.
92. Spender and Asquith, *Asquith*, II, pp. 253–4.
93. Blake, *Bonar Law*, p. 313; Beaverbrook, *Politicians and the War*, pp. 404–9.

On Sunday, 3 December, a sensational article appeared in the radical newspaper *Reynolds News*. It purported to be an interview with Lloyd George, in which he threatened to resign and challenge the government's record before the court of public opinion unless his demands were met. The impression was also given that his action would be supported by Bonar Law, Carson and Derby.[94]

Reynolds News was owned by Sir Henry Dalziel. He was well known as a friend of Lloyd George. It took little imagination to work out who had inspired the article. Bonar Law's Unionist colleagues were furious at what they regarded as Lloyd George's 'trafficking with the press'. After a confused meeting at Bonar Law's house, Pembroke Lodge, they passed a resolution calling on the Prime Minister to resign. This was intended to allow a reconstruction of the government which would strengthen Asquith's position against Lloyd George.[95]

Bonar Law informed Asquith of the resolution the same day.[96] Asquith chose not to resign but to compromise. He agreed to the formation of a small War Council with Lloyd George as Chairman. Bonar Law's wish for Asquith to accept this arrangement was genuine. He had no desire to force him out of office. From Law's point of view, this was the ideal solution. It did not last. Within twenty-four hours, fortified by the unanimous support of his Liberal Cabinet colleagues, Asquith repudiated the agreement and prepared to fight.

Lloyd George received Asquith's letter of repudiation on the morning of Tuesday, 5 December. His moment of decision had arrived. He had threatened resignation many times before, but he had always recoiled from its consequences. This time he did not hesitate. He resigned. He did so with a certain amount of confidence. This owed much to the activities of his most important parliamentary supporter, the radical East End doctor, Christopher Addison.

The events of 1916 provided Lloyd George with a power base in the parliamentary Liberal party, but its existence was not the result of his deliberate intent. His awareness of it came from Addison. On 4 December Addison began canvassing the Liberal party. He found 49 Liberal MPs who were willing to support Lloyd George unconditionally. This figure was the approximate membership of the Liberal War Committee. By 6 December he had identified another 126 who would support Lloyd George if he succeeded in forming a government. 'By this canvass Addison became the real maker of the Lloyd George government,' wrote A.J.P. Taylor. 'The Unionist rebels forced Bonar Law into action. Max Aitken brought Lloyd George and Bonar Law together. It was Addision, and the Liberal rebels, who put Lloyd George in the first place.'[97]

Lloyd George's resignation had immediate consequences for Bonar Law. He could no longer hope to arrange a compromise through which Asquith and Lloyd George could continue to work together. He had to choose. He chose Lloyd George.

Bonar Law's decision was fundamental. The odds began to shorten in Lloyd George's favour. Asquith was now faced with the united and implacable

94. For the Press in general, see J.M. McEwen, 'The Press and the Fall of Asquith', *Historical Journal*, XXI (1978), pp. 863–83.
95. Blake, *Bonar Law*, p. 318.
96. Accounts of what took place at this meeting differ, see Blake, *Bonar Law*, pp. 316–20; Spender and Asquith, *Asquith*, II, pp. 258–9; Beaverbrook, *Politicians and the War*, pp. 425–36.
97. Taylor, 'Politics in the First World War', p. 84.

6 The End of an Era:
Asquith photographed
after his resignation in
December 1916 (*BBC
Hulton Picture Library*)

opposition of Bonar Law, Carson and Lloyd George. News of this disconcerted the Unionist ministers. On the afternoon of 5 December, Curzon, Cecil and Austen Chamberlain informed Asquith that they could not serve with him in a government from which both Bonar Law and Lloyd George had resigned. Later that day Bonar Law wrote to Asquith with the full agreement of his Unionist colleagues and told him that the government could no longer go on. Asquith resigned.

He did so, according to Trevor Wilson, 'not [as] a manoeuvre to strengthen his hold on office, but [as] a despairing act of recognition that the process of retreat and surrender could go no farther, and that the time had come to abandon a position from which dignity and authority had already departed'.[98] This may be doubted. Asquith's resignation was not a submission to his adversaries; it was a challenge. His position was still strong. He was certain of the support of his Liberal ministerial colleagues. He was aware of Unionist hostility to Lloyd George. He was confident that no government could be formed which did not enjoy his own support, and he was unwilling to lend this either to Bonar Law or to Lloyd George.

Asquith's resignation left Bonar Law and Lloyd George to test the validity of these assumptions. Bonar Law promised Lloyd George that he would not attempt to form a government unless Asquith was willing to support him.

98. Wilson, *Downfall of the Liberal Party*, p. 105. See also pp. 110–11.

Asquith refused. Responsibility now fell on Lloyd George. His task was not an easy one. The Liberal ministers all remained faithful to Asquith. The only major Liberal figure whose services were available was Churchill, but he was completely unacceptable to the Unionists.[99] Lloyd George had no choice but to try and find an administration from among the Unionist ministers of the former Coalition. They included men whose animosity towards him had been vehemently expressed only days before.

Lloyd George's cause was greatly helped by the early adherence of Balfour, who accepted the offer of the Foreign Office made to him by Bonar Law. Balfour had played no part in the crisis because of illness. He was a close friend of Asquith. He had no reason to love Lloyd George, who was planning to replace him as First Lord of the Admiralty. When Balfour learned of this, on 5 December, he immediately resigned. He seemed unpromising material for Lloyd George's purposes. His 'defection' was therefore something of a *coup*. It did much to influence the views of other Unionists and came as a real shock to Asquith.[100]

In seeking the support of the other Unionist ministers Lloyd George chose to do battle on his favourite ground: individual meetings, face-to-face. Lloyd George had enormous charm and formidable powers of manipulation. His personality assumed whichever guise would be most effective in insinuating himself into his listener's trust. 'When Lloyd George was alone in a room,' remarked Asquith's daughter, Lady Violet Bonham-Carter, 'there was really no one there.' Bonar Law had twice discovered how difficult it was to say 'no' to Lloyd George; now, in the face of Lloyd George's blandishments, Law's colleagues showed no more resolution than their leader. On 7 December Lloyd George announced that he had succeeded in forming a government.

Lloyd George's triumph was a watershed in British politics. The formation of the Lloyd George Coalition was not only a personal defeat for Asquith. It was also a defeat for the Liberal party, which was split between the supporters of Lloyd George and those of Asquith. Apart from Lloyd George himself the only Liberal to obtain a key post was Addison, rewarded with the Ministry of Munitions. All the other important ministries – the Admiralty, War Office, Foreign Office and Exchequer – were held by Unionists. Lloyd George was Prime Minister, but he led no political party. Despite Addison's promptings, he made no attempt to create a Coalition Liberal organization. His continuance in office depended on the goodwill of his Unionist colleagues and the votes of their supporters. In the case of Curzon, Lord Robert Cecil and Austen Chamberlain ('the three Cs'), this goodwill was made contingent on the continuance of Sir Douglas Haig as Commander-in-Chief of the British Expeditionary Force. Lloyd George's position was therefore one of limited independence and room for manoeuvre. The consequences of this dominated the politics of the next two years – and beyond.

'Do it Now'

The new Prime Minister wasted no time. He immediately abolished the 'full' Cabinet and the War Committee. They were replaced by a small War Cabinet.

99. Blake, *Bonar Law*, p. 340. See also Beaverbrook, *Politicians and the War*, pp. 494–514.
100. Beaverbrook, *Politicians and the War*, p. 503, described Asquith as 'thunderstruck' when he was told the news.

This was composed largely of men freed from departmental responsibilities and it enjoyed complete executive authority. Within a month, the departmental system below Cabinet level was also transformed by the creation of new ministries of Shipping, Labour, Food, and Pensions. These were followed in 1917 by a Ministry of National Service and Reconstruction.

Changes were not confined to the structure of administration. There were also important changes of personnel. Lloyd George showed his determination not to be inhibited by the familiar political constraints in constructing his government. He cast his net wide. In reality he had little choice. Most governments exist for many purposes. Lloyd George's existed for only one – to win the war. It would stand or fall on its ability to deliver victory. Victory, however, was not in the gift of parliament. It required the mobilization of the nation's entire economic, industrial and social resources. This could only be achieved with the collaboration of the representatives of organized labour, whose parliamentary insignificance belied their real power. Lloyd George's ministerial appointments reflected this need.[101]

The Lloyd George Coalition provided the greatest opportunity the Labour movement had known to exert influence on the counsels of state. Eight Labour men entered the new government, compared with three in the Asquith Coalition. Arthur Henderson, principal voice of trades unionism, joined the War Cabinet itself. George Barnes became Minister of Pensions and John Hodge Minister of Labour. Businessmen were also recruited to instill urgency and purpose into key areas of wartime administration. The Glasgow shipping magnate, Sir Joseph Maclay, became Director of Shipping and played a major rôle in the defeat of the U-boats. The coal owner, Lord Rhondda, seventeenth child of a Welsh grocer, became President of the Local Government Board. The civil engineering contractor, Lord Cowdray, became Chairman of the Air Board. These were the men of 'push and go' in whose company Lloyd George felt the sympathy of kindred spirits and whose kind had contributed much to his success at the Ministry of Munitions.[102] The criteria of appointment were merit and relevant expertise. This is what brought the agricultural reformer, R.E. Prothero, to the Board of Agriculture and the historian, H.A.L. Fisher, Vice-Chancellor of Sheffield University, to the Board of Education.

Lloyd George's most significant and dramatic appointment, however, was that of the German-born Imperial pro-consul and apostle of 'social-imperialism', Lord Milner, to the War Cabinet.[103] It was a surprising choice. Lloyd George and Milner had spent much of their careers in conflict. Lloyd George was a bitter critic of Milner's conduct of his South African High Commission, especially during the Boer War; Milner urged the House of Lords to reject Lloyd George's budget in 1909. But there also existed between them a community of sentiment about the future of social reform and the importance of 'organization'. Both cared about the welfare of 'the masses'. Both were hostile to the suffocating weight of the past on British life. Both desperately wanted to win

101. Lloyd George, *War Memoirs*, I, pp. 635–44. For a critical view of Lloyd George's choices, see Taylor, 'Politics in the First World War', pp. 84–7.

102. See D. Crow, *A Man of Push and Go: the Life of George Macaulay Booth* (London, Rupert Hart Davis, 1965).

103. See P.A. Lockwood, 'Milner's entry into the War Cabinet, December 1916', *Historical Journal*, VII (1964), pp. 120–34. For Milner's career, see A.M. Gollin, *Proconsul in Politics* (London, Blond, 1964) and T.H. O'Brien, *Milner* (London, Constable, 1979).

7 In harness: Lloyd George drives the forces of capital and labour down the road to 'total war'. (*Punch, 21 April, 1915*)

the war. Milner's appointment had particular political advantages. He had the almost unique ability to attract the enthusiasm of diehard Tories as well as 'patriotic Labour' and the young intelligentsia. The country would need the support of all three if it was to win the war.

Many of Milner's 'Kindergarten' of young intellectuals found their way into either Lloyd George's 'Garden suburb' of unoffical advisers or into the Cabinet

Secretariat which the Prime Minister established under the inevitable Maurice Hankey in order to give substance and clarity to the decisions of the War Cabinet.[104]

Lloyd George's claim to be 'the man who won the war' rests principally on the utility of the administrative changes which he effected during his first few weeks as Prime Minister. The self-conscious innovation of his actions, however, disguised an underlying administrative continuity between his government and its wartime predecessors.

The need for a small War Cabinet was at the heart of the concerns which undermined Asquith's leadership. Asquith's opponents were united in their belief that a successful prosecution of the war demanded the centralization of decision making in a few hands in order to avoid muddle and confusion. The actual War Cabinet which Lloyd George established disappointed these expectations. It did little to make government more 'streamlined'. The proliferation of sub-committees continued. There were 102 at the time of Asquith's fall; Lloyd George added another 63.[105] Much executive authority was necessarily delegated to them. The War Cabinet acted more as a supervisory body regulating the decisions of its subordinate committees rather than taking decisions itself.

The real differences between Lloyd George's government and Asquith's were of style rather then substance. This was to be expected. All the most important decisions of the war – the despatch of the British Expeditionary Force to France, the raising of an army on the Continental scale, the initiation of the Mesopotamia, Gallipoli and Salonika campaigns, the abandonment of Gallipoli and the introduction of conscription – were taken before Lloyd George became Prime Minister and necessarily limited his options. There remained the vital matter of national morale. Asquith ignored Bonar Law's advice that 'in war it is necessary not only to be active but to seem active'.[106] Lloyd George had no intention of repeating the mistake. His energy and dynamism infused the whole of the British war effort with a new sense of purpose and direction and a belief in ultimate success. The importance of this should not be underestimated.[107]

The increased effectiveness of government, however, was brought about by more than a change of personality at the helm. It was the result of a change in the atmosphere of political life.

Asquith's failure was essentially political. Even Hankey professed admiration for Asquith's administrative arrangements. What rendered them ineffective was not their inherent inadequacies but the political divisions and personal animosities which undermined Asquith's government after April 1916.[108] The fall of Asquith delivered Lloyd George from these frustrations. He had no artificial balance to maintain between contending factions. Lloyd George in December 1916 – like Churchill in May 1940 – was the symbol of the nation's

104. See J. Turner, *Lloyd George's Secretariat* (Cambridge, Cambridge University Press, 1980). See also, J.F. Naylor, *A Man and an Institution: Sir Maurice Hankey, the Cabinet Secretariat and the Custody of Cabinet Secrecy* (Cambridge, Cambridge University Press, 1984) and Lord Hankey, *The Supreme Command* (2 vols., London, Allen & Unwin, 1961), II, pp. 582–91.
105. Hankey, *Supreme Command*, I, p. 226.
106. Blake, *Bonar Law*, p. 290.
107. Ehrman, 'Lloyd George and Churchill', p. 105, defines 'sustaining the morale of the nation' as one of the three main functions of a prime minister in wartime.
108. Jenkins, *Asquith*, p. 411; Hankey, *Supreme Command*, II, pp. 543–4.

determination to prevail over its enemies. His government was a 'dictatorship in commission' which enjoyed both a popular and a parliamentary mandate.

Lloyd George had nothing to fear from the official Opposition. Asquith was in a difficult position.[109] He was unwilling to contemplate the consequences of open criticism of the government, but compelled to maintain the appearance of offering a constructive alternative if only to remind the country that he was still alive. This was not easy. Asquith's fall – however squalid and conspiratorial the circumstances – represented a clear repudiation of his leadership. In 1917 the Reports of the Commissions of Inquiry into the Dardanelles and Mesopotamia campaigns which Asquith had established – against Hankey's advice – as a sop to his critics in the aftermath of the Irish *débâcle* turned into a damning indictment of the muddle and timidity of his government.[110] Asquith was yesterday's man. The only alternative he had to offer was a proven record of failure. During the next two years fate dealt him one opportunity to embarrass – and possibly to unseat – the government without incurring the stigma of being 'unpatriotic' and this was firmly bungled.[111]

The moribund nature of the Opposition reflected the general mood of parliamentary quiescence. On 7 December 1916 normal parliamentary politics ceased for the remainder of the war. Parliamentary discontent with the political conduct of the war was instrumental in Lloyd George's rise to power. But having played its part in putting the new Prime Minister into 10 Downing Street, parliament wished only to allow him to get on with the job. This suited Lloyd George admirably. He rarely attended the Commons. The position of Leader of the House was delegated to Bonar Law.[112] The Prime Minister was free to concentrate the whole of his formidable energy on winning the war.

Lloyd George had strong opinions on how this was to be done. Unfortunately, they were not shared by the military high command. For the next fifteen months the most important political battle was fought not on the floor of the House of Commons or even in the Cabinet but between the Prime Minister and his principal military adviser, the Chief of the Imperial General Staff, Sir William Robertson.

109. McGill, 'Asquith's predicament ', p. 297.
110. Hankey, *Supreme Command*, II, pp. 522–9.
111. This was the Maurice Debate of 9 May 1918, when Lloyd George was accused of misleading the House of Commons about the strength of the British Expeditionary Force prior to the German Spring Offensive.
112. Lloyd George was the first commoner Prime Minister to delegate this function.

6

Soldiers and Statesmen[1]

> For armies can signify but little abroad unless there be counsel and wise management at home.
>
> *Cicero*[2]

> It is a hard war – not because of the Boche but because of these people here!
>
> *General Sir William Robertson*[3]

The formation of the Lloyd George Coalition represented the triumph of those – including Lloyd George himself – who wanted an end to 'divided councils, half-hearted measures, grudged resources [and] makeshift plans',[4] and who were willing to pursue a ruthless strategy of 'victory at all costs'. Asquith was a victim of what Raymond Aron has called 'the dynamism of total war'. So, too, was Lloyd George. The events of the next two years showed his choice as the instrument of the policy of 'ruthlessness' to be richly ironic. At home, he was prepared to sacrifice any number of sacred cows in pursuit of victory; but abroad, he recoiled from the consequences of trench warfare, whose 'futile massacres' served only to pile up 'the ghastly hecatombs of slaughter'.[5] His struggle to restrain Field-Marshal Haig from launching further costly offensives on the Western Front and to find an alternative strategy for the defeat of Germany dominated the politics of his wartime prime ministership.

Lloyd George's dilemma was symptomatic of general British bewilderment with the course of the war and its appalling human and material costs. The

1. The standard account of British strategy during the Great War is P. Guinn, *British Strategy and Politics 1914–1918* (Oxford, Clarendon Press, 1965). This is now threatened by D. French, *British Strategy and War Aims 1914–1916* (London, Allen & Unwin, 1986). Lord Beaverbrook's *Men and Power 1917–1918* (London, Hutchinson, 1956) is a compelling account of the politics of civil-military relations during the last two years of the war by a contemporary participant. See also, V.H. Rothwell, *British War Aims and Peace Diplomacy 1914–1918* (Oxford, Clarendon Press, 1971) and D.R. Woodward, *Lloyd George and the Generals* (London and Toronto, Associated University Presses, 1983).
2. Quoted in Lord Hankey, *The Supreme Command* (2 vols., London, Allen & Unwin, 1961), II, p. 439.
3. Robertson to Haig, 6 October 1917, quoted in J. Terraine, *The Road to Passchendaele. The Flanders Offensive of 1917: a Study in Inevitability* (London, Leo Cooper in Association with Secker & Warburg, 1984), p. 284.
4. W.S. Churchill, *The World Crisis. The Aftermath* (London, Thornton Butterworth, 1929), p. 447.
5. D.Lloyd George, *War Memoirs* (2 vols., London, Odhams, [1938]), I, pp. 289–93 for the 'futility' of Western Front offensives.

British were psychologically unprepared for Armageddon. This owed much to their history and to the 'lessons' which were distilled from it.

'The British Way in Warfare'[6]

'The British way in warfare' did not envisage the need for mass armies or mass casualties – at least not British ones. The reason for this was seapower. 'He that commands the sea is at great liberty,' wrote Francis Bacon, 'and may take as much and as little of war as he will.'[7] The British preferred to take as little as possible and to leave the bulk of the fighting to Continental allies. Their ideal was the Seven Years' War against Louis XV's France.

The Seven Years' War was a British triumph. France was incomparably the greatest military power in the world, but this did not save her from a humiliating defeat. Britain achieved her victory without attempting to raise military forces on the French scale, which was in any case beyond her resources. British military operations on the continent of Europe were strictly limited. A small expeditionary force was sent to Germany to fight alongside Britain's ally King Frederick II of Prussia. Direct military support of Prussia was essential in order to ensure the diversion of French strength from the defence of Canada, the conquest of which was the principal aim of British strategy, and to prevent French territorial gains in Europe for which Britain would have to exchange her own colonial annexations when peace was made. 'Commando' raids were also launched against the French coast in an attempt to tie down troops which would otherwise be deployed against Prussia. The remainder of Britain's military forces were used for offensive operations against the French empire not only in North America but also in the West Indies where French possessions were rich and vulnerable.

The success of this strategy was made possible by seapower. Admiral Hawke's victory at Quiberon Bay in November 1759 removed any possibility of a French invasion of Britain, isolated French colonial garrisons from effective support and reinforcement and permitted British prosecution of a ruthless trade war, the basis of which was the blockade.

The strategy proved itself at the Peace of Paris in 1763. The advance of French armies in Europe counted for little. France was forced to evacuate the territory she had conquered in Hanover, Hesse and Brunswick in return for the restoration of her much-valued West Indian possessions of Martinique, St Lucia and Guadeloupe. Ostend and Nieuport were returned to Austrian control. British colonial gains were dramatic. In North America, France surrendered Canada and Cape Breton Island. Her ally, Spain, surrendered Florida and was compensated with the French territory of Louisiana. This put an end to French colonial ambitions on the American continent. Her position in North America was reduced to the islands of St Pierre and Miquelon and a share in the fishing

---

6. See B.H. Liddell Hart, *The British Way in Warfare* (London, Faber, 1932). His thesis is summarized in 'Economic pressure or Continental victories?' *Journal of the Royal United Services Institute for Defence Studies*, LXXVI (1931), pp. 486–503. See also M. Howard, *The British Way in Warfare* (Neale Lecture in English History, University of London, 1974; London, Jonathan Cape, 1975) and H. Strachan, 'The British way in warfare revisited', *Historical Journal*, XXVI (1983), pp. 447–61.
7. F. Bacon, 'Of the True Greatness of Kingdoms', in *Essays* (1625; London, Grant Richards, 1902), p. 88.

rights of the St Lawrence and the Grand Banks. France also lost the West Indian islands of Grenada, Dominica, St Vincent and Tobago, the key Mediterranean island of Minorca, and Senegal. The conquests of the British East India Company in Bengal were retained and the French position in India fundamentally undermined.

These stunning successes exercised a beguiling influence on British strategic thought. The Seven Years' War seemed to offer a blueprint for the conduct of war which accorded exactly with 'the conditions of [British] existence'.[8] So long as Britain was a great naval power she had no need to become a great military power even to prevail in a war against an enemy which counted its armies by the hundred thousand. The maintenance of maritime supremacy would guarantee immunity from invasion and permit the release of military forces for offensive operations elsewhere. In Europe these could be confined to the despatch of a small expeditionary force in support of an ally which was a major military power in its own right and whose army would occupy the bulk of the enemy's main forces. The success of enemy armies in Europe would be negated at a peace settlement in exchange for the return of colonial annexations which it was within the power of even small British military forces to effect because of the mobility and surprise afforded by command of the sea. Such conclusions were deeply congenial to public opinion in a country whose political culture was hostile both to standing armies and to high taxation. They appeared to be confirmed by experience of the long struggle against Napoleon.

During the revolutionary and Napoleonic wars the Earl of Chatham's 'maritime strategy' was implemented with almost slavish fidelity by his successors, including of course his own son. It met with less immediate success than in the Seven Years' War. The cause was simple. Britain's Continental allies had less skill and considerably less luck than Frederick the Great. British expeditionary forces could do nothing to prevent the repeated ignominious collapse of their allies before the armies of the Republic and Empire. Britain often found herself expelled from Europe and challenged by hostile coalitions which threatened her national survival. The success of British arms against the French colonies was powerless to prevent this. But, in the end, the strategy was seen to prevail. Maritime supremacy *did* protect Britain herself from defeat and invasion. The maintenance of Britain's independence *did* encourage her allies and help to bring about the coalition which eventually overthrew Napoleon. The blockade *did* undermine French economic power and political control. After 1809, Wellington's peninsular expeditionary force *did* make a significant contribution to the military weakening of France. Austria, Prussia and Russia *did* bear the major share of the military burden and suffered most of the casualties. Britain's colonial empire *did* expand further, largely at French expense. British command of the sea and preservation intact of her military manpower *did* ensure her a voice in the post-war settlement and a resolution satisfactory to British interests.

In so far as the statesmen responsible for British entry into the Great War had given any thought to how the war was to be won, they favoured the 'maritime strategy'. The shift towards a 'Continental commitment' and the creation of the British Expeditionary Force[9] were not a repudiation of traditional doctrine but a

8. Sir J.S. Corbett, *Some Principles of Maritime Strategy* (2nd edn, London, Longmans Green, 1919), pp. 11–12.
9. See above, pp. 13–14.

necessary concomitant to it. Field-Marshal French's troops were merely required to follow in the strategic footsteps of the Marquis of Granby and the Duke of Wellington. The attachment to this strategy is not surprising. It had behind it not only the weight of history but also the appeal of fashion.[10] Above all, there seemed to be no realistic alternative. The 'conditions of [British] existence' had not changed.[11] Britain's naval power was still great; her military power, by Continental standards, was still contemptible. Other strategies were dependent upon British willingness to raise armies on the Continental scale. Few men believed this wise. Fewer still believed it possible. The British would hold fast to their 'way' in warfare. The BEF would be sent to France. Germany would be blockaded. Her deep-sea commerce would be wiped from the oceans of the world. Her colonies would be systematically annexed. Britain's allies would be reinforced with raw materials, credit and the certainty of eventual success. Britain's trained manpower would be conserved for the decisive blow. This would ensure victory not only on the battlefield but also at the conference table.

It was not to be.

The Realities of War

Liddell Hart defined strategy as 'the art of distributing and applying military means to fulfil the ends of policy'.[12] British 'policy' during the Great War was far from straightforward. There was a 'hidden agenda'. This bore little relationship to the public proclamation of international pieties which accompanied the British declaration of war. The real issue was Britain's survival as a Great Power. This had been under serious challenge for many years. The hey-day of effortless Palmerstonian supremacy was long gone. There were wolves at the door. The threat did not come solely – or even primarily – from Germany. Britain's allies – France, Russia and Japan – and the neutral United States were also a grave cause for concern. A British 'victory' required more than the defeat of Germany; it also required a peace settlement which would provide the British Empire with long-term security against its 'friends' as well as its 'enemies'.[13]

The 'maritime strategy' seemed peculiarly suited to this dual purpose. Certainly, Liddell Hart thought so. He attributed Britain's 'catastrophic' losses during the Great War to the abandonment of 'the British way in warfare' in favour of the bloody logic of the false 'Continental' prophet, Clausewitz.[14] Britain's policy aims made it imperative that she emerge from the war as the strongest power. Only then could she hope to realize her ambitions for long-term security in a dangerous world. The difficult years of readjustment to the realities of international competition made it clear that Britain's resources were finite and in many respects markedly inferior to those of her major rivals. It was therefore essential that she husband her strength in order to win the peace while encouraging her allies to expend theirs in order to win the war. This was axiomatic among the 'principles of maritime strategy'.

The implementation of such a strategy, however, faced many difficulties. Chief among these was Britain's main enemy.

10. See above, p. 28.
11. See above, p. 134.
12. B.H. Liddell Hart, *Strategy: The Indirect Approach* (London, Faber, 1954), p. 335.
13. This is a major theme of David French's *British Strategy and War Aims*, see pp. xii–xiii.
14. Howard, 'British way', p. 7.

Critics of British conduct of the war often ignore the existence of an enemy. British soldiers and statesmen could not. German power was the fundamental reality of the war. It had many aspects. One of these was geographical location. Germany's position in the centre of Europe, adjacent to the territory of her major ally, Austria-Hungary, gave her the enormous strategic advantage of being able to operate on internal lines of communication in a war against France and Russia. Another was size. Germany was a big country. Her human and material resources were correspondingly large. The population in 1914 – 67M – was only 16M less than that of Britain and France combined. Among advanced industrial nations only Russia and the United States were more populous. Poles formed the only substantial ethnic minority with independent nationalist aspirations and they were fiercely anti-Russian. The German people were the best-educated and the best-trained in Europe. The duty of military service to the state was the accepted obligation of all adult males. This helped to make the German Army a most potent instrument. Germany owed its nationhood to success in war. The Army was the focus of German national identity. Its officer corps attracted the country's social and intellectual élite. The Army enjoyed paramount political power and lavish material provision. And it had a record of victory unbroken since the Prussian disasters at Jena and Auerstädt in 1806. The German economy was second only to that of the United States and much more militarized. Germany was a world leader in heavy engineering and chemicals, sectors vital in modern war. Political development was less impressive. Parliamentary democracy was shallow-rooted. Political culture remained essentially monarchical and authoritarian. This was somewhat anomalous in a society which prided itself on being modern, rational and scientific. It was also a cause for concern, not least among the supporters of monarchy and authority. Many scholars have seen the German governing élite's fears for the future as a major stimulus to the 'will to war'.[15] But these tensions were well hidden. Germany gave every appearance of political stablility. The large socialist movement was docile and patriotic. There was nothing to match the poisonous political and social divisions of the Third Republic or even the bitter party strife of pre-war Britain. Germany was, in short, a formidable adversary.

The success of Britain's 'maritime strategy' depended upon two things. The first of these was the effective direct application of seapower to the defeat of Germany. This required the imposition of a blockade designed to destroy German seaborne commerce and to undermine the German economy and the annexation of German colonial possessions to use as bargaining counters against German territorial acquisitions in Europe at a future peace conference. The second was the power of resistance of Britain's Continental allies. Germany presented problems to both.

Germany was less vulnerable than Bourbon or Napoleonic France to the direct application of British seapower. Germany did not possess a navy on the same scale as Britain's. Her attempt to create one had been quietly abandoned in 1912. But the High Seas Fleet remained a source of danger and concern. The strength of the German navy, with its impressive array of modern ships of all classes, and the geographical position of Germany were sufficient to exclude

15.   V.R. Berghahn, *Germany and the Approach of War in 1914* (London, Macmillan, 1973); F. Fischer, *The War of Illusions. German Policy from 1911 to 1914* (New York, Norton, 1975).

Britain from the Baltic. This complicated the question of supplies to Britain's ally, Russia, and confined the possibility of Anglo-Russian amphibious operations against the German Baltic coast to the rabid imaginings of Admiral Fisher.[16] German naval defences, changes in naval technology and the realities of international politics conspired also to make a ruthless British blockade of the Nelsonic type impossible.[17] An economy as highly developed and as well endowed as that of Germany was unlikely to surrender tamely when confronted by the threat of mere 'contraband control'. There existed the possibility that blockade, far from destroying the German economy, would act as an incentive to the more efficient exploitation of German economic resources, both in Germany itself[18] and in any territories conquered by the German Army.[19] There was also a more worrying prospect. Britain herself had become dangerously vulnerable to economic warfare. During the Napoleonic wars Britain had been almost self-sufficient in food. This was no longer true by 1914. Britain imported four-fifths of her wheat and lard, three-quarters of her cheese, two-thirds of her bacon, half of her condensed milk and all of her sugar from abroad.[20] These were items vital to the diet of the working class, which constituted 80 per cent of the population.[21] The potential for Germany to impose a crippling 'reverse blockade' on Britain was apparent, and the submarine provided the means by which she could do it.

German colonial possessions in east, west and south-west Africa and the Pacific were all vulnerable to British attack. Most of them succumbed soon after the war began. But this was of little consequence. Germany was not a major colonial power. She had come late into the great game of Imperialism after the choicest prizes had already been won. Colonies had been acquired principally as tokens of national prestige and international recognition. They contributed nothing material to German power. Only German East Africa appeared to have much economic potential and this was where German settlement was thickest and German resistance strongest.[22] It was therefore difficult to gain the kind of colonial 'leverage' on Germany that Chatham had used so successfully against France during the Seven Years' War. Germany's colonies were bastard children, sickly and unloved. They made poor hostages.

This did not mean that colonial calculations were irrelevant. Germany retained grandiose Imperial ambitions. If she succeeded in occupying Belgium she was unlikely to vacate it in return for the *restoration* of the Bismarck Archipelago or the Namib Desert, but she might vacate it in return for the *acquisition* of the Belgian Congo or the Portuguese colonies of Angola and

---

16. See above, p. 28.
17. See above, p. 29.
18. See N. Stone, *The Eastern Front 1914–1917* (London, Hodder & Stoughton, 1975), pp. 163–4.
19. See above, pp. 66–7.
20. L. Margaret Barnett, *British Food Policy During the First World War* (Boston, Mass., Allen & Unwin, 1985), p. 3.
21. *ibid*.
22. For this, see British Official History, *Military Operations in East Africa August 1914–September 1916* (compiled by Lt. Col. C. Hordern, London, HMSO, 1941). (This was to have been the first volume in a series, but no more were published.) See also, C. Miller, *The Battle for the Bundu. The First World War in East Africa* (New York, Macmillan, 1974); F. Brett Young, *Marching on Tanga* (London, Collins, 1917). Small German forces under General von Lettow-Vorbeck conducted a brilliant guerrilla campaign and did not surrender until after the Armistice in Europe – on 25 November 1918.

Mozambique. The prospect of this kind of colonial bargaining, however, was disturbing to the British. It was not at all what they envisaged. The security of Britain in Europe was not to be purchased at the price of the security of the British empire in Africa. If such payment was to be avoided much would depend on the fighting capacity of Britain's Continental allies. Herein lay the fundamental British dilemma of the war.

This, simply put, was 'what should Britain do if the fighting capacity of her allies proved inadequate to prevent a German victory or to inflict a German defeat?' There were two possibilities.

The first was to conform to the 'principles of maritime strategy'. These were clear: resist French and Russian demands for increased military support, maintain the blockade, utilize the opportunities of mobility and surprise afforded by command of the sea to make harassing attacks against the Central Powers on terms of military advantage, conserve manpower, and wait. This was the pattern of the Napoleonic wars. It was full of dangers. The willingness to risk a French or Russian defeat was implicit. The consequences of a French collapse, however, would be very grave. France would either be occupied or compelled to sign a separate peace on German terms. These would almost certainly mean the German annexation of Belgium. Britain would be expelled from western Europe and threatened with invasion. The blockade would be rendered nugatory. Neutral opinion would be cowed. The possibility of British offensive operations elsewhere against Germany – in the Balkans or the Middle East – without French support would be slight. The bulk of the German Army would be free to concentrate against a British landing and to move supplies and reinforcements more quickly by rail than could the British by sea. The best the British could hope for would be to survive through long years of perilous isolation and economic distress until the day of some distant deliverance. This was precisely the situation in which she found herself a generation later after the Fall of France in June 1940.

The second possibility was to do everything necessary to prevent the defeat of France and Russia even if this meant raising a mass army to fight on the Continent against Germany. This had two advantages. It would lessen the German Army's chances of inflicting defeats of total annihilation on France and Russia. And it would prevent France from withdrawing from a military stalemate through a separate peace. There could be no better guarantee of French fidelity to the alliance than the presence of sixty British divisions on French soil. But there were also dangers. Such a fundamental departure from the 'principles of maritime strategy' was bound to be politically divisive. The raising of British armed forces on a Continental scale was an unprecedented undertaking. Its consequences were unpredictable but they were likely to permeate every aspect of British life. An army of a million men engaged against the main force of a country as powerful as Germany would also be a fearful hostage to fortune. A mass army risked the possibility of mass casualties and the dissipation of the reserves of strength on which British hopes for long-term security were based.

This is, of course, what happened. The British have regretted it ever since.

'Limited Liability'

The first British statesman to contend with the realities of the Great War was Lord Kitchener.[23] His appointment as Secretary of State for War on 5 August 1914 was the first of Asquith's many war-time expedients.

British history offers few rivals to the popular esteem in which Kitchener was held. His membership of the government resounded with political advantage. The outbreak of war made the appointment of a new Secretary of State imperative. Asquith himself had held the office on a temporary basis since the resignation of Col. J.E.B. Seely in the aftermath of the Curragh Mutiny in March.[24] Kitchener's appointment would relieve him of an unacceptable burden and preclude the need for difficult ministerial changes. It would fortify the government with the reputation of England's greatest soldier. Kitchener's presence would be a symbol of national unity and a token of the government's seriousness of purpose. His appointment would be popular with public, press and Opposition. The government's detractors would find it more difficult to attack.

There were also dangers. Asquith realized that he was taking a risk. Kitchener was a man of action, used to the exercise of power. He was unlikely to be a passive figurehead. He was bound to have views of his own on the conduct of the war, but no one knew what they were or what their consequences might be. His reputation was that of an autocrat. His willingness to submit to the constraints of Cabinet government was unknown. He was 'above party' in a political system in which the disciplines and incentives of party were essential to smooth government. He admitted his ignorance of England, its army and its politics.[25] Who knew what he might do?

Kitchener entered the government with an immense burden of public expectation. His cabinet colleagues regarded him warily, with a mixture of curiosity and trepidation. He did not take long to disappoint them. 'My own belief is that K . . . is a most overrated man,' the Postmaster-General, Christopher Hobhouse, confided to his diary on 22 December 1914, 'very conceited, and though hard-working, much over-weighted by the character of his labours. He is a pessimist and a bad *soldier*.'[26] The 'character of his labours' was indeed severe. He 'undertook to raise, train and equip new armies of unprecedented size; to mobilize the nation's industries for war; and to supervise the conduct of British military strategy in every part of the globe'.[27]

The 'shells scandal' of May 1915[28] confirmed the doubts of Kitchener's critics. The creation of the Ministry of Munitions imposed the first serious restraint on his powers. By the second autumn of the war Churchill was ready to conclude that Kitchener's appointment had been a mistake. 'We have suffered most terribly . . . from his conduct of the War Office,' Asquith was informed on 4

23. For Kitchener, see Sir G. Arthur, *The Life of Lord Kitchener* (3 vols., London, Macmillan, 1920), Volume III; Sir P. Magnus, *Kitchener. Portrait of an Imperialist* (London, John Murray, 1958); and G.H. Cassar, *Kitchener: Architect of Victory* (London, William Kimber, 1977).
24. See above, p. 18, n. 43.
25. Cassar, *Kitchener*, p. 185.
26. C. Hobhouse, *Inside Asquith's Cabinet. From the Diaries of Charles Hobhouse* ed. E. David (London, John Murray, 1977), p. 214.
27. Magnus, *Kitchener*, p. 283.
28. See above, p. 108.

8 The Weary Titan:
Kitchener showing the
signs of strain (*Mansell
Collection*)

October. 'The composition of our new armies, the preparation of munitions, the strategic & professional advice at the disposal of the Cabinet are three salient examples.'[29] Asquith needed no convincing. In December 1915 he appointed Sir William Robertson Chief of the Imperial General Staff specifically to restrict Kitchener's independence and to provide the government with an alternative source of military opinion. By the summer of 1916 Kitchener's continuance in office was something of an embarrassment to his colleagues and his tragic death came almost as a relief.

The verdict of posterity has been equally unkind. Kitchener's principal biographers, Sir George Arthur and Sir Philip Magnus, have regarded his tenure of the War Office merely as an unhappy postscript to his Imperial career. His reputation is that of a wrecker, carelessly undoing the patient work of pre-war reform which produced the General Staff and the Territorial Army.[30] Only his undoubted contribution to the recruitment of the great new volunteer armies has endured. 'If Kitchener was not a great man,' declared Elizabeth Asquith, 'he was certainly a great poster.'

29. Quoted in M. Gilbert, *Winston Churchill Volume III 1914–1916* (London, Heinemann, 1971), p. 543.
30. See below, Chapter 8.

Kitchener was an easy man to poke fun at. His ignorance of many of the basic facts of British life exposed him to the ridicule of the sophisticated and shallow. 'Tell me,' he is supposed to have said, 'is the *Morning Post* a Conservative or a Liberal newspaper?'[31] His inarticulateness, secrecy and resentment of interference isolated him from his colleagues. The immensity of his burdens eroded his health and strength and revealed his weaknesses. Lesser men delighted to point out that the idol had feet of clay. His death left the field to his detractors. His case has still to be made.[32]

Kitchener's claims to be the 'architect of victory' are substantial. Lloyd George, in a famous passage, likened him to 'one of those revolving lighthouses which radiate momentary gleams of revealing light far out into the surrounding gloom and then suddenly relapse into complete darkness'.[33] These 'momentary gleams' exercised a profound influence on British conduct of the war.

Kitchener's most important contribution was made before a shot was fired. Within two days of his appointment he advocated the raising of a 'new army' numbered in millions. The acquiescence of his Cabinet colleagues in this fundamental departure from British tradition was almost laconic. Kitchener's reasons for making the proposal were the product of intelligent speculation.[34] He rejected the fashionable view that economic dislocation would compel the belligerents to bring the war to a speedy conclusion.[35] He believed the struggle would be long. In a rare press interview in December 1914 he suggested a duration of three years. This was based upon his assessment of the relative strengths of the opposing powers. Kitchener knew his enemy. Germany was prepared for war. She possessed a magificent army and a powerful industry. She would not be defeated easily.[36] He was less impressed with Britain's allies. The French were a particular concern. During the Franco-Prussian War of 1870 Kitchener had enlisted as a private soldier in the French Army. His experience left him with a low opinion of French military prowess. This was determined as much by political as by military considerations. He regarded French 'democracy' as divisive and enervating. The 'disciplined legions' of Germany would be more than a match for the French 'rabble'; they would 'walk through them like partridges'. Kitchener did not believe that the small British Expeditionary Force was adequate to redress the military imbalance between France and Germany. Nor did he share the confidence of his countrymen in the ability of seapower to redeem the poverty of British military resources. The security of the alliance required Britain to increase her military contribution. This was a denial of one of the basic assumptions of the 'maritime strategy', restated with renewed cogency and force by the naval historian Sir Julian

---

31. Lloyd George, *War Memoirs*, I, p. 451, provides a similar illustration of Kitchener's ignorance of the nuances of British religious life.

32. Cassar's *Kitchener* is, however, a robust defence.

33. Lloyd George, *War Memoirs*, I, p. 450.

34. Kitchener's decision-making processes are most often attributed to instinct rather than to calculation, see Viscount Grey of Fallodon, *Twenty-Five Years, 1892-1916* (London, Hodder & Stoughton, 1925), II, pp. 71-2.

35. This view was held even by those who, in other respects, predicted the nature of the war with chilling accuracy, see J. Bloch, *Is War Now Impossible?* (London, Grant Richards, 1899), p. lx. For Bloch, see T.H.E. Travers, 'Technology, tactics and morale: Jean de Bloch, the Boer War, and British Military Theory, 1900-1914', *Journal of Modern History*, LI (1979), pp. 264-86.

36. Cassar, *Kitchener*, p. 197.

Corbett in 1911, that command of the sea permitted the successful 'application of limited [military] force to the attainment of an unlimited [military] object'.[37] The assumption was always dubious.[38] Kitchener would have none of it. In his judgement, the war would be decided on land. The decision would be expensive to both sides. And, without a major British military presence, it would be decided in favour of Germany.

The fate of Kitchener's armies was to be expended in the bloody battles on the Somme and in the Ypres Salient in 1916 and 1917.[39] This was never Kitchener's intention. He had no doubt that the war could only be won on the Western Front. The contribution of his armies would be to strike the 'decisive blow'. They would not be able to do this until they were properly trained and equipped. Kitchener did not expect this to be until 1917. Before then the rôle of the French and Russian armies was to prepare the way by eroding the moral and material strength of the German Army and making it ripe for defeat. Theirs would be the 'wearing out fight'. This strategy accorded exactly with Britain's war aims.[40] It would leave Britain's enemy beaten and her allies exhausted. Britain would end the war as the strongest power and be free to dictate the peace. Unfortunately, France and Russia showed a depressing reluctance to conform to British ambitions.

It was the Russians who presented Kitchener with his first major dilemma. The conduct of the war on the Eastern and Western fronts was inseparable in Kitchener's mind. He indulged no fantasies about the power of the 'Russian steamroller'. Like Marshal Saxe, he understood that in war 'great numbers sometimes serve only to bewilder and perplex'. He did not expect the Russians to overwhelm Germany. But he was certain that with Russia out of the war Germany would be able to overwhelm France. It was vital to keep Russia in the war in the East until trained British manpower appeared in the field in large numbers in the West. Grand Duke Nicholas's call for a British 'demonstration' against Turkey, which was received on 2 January 1915, was an uncomfortable intimation of Russian vulnerability.

The war went badly for Russia. A reckless incursion into East Prussia in August 1914 caused consternation in the German Court and High Command and disrupted the execution of the Schlieffen Plan,[41] but ended in humiliating defeat at Tannenberg (26–30 August) and the Masurian Lakes (9 September). No Russian soldier stood on the soil of the Reich for the rest of the war. Russian armies enjoyed greater success against the Austrians in Galicia, but the attempt to mount an attack on Silesia through Poland was crushed by the German Ninth Army at the Battle of Lodz (18–25 November). Turkey's entry into the war on the side of the Central Powers at the beginning of November opened another front on Russia's southern flank in the Caucasus and closed her Black Sea ports to trade with the outside world.

Russia's need for help was apparent. Kitchener's course of action was not. Trained British manpower was at a premium in January 1915. The Regular

37.　Howard, 'British way', p. 10.
38.　*op cit. passim.* See also, P.M. Kennedy, *The Rise and Fall of British Naval Mastery* (London, Allen Lane, 1976), pp. 177–204, 239–66.
39.　See above, pp. 59–65.
40.　See above, p. 135.
41.　See above, p. 19.

Army had already suffered severe losses.[42] The 'New Army' was very far from ready. Most units still lacked basic equipment and their training was virtually non-existent.[43] Much British frustration in 1915 stemmed from a failure to recognize that Britain lacked the capacity to make decisive military interventions.[44] Kitchener understood this. It made him cautious.

The obvious way to help the Russians was to reinforce the British Expeditionary Force in France and to press the Germans hard on the Western Front. Kitchener was reluctant to do this. There was no prospect that the British army could win the war in 1915. To expose its accumulating reserves to the wrath of the German Army too soon might prevent it from winning the war in 1917. He had also to consider the Empire. Kitchener's belief that the war could only be won on the Western Front made him a 'Westerner', but (like other 'Westerners') he was also an Imperialist. Turkey's entry into the war complicated calculations for Britain as well as Russia. British interests in Egypt and Mesopotamia were threatened by Turkish belligerency. They had to be secured. Kitchener was thus confronted with three problems: to provide effective assistance to Russia; to protect the Empire in the Middle East; and to prevent premature dissipation of British manpower on the Western Front. He found, in support for Churchill's Dardanelles scheme, a solution for all three.

Kitchener's resolution of his difficulties was intellectually neat. An attack on the Dardanelles would make limited demands on manpower. It would satisfy the Russian request for a British 'demonstration' against Turkey. It would silence the domestic political clamour for British offensive action. And it would delay the decision to deploy Britain's reserves until the New Army was ready and more favourable opportunities presented themselves on the Western Front.[45] The solution had only one drawback. It did not work.

The Dardanelles campaign itself turned into a nightmare.[46] The drain on manpower became significant. Casualties were high. There was no apparent gain. Russian fortunes continued to deteriorate. In May a massive Austro-German offensive was launched in Galicia. The Russians suffered a major defeat at the Battle of Gorlice-Tarnow and were ejected from Galicia and Poland. Half a million Russian soldiers were taken prisoner. In October an Austro-German-Bulgarian army overran Serbia. Austria was relieved of the complications of a two-front war and free to concentrate her forces against Russia. The fall of Serbia made possible direct rail communication between Berlin and Constantinople and opened up the prospect of German reinforcement of Turkey. If Russia was to be kept in the war she would require more help than a 'sideshow' could provide. Kitchener's attention was drawn back inexorably to the Western Front. There, he could find no escape from the obligations of Britain's alliance with France.

France was at the heart of Kitchener's strategy. He believed that if France was defeated Britain must also lose the war. It followed that Britain's limited military resources should be devoted to the prevention of a French defeat. In practice, this meant maintaining British forces on the Western Front, the only place where

42. See above, p. 26.
43. See below, Chapter 7.
44. K. Neilson, 'Kitchener: a reputation refurbished?' *Canadian Journal of History*, XV (1980), pp. 226–7.
45. Neilson, 'Kitchener', p. 213.
46. See above, pp. 40–8.

France could be knocked out of the war. Kitchener recognized that this imposed restrictions on Britain's freedom of action, not least on that of the BEF. This was reflected in his turbulent visit to Field-Marshal French in August 1914, when the British Commander-in-Chief was prevented from withdrawing from the French line and ordered to conform to the movements of the French army.[47] This has been described as 'one of the most pregnant episodes of the war'.[48] Its progeny were the Somme and Passchendaele.

Kitchener's strategy was essentially prudent. He wished to fight the war on principles of 'limited [British] liability'. But there was a fundamental flaw. The rôle he envisaged for the French Army was unacceptable to France. General Joffre was not content to prepare the way for the British to strike the decisive blow at some future time convenient to themselves. He wished to strike the decisive blow himself and as soon as possible. This was understandable. His country had already suffered grievous losses. The German Army occupied a fifth of the soil of France. Their line was as close to Paris as Canterbury is to London. Kitchener's favoured strategy of 'attrition' was psychologically and politically impossible for the French, and there was no means by which they could be made to adhere to it.[49] The British could not escape the consequences of this. The French Army's massive offensives in the spring and autumn of 1915 resulted in equally massive casualties for no tangible reward. The German front was not broken. The Germany Army showed no signs of irreparable moral or material damage. Its attacks on the Eastern Front did not cease. The French Army's demands for British support became ever more urgent and insistent. Kitchener's strategy depended upon the willingness of the French Army to exhaust itself in order to weaken the German Army's power of resistance. It did not allow for the French Army's exhausting itself and leaving the German Army's power of resistance intact. By the late autumn of 1915 Kitchener – and the British people – reached their Rubicon. Kitchener was not among those who wished to cross, but he did so all the same.

In 1916 the British Expeditionary Force was prepared, a year earlier than expected and long before it was ready, to strike the 'decisive blow'. David French has described this as an 'enormous gamble'.[50] The precondition for its success did not exist. The Battle of the Somme took place not because the German Army was weak and ripe for defeat, but because the French Army was threatened with extinction.[51] The gamble failed. Far from striking the 'decisive blow', the British Expeditionary Force was dragged into a 'wearing out fight' which damaged its own moral and material strength. This, it had been the aim of all British statesmen to avoid. The consequences were profound.

The Somme changed everything. Kitchener's strategy of 'limited liability' was bankrupt. Britain's unprecedented military efforts had met with no success. The future looked bleak. France and Russia were nearing the point of exhaustion. German powers of resistance were still great, though she too had suffered much. The danger that one or more of Britain's allies would seek a separate peace was very real. Such agreements could only be on German terms. These would be

47. See above, p. 22.
48. Cassar, *Kitchener*, p. 486.
49. French, *British Strategy and War Aims*, p. xi.
50. *op. cit.*, p. xiv.
51. See above, pp. 50–1.

inimical to British interests, which could not be served until 'German military power was broken'.[52] By the end of 1916 it seemed that only Britain could break it. The price of doing so was unlimited liabilities, both at home and abroad.

Recognition of this brought to a final and irredeemable conclusion the 'maritime strategy' and Asquith's attempts to find acceptable compromises between its supporters and their opponents. Advocates of 'the British way in warfare' remained prominent in Asquith's government despite the body blow dealt by the decision to raise a mass army. Chief among them were Reginald McKenna and Walter Runciman.[53] The events of 1915 and 1916 proved destructive to their hopes. The traditional aspects of British power were employed with no more effect than the sacrifice of Kitchener's armies. The Royal Navy fumbled its opportunity at Jutland.[54] The success of the blockade appeared remote. Diplomacy was a grave disappointment. Russian hostility made it impossible to secure Greek support against Turkey. Italy was attracted to the Entente but her military performance became a source of embarrassment. The Austro-Hungarian army actually seemed to enjoy fighting Italians and did so to great effect. Bulgaria was lost to the enemy camp. Romania's entry into the war was a disaster for the Allied cause. Worst of all was the profligate expenditure of British economic resources which resulted from the attempt to become a major military power. Economic strength was one of the key elements of the 'maritime strategy'. 'Our ultimate victory is assured if, in addition to our naval and military activities, we retain unimpaired our power to assist in financing, supplying and carrying for the Allies,' McKenna reminded his colleagues in December 1915, 'but the retention of that power is probably the most indispensable element of success.'[55] The power, however, was not retained. The strain even of 'limited liability' proved too much. British economic independence was surrendered to the United States.[56] America replaced Britain as banker to the Entente. American credit would pay for the tools. British soldiers would die in large numbers to finish the job.

It was in these circumstances that Lloyd George entered upon his ambivalent inheritance.

'Guerre à outrance'

In the Preface to his *War Memoirs* Lloyd George singled out those whose 'great services' had contributed to Allied victory. Among British soldiers he commended Plumer, Allenby, Maude, Monash and Cowans. Conspicuous only by their absence were the names of Sir Douglas Haig, Commander-in-Chief of Britain's largest ever army in the most important theatre of the war, and Sir William Robertson, principal architect of the strategy of which Haig's army was the instrument. This was not an oversight. Lloyd George regarded Haig and Robertson as co-authors of the 'dismal narrative of military ineptitude' which he believed distinguished British conduct of the war in 1916 and 1917. His memoirs

52. Lloyd George, *War Memoirs*, II, p. 1242.
53. French, *British Strategy and War Aims*, p. 247.
54. See above, pp. 55–58.
55. Quoted in French, *British Strategy and War Aims*, p. 247.
56. For this, see K. Burk, *Britain, America and the Sinews of War, 1914–1918* (Boston, Mass., Allen & Unwin, 1985).
57. Lloyd George, *War Memoirs*, I, p. 536, and II, pp. 2010–31.

were a systematic indictment of their professional incompetence, stupidity and inhumanity.[57] He was less than just.[58]

Sir William Robertson became Chief of the Imperial General Staff on 23 December 1915. The appointment made him professional head of the British army. This was a remarkable achievement for the son of a tailor who entered the army as a private soldier.[59] Nevertheless, he did not rush to accept Asquith's offer. The post had neither authority nor prestige. The British army did not acquire a General Staff until 1904. When the war broke out most of its officers were allowed to disperse to regimental duties. Kitchener virtually ignored its existence and treated the CIGS, Sir James Wolfe-Murray, as a clerk. Nature had not intended Robertson for a cipher. His conditions of acceptance were stringent. He was appalled by the division of responsibility for the military conduct of the war.[60] He believed that the Chief of the Imperial General Staff was the only proper repository for such responsibility.[61] He therefore made three demands: to be the 'one authoritative channel' of military advice to the Cabinet, independent of the Secretary of State for War; direct access to the army's field commanders, independent of the Army Council; and a reorganization of War Office duties designed to free him from administrative routine.[62] The result was to confer on him powers enjoyed by no other holder of the office before or since. It was convenient for Asquith to acquiesce in these demands because their effect was to subordinate Kitchener and this was the main object of the exercise. Only after Kitchener's death and the appointment of Lloyd George as Secretary of State for War was the potential for civil–military conflict in the expedient realized.

Robertson worked smoothly enough with Kitchener. They were both soldiers. They had served together before. They shared a suspicion of civilian politicians. They were united in their belief that the war could only be won on the Western Front. They recognized that coalition warfare imposed constraints on British freedom of action. They were alike in their contempt for attempts to find an 'easy' way of winning the war. There was, however, an important difference between their strategies. The significance of this did not emerge until after Kitchener's death.

The difference concerned their views of the 'wearing out fight'. In Kitchener's plan this was the task of the French and Russian armies. The rôle of the British army would be to apply the *coup de grâce*. Robertson was more pessimistic. By the time he became CIGS he believed that the French and Russian armies were already dangerously exhausted. It was in order to relieve pressure on them and to strengthen the morale of their leaders, that the British Expeditionary Force had been compelled to launch an attack at Loos in September 1915 which resulted in casualties shocking to British opinion.[63] Loos was painful evidence that the BEF could not be sheltered from full participation in the preparation of the German Army for defeat.

58. For a devastating account of the composition of Lloyd George's *War Memoirs*, see P. Fraser, 'Cabinet secrecy and war memoirs', *History*, LXX (1985), pp. 397–409.
59. For Robertson's own account of his career, see *From Private to Field Marshal* (London, Constable, 1921).
60. Sir W.R. Robertson, *Soldiers and Statesmen 1914–1918* (2 vols., London, Cassell, 1926), I, p. 160.
61. Robertson, *Soldiers and Statesmen*, I, pp. 161–2.
62. *op. cit.*, pp. 168–71.
63. See above, pp. 38, fn 21.

Robertson also disagreed with Kitchener's method for conducting the 'wearing out fight'. Kitchener favoured a strategy of 'active defence'. He realized that to adopt a policy of pure passivity by retreating behind strong defences and waiting for the German Army to break itself against them was impossible on the Eastern Front and imprudent on the Western Front. It would surrender all initiative to the enemy. Instead the Allies must seek to deny the German Army respite and to wear down its strength through repeated small-scale attacks for limited objectives at places of tactical advantage. This had much to recommend it, but as we have seen it was unacceptable to the French and was never implemented. Robertson did not believe that it would be enough. Only major Allied offensives, preferably co-ordinated, offered any prospect of bringing about a German defeat. It was his advocacy of this strategy of 'offensive attrition' and its human costs that brought him into bitter conflict with Lloyd George.

Robertson emerges from the pages of Lloyd George's *War Memoirs* as a sinister buffoon with no idea how to win the war except to render optimistic and uncritical support to his master Haig's 'stubborn infatuation' with the efficacy of repeated frontal assaults on the German line. Nothing could be further from the truth. Robertson's loyalty to Haig – who outranked him throughout the war – was total, but he remained his own man. He was a formidable personality, irascible, stubborn and shrewd.[64] His support for Haig's unflagging optimism was a public front maintained for political purposes of military solidarity.[65] Privately, he warned Haig against making grandiose claims.[66] He made none of his own. His view of the war was carefully thought out, clear, consistent and remorselessly bleak.

Robertson was not the blinkered 'Westerner' of Lloyd George's caricature. His conviction that the war could only be won on the Western Front was not the result of personal preference. He lacked Haig's proprietorial interest in the location of the battlefield. An ideological belief in the need for a 'bloodletting' as the prelude to victory was alien to his empirical cast of mind. His conversion to the strategy of 'attrition' was reluctant.[67] He admitted that the British army's weaknesses of training, doctrine and organization made it a less than perfect instrument with which to conduct the kind of war attrition involved.[68] He was less confident than Haig that all would proceed according to plan. Robertson was not a 'Westerner' because he wanted to be, but because he had to be. This arose not only from his response to the logic of events but also from his perception of the purpose of the war.

Robertson believed that the fundamental aim of British strategy was the defeat of the German Army. Without this there could be no 'victory' and no peace satisfactory to British interests.[69] Germany had to be deterred from contemplating future acts of military adventurism. Only the material destruction of the German Army – the source of that military adventurism – could achieve this. The German Army's destruction could only be accomplished on the Western Front where its main forces were deployed.[70] This would require the maximum concentration of British effort in the 'main theatre of operations'.[71] Robertson was aware that the security of the Empire necessitated the retention of some forces in the Middle East and elsewhere, but he believed they should be kept to a minimum. It was better to try and detach Turkey and Bulgaria from the Central Powers by diplomacy than to dissipate British strength in trying to defeat them.[72] This aim was essentially modest and limited. It envisaged neither the destruction nor the democratization of Germany, foreseeing the need for a strong bulwark in central Europe against the post-war spread of Bolshevism. The co-ordination of ends and means showed remarkable coherence. In comparison, Lloyd George's strategic aims were riven with ambiguities.[73]

64. For a vivid portrait, see E.L. Spears, *Prelude to Victory* (London, Jonathan Cape, 1939), pp. 33–5.
65. See Robertson's letter to Haig, 8 March 1916, quoted in J.Gooch, 'Soldiers, strategy and war aims in Britain 1914–1918', in B.D. Hunt and A. Preston, eds., *War Aims and Strategic Policy in the Great War* (London, Croom Helm, 1977), p. 23.
66. F-M Earl Haig, *The Private Papers of Douglas Haig 1914–1919* ed. R.N.W. Blake (London, Eyre & Spottiswoode, 1952), p. 239.
67. Gooch, 'Soldiers, strategy and war aims', p. 31.
68. *ibid.*
69. This was also the view of Haig and Wilson, see Terraine, *The Road to Passchendaele*, p. 290; and C.E. Callwell, *Field-Marshal Sir Henry Wilson: His Life and Diaries* (2 vols., London, Cassell, 1927), I, p. 119.
70. Robertson, *Soldiers and Statesmen*, I, p. 75.
71. See Robertson's 'Paper Submitted to the War Committee by the Chief of the Imperial General Staff, 31 March 1916', in *OH 1916, Appendices*, Appendix 4, pp. 30–1.
72. Gooch, 'Soldiers, strategy and war aims', p. 28.
73. *op. cit.*, pp. 21–38.

Lloyd George owed his rise to power not only to a successful political conspiracy but also to a change in the climate of opinion. He both represented and articulated the views of those who believed that victory would go to the side which succeeded in mobilizing its resources to their fullest extent and that further British delay in implementing the necessary measures was dangerous and irresponsible. The contribution which he made to the organization of British society for 'total war' is undeniable. His attempts to change the ends to which British resources were put, however, were doomed to frustration. Both the conflict which this provoked and its resolution were inherently probable from the outset of his prime ministership.

Lloyd George was always an 'Easterner'. His preference was to wage war against Germany's allies rather than Germany herself. This was partly because he wished to preserve Britain's freedom of action. He demonstrated an early unease at the constraints of coalition warfare. 'Are we really bound to hand over the ordering of our troops to France as if we were her vassal?' he complained to Churchill in January 1915.[74] If Britain continued to maintain the bulk of her forces on the Western Front the answer appeared to be an unpalatable 'yes'. The appeal of an 'Eastern' strategy was also reinforced by Lloyd George's war aims. These were much more ambitious than Robertson's. They embraced nothing less than the destruction of 'Prussian militarism'.[75] This could not be achieved simply by the deterrent effect of giving the German Army a 'bloody nose'. It required the dismantling of Germany's entire sphere of influence and the democratization of her society and institutions. His confidence that Britain could inflict a defeat of such magnitude reflected a residual faith in the ability of seapower to permit the deployment of British forces in places where limited effort would produce unlimited effects.

Asquith's governments' attempts to find such places met with little success. The failure of the Gallipoli campaign was a permanent embarrassment to all those who advocated an 'indirect approach' to strategy.[76] The Anglo-French landing at Salonika in October 1915 did nothing to accomplish its aim of saving Serbia from defeat. French involvement owed most to the political need to satisfy the supporters of the 'Republican' general, Sarrail, by finding him a suitable command. The Salonika contingent became the 'forgotten army' of the Great War. The campaign was vitiated by Allied bickering, indifference and indecision as well as chronic problems of supply. The army was unable to break out of its bridgehead. The real war was waged against the malarial mosquito. The Germans called Salonika 'the biggest internment camp in Europe' and treated the whole thing as a joke.[77]

The Greeks, however, were not amused. Their pro-Entente Prime Minister, Venizelos, resigned the day before the landing, which went ahead without permission. A campaign whose aim was to restore the rights of one small nation began by infringing those of another. The difference between the uninvited

74. M. Gilbert, *Winston S. Churchill Volume III, Companion Volume I* (London, Heinemann, 1971), p. 472.

75. Gooch, 'Soldiers, strategy and war aims', p. 24; for the text of Lloyd George's 'war aims' speech of 5 January 1918, see *War Memoirs*, II, pp. 1492–3.

76. See above, p. 47.

77. For the Salonika campaign, see British Official History, *Military Operations Macedonia* (2 vols., London, HMSO, 1934–5). The volumes were compiled by Captain Cyril Falls. See also, A. Palmer, *The Gardeners of Salonika* (London, Andre Deutsch, 1965).

presence of 75,000 British and French troops on Greek soil and the German violation of Belgian neutrality was a distinction too subtle for many Greeks. This was merely the prelude to growing contradictions between a 'Western' strategy sustained by proclaimed principles of international justice and national self-determination and an 'Eastern' strategy which had as its main political purpose the increase of Imperial influence and control.[78] By the end of 1917 the British government, in its anxiety to dismantle the Ottoman Empire, was simultaneously sponsoring Arab nationalism,[79] Zionism[80] and French Imperial ambitions in Syria and the Levant. The result was a vast increase in British Imperial commitments and the creation of regional enmities so bitter as to become in our own time a major threat to world peace.

Conflict between Lloyd George and Robertson was inevitable. It is difficult to know to what extent, if any, during the intrigues that brought him to power, Lloyd George appreciated the magnitude of the dilemma which would confront him as Prime Minister. As far as strategy was concerned this was no less than responsibility without power. Lloyd George was faced with military advice which he found unacceptable and a military adviser whom he could not remove. The ensuing struggle was neither edifying nor helpful to the British war effort.

Lloyd George's campaign against 'the generals' was, appropriately enough, one of feint and manoeuvre. He recognized the futility of frontal assaults. Robertson's dismissal was fraught with political difficulties, Haig's even more so. The 'Western' strategy was approved by the Unionist leadership, much of the Liberal hierarchy and most of the press. Like Haig, Robertson also had the ear of the King. Lloyd George found himself isolated and alone. Even the out-and-out Imperialists in his government deferred to the General Staff. Celtic eloquence was to no avail. Robertson was impossible to persuade. Once convinced of the 'soundness' of a position he was unmovable. Lloyd George's 'reasoned doubts' were dismissed as 'fatuous criticism', his attempts to engage in 'constructive dialogue' received only with grunts. It was like talking to the deaf. Robertson was equally impossible to ignore. His conditions of appointment ensured that. He was the government's sole military adviser and there was an Order in Council to confirm his authority. Lloyd George was left with one recourse – subordination.

His first attempt ended in failure. On 26 February 1917 the Allied political and military High Command met at Calais, ostensibly to discuss problems of rail transport on the Western Front. Lloyd George's purpose, however, was to effect the submission of the British Expeditionary Force to the control of the new French Commander-in-Chief, General Nivelle, whose agreement had already been secured. He hoped that this would reduce Robertson's influence and curb the 'excesses' of Haig's generalship. It did neither. Robertson was apoplectic when he discovered the plot. 'His face went the colour of mahogany,' Sir Edward Spears recalled, 'his eyes became perfectly round, his eyebrows slanted outwards like a forest of bayonets held at the charge.'[81] Lloyd George was forced

78. It is instructive to compare Lloyd George's 'war aims' speech (see above n. 75) with the text of the Sykes-Picot Agreement for the Partition of the Ottoman Empire by Britain, France and Russia, April-October 1916 (in J.A.S. Grenville, comp. and ed., *The Major International Treaties 1914–1973* (London, Methuen, 1974), pp. 30–2).

79. See above, p. 95.

80. The Balfour Declaration of 9 November 1917 pledged British support for the 'establishment in Palestine of a national home for the Jewish people'.

81. Spears, *Prelude to Victory*, p. 143.

to compromise. Haig was to conform to Nivelle's orders only for the duration of the French offensive.[82] This was an unmitigated defeat. Robertson and Haig were alerted to Lloyd George's intentions. They never trusted him again. Lloyd George's resort to such blatant intrigue was an admission of weakness. His climb-down was a reminder of the soldiers' strength. It took until the end of the year before Lloyd George could free himself from the 'yoke of Calais' and resume his attack.[83] This time he was more successful.

Lloyd George was appalled by the results of Haig's Flanders Campaign. The continuation of the fighting through the rain and mud of October gave even Robertson qualms. The collapse of the Italians at Caporetto, the British *débâcle* at Cambrai[84] and Allenby's triumphant entry into Jerusalem without the massive reinforcements that Robertson insisted he would need[85] put the High Command on the defensive and gave Lloyd George renewed encouragement. In November he had finally secured agreement for one of his pet schemes, the establishment of a Supreme War Council (meeting at Versailles) to co-ordinate Allied military operations and to allocate the distribution of reserves. This reflected his conviction that the Allied war effort could never be made effective without 'unity of command'. But it was also a device. This was immediately apparent to some. '[The Supreme War Council] is utter rubbish as far as fighting is concerned,' Haig's chief intelligence officer, Brigadier-General John Charteris, noted in his diary. 'It will mean delay in any attack on the Germans and will break down at once if the Germans attack us. But it also means that the Cabinet is going to oust [Haig] or Robertson or both.'[86] The target was, in fact, Robertson. There could be no prospect of getting rid of Haig while Robertson remained as his shield. The trap was sprung in February 1918.

All the Allied military representatives on the Supreme War Council were the Chiefs of Staff of their respective armies. All, that is, except Britain's. Lloyd George chose, instead of Robertson, Sir Henry Wilson, who had been acting for some time as his unofficial adviser. This arrangement did not immediately concern Robertson. He thought the War Council would be nothing more than a talking shop. He even applauded its attempts to set up an Allied General Reserve. But when he discovered that the Chief of the Imperial General Staff would have no control over this he became alarmed. He demanded to be appointed to the War Council himself. Lloyd George called his hand. On 11 February Robertson received a note from the Prime Minister informing him that he had been made British Military Representative at Versailles, but that Wilson had been appointed CIGS in his place with 'pre-Robertson' powers. Robertson refused to comply. After some confused manoeuvrings, he was given the opportunity to remain CIGS, but only on the same terms as Wilson. He again refused. On 16 February it was officially announced that his 'resignation' had been accepted. He had, in fact, been dismissed.

Lloyd George had no time to consummate this success with an attack on Haig. A little over a month later the German Army – ultimate source of the strategic

82. For the agreed text, see *OH 1917 I, Appendices*, Appendix 19, pp. 64–5.
83. D.R. Woodward, 'Britain in a continental war: the civil-military debate over the strategical direction of the great war of 1914–1918', *Albion*, XII (1980), p. 56.
84. See above, pp. 79–80.
85. See above, p. 95. Robertson had deliberately encouraged Allenby to inflate his troop requests in order to obstruct Lloyd George's plans, see Woodward, 'Britain in a continental war', pp. 54–5.
86. J. Charteris, *At GHQ* (London, Cassell, 1931), p. 267.

frustrations of Lloyd George's prime ministership – rendered further civil–military conflict irrelevant by launching its massive Spring Offensive.[87] All strategic debate ceased. The pressure of events compelled Haig to accept the 'unity of command' which he had always opposed.[88] There could now be no doubt which should be the 'main theatre of operations'. Two divisions returned from Italy to the Western Front. Even Lloyd George's favourite campaign in Palestine was denuded of its British infantry. Reinforcements also poured in from the United Kingdom, over half-a-million men between 21 March and 31 August.[89] No one would again be able to accuse Lloyd George of denying Haig men. His successful rebuttal of General Maurice's accusation that he had deliberately misled the House of Commons about the strength of Haig's army before the German attack, in the famous Maurice Debate of 9 May, demonstrated the real authority of his Coalition and ensured it a life beyond the duration of the war.[90]

87. See above, pp. 85–92.
88. See above, p. 87.
89. J. Terraine, *The Western Front 1914–1918* (London, Hutchinson, 1964), p. 111.
90. For the political significance of the Maurice Debate, see Lord Beaverbrook, *Men and Power*, p. 260. See also, J. Gooch, 'The Maurice Debate 1918', *Journal of Contemporary History*, III (1968), pp. 211–28.

7

A New Army[1]

Most British defeats have been caused by stupidity.

Correlli Barnett[2]

Looking round the faces opposite me, I felt what a fine hard-looking determined lot of men the war had brought to the front.

Field-Marshal Sir Douglas Haig[3]

Lloyd George's disquiet with the High Command's 'Western' strategy was symptomatic of his doubts about the capacity of the army as a whole to adapt to the demands of 'total war'.

Lloyd George had no affinity with soldiers. His upbringing in rural Welsh Nonconformity was not an ideal preparation for acquiring one. Neither his career as a provincial solicitor nor his pre-war ministerial experience at the Board of Trade and the Treasury did anything to remedy this. His first real contact with the military – over the munitions question[4] – was inauspicious. His struggles with the War Office created in his mind the image of a class of men who were hidebound and inflexible, floundering out of their depth in a crisis which they lacked the imagination to anticipate and the initiative to resolve. Subsequent events did little to correct this impression. Despite the unprecedented human and material resources which the war placed at the army's disposal it won nothing which could remotely be made to resemble a victory until Maude's capture of Baghdad in March 1917.[5] Looking back on the

1. The organizational and tactical evolution of the British army during the Great War has attracted little scholarly attention, but this is now happily being remedied. S. Bidwell and D. Graham, *Fire-Power. British Army Weapons and Theories of War 1904–1945* (London, Allen & Unwin, 1982) is a major contribution to understanding the British army's problems during the war, emphasizing the lack of any tradition of all-arms co-operation and any British doctrine of warfare. T. Travers, *The Killing Ground. The British Army, the Western Front and the Emergence of Modern Warfare 1900–1918* (London, Allen & Unwin, 1987) stresses the weakness of the army's hierarchical and personalized structure, which encouraged the persistence of pre-war ideas and a view of battle which attached importance to order and regularity. I.F.W. Beckett and K. Simpson, eds., *A Nation in Arms. A Social Study of the British Army in the First World War* (Manchester, Manchester University Press, 1985) also contains some important articles.
2. C. Barnett, *The Desert Generals* (London, Pan, 1983), p. 342.
3. Haig's Diary, 20 July 1917. Quoted in J. Terraine, *The Road to Passchendaele. The Flanders Offensive of 1917. A Study in Inevitability* (London, Leo Cooper in Association with Secker & Warburg, 1984), p. 197. The 'determined lot of men' were the Staffs of Sir Claud Jacob's II Corps and of the 18th, 24th, 25th and 30th Divisions.
4. See above, p. 112.
5. See above, pp. 94–5.

war, Lloyd George could find only in the career of Sir John Monash the faintest gleam of 'military genius' and he believed that had been deliberately concealed from him by an army hierarchy embarrassed by the success of a man who was a civilian when the war began.[6]

Posterity has generally been content to follow Lloyd George down the same road. Popular opinion still indicts the High Command and lays the entire blame for the human tragedy of the Western Front on the 'stupidity' of the generals. This explanation is often supported by a crude sociological determinism which asserts that all British generals were stupid because only stupid people joined the army, whose officer corps was nothing more than a dumping ground for upper-class chumps with neither the wit nor the energy to pursue careers in more intellectually demanding and competitive professions. It will not do. A true understanding of the inadequacies of British military performance must be sought elsewhere, above all in the army's peculiar institutional inheritance and its legacy of material weakness.

'An Unprofessional Coalition of Arms and Services'[7]

British pre-war military arrangements were curious and singular. Britain was alone among the European Great Powers in her reliance upon a small, long-service, volunteer army. This was made possible by the Royal Navy's maintenance of maritime supremacy. Seapower guaranteed the nation's independence and security. There was no need for a large standing army for national defence and consequently no tradition of compulsory military service. Seapower was also the means by which Britain acquired a great colonial empire.[8] From 1815 onwards parliament identified defence of these varied and scattered possessions as the main rôle of the British army. The demands of Imperial policing which this involved exercised a decisive influence on Britain's military ethos and organization.

Colonial service cut the army off from the mainstream of civilian life and emphasized its separateness. The army's real home was not England but India. The cap badge of the Leicestershire Regiment – a tiger superscribed with the legend 'HINDOOSTAN' – commemorates nineteen successive years spent there. A soldier who joined the Victorian army abandoned his citizenship. This restricted the army's appeal to the footloose and desperate. It also reinforced the national distaste for recruitment by compulsion. Short-term conscripts seemed ill-suited to the duties of colonial garrison troops, something the French also recognized with the creation of their mercenary Foreign Legion. Edwardian supporters of British National Service advocated it only for home defence, which they believed threatened by the emergence of Germany as a naval power. The Regular Army was to be left to do what it did best – policing the Empire.

Colonial campaigns of counter-insurgency provided few opportunities for large-scale operations. The army was permanently fragmented. Its basic unit was the battalion, at most 1,000 officers and men, usually far less. This, and the

---

6. D. Lloyd George, *War Memoirs* (2 vols., London, Odhams, [1938]), II, pp. 2016, 2041–2.
7. The phrase is taken from Bidwell and Graham, *Fire-Power*, p. 295. For an admirably succinct analysis of the Regular Army on the eve of war, see E.M. Spiers, 'The Regular Army in 1914', in Beckett and Simpson, eds., *Nation in Arms*, pp. 38–61.
8. See above, pp. 133–4.

obligation for long periods of isolated service abroad, made for a certain degree of intimacy. 'The old Army,' recalled Lord Moran, 'was a small family affair.'[9] It also meant that a soldier's loyalty was not to the abstract concept of the 'Army' but to the concrete reality of the 'Regiment'. This was unique to the British army both in its advantages and disadvantages.

The 'regimental system' and the experience of colonial policing produced superb battalions but a poor army. The loyalty of officers and men to the 'honour of the Regiment' often repaired the inadequacies of official provision.[10] It did much to create and foster the high morale and exemplary discipline displayed by the BEF in 1914.[11] But it did little to prepare officers for high command. Few looked beyond their battalions for professional fulfilment and recognition. Prior to the establishment of the General Staff in 1904 there was little official incentive for them to do so. Even then the Staff was regarded by regimental officers with ill-concealed disgust as a haven for the self-interested and dishonourably ambitious.[12] As a result the British army embarked upon the Great War with only 447 trained staff officers.[13] One of the most able of them, Tim Harington, admitted that he had not been prepared to 'think in "Armies"'. He had 'never even in theory' contemplated the problems of commanding a force bigger than the original BEF, but within less than two years of the outbreak of war he found himself responsible for the Staff work of an Army which 'two or three times in [his] tenure exceeded thirty divisions'.[14] Small-scale colonial operations were ideal for inculcating the standards of musketry and fieldcraft which so impressed the Germans in 1914, but they were ill-suited to the training of troops and their commanders in the kind of all-arms co-operation vital to success in Continental war. 'We live in watertight compartments,' wrote Sir Henry Rawlinson in 1892, 'the infantry know nothing about the artillery, nor the artillery anything about the infantry, the cavalry nothing about either.'[15]

Britain's was a small army for fighting little wars. Previous experience – in the Crimea and in South Africa – provided painful evidence of the cost of improvising large armies to fight big wars. But this was precisely the challenge which confronted the British High Command on the Western Front once the obligations of the Entente compelled Britain to undertake, for the first – and only – time in her history, major military operations against the main forces of a major military and industrial power.

'To Have a Giant's Strength'[16]

When the war began Britain could claim to have a million men 'under arms'. This gave a very misleading impression of her military strength. Kitchener's

9. Lord Moran, *The Anatomy of Courage* (London, Constable, 1945), p. 60.
10. This is one of the themes of M. Weaver's 'The Regimental Structure of the Victorian Army' (unpublished MA thesis, University of Birmingham, 1981).
11. J. Baynes, *Morale: A Study of Men and Courage* (London, Cassell, 1967) is an excellent study of the ethos of a pre-war Regular battalion, the 2nd Scottish Rifles.
12. Baynes, *Morale*, Chapter 11.
13. B. Bond, *British Military Policy Between the Two World Wars* (Oxford, Clarendon Press, 1980), p. 2.
14. Sir C.H. Harington, *'Tim' Harington Looks Back* (London, John Murray, 1940), p. 53.
15. Sir F.D. Maurice, *The Life of General Lord Rawlinson of Trent* (London, Cassell, 1928), p. 78.
16. The first major study of the expansion of the army, P. Simkins, *Kitchener's Army. The*

declaration 'There is no Army' came closer to capturing the reality of the situation.[17]

British forces were divided into First and Second Line units. The First Line consisted principally of the Regular Army. This had less than 250,000 fully trained and officered men at the beginning of August 1914.[18] Nearly half of these were committed to colonial garrison duties and stationed abroad. The remainder formed the core of an organized Expeditionary Force of six infantry divisions and a cavalry division,[19] but their numbers were too small to allow them to take the field without reinforcement from the limited supply of reserves. There were about 210,000 of these. One-hundred-and-fifty-thousand of them were ex-Regular soldiers who had served their seven years with the colours and returned to civilian life, from which they were subject to recall for a period of five years. A further 60,000 belonged to the Special Reserve created by Haldane out of the old Militia in 1908. Its members enlisted for six years, of which only six months were spent in full-time training, apart from an annual fortnight's refresher course under canvas.[20] Reservists provided two-thirds of the BEF's infantry strength. Their contribution to the British military effort in 1914 was crucial.

Britain's Second Line forces were even weaker. Their most important element was the part-time Territorial Army.[21] This was organized along the same lines as the Regular Army and was divided into fourteen infantry divisions commanded by Regular Major-Generals with small professional Staffs. There were also fourteen brigades of Yeomanry cavalry. Responsibility for recruitment and administration was delegated to County Territorial Associations. Haldane believed they provided a framework for an almost infinite expansion of the Force if the need arose, but in 1914 most of them were undermanned and short of equipment. This reflected the state of the Territorial Army as a whole. Its 269,000 officers and men were 36,000 below establishment. Their training left much to be desired. The statutes which governed the Army recognized this. They required a six-months' training period to be undertaken after the Force had been embodied on the declaration of war in order to bring it up to a respectable level of efficiency.[22] There was also another important drawback. It was never the intention or the expectation that the Territorial Army would serve

Raising of the New Armies 1914-16 (Manchester, Manchester University Press, 1988) appeared too late for consideration in writing this book. See also P. Simkins, 'Kitchener and the Expansion of the Army', in J. Gooch and I.F.W. Beckett, eds., *Politicians and Defence* (Manchester, Manchester University Press, 1981), pp. 87–109, and Beckett and Simpson, eds., *Nation in Arms, passim*.

17. Sir G. Arthur, *The Life of Lord Kitchener* (3 vols., London, Macmillan, 1920), III, p. 7.

18 The figures on army strength, except where otherwise stated, are taken from *Statistics of the Military Effort of the British Empire during the Great War 1914–1920* (London, HMSO, 1922).

19 See above, pp. 13–14.

20 R.J.Q. Adams and P.P. Poirier, *The Conscription Controversy in Great Britain, 1900–1918* (London, Macmillan, 1987), p. 29.

21 For the Territorial Army, see P. Dennis, *The Territorial Army 1906–1940* (London, Royal Historical Society, 1987) and I.F.W. Beckett, 'The Territorial Force', in Beckett and Simpson, eds., *Nation in Arms*, pp. 128–63. See also Patricia Morris's 'Leeds and the Amateur Tradition. The Leeds Rifles and their antecedents, *c.* 1850–1918' (unpublished PhD thesis, University of Leeds, 1983).

22. J. Terraine, *White Heat. The New Warfare, 1914–1918* (London, Guild Publishing, 1982), p. 29.

abroad. Its rôle was home defence. By 1 July 1914 only 18,683 Territorials had accepted the Imperial Service obligation. They included a mere five complete units.[23]

The remainder of the Second Line existed only on paper. This was the National Reserve, established by 'private enterprise' in August 1910.[24] It was little more than a register of some 350,000 men with military experience who had expressed a willingness to serve with either the Regular or Territorial armies in the event of war.[25]

The military resources of the Empire did nothing to remedy British weakness. The British-officered Indian Army had almost 160,000 Regulars, but they were committed to the defence of India's frontiers. Its reserves were paltry. Elsewhere, the situation was even more embarrassing and threadbare. Canada had only 3,000 Regulars, 500 more than South Africa. Australia and New Zealand had none at all.

The contrast with Britain's principal adversary could not have been greater. Germany could call on 4.3M trained men. Within two weeks of the outbreak of war 1.5M of these were deployed on the Western Front, where they outnumbered the BEF by more than ten to one.[26]

No one was more alarmed by this disparity than Lord Kitchener.[27] He immediately set about removing it. He succeeded with dramatic effect. On 7 August 1914 he called for 100,000 volunteers between the ages of nineteen and thirty to reinforce the Regular Army. He got them within three weeks. On 28 August he called for another 100,000 and raised the upper age limit to thirty-five. Before the war was two months old 761,824 men had volunteered. They doubled the combined pre-war strength of the Regular Army, Reserve, Special Reserve and Territorial Force. The million mark was exceeded well before Christmas.

The Empire also began to rally to the flag. Thirty thousand troops arrived in England from Canada in October, the vanguard of 630,000 Canadians, 412,000 Australians, 136,000 South Africans and 130,000 New Zealanders who fought in the British army during the war.[28]

This rapid expansion of Britain's military forces was a remarkable achievement. Churchill described it as one of 'the wonders of the time'.[29] By the end of 1914 the British army had attained a giant's size for the first time in its history. The problem of acquiring a giant's strength remained. Numbers alone were not enough. Kitchener's volunteers would have to be formed into military units, housed, fed, clothed, armed, equipped, disciplined and taught the technical skills necessary for them to survive in the unforgiving environment of modern war.[30] They would, in short, have to be turned into soldiers. This proved to be an even more formidable undertaking.

23. Beckett, 'Territorial Force', pp. 130, 135.
24. British Official History (henceforth *OH*), *Military Operations France and Belgium 1914, Volume 1* (London, Macmillan, 1925), p. 11.
25. *OH 1914, I,*, p. 12.
26. *op. cit.*, p. 21.
27. See above, pp. 140–42.
28. Terraine, *White Heat*, p. 136.
29. W.S. Churchill, *The World Crisis 1911–1914* (London, Thornton Butterworth, 1923), p. 236.
30. B. Williams, *Raising and Training the New Armies* (London, Constable, 1918), p. 44.

Making a New Army[31]

Obstacles to the creation of a New Army capable of taking on and defeating the German Army in the field were numerous and severe. The astounding response to Kitchener's call-to-arms overwhelmed the existing facilities for processing, equipping and training recruits. This is hardly surprising. They were never designed for the task with which they were now charged. The Cabinet's fateful acquiescence in Kitchener's decision to raise a mass army opened a new and unprecedented chapter in British history. Neither the army nor the country was prepared. There was no reason why they should have been.

Responsibility for recruitment to the Regular Army rested with the War Office Recruiting Department. This employed barely 500 people, mostly retired army officers and soldiers. Their job was to produce a steady supply of recruits amounting to no more than 37,000 a year. This quota was fixed and permanent. It was often difficult to fill. There was no incentive to exceed it. Unusually heavy flows of recruits were staunched simply by raising the army's physical demands. The conduct of recruiting officers was strictly controlled and enterprise was not encouraged. This became painfully obvious as soon as the war-time rush to the colours began. By the middle of September the strain of attesting 30,000 men a day proved too much. The Recruiting Service collapsed amid a welter of muddle, confusion and recrimination. The situation was saved by an impressive display of local civilian initiative, co-ordinated by an all-party Parliamentary Recruiting Committee in which advocates of conscription, such as Leo Amery, played an important part.[32]

Local civilian initiative, however, could do little to repair the inadequacies of material provision inherited from the pre-war army. When the war began barrack accommodation existed for only 175,000 troops.[33] More than 800,000 of Kitchener's volunteers received their introduction to army life in billets, hired buildings or makeshift tented encampments wholly unsuitable for the establishment of military discipline and the conduct of serious training. They were denied even the appearance of soldiers. The pre-war army was accustomed to ordering a quarter of a million pairs of boots, 220,000 shirts and less than a million pairs of socks a year.[34] This modest scale of supply left no reserves of spare uniforms capable of equipping the new recruits. The expedient of issuing temporary uniforms made from Post Office blue serge was not popular with the men. Wearers were greeted with cries of 'How long have you got, Bill?' and 'Where is your number?' owing to its resemblance to convict clothing.[35] The situation with regard to weapons was even worse. The army's total stock of

31. The raising and training of the New Army has received little attention. The contemporary semi-official account by the historian Basil Williams, himself a Kitchener volunteer (see above, n. 30), has not been superseded. See also, I. Hay, *The First Hundred Thousand* (London, Blackwood, 1915) and *Carrying on After the First Hundred Thousand* (London, Blackwood, 1917); R. Kipling, *The New Army in Training* (London, Harrap, 1916); and, E. Wallace, *Kitchener's Army and the Territorial Forces* (London, George Newnes, 1915), which contains many interesting photographs.
32. See J.M. Osborne, *The Voluntary Recruiting Movement in Britain 1914–1916* (New York, Garland, 1982); see also, R. Douglaş, 'Voluntary enlistment in the First World War and the work of the PRC', *Journal of Modern History*, XLII (1970), pp. 564–85.
33. Williams, *New Armies*, p. 44.
34. D. Chapman-Huston and O. Rutter, *General Sir John Cowans* (2 vols., London, Hutchinson, 1924), II, p. 20.
35. G. Paget, *History of the Raising of the 7th (Service) Battalion Northamptonshire Regiment (48th and 58th Foot) and its Records from the Formation until it Proceeded on Active Service,*

rifles amounted to less than 800,000. Half of these were obsolete. Output was less than 2,000 a week.[36] Hand grenades were virtually non-existent. The army in the field was receiving only forty a week by November 1914.[37] The standard 18-pdr field gun was in very short supply. Some New Army units had none at all.[38] Production of high explosive was negligible.[39] Shortages of specialist signals and engineering equipment were acute.

Months were to elapse before significant improvements could be effected. Plans for building hutted camps to provide accommodation and training facilities for a million men were laid as early as 14 August 1914, but it was a year before three-quarters of them were ready.[40] Infantry battalions of 'K1' ('the first hundred thousand') had only 400 rifles each – less than half their requirement – by January 1915. 'K2' battalions had only 100.[41] The artillery were still worse off. By March 1915 some divisions had only two guns per battery, making realistic training almost impossible.[42] Artillery resources did not become adequate to the conduct of major battles until the middle of 1916. Even then ammunition supplies had to be carefully monitored. Unlimited quantities of good quality high-explosive shell did not become available until 1917;[43] and it was not until 1918 that the provision of guns was wholly satisfactory, finally freeing artillery operations from material constraints.[44]

Most units were equipped slowly and in dribs and drabs. The experience of the 7th Northants – a 'K3' battalion – was typical. The battalion reached establishment on 14 September 1914. It received no equipment of any kind until 6 October, when the first issue of blue serge arrived. The first suit of khaki was not issued until 5 January 1915 and the second not until 19 March. Leather equipment did not become available until the end of April. Pack mules arrived on 21 April, their harness on 2 July. Three-hundred-and-thirty-three drill purpose rifles were issued on 14 October 1914, followed by another sixty-six nine days later. The battalion had no weapons capable of being fired until January 1915, when it received an issue of 500 obsolete 'long' Lee Enfields. The standard Short Magazine Lee Enfield service rifle was not issued until 8 – 10 July, and the 1907 'Sword' bayonet not until a fortnight later.[45] Despite this the battalion was posted abroad on 31 August and arrived at Boulogne on 2 September. Twenty-four days later it was thrown into the battle of Loos and suffered heavy casualties.[46]

14th September 1914–31st August 1915 (Aldershot, Gale & Polden, 1915), p. 15. I owe my awareness of this interesting little book to Dr R.W. Bushaway and am indebted to him for the loan of his copy.

36. Williams, *New Armies*, pp. 55–6.
37. *OH 1914*, II, p. 7.
38. Williams, *New Armies*, pp. 55–6.
39. 'GSO', *GHQ (Montreuil-sur-Mer)* (London, Philip Allan, 1920), p.67. 'GSO' was Sir Frank Fox (1874–1960), journalist and author; military correspondent of the *Morning Post* in Belgium, 1914; subsequently an officer in the Royal Field Artillery and a member of the Quartermaster-General's Staff at Montreuil.
40. Williams, *New Armies*, p. 44.
41. *op. cit.*, p. 54.
42. *op. cit.*, pp. 55–6.
43. See above, p. 72.
44. G.A.B. Dewar and Lt Col. J.H. Boraston, *Sir Douglas Haig's Command* (2 vols., London, Constable, 1922), I, p.59.
45. Paget, *7th Northants*, p. 25.
46. See above, p. 39.

Shortages of equipment were not the only problem. The conversion of the New Army's volunteers from civilians into soldiers was also inhibited by a lack of trained instructors. 'Kitchener's men' were desperately keen and anxious to learn, but there was no one to teach them. The Regular Army's cadre of training instructors, including those on Territorial attachment, were allowed to disperse to their regiments on the outbreak of war. The exigencies of the army in the field made it impossible to get them back. Their experience was difficult to replace. Every effort was made to scrape together a nucleus of professional officers and to send at least one to each New Army unit. Former Regulars were 'dug out' of retirement. Sandhurst and Woolwich were emptied of their cadets. Officers of the Indian Army home on leave were seconded to New Army duties. It was not enough.

The bulk of the New Army's officers were young men without military experience.[47] They found themselves in their positions of authority by reason of education, social class, family connexion, sporting prowess or popularity. 'For all practical purposes,' wrote Basil Williams, 'most of the infantry subalterns of the new armies had to train themselves during the first five months of the war as best they could in the intervals of training their men.'[48] The consequences of this were both predictable and tragic.

The fate of the 7th Northants merely anticipated that of many other New Army battalions whose training was too little and too late. The condition of the British Expeditionary Force on the eve of its greatest battle fully justified Sir Douglas Haig's fears.[49] Fewer than a quarter of his troops had received any pre-war military training.[50] Marksmanship was abysmal by Regular Army standards.[51] Six of the eleven Fourth Army infantry divisions which attacked the German position on the Somme on 1 July 1916 had no previous experience of battle.[52] The level of training afforded to three of them, the 30th, 32nd, and 34th, bordered on the scandalous.[53] Their twenty-eight front-line New Army battalions belonged to 'K4', 'the fourth hundred thousand', units raised right at the end of 1914. They had been last in the queue for everything. Their allocation of Regular Army officers and NCOs was meagre. Their full complement of arms and equipment did not arrive until late in the autumn of 1915. Their exposure to the kind of careful, progressive training which had honed the skills of the original BEF was virtually nil by the time they were posted abroad. Their war was a cruel one. Fifteen of them failed to survive it as fighting units and were either disbanded or reduced to training cadres.[54] This is a compelling indictment of the inadequacies of their preparation.

47. For the officer corps during the war, see K. Simpson, 'The Officers', in Beckett and Simpson, eds., *Nation in Arms*, pp. 64–97.
48. Williams, *New Armies*, p. 69.
49. See above, p. 51.
50. J. Keegan, *The Face of Battle* (London, Cape, 1976), p. 225.
51. A. Farrar-Hockley, *The Somme* (London, Batsford, 1964), p. 69.
52. Keegan, *Face of Battle*, p. 225.
53. *op. cit.*, p. 222.
54. In the 30th Division, these included the 7th, 18th and 19th Manchesters and the 19th and 20th King's (Liverpool); in the 32nd Division, the 11th Border, the 16th Northumberland Fusiliers and the 17th Highland Light Infantry; in the 34th Division, the 15th and 16th Royal Scots and the 20th, 21st, 24th, 26th and 27th Northumberland Fusiliers. See Brigadier E.A. James, *British Regiments 1914–1918* (London, Samson Books, 1978), pp. 96–7, 52, 77, 46, 103, 43, 47.

These inadequacies were not the fault of the military High Command. They were not the fault of anyone. They were inherent in the unparallelled effort of improvisation undertaken by the British government and people after 7 August 1914. Fate dealt the generals a weak hand. The army which nurtured them provided neither relevant practical experience nor theoretical doctrine to guide their actions. Its legacy of numerical and material weakness was beyond the generals' capacity to remedy and beyond anyone's capacity to remedy quickly. The war in which they found themselves ushered in complex new military technologies which added immeasurably to the problems of tactical understanding and control. The army which they faced was a formidable one, millions strong, superbly equipped, well entrenched in positions of immense natural advantage skilfully reinforced with all the ingenuity of German military engineering, manned by the best trained army in the world recruited from a society with a long history of compulsory military service, commanded by a large professional officer corps and sustained by the world's greatest strategic railway system designed and operated by soldiers. France, the principal ally alongside whom they fought, was too weak to defeat Germany without massive British support but too strong both militarily and politically to allow strategic initiative and independence to British commanders for most of the war.

The nature of their problem was not lost on the generals themselves. 'The greatest of all errors was that of not providing before the war an Army adequate to enforce the policy adopted,' wrote Sir William Robertson in 1917. 'To our absurdly weak pre-war Army can be attributed practically all the difficulties which now face us.'[55] There is much truth in this argument. It became the foundation upon which the Official Historian, Sir James Edmonds, erected his defence of the 'Western' generals. 'External' factors, beyond the control of the High Command, undoubtedly exercised a malign influence on their conduct of the war and helped to swell the casualty figures. But it is not the whole truth. Much necessarily remained within the generals' judgement and discretion. This included 'technical' military matters, such as tactics and systems of command and control, which were of major importance in deciding the question of victory or defeat. The war was profligate with difficulties for the High Command, but it also provided them with a British army of unprecedented size, with soldiers of unusual intelligence, and from 1917 onwards with an almost inexhaustible supply of material resources. It is on their ability to find a proper application of this eventually overwhelming force that they should be judged.

The High Command and the Western Front: Theory[56]

It is currently unfashionable to believe in the existence of 'principles of war'.[57] It

---

55. Quoted in Terraine, *Road to Passchendaele*, pp. 170–1.
56. One of the most useful short summaries of British tactical development is S. Bidwell, *Gunners at War. A Tactical Study of the Royal Artillery* (London, Arms & Armour Press, 1970), pp.31–46. The following articles were also illuminating: D. Graham, 'Sans doctrine: British army tactics in the First World War', in T.H.E. Travers and C. Archer, eds., *Men at War* (Chicago, Precedent, 1982), pp. 69–92; T.H.E. Travers, 'Technology, tactics and morale: Jean de Bloch, the Boer War and British military theory, 1900–1914', *Journal of Modern History*, LI (1979), pp. 264–87, and 'The offensive and the problem of innovation in British military thought', *Journal of Contemporary History*, XIII (1978), pp. 531–53.
57. See Shelford Bidwell's editorial, 'Whizz-kids, academic strategists and the principles of war', in the *Journal of the Royal United Services Institute for Defence Studies* (June, 1973).

is even more unfashionable to believe that such principles can be deduced from military history. This was not the case before the First World War. Napoleon, greatest of all military maxim-makers, exercised a beguiling influence on military thought. The nineteenth century was an age of military theory. Clausewitz, Jomini and the elder Moltke, together with those who popularized and vulgarized their ideas, encouraged the belief that success in war depended upon adherence to certain fundamental principles, deducible from experience, which could only be ignored at the risk of defeat. Even the pragmatic and empirical British were not immune from this development. Sir John French, the least intellectual of soldiers, admitted that his wise decision not to retreat to the 'security' of the fortress of Maubeuge in August 1914 owed much to his reading of Sir Edward Hamley's *The Operations of War*.[58] This book was published in 1866. By 1914 it had gone through six editions and numerous impressions. The 1907 edition was edited by Colonel L.E. Kiggell, later Haig's Chief of Staff. Kiggell's interests reflected those of Haig himself.

John Terraine described Haig as 'the army's most educated soldier'.[59] The description is fully justified. Haig regarded his profession with seriousness and dedication. He immersed himself in its study. To this task he brought a clear and logical mind and a personality of rare determination and force. Intelligence takes many forms. Haig was a simplifier. He saw things clearly and had the strength of character to maintain his beliefs in adversity. These beliefs were fully developed before the war began. He clung on to them throughout the conflict. His confidence in them sustained him through every crisis. Victory convinced him of their validity. They were enunciated with remarkable lucidity in his Final Despatch.[60]

Haig's study of military history led him to conclusions which influenced his entire conduct of the war as Commander-in-Chief. The first, and most important, of these was that the main army of the main enemy was the principal objective of military operations. The second was that military operations necessarily fell into four stages: the manoeuvre for position; the first clash of battle; the wearing-out fight; and the eventual decisive blow. The third was that the 'wearing-out fight' was the crucial stage, in which the successful erosion of the enemy's material and moral reserves could alone prepare the path to victory. The fourth was that between opposing forces approximately equal in numbers, courage, morale and equipment the 'wearing-out fight' would be long, arduous and bloody. And the last, that victory would go to the army which preserved its discipline, its morale and, above all, its capacity for offensive action during the battle of attrition.

Haig's application of these principles to the strategy of the war was remorseless and coherent. Germany was the main enemy. The main German army was deployed in France and Belgium. The war could only be won and lost on the Western Front: to pretend otherwise was to indulge in escapist fantasy. The German Army on the Western Front could only be defeated after the erosion of its material and moral reserves. The occupation of French and Belgian territory rendered the German Army's position so strong, both militarily and politically, that its material and moral reserves could only be eroded by

58. F-M Viscount French, *1914* (London, Constable, 1919), p. 71.
59. J. Terraine, *Douglas Haig. The Educated Soldier* (London, Hutchinson, 1963), p. xviii.
60. J.H. Boraston, ed., *Sir Douglas Haig's Despatches* (London, Dent, 1919), pp. 319–57.

10 The Chief: Haig
(*Mansell Collection*)

constant offensive pressure. After the summer of 1916 the maintenance of this constant offensive pressure became increasingly beyond the power of the French Army. The British army would have to win the war.

Haig's strategy has withstood the test ot time. Few now seriously dispute the logic (or, at least, the logic of events) which compelled the British army to fight on the Western Front and, from mid-1916 onwards, to assume an ever greater part in the fighting. The hoary old debate between 'Easterners' and 'Westerners' rumbles on, but there can be little doubt that the 'Westerners' have won the argument. This has done nothing to redeem Haig's battered reputation. The fundamental issue at the heart of the condemnation of his generalship is not his overall perception of the war but his conduct of it, not his strategy but his tactics. Here, his study of military history proved to be an unreliable guide.

The battlefields of the Western Front were the product of a century of technological progress. Breech-loading rifles, machine-guns, quick-firing rifled cannon and railways transformed the practice of war. Their main effect was massively to augment the strength of the defence. Breech-loading rifles and machine-guns allowed troops to fire rapidly while lying down, under cover or entrenched. This meant that attacking infantry would have to cross a murderous fire-swept zone unprotected before they could bring to the point of assault defenders who were difficult to see and even more difficult to hit. It also meant that far fewer men could hold a much longer defensive line than was previously possible, leaving others to be held in reserve for counter-attack. Quick-firing rifled cannon extended the width and depth of the fire-swept zone.

Attacking infantry were compelled to deploy into attack formation at a greater distance from their objective and to extend that formation over a greater width than ever before. The extension of the battlefield forced the artillery to fire 'indirect' at targets which the gunners could not see for themselves. This exacerbated the problems of command and control and reduced the artillery's accuracy and effectiveness, especially in attack. Railways permitted the rapid movement and deployment of reserves and made it difficult for the attacker to exploit a breakthrough, even supposing he could effect one.

The significance of these changes was not lost on thinking soldiers. The revolution in firepower was well understood. It caused an immediate problem for military theorists. The advantages which it gave to the defence challenged one of the cardinal principles of contemporary theory, the superiority of the offensive. Analysis of the Russo-Japanese War, however, appeared to resolve the dilemma.

The outcome of the Russo-Japanese War offered a 'human' solution to the problems of the technological battlefield which was compatible with an offensive strategy.[61] The war demonstrated beyond question the destructive effects of defensive fire-power. Soldiers who studied it became convinced that huge casualties would be the necessary and inevitable consequence of large-scale conflict between advanced industrial states. But this conviction did not lead them to find urgent ways of improving the attacker's chances of survival while crossing the fire-swept zone or to reject the 'spirit of the offensive' as the key to victory, indeed quite the reverse. The reason was simple. The attacking side – Japan – won. And its success owed nothing to superior technology or tactics. It owed everything to superior morale. Future wars would be decided by troops whose discipline and training allowed them to prevail despite heavy losses and by commanders with the moral courage to press home the attack regardless of cost. This was a tragic misjudgement. French soldiers died by the hundred thousand across the rolling fields of Lorraine and the heights of Champagne to give the lie to its conceit.

The war on the Western Front represented the triumph of fire-power over mobility. The problem which this posed was a simple one: how to maintain an advance through entrenched positions of ever-increasing depth, defended by dense belts of barbed wire, intersecting arcs of machine-guns and abundant artillery. The solution was far from simple. Millions died in the attempt to find it. And even when it was found the human costs were not cheap.

Faith in the 'human' solution died hard. It was killed by failure. Brave soldiers, well led, always found it possible to break into the German trench system. Breaking through it was another matter. Once attacking troops penetrated the first line of German trenches they became trapped in a killing ground out of range of the observed fire of their own artillery. The Germans were adept at placing an artillery barrage just in front of their first line trench after it had been captured.[62] This made reinforcement of attacking troops from the rear extremely hazardous and reduced the wire-bound communications

---

61. Travers, 'The offensive and the problem of innovation', p. 537.
62. C. Messenger, *Trench Fighting, 1914–1918* (London, Pan Books, 1972), p. 56. The technique was known as *sperrfeuer* and was one part of a defensive artillery technique which also included bombardment of the enemy's forming up positions (*zerstörungsfeuer*) and sharp fire on the enemy's front line at the moment of attack (*vernichtungsfeuer*).

system to a shambles. Denied covering fire, reinforcements, orders and supplies, attacking troops lost all forward momentum and became dangerously vulnerable to counter-attack. French troops of high morale were thrown against the German trench system in this way by a commander of iron resolve throughout 1915. They achieved virtually nothing. The German line was inched backwards but no positions of strategic importance were captured. Casualties were enormous. The 'offensive spirit' was not enough.

The High Command and the Western Front: Practice[63]

The ability of attacking troops to break into the German front line gave the first clue to a possible solution. Their success was explained by the achievement of effective co-ordination between attacking infantry and attacking artillery. Once the infantry broke into the German position co-ordination disintegrated with fatal consequences. The problem was how to maintain infantry–artillery co-operation beyond the 'break-in' in order to achieve a 'break-through'. This presented particular difficulties to the British.

The British army had no tradition of 'scientific' gunnery. In the Royal Field Artillery and the Royal Horse Artillery everything was subordinated to speed and to the need to maintain close support for the infantry. This left little time for calculation and often no call for it. 'Scientific' gunnery was confined to the despised Royal Garrison Artillery, created only in 1891, whose primary responsibility was the mundane one of manning the big guns of the coastal defences. The future lay with them, nevertheless. The techniques which they developed in order to hit moving targets at long range provided an invaluable source of experience and expertise from which the rest of the artillery was able to benefit. The conversion of the Royal Regiment of Artillery as a whole to the principles of 'slide-rule' gunnery was one of the fundamental British military achievements of the war, without which no victory was possible.

Much nonsense has been written about Sir Douglas Haig's 'cavalry obsession'. By September 1916 there were only five cavalry divisions on the Western Front. Two of these were Indian. This represented a mere 2.5 per cent of the BEF's total strength.[64] The contrast with the fortunes of the Royal Artillery could not be more marked. In August 1914 the Regiment had 4,083 officers and 88,837 men. By November 1918 this had risen to 29,990 officers and 518,790 men, more than twice the size of the entire British Army at the outbreak of war.[65] By the end of 1915 Haig understood, as did many others, that it was a gunners' war. He became a convinced and enthusiastic artillerist. For most of 1916 and 1917 he attempted to turn his proliferating artillery resources into a war-winning weapon. He failed.

There were three reasons for this. The first was that artillery was a very imperfect weapon, and remained so despite impressive improvements in the provision of guns and ammunition made by 1918. The second was the failure to

63. Bidwell and Graham, *Fire-Power*, is essential to any understanding of British tactical development on the Western Front. I find their general thesis more persuasive than that of Travers, *Killing Ground*.

64. J. Terraine, *The Smoke and the Fire. Myths and Anti-Myths of War 1861–1945* (London, Sidgwick & Jackson, 1980), p. 162.

65. General Sir M. Farndale, *History of the Royal Regiment of Artillery. Western Front, 1914–1918* (Woolwich, The Royal Artillery Institution, 1986), p. 342.

recognize this imperfection or to consider its tactical and strategical consequences. The third was the neglect of the tactical possibilities of other arms,
especially the infantry, occasioned by the exaggerated faith in the power of
artillery.

Artillery depends for its effect upon speed of fire, accuracy, lethality, range
and mobility. It must be able to shoot quickly, hit and destroy targets deep in an
enemy position, and move rapidly either to support an advance or to evade the
counter-fire of hostile guns. First World War artillery was deficient in all but one
of these important characteristics.[66]

The speed of fire of field guns was one of the war's fundamental tactical realities, responsible more than any other single factor – including machine-
guns – for the costly ineffectiveness of infantry assaults. The French led the way
with their famous '75', the first truly modern gun, introduced in 1897, and
capable of firing twenty rounds a minute. The Germans followed with their '77'
and the British with their 18-pounder. In other respects, however, artillery
remained extremely primitive.

Inaccuracy was a major weakness. This was partly a fault of the guns themselves, but it owed most to the absence of a reliable system of signals communications through which the fire of the guns could be controlled.

Despite their appearance of mass-produced similarity and rugged power,
guns were idiosyncratic and sensitive machines whose performance could be
easily impaired by wear and tear and the vagaries of wind speed and direction,
temperature and humidity. In order to overcome this it became necessary to
'calibrate' the individual peculiarities of each weapon, to keep a permanent
record of its operating history and to adjust for climatic conditions on the basis
of information regularly supplied by telegram from the Meterological Service to
every battery.

Solving the problem of 'fire-control' was more difficult. The destructive effect
of modern fire-power at short range prevented the British field and horse artillery from providing its traditional close support for the infantry. The need for
such a change was accepted in principle before the war began, but it took the
actual experience of combat to compel its adoption in practice. The battle of Le
Cateau on 26 August 1914 marked the moment of realization and opened a new
era in the history of the Royal Artillery.[67] The artillery could not support the
infantry unless its own survival was assured. And the artillery could not survive
unless it retreated beyond the reach of German rifles and machine-guns and
sought sanctuary from German shells by taking maximum advantage of
available cover. This meant that the gunners would not be able to see their
targets. Their fire would be 'indirect'. Finding a reliable method of locating
enemy targets and observing the effect of fire on them became the army's most
urgent task. There was no shortage of expedients.

Target location witnessed many improvements. In the early part of the war
much depended on the skill, courage and good fortune of Forward Observation
Officers (FOOs). Theirs was hazardous work. It took them close to the German
lines or on to vantage points such as hills, trees and high buildings whose very

---

66. I should like to thank Major D. Thomas, RA, for helpful instruction on the strengths and
weaknesses of modern artillery.
67. Bidwell, *Gunners at War*, pp. 13–30.

utility rendered them immediately suspect in German eyes.[68] Locating German guns was particularly difficult. They were carefully sited and camouflaged to avoid detection and only really betrayed their positions through the muzzle 'flash' which accompanied actual firing. But when they were firing their target was often the FOO himself. The German Army had a vested interest in wishing to effect his speedy demise. It was an occupation which held out no prospect of longevity.

Ground observation was soon supplemented by aerial spotting. The advantages of this were readily apparent. Observers could see much further from the air. They could also photograph what they saw. Photographs became the major source of artillery 'intelligence'.[69] Detailed and accurate maps of the German position were constructed from them. These later made possible the sophisticated and effective technique of mathematically calculated or 'predicted' fire.[70] The war in the air came to revolve round this vital activity.[71] Defence of reconnaissance aircraft was the essential task of the more glamorous 'fighter' squadrons and their famous 'aces'.[72] By 1916 neither side could contemplate launching an offensive unless it had first managed to obtain local air superiority. The great British advance in the second half of 1918 owed much to the Royal Air Force's having finally achieved air superiority over the whole of the Western Front.

Mathematical calculation was also central to the important innovation known as 'sound ranging', the brain-child of one of Britain's leading scientists, the Nobel Prize winning physicist, Lawrence Bragg. This involved placing a series of microphones in carefully surveyed positions across the sound track of hostile gun fire. An electronic device measured the time intervals as the sound passed over each microphone. From this information it was possible not only to locate individual enemy guns but also to establish their type.[73]

Improvements in 'fire-control' were less impressive. They were inhibited by the inadequacies of a communications system based on the electric telegraph.[74] The accuracy of British artillery depended on the ability of Forward Observation Officers to observe the fall of shot and recommend corrections. To do this, they had to be able to communicate with their guns. They were linked to these by miles of telegraph wire. This was hopelessly vulnerable to German shell fire and contact was frequently lost, often for long periods. During this time the guns were reduced to firing 'blind'. The Signal Service of the Royal Engineers went to prodigious lengths to prevent such an occurrence.[75] During preparations

---

68. I should like to thank Bombardier George Burcombe (late Royal Field Artillery) for sharing with me his recollection of forward artillery observation.
69. See Farndale, *Royal Artillery*, pp. 368-9, for the development of artillery intelligence.
70. See above, pp. 79, 98.
71. One of the best accounts of the war in the air as it affected the land battle is S.F. Wise, *Canadian Airmen and the First World War: Official History of the Royal Canadian Airforce. Volume 1* (Toronto, University of Toronto Press, 1980), especially pp. 334-579.
72. D. Winter, *The First of the Few. Fighter Pilots of the First World War* (London, Allen Lane, 1982) is a brilliant account of the pilots and their machines.
73. Sir L. Bragg, 'Sound Ranging in France 1914-1918', in Farndale, *Royal Artillery*, pp. 374-79.
74. R.E. Priestley, *The Signal Service in the European War of 1914 to 1918* (Chatham, Royal Engineers, 1921) is tedious but indispensable for an understanding of the difficulties of communications and the expedients taken to try and remedy them. M. Van Creveld, *Command in War* (Cambridge, Mass., Harvard University Press, 1985) has an important chapter on the British command system on the Somme.

for the Somme battles in 1916 they laid 50,000 miles of cable, 7,000 miles of which was buried to depths of up to ten feet.[76] The result was a system of labyrinthine complexity and extreme rigidity.[77] But even this was something. Beyond the British front line there was nothing. There, the wire petered out. Attacking troops left their communications behind them and entered a void. Infantry–artillery co-ordination became dependent upon the infantry's ability to conform to a predetermined programme of artillery support which proceeded according to a fixed timetable. This was usually impossible. The 'umbrella' of covering artillery fire raced ahead of the infantry it was designed to protect and left them vulnerable and helpless.[78]

Artillery was not only inaccurate but also inefficient. Captain Sidney Rogerson commented with some satisfaction on the 'enormous number of projectiles necessary to destroy one human life'.[79] This owed much to the type of ammunition used. The greater part of the British artillery consisted of shrapnel-firing field guns. Shrapnel was a devastating anti-personnel weapon, but largely ineffective against barbed wire, earthworks and concrete dug-outs. It was also temperamental. A report of 1918 claimed that 50 per cent burst uselessly in the air and recommended total conversion to high explosive.[80] For much of the war this was little better. Until the introduction of the '106' fuse in the spring of 1917 its main effect was to disfigure the landscape with craters. These soon filled with mud after rain, making the forward movement of troops difficult and the forward movement of guns impossible.

The theoretical range of a field gun was about 7,000 yards. Its effective range was often far less because of the limitations imposed by the need for observed fire. This allowed the Germans to respond to the increasing weight of British bombardments simply by deepening their position and keeping the bulk of their infantry beyond the reach of British guns. From this position of safety they could counter-attack any British troops rash enough to stray into the killing ground beyond the protection of their own artillery or regroup further back to await another more cautious set-piece attack.[81]

The artillery's lack of mobility hampered its movement forward to support an infantry advance. The principal motive power of the Great War was the horse. There were 510,098 serving with the British army by the end of 1918, including 305,664 in the BEF alone.[82] Every battery of field guns had at least fifty.[83] The ravished landscapes of the Western Front did not provide easy going for them and they were extremely vulnerable to gun fire of all kinds. The movement of heavy siege guns was even more fraught with difficulty. They took days to dig in to special pits and light railways had to be constructed to bring up their ammunition. The vast quantities of stores and ammunition which the artillery consumed required the establishment of huge dumps. The scale of activity which this

75. Priestley, *Signal Service*, Chapter IX.
76. *op. cit.*, p. 121.
77. Van Creveld, *Command in War*, p. 158.
78. See above, p. 39.
79. S. Rogerson, *Twelve Days* (London, Arthur Barker, 1933), p. 61.
80. Bidwell, *Gunners at War*, p. 35.
81. I.D. Houghton, 'The Evolution of British Army Tactics on the Western Front 1914–1918' (Unpublished BA thesis, University of Birmingham, 1982), p. 26.
82. I owe this information to Mr G.R. Winton, who is researching the subject.
83. I should like to thank Driver Henry Harrison (late Royal Field Artillery) for discussing with me his experiences in the horse lines of an 18-pdr battery between 1915 and 1918.

involved was difficult to conceal and unconducive to the achievement of secrecy and surprise. There was also the problem of psychological immobility. Trench warfare often proceeded with industrial regularity. Gun crews fired according to strict plans which neither permitted nor encouraged initiative. They became incapable of taking advantage of tactical opportunities even when they presented themselves.[84]

For most of 1916 and 1917, during the great 'wearing-out fight', the British High Command based its conduct of the war on the simple proposition that 'artillery conquers, infantry occupies'. The actual power of artillery provided no justification for this belief. The experience of battle refuted it. The weakness of artillery was inherent. It could not be compensated by the mere accumulation of greater and greater numbers of guns which characterized the Somme and 'Passchendaele' campaigns. 'Even these [unprecedented] quantities of steel did not destroy all life, 'wrote Ludendorff, 'the infantry always found far too much to do.'[85] It only needed a handful of German machine-gunners to survive to bring an entire British offensive to a halt. The failure to recognize the probability of this beforehand stemmed from an essentially 'human-centred' view of war which emphasized the importance of morale and the idea of the 'breakthrough'. This was an act of faith. It had no foundation in a careful analysis of the tactical possibilities of artillery as a 'weapons-system'. The result was tactics which were not devised to fit the weapons and a strategy which was not developed to fit the tactics.

The conversion of the High Command to a 'weapons-centred' view of war was cautious and empirical. Evidence of it may be found in the gradual acceptance of the 'limited objective'.[86] This had many advantages over the strategic grandiosity of the 'breakthrough'. It recognized the limitations of artillery and the difficulties of communications. But it had disadvantages too. Progress was painfully slow and costly. It was a long way to Berlin at a thousand yards a time. It also led to a dangerous obsession with holding ground at all costs and for its own sake. 'Capture a pig sty at the bottom of a hill, overlooked on three sides by the enemy, the sump for the local drainage, and hold it we must and did,' recalled Lord Chandos. 'Any local commander who wished to withdraw 500 yards to the ridge behind him would have been in danger of being relieved of his command. Even to suggest it provoked questions about his competence and courage.'[87] Nothing was more likely than this to erode soldiers' morale, confidence in the wisdom of 'orders' and capacity for offensive action, preservation of which the Commander-in-Chief himself deemed essential to ultimate success.

The infantry 'always found far too much to do' not only because of the weakness of artillery but also because over-confidence in it led to their own tactical development becoming the subject of official neglect. As a result, when the artillery failed to 'conquer' a position the infantry lacked the battlecraft, leadership, initiative and indigenous fire-power to 'occupy' it at acceptable cost and became dependent upon ever greater levels of artillery 'preparation'. The

84. See above, p. 63.
85. E. Ludendorff, *My War Memories 1914–1918* (2 vols., London, Hutchinson, n.d.), II, p. 577.
86. See above, pp. 38, 62, 99.
87. Oliver Lyttelton, Viscount Chandos, *From Peace to War. A Study in Contrast 1857–1918* (London, Bodley Head, 1968), p. 133. I owe this reference to Dr R.W. Bushaway.

British victories of 1918 were due in no small part to the rediscovery of infantry as 'queen of the battlefield' and to a renewed interest in its methods of attack and fire support.

Haig escaped from the tactical vicious circle only in 1918. His handling of the BEF during the Great Advance showed that he had learned the principal tactical lesson of the war. This taught the need for direct, close fire support for the infantry. The artillery firing 'indirect' could not guarantee to do enough damage to enemy machine-guns or gun emplacements to permit effective infantry assaults. The vain attempt to obliterate German fire-power was abandoned. The British army began instead to cultivate its own. By 1918 Lewis guns, hand grenades, rifle grenades and mortars at last became available in sufficient quantities. They added enormously to the fire-power directly available to attacking infantry. Musketry skills were again encouraged. Mobile artillery was provided by tanks, whose most effective use was finally understood, though there were never enough of them. Swarms of aircraft carried hostile fire deep into the enemy position, shooting up communications centres, command posts, supply lines, and bringing German reserves once more within the range of British guns. The sense of powerlessness which this induced in German troops was a crucial element in their eventual demoralization and defeat.[88] The emergence of the platoon, rather than the company, as the focus of tactical planning and control acknowledged the realities of what Lord Wavell called a 'platoon commanders' war' and made possible greater flexibility and enterprise in infantry tactics.[89]

The use of artillery did not diminish. Guns continued to arrive at the front in ever increasing numbers. Production figures for 1918 showed a 64 per cent rise on those for 1917. Forty-two per cent of all guns and howitzers manufactured in Britain during the war were completed in its last year. By November 1918 the BEF had 6,437 guns of all types, including 2,562 howitzers.[90] The expenditure of ammunition was prodigious. Almost 258,000 tons were issued from depots in France to the front line batteries each month. During the key months of August and September more than 8,800 tons were used daily. The 18-pounder field guns fired 100,000 rounds in an average day and twice as many when the fighting was heavy.[91]

The end to which this colossal fire-power was directed, however, was no longer the annihilation of the enemy but the suppression and dislocation of his fire. Gas shells, essentially a harassing rather than a killing weapon, were particularly effective for this purpose. Once it was achieved, the infantry and tanks could close with the defenders, using the pre-war tactics of 'fire and manoeuvre', and destroy them and their defences at short range. The continuance of offensives long past their usefulness ceased. The holding of ground simply because it has been captured lost its mystical significance. The

88. Ludendorff, *War Memories*, II, pp. 599–601. See also, B. Greenhous, 'Evolution of a close ground support role for aircraft in the First World War', *Military Affairs*, XXXIX (1975), pp. 22–8.
89. This, like many of the other 'innovations' of 1918, actually originated in 1917. See *The Organization of an Infantry Battalion and the Normal Formation for the Attack* (London, War Office, 1917).
90. Farndale, *Royal Artillery*, p. 342.
91. 'GSO', *GHQ*, p. 75.

lives of trained British troops were recognized as an irreplaceable asset. Fire-power fought fire-power. The German Army broke under the strain.[92]

'The Name of the Game'

Why did it take so long to arrive at this successful tactical formula? Why was the learning process so expensive in human life? There are no simple answers. Haig would not even agree with the questions.

Part of the explanation may lie in the BEF's command structure. This was based on 'line management'. The 'managing director' (the Commander-in-Chief), after discussion with his board (GHQ), decided the main lines of 'company policy' (strategy), detailed implementation of which (tactics) was left to 'senior line managers' (army commanders), and then transmitted along a chain of command through 'junior line managers' (corps, division and brigade commanders) to the 'factory manager' (battalion commander) and his 'shop floor workers' (front line infantry). It was, in the jargon of systems analysis, a 'rigid people-centred' structure, fundamentally hierarchical and dependent for its success upon the initiative and driving power of those at the top. This was unfortunate.

Haig was a poor 'driver'. He was notoriously reluctant to interfere in the arrangements of his 'senior line managers' even when he believed they threatened 'company policy'. On at least two occasions his failure to insist on the implementation of his own better judgement had tragic results.[93] He saw himself and his Staff as 'master planners'. He preferred to issue generalized instructions.[94] These were intended to reduce the inevitable chaos of war to a set of certainties which made interference in the actual conduct of battle unnecessary. Problems arose when things did not go according to 'plan'. Haig's unwillingness to 'drive' meant that he abdicated control. Battles developed according to their own momentum. GHQ, the 'brain' of the army, ceased to direct the progress of events.

This tendency was exacerbated by failures in the army's 'nervous system'. When German shelling interrupted communications paralysis set in. The inability of British troops to act independently and effectively without orders was commonly observed during the war.[95] It was to be expected. 'Line management' discouraged initiative. It provided no means by which the views of 'junior line managers' could be consulted or their experience and that of 'factory managers' and 'shop floor workers' analysed and fed back into the system. The BEF's command structure depended solely on initiative from above, which could not be relied upon, and on the maintenance of a chain of command, which was bound to be broken under battlefield conditions. It thus added to the inherent difficulties of trench warfare.

The German system was completely different, especially after the Somme. Even before the war the Germans had gone a long way towards breaking up the

---

92. See above, pp. 97–101.
93. See above, pp. 64, 74.
94. Travers, *Killing Ground*, pp. 101–27.
95. See, for example, British Official History, *Military Operations France and Belgium 1917 Volume 1* (London, Macmillan, 1932), p. 554, and Sir E.L. Spears, *Prelude to Victory* (London, Cape, 1939), p. 428.

chain system of command and giving more initiative to subordinate commanders. This owed much to Moltke's awareness of the problems of command and control experienced during the Franco-Prussian war. In 1916 Lossberg's discovery that it took, on average, eight to ten hours for messages to reach the front line from divisional HQ when a battle was in progress led him to take things a stage further. Primary responsibility for the conduct of battle was delegated to divisional commanders. They were given total control of all available forces in their sector, including field and heavy artillery.[96] The outcome of the fighting rested on the decisions which they took in the light of information supplied by their front battalion commanders. The power of the battalion commanders was also greatly increased. 'They were given as full a control over their sector of the battle area as has a captain over his ship,' wrote Captain G.C. Wynne, 'and their decisions were to be accepted *by superiors and subordinates alike*, as final and unquestioned while the battle lasted.'[97]

The German system was 'work-oriented'. It was designed to function from the bottom up rather than the top down. It was much superior to 'line management'. It recognized the difficulties of maintaining a chain of command and sought to avoid them. It kept key decision makers in contact with battlefield realities, allowed them to learn from experience and to pass the experience on to others. It was useless without initiative, the inculcation of which became a cardinal element in German training. The simplicity of the system and its encouragement of troops to fight intelligently within a generally understood overall doctrine does much to explain the German Army's incredible resilience during two world wars. The reality of the independent, initiative-taking German soldier is the complete opposite of the traditional British stereotyping of him as a disciplined military automaton who does only what he is told and never complains.

Some have seen in the British Expeditionary Force's command structure a reflection of the values of the Regular Army and yet another example of its failure to respond to the challenge of war.[98] This may be doubted. There was nothing distinctively 'military' about the system under which it operated. 'Line management' was commonplace among British civilian institutions and deeply rooted in cultural values which emphasized class distinction, hierarchy and deference. The failure to encourage initiative was peculiar neither to the army nor to the Great War. It is the British vice.

The Great Advance did witness some simplification of the command structure. This was most apparent in artillery organization, where the principle that artillery must be handled at the highest level at which control is possible – however low the level – found eventual acceptance.[99] This, in practice, was the division, rather than the corps, as on the Somme.[100] Elsewhere, British victories owed little to changes in the command structure. On the contrary, they were achieved within a framework of *increasing* tactical rigidity.

96. G.C. Wynne, *If Germany Attacks. The Battle in Depth in the West* (London, Faber, 1940), p. 126.
97. *op. cit.*, p. 125.
98. D. Winter, *Death's Men. Soldiers of the Great War* (London, Allen Lane, 1978), especially pp. 37–50, is a brilliant and savage attack on the Regular Army's lack of imagination; Travers, *Killing Ground*, is a more subtle analysis of the Regular Army's institutional weaknesses, see above n 1.
99. Bidwell, *Gunners at War*, p. 44.
100. See above, p. 63.

This was truest in Sir John Monash's ANZAC Corps, whose success depended not on the free-wheeling independence and initiative of its insubordinate 'diggers', but on their explicit adherence to orders which allowed nothing to the judgement of front line troops.[101]

Haig himself offered no explanation for the duration and cost of the BEF's 'learning process'. None was necessary. He did not attribute victory to the 'improved' tactics which issued from the 'learning process' in 1918, but to the cumulative effect on the German Army of the battles of attrition in 1916 and 1917. There was no reason to think that an earlier introduction of the 'improved' tactics – even if the availability of material resources permitted it – would have resulted in a quicker or cheaper victory. Fighting the German Army was never easy. Crude as the British tactics were in 1916 and 1917 they would have broken troops less skilful, courageous and well-led than those of Germany. No army that has fought the main forces of the German Army in this century has avoided mass casualties except at the price of rapid and humiliating defeat. The human costs of battle remained severe until the very end. During the last 96 days of the war the British Expeditionary Force lost 350,000 men, including a third of all officers and men of the Tank Corps. This represented a daily loss of 3,645 men, greater than for either the Somme or 'Passchendaele'.[102] 'Whatever you do,' wrote the French general, Mangin, 'you lose a lot of men.'[103]

The Chief[104]

The size of these losses has made Douglas Haig the most controversial and hated soldier in British history. Responsibility for them has fallen mainly on him. This has disguised the scale of his achievements.

Haig began the war as a corps commander in an expeditionary force of six divisions. He ended it as the Commander-in-Chief of an army of fifty-nine divisions. His supervision of this transformation was an administrative triumph.[105] The transport, supply and medical disasters which litter British military history, including that of the Great War, were absent from the Western Front.[106] The army's tactical evolution was more difficult, but within less than three years he succeeded in incorporating the new technologies of chemical, aerial and armoured warfare into an effective operational 'doctrine' without precedent in pre-war military experience and material provision. The constraints of coalition warfare demanded from him diplomatic skills of a high

101. Terraine, *Road to Passchendaele*, p. 224.
102. Terraine, *Smoke and the Fire*, p. 46.
103. *op. cit.*, p. 45.
104. Haig has, to a certain extent, defied all his biographers. He is not an easy man to understand and almost impossible to like. A. Duff Cooper's *Haig* (2 vols., London, Faber, 1935) remains the best full life; J. Charteris, *Field Marshal Earl Haig* (London, Cassell, 1929) is mainly interesting for what it leaves out than for what it puts in; Terraine's *Douglas Haig* is a formidable defence of Haig's generalship which no one has seriously sought to challenge until, perhaps, Travers's *Killing Ground*. G. de Groot's *Douglas Haig 1861–1928* (Larkfield, Maidstone, Unwin Hyman, 1988) appeared too late for consideration in writing this book.
105. See, for example, C.E. Carrington, *Soldier From the Wars Returning* (London, Hutchinson, 1965), p. 105, and Rogerson, *Twelve Days*, pp. 116, 140–1.
106. The medical history of the war on the Western Front is particularly interesting. Sally-Ann Vardy's 'The Army Medical Service on the Western Front during World War One' (Unpublished BA thesis, University of Birmingham, 1981) is a concise introduction.

order. The mischief-making conspiracies of his own Prime Minister tested his political judgement to the full. His personality was rooted in a deep religious faith.[107] He bore a crushing burden with equanimity and calm. He remained supremely confident in his own abilities. His subordinates' faith in him never wavered. He was not the stupid, unimaginative butcher of Lloyd George's caricature.

Generalship is the most arduous and exacting of all human activities. It is a zero-sum game: win or lose. There is no in-between. What is not a victory is a defeat. And military defeat in this century has been followed not only by national humiliation but also by occupation, oppression and genocide. Douglas Haig fulfilled the most important criterion of generalship. He won. The scale of his victories was the greatest in British military history. His countrymen have never forgiven him.

---

107. For this important aspect of Haig's character, see G.S. Duncan, *Douglas Haig as I Knew Him* (London, George Allen & Unwin, 1966). Duncan, a Scots Presbyterian Minister, was Haig's Chaplain at GHQ.

PART III

'We are Making a New World':
A Social History of the Great War

8

Men and Munitions[1]

Lend your strong right arm to your country. Enlist now.

Recruiting Poster, 1914[2]

Your King and Country need men to manufacture the munitions of war . . . You can help Lord Kitchener by filling a vacancy at the Clyno Engineering Co. Highest wages paid.

Newspaper Advertisement, 1915[3]

British society as a whole was even less prepared for war than the army. This owed much to the limited nature of pre-war military demands. The six infantry divisions and one cavalry division of the original BEF comprised 120,000 men, 40,000 animals, 334 lorries, 133 cars, 166 motor cycles, 300 guns and 63 aircraft. Provision for an army of this size caused scarcely a ripple on the surface of British economic and social life.

The changes effected by the war were extraordinary. By November 1918 the BEF had 2,360,400 men, 404,000 animals, 31,770 lorries, 7,694 cars, 3,532 ambulances, 14,464 motor cycles, 6,437 guns and 1,782 aircraft.[4] This made it the second largest administrative unit in the British Empire after the London County Council.

British armies numbered by the hundred thousand were also to be found in Mesopotamia, Egypt and Salonika.[5]

The BEF's logistical arrangements were prodigious. The Medical Service supervised 95,000 hospital beds.[6] The Transport Directorate controlled more than 4,000 miles of road, a standard-gauge railway operating 900 locomotives,

1. Arthur Marwick's *The Deluge. British Society and the First World War* (London, Bodley Head, 1965; Harmondsworth, Penguin, 1967) remains the starting point for the social history of the war. Support for Marwick's views has recently been provided by J.M. Winter, *The Great War and the British People* (London, Macmillan, 1986), which, although not the book of its title, contains much new and valuable material.
2. The poster is illustrated in C. Haste, *Keep the Home Fires Burning. Propaganda in the First World War* (London, Allen Lane, 1977), p. 51.
3. *Wolverhampton Express & Star*, 24 March 1915. I owe this reference to Mr Neil Werrett.
4. The above figures are based on: D. Chapman-Hutson and O. Rutter, *General Sir John Cowans: The Quartermaster-General of the Great War* (2 vols., London, Hutchinson, 1924), II, pp. 342, 343; and General Sir M. Farndale, *History of the Royal Regiment of Artillery. Western Front 1914-1918* (Woolwich, The Royal Artillery Institution, 1986), p. 342.
5. Chapman-Hutson and Rutter, *Cowans*, II, p. 342.
6. Major-General Sir W.G. MacPherson, ed., *History of the Great War Based on Official Documents. Medical Services. General History* (4 vols., London, HMSO, 1921), II, diagram facing p. 68.

a light railway carrying 175,000 tons a week,[7] a network of inland waterways, a fleet of coastal barges and a cross-Channel ferry.[8] The Signal Service of the Royal Engineers despatched 40,000 telegrams and connected 80,000 telephone calls a day.[9] In preparation for the attack on Vimy Ridge in April 1917 First Army alone required 3,600 tons of supplies and 2,960 tons of ammunition a day and 190,000 gallons of petrol a month. Its Forward Depots stored 828,000 full days rations for men, 100,000 full days rations for horses and 200,000 iron rations.[10] A single square mile of trench system contained 900 miles of barbed wire, 6M sandbags, 1M cubic feet of timber and 360,000 square feet of corrugated iron.[11]

Casualties were equally enormous. More than 670,000 British soldiers were killed or died during the war, almost 13 per cent of those who served.[12] A memorial plaque on the 'Dog and Partridge' public house in the Staffordshire township of Cobridge records those killed in the war who came from just two small streets nearby. It contains thirty-six names.[13] The male generation aged 25–45 was decimated. One-hundred-and-sixty-thousand wives lost their husbands. Over 300,000 children lost their fathers. Millions were wounded and often permanently maimed or disfigured.[14] By 1921 the government was distributing 3.5M war pensions.

No section of British society was immune from the repercussions of war conducted on such a scale.[15]

Challenge

The rapid growth of the army's demands confronted British society and its institutions with a serious challenge.

British strategy did not anticipate a long war. The social and economic implications of fighting one had not been considered.[16] 'Man-power planning' formed no part of pre-war defence arrangements. The government had neither the power nor the desire to compel men to undertake military service. Its ability to control the labour force was even more problematical. Ministerial intervention in labour matters (particularly labour disputes) was well

7. For this, see K. Taylorson, *Narrow Gauge at War* (Croydon, Plateway Press, 1987).
8. 'GSO' [Sir Frank Fox], *GHQ* (London, Philip Allan, 1920), p. 40.
9. This is based on an interpolation of the figures in M. Van Creveld, *Command in War* (Cambridge, Mass., Harvard University Press, 1985), p. 158.
10. British Official History, *Military Operations France and Belgium 1917. Volume 1 Appendices* (London, Macmillan, 1932), pp. 157–8.
11. D. Winter, *The First of the Few. Fighter Pilots of the First World War* (London, Allen Lane, 1982), p. 15.
12. Winter, *Great War and the British People*, p. 73.
13. The pub is now closed. After many years of dereliction it became a Scout Hut. The memorial is well cared for.
14. D. Winter, *Death's Men. Soldiers of the Great War* (London, Allen Lane, 1978), pp. 251–4, gives poignant examples. See also Wilfred Owen's poem 'Casualties'.
15. See A. Clark, *Echoes of the Great War. The Diary of the Reverend Andrew Clark 1914–1919* ed. J. Munson (Oxford, Oxford University Press, 1985) for the impact of the war at village level (Great Leighs in Essex).
16. See D. French, *British Economic and Strategic Planning 1905–1915* (London, Allen & Unwin, 1982), pp. 74–84 for the limits of pre-war planning. For wartime developments, see C. Wrigley, 'The First World War and state intervention in industrial relations, 1914–1918', in *A History of British Industrial Relations*, vol. 2 (Hassocks, Harvester, 1987).

established, but a systematic administrative machinery was lacking.[17] Attempts to create one were likely to meet with opposition from a trade-union movement increasing in size and self-confidence. Trade-union ideology was deeply attached to the principle of free collective bargaining, sensitive to the prerogatives of skilled workers and hostile to the introduction of new technology.[18]

Much of British industry, especially in the engineering sector, was small-scale and family owned, manufacturing limited runs of specialized products for markets where there was little competition. The industrial élite was conservative. The 'cult of the amateur' still prevailed over American notions of 'scientific management'. Scientific and technical education was neglected and despised.[19] Weaknesses were apparent in areas vital to the production of weapons and military equipment. Iron and steel technology lagged behind that of other major producers. Coal mining remained in the era of the pick and shovel and was riven with class bitterness and labour unrest. The chemical industry was greatly inferior to that of Germany, on which it had become dependent for some of the chief materials used in the manufacture of explosives.[20]

Agriculture was in the grip of a long-term depression. Home production was sufficient to feed the country for only 125 days a year.[21]

Manufactured goods, raw materials and food would have to be imported from abroad in huge quantities. This would be inherently expensive. The threat of enemy action against shipping would make it more expensive still.

Even the temper of the people was uncertain. Much has been made in recent years of the 'psychological preparation' of the British people for war by the creation of a 'climate of militarism' through the activities of organizations such as the Boy Scouts, the Boys' Brigade and the Lads' Drill Association.[22] This may be doubted. The British working class was the least militarized in Europe. Its attitude to the army was almost wholly negative even when not openly hostile. The growth of quasi-military youth movements during the Edwardian period reflected rather than resolved right-wing concern about the 'unsuitability' of the urban working class for war.

17. S.J. Hurwitz, *State Intervention in Great Britain. A Study of Economic Control and Social Response, 1914-1919* (New York, Columbia University Press, 1949), p. 83.
18. The best study of trade union ideology is R. Currie, *Industrial Politics* (London, Oxford University Press, 1979).
19. A.L. Levine, *Industrial Retardation in Britain 1880-1914* (London, Weidenfeld & Nicolson, 1967), *passim*.
20. D.S.L. Cardwell, *The Organisation of Science in England* (Revised edn., London, Heinemann, 1972), p. 221. I should like to thank Dr D.M.G. Wishart for drawing this book to my attention.
21. Sir E.L. Woodward, *Great Britain and the War of 1914-1918* (London, Methuen, 1967), p. 498.
22. See J.O. Springhall, *Youth, Empire and Society* (London, Croom Helm, 1977). See also Springhall's articles 'The Boy Scouts, class and militarism in relation to British youth movements, 1908-1930', *International Review of Social History*, XVI (1971), pp. 125-58, and 'Lord Meath, youth and empire', *Journal of Contemporary History*, V (1970), pp. 97-111. See also P. Wilkinson, 'English youth movements, 1908-1930', *Journal of Contemporary History*, IV (1969), pp. 3-24; A. Summers, 'Militarism in Britain before the Great War', *History Workshop*, II (1976), pp. 104-23; and M.D. Blanch, 'Imperialism, nationalism and organised youth', in J. Clarke *et al.*, eds., *Working Class Culture* (London, Hutchinson, 1979), pp. 103-20.

Response

The fundamental challenge was that of ensuring an adequate supply of men for the armed forces and for the civilian and military economies. The response was cautious and fraught with difficulties. The adoption of 'manpower planning', and of the controls needed to make it work, was piecemeal and pragmatic. It was extended step-by-step by the compelling force of circumstances. The influence of Lord Kitchener was again immense.

The first demand on the nation's manpower was for more soldiers. The need was immediately recognized.[23] Subsequent events on the battlefield confirmed it.[24] This had important consequences. The priority accorded to the military demand for men made it difficult to establish the legitimacy of other claims. Kitchener's insistence on a policy of voluntary recruitment made it more difficult still. This influenced the whole British conduct of the war and the ways in which it was perceived, then and since.[25]

Kitchener's method of raising the 'new armies' lies at the heart of his reputation as a wrecker. There are two charges against him. The first concerns his 'failure' to utilize the machinery of the Territorial Army in expanding Britain's military forces. He has been accused of missing the opportunity to achieve an orderly expansion by this 'total divergence' from the 'established military structures of the War Office'.[26]

The charge is rather strange. There were no 'established military structures' capable of effecting a rapid and orderly expansion of the army. Kitchener was navigating through uncharted territory. He set course by the few familiar landmarks that remained. The most important of these was the Regular Army. Far from 'bypassing' its structures, he was careful to preserve them.

The basic unit of the New Army was the 'Service' battalion which volunteers joined for three years or the duration of the war. These battalions were attached to existing Regular Army regiments. When possible, they received an allocation of Regular Army officers and NCOs.[27] No new regiments were created. The way in which the system worked is apparent from the example of the North Staffordshire Regiment. When the war began the regiment had six battalions. The 1st and 2nd were part of the Regular Army. The 3rd and 4th were part of the Regular Army Reserve and existed as little more than training cadres. The 5th and 6th were part of the Territorial Force. By the end of October 1914 the regiment acquired another five battalions. These were numbered consecutively and became the 7th, 8th, 9th, 10th and 11th (Service) Battalions, the Prince of Wales's Own (North Staffordshire) Regiment.[28] This arrangement ensured that the New Army was grafted on to the old. It was logical and consistent with previous practice.

Kitchener's reliance upon the Regular Army's organization was not only the instinctive response of a lifelong professional soldier but also the result of

23. Asquith asked the House of Commons to sanction an increase of 500, 000 men for the army on 6 August 1914.
24. See above, p. 26.
25. This theme is pursued in Chapter 10, below.
26. R.J.Q. Adams and P.P. Poirier, *The Conscription Controversy in Great Britain, 1900–1918* (London, Macmillan, 1987), p. 57.
27. See above, p. 160.
28. E.A. James, *British Regiments 1914–1918* (London, Samson Books, 1978), p. 98.

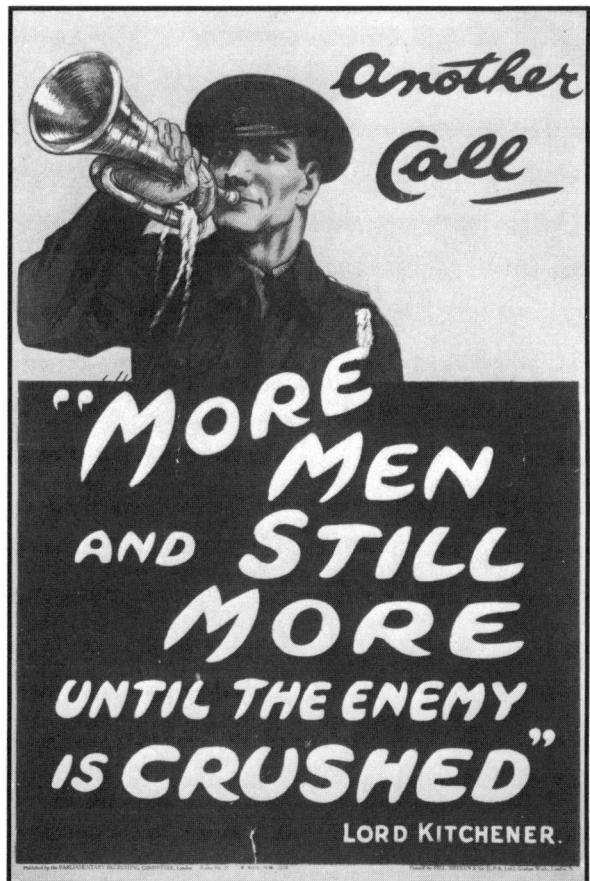

prudent calculation. The Territorial Force was intended solely for home defence. The departure of the British Expeditionary Force to France left the country denuded of Regular troops. If Germany succeeded in landing an army on the east coast of England – which many feared – the Territorials would be needed to repulse it. They could not do this and undertake a massive programme of recruitment and training at the same time. Equally, the Territorial Army's expansion would serve no purpose if it could not be used abroad. It seemed more sensible to leave the Territorial Army alone and make a fresh start uninhibited by these complications.[29]

This was not, however, the end of the story. Far from withering in the frost of Kitchener's supposed irrational hostility, the Territorial Army prospered. On 10 August 1914 units were invited to volunteer for overseas service. After 31 August, where 60 per cent of a unit had volunteered, permission was granted to establish 'second line' battalions of 'home service' men. Once Kitchener got his 'first hundred thousand' New Army volunteers, the Territorial Army was

29. G.H. Cassar, *Kitchener: Architect of Victory* (London, William Kimber, 1977), p. 201.

allowed to continue recruiting either for overseas service or (until March 1915) for home service. In areas such as the Black Country where the TA had a strong popular appeal, its administration and personnel played a key role in the voluntary recruiting movement.[30] More than 700,000 of the 2.5M volunteers who enlisted before the introduction of conscription joined the Territorials. Territorial divisions began to take up colonial garrison duties from September 1914 onwards, releasing Regular troops for service elsewhere. A few handpicked units – led by the London Scottish – joined the BEF in France before the end of the year. The Territorial Force was in the field in strength by the Spring of 1915. Three-hundred-and-eighteen Territorial battalions served abroad by the end of the war, compared with 404 from the New Army. This' represents a major contribution to the British war effort.[31]

The second charge against Kitchener is more serious. It concerns conscription. British experience between 1914 and 1918 proved conclusively that it was impossible to fight a major modern war without compulsory military service. In retrospect, the delay in introducing it appeared to be a fundamental mistake, leading to muddle and confusion and prolonging the war. Churchill held Kitchener primarily responsible. He believed that if Kitchener had thrown his immense authority and prestige behind the conscription cause as soon as the war began the Liberal government would have been compelled to adopt it.

Kitchener was not even tempted to try. He preferred a voluntary system. He did not trust conscripts, at least not those from liberal democracies, the Franco-Prussian War having left him with a deep suspicion of their fighting prowess.[32] And he did not think conscription was necessary. Kitchener did not enter office armed with a coherent manpower plan. Only later did he formulate the concept of an army of seventy divisions. His initial call-to-arms was essentially modest. Even he realized that conscription was likely to be politically controversial and divisive. Why risk this for the sake of a mere 100,000 men whom he was certain he could obtain without recourse to compulsion? The astounding response to Kitchener's call made the resort to conscription seem even less necessary, at least in the short term.

Churchill's belief that Kitchener ought to have insisted on conscription in August 1914 is as unfair as his contention that the Liberal government would have acquiesced in it is unfounded. Recent research does not support him.[33] The real criticism of Kitchener is not that he failed to bring about conscription in 1914 but that he continued to oppose it as late as 1916. His 'conversion' was as slow and reluctant as that of any major political figure. The maintenance of the voluntary system became inseparable from his own reputation. Even so, it is difficult to imagine that conscription could have been introduced with such little public dissent unless voluntary methods had been tried first. Without Kitchener's intervention in August 1914 it is doubtful whether they would have been tried so soon or on such a scale. It was, above all, the size of the armies which Kitchener raised by voluntary means, and the consequent disturbance which this caused to the social and economic norms of British life, that

30. I owe this information to Mr Neil Werrett, who is researching the subject.
31. I.F.W. Beckett, 'The Territorial Force', in I.F.W. Beckett and K. Simpson, eds., *A Nation in Arms* (Manchester, Manchester University Press, 1985), p. 132.
32. See above, p. 141.
33. French, *British Economic and Strategic Planning*, p. 128.

eventually demonstrated not only the inevitability but also the justice of conscription.

Voluntary enlistment was a great numerical success. During the period of its operation, from August 1914 to January 1916, the voluntary system brought into the army, on average, twice the number of men per month as that attained by conscription during the remainder of the war.[34] The social and economic costs, however, were high. The voluntary recruiting movement, which grew up after the initial rush to the colours overwhelmed the Regular Army's capacity for processing recruits,[35] gradually found itself having to resort to greater and greater degrees of organized persuasion in order to maintain the flow of men. This included the encouragement of locally raised units – the famous 'Pals' and 'City' battalions – the holding of monster rallies and, finally, 'economically influenced individual pressure'.[36] The last offended deep British notions of fair play and caused enormous resentment. 'If the government want more men,' William Milton, an Essex farm foreman, told the Reverend Andrew Clark, 'let them take idlers, not workmen.'[37]

The government began to agree. By the end of 1914 it was apparent that too many 'workmen' had been taken already and that the indiscriminate nature of voluntary enlistment was hampering the war effort. On 23 December the Cabinet Committee on munitions met for the first time in two months. It discovered that the supply of labour had become 'a matter of acute difficulty'.[38] Sixteen per cent of all employees in small-arms factories and 23 per cent of those in chemical and explosive works had been allowed to join the army.[39] The armaments industry was short of 6,000 workers.[40] The demand for munitions was increasing at an unprecedented rate at the same time that the number of men available to produce them was declining. Something had to be done.

Lloyd George pointed the way ahead. The enlistment of skilled men into the army would have to be checked. More efficient use of the skilled men who remained would have to be sought. Tasks currently performed by skilled men would have to be opened up to the semi-skilled and unskilled. Women would have to be employed in industry in large numbers.[41]

Most of this 'programme' was anathema to the trade-union movement, without whose co-operation nothing could be achieved. The war confronted the unions with both difficulty and opportunity.[42] 'Dilution' of the 'restrictive

34. *Statistics of the Military Effort of the British Empire during the Great War* (London, HMSO, 1922), p. 364: 2,466, 719 men were enlisted voluntarily between August 1914 and January 1916; 2,504,183 by conscription between January 1916 and November 1918.

35. See above, p. 158.

36. J.M. Osborne, *The Voluntary Recruiting Movement in Britain 1914–1916* (New York, Garland, 1982), p. 128.

37. Clark, *Echoes of the Great War*, p. 58.

38. D. Lloyd George, *War Memoirs* (2 vols., London, Odhams, [1938]), I, p. 172.

39. Woodward, *Great Britain and the War of 1914–1918*, p. 464. For recruitment and the labour force in general, see P.E. Dewey, 'Military recruiting and the British labour force during the first world war', *Historical Journal*, XXVII (1984), pp. 199–223.

40. Lloyd George, *War Memoirs*, I, p. 172.

41. *op. cit.*, p. 173.

42. There is no study dealing specifically with the Trade Unions and the Great War, but see R. Currie, *Industrial Politics* (London, Oxford University Press, 1979); J. Hinton, *The First Shop Stewards Movement* (London, Allen & Unwin, 1973); R.I. McKibbin, *The Evolution of the Labour Party, 1910–1924* (Oxford, Oxford University Press, 1974); and J.M. Winter,

practices' on which the dominance of skilled workers was based threatened the whole foundation of the unions' hard-won industrial power. Women also posed a danger. Traditional male trade-union opposition to the employment of women rested on the belief that they were prepared to work for a pittance and would become a source of cheap labour through which unscrupulous employers could drive down wages. The obvious solution to this – that women should receive equal pay to men for equal work – did not commend itself. It offended notions of masculine superiority and challenged the male rôle of 'breadwinner'. It had no serious support.[43] The wholesale introduction of women into industry might have the effect of accomplishing either or even both of these unappealing prospects.

On the other hand, the very appearance of these proposals on the political agenda was indicative of a major change in the 'economy' of industrial relations. The reduction of the workforce through military enlistment made 'labour' an appreciating asset. Neither the employers nor the government could avoid the consequences of this. For the employers it meant competing for labour in a seller's market. The price of success would have to be paid in higher wages and better working conditions. For the government it meant seeking the co-operation of the trade-union leadership. The price of this would be to admit the trade-unions to a share in political decision making at the highest level. It was a price which Lloyd George, for one, was willing to pay.

Ever since the foundation of the TUC in 1868 the elected representatives of organized labour had sought respectability and recognition. The obstacles across their path had been very great. But now their chance had come. The future beckoned. The past echoed with old fears and animosities and whispered 'caution'.

Trade-union worries in December 1914 were premature. Attempts to expand and dilute the labour force following the meeting of the Cabinet Committee on munitions amounted to very little. The fullest possible use was made of the skills of Belgian refugees.[44] This presented few political difficulties. Elsewhere, progress was slight. In January 1915 arrangements were made to permit the release of skilled munitions workers from the army. The results were disappointing. Kitchener was reluctant to countenance the rejection of any willing recruit. Rationalization of recruitment foundered on his opposition. A system of providing badges to workers, indicating that they were involved in production vital to the war effort and designed to protect them from the increasingly strident moral pressure of the voluntary recruiting movement, was not introduced until March. The Board of Trade's efforts to attract skilled workers to the limited number of armaments manufacturers with whom the War Office was prepared to place contracts met with little success. Skilled workers represented the major capital investment of many engineering firms. Employers had every reason to cling on to them. The workers themselves had no incentive to move. Considerable dislocation of family life was involved and housing problems were severe. On 16 March the Board of Trade made the first

Socialism and the Challenge of War. Ideas and Politics in Britain, 1912–18 (London, Routledge & Kegan Paul, 1974).

43. G. Braybon, Women Workers in the First World War. The British Experience (London, Croom Helm, 1981), p. 30.

44. Eventually, a complete Belgian factory community (named 'Elizabethville' in honour of the Queen of the Belgians) was established near Birtley in County Durham.

systematic attempt to enrol women for war work. By June 78,946 had been placed on the Special War Register, but only 1,816 were actually given jobs.[45] On 19 March Lloyd George and Walter Runciman signed the 'Treasury Agreement' with the union representatives Arthur Henderson and William Mosses. The unions agreed to accept 'dilution', the suspension of 'restrictive practices' and compulsory arbitration. The government agreed to maintain the skilled wage rate even when a job was no longer performed by a skilled man and to impose a limit on private profits. A return to traditional arrangements after the war was guaranteed. The agreement was important, but its implementation was not immediate. This had to await the establishment of the Ministry of Munitions in the wake of the 'shells scandal' and the formation of the Asquith Coalition government in May.[46]

Once he became Minister of Munitions Lloyd George pursued with customary zeal implementation of the proposals which he first expounded in December 1914. 'Dilution' was introduced. Resistance was stiff, despite the 'Treasury Agreement' and the powers afforded to the Minister by the Munitions of War Act, 1915. But the facts were on Lloyd George's side. The results of the National Registration of Manpower, which took place on Sunday, 15 August 1915, and the failure of the Munitions Volunteer Programme established them for all to see. It was clear that there was no 'surplus' of skilled workers who could be transferred to munitions work. The inevitability of 'dilution' was established. It was also clear that it was impossible to produce munitions on the scale required using only male labour and maintain an army of seventy divisions. The commitment to a Continental-size army could not be abandoned. That left one solution. Women were at last admitted to the industrial war effort. The numbers employed in munitions production rose from 82,589 in July 1914 to 340,844 by July 1916.[47]

These were impressive achievements, but they fell short of the establishment of a coherent national manpower plan. The free market in labour remained. The Ministry of Munitions simply intruded a new element of competition into it. This guaranteed that the army would not have everything its own way, but it did not make for the most effective use of national manpower resources. The Ministry of Munitions and the War Office were would-be monopolists concerned only with cornering the market in labour to their own advantage. The Ministry of Munitions proved no more able to take a 'national' view of manpower demands than the army. Far from resolving the manpower problem, the Ministry became part of it. Conscription was essential.

The military high command saw conscription as the ultimate solution. Sir William Robertson, Chief of the Imperial General Staff, was foremost among its advocates. He believed that conscription would curb the depredations of the Ministry of Munitions, draw the 'shirkers' out of industry and provide more men for the army. He was mistaken. Once conscription was introduced, men with industrial and agricultural skills vital to the war economy were systematically exempted from military service.[48] From mid-1916 onwards, after the huge losses of the Somme battles, the army found itself chronically short of

45. Lloyd George, *War Memoirs*, I, p. 174.
46. See above, pp. 107ff.
47. Lloyd George, *War Memoirs*, I, p. 175. By November 1918 the figure stood at 1,587,300.
48. Dewey, 'Military recruiting', p. 218. Occupations receiving the greatest degree of 'protection' were mining, metals, transport (railways, docks and canals) and agriculture.

men. Once Lloyd George became Prime Minister he was happy to see this situation continue. There is now no doubt that in 1917 he sought to restrain Haig by limiting the flow of men into the army.[49] This resulted in a dramatic reduction of the BEF's infantry strength by 1918.[50]

The advent of compulsion marked an important step in the 'civilianization' of manpower planning, but it did nothing to bring civilian 'recruiting' under control. The Ministry of Munitions and its sub-departments retained autonomous powers. Some overall authority which could fairly determine the competing demands for manpower was urgently required.

A start was made in August 1916 with the establishment of the Man-Power Distribution Board. Lloyd George carried the logic of this further in December. One of his first acts as Prime Minister was to create a Department of National Service. Neville Chamberlain was made its Director-General. He was given an impossible task. Lloyd George's instincts told him to extend compulsion to civilian life. They also told him that this was politically unacceptable. The legislation which embodied the Ministry of National Service in March 1917 specifically incorporated pledges designed to allay fears of 'industrial conscription'. Chamberlain was expected to achieve results which only the power of compulsion could produce while actually being constrained by the retention of the voluntary principle. He was given no authority at all over military recruiting where compulsory powers did exist. Muddle and confusion ensued. Chamberlain took the blame. He resigned in August. His treatment left him with a deep and abiding distrust of Lloyd George.

Chamberlain's departure gave Lloyd George the opportunity to reconstruct the ministry. Sir Auckland Geddes was made Director-General. The War Office yielded control of military recruiting. The relationship of the Ministry of National Service to the equally new Ministry of Labour over such questions as labour supply, priority, enrolment, allocation, transfer and substitution was clarified. The Germans did the rest. Their great Spring Offensive in March 1918 brought an end to three years of cautious experiment and compelled the adoption of centralized and coherent manpower planning. It was almost too late.

The manpower situation deteriorated throughout 1917. By the end of the year it reached crisis-point. Geddes placed the grim arithmetic before the War Cabinet in October in a paper entitled 'Recruiting Problems and Prospects'. There were 8M males in civilian life. Three point six million were of military age. Eight-hundred-thousand of these were aged 18–25, of whom only 270,000 were Category A. No more than 160,000 could be safely withdrawn from their civilian employment. Geddes estimated that only 120,000 men could be recruited for the army in the next eight months unless conscription was extended to men over the age of 41 and to Ireland.[51]

Both these expedients were adopted in 1918. The Military Service Act, which was passed in April, extended conscription to all males aged 18–51 and gave the Director of National Service power to cancel exemptions. The Act disturbed

49. D.R. Woodward, 'Did Lloyd George starve the British Army of men prior to the German offensive of 21 March 1918?' *Historical Journal*, XVII (1984), pp. 251–2.
50. See above, p. 90.
51. Adams and Poirier, *Conscription Controversy in Britain*, p. 214. For the Irish dimension, see A.J. Ward, 'David Lloyd George and the Irish conscription crisis', *Historical Journal*, XVII (1974). pp. 107–29.

trade-union opinion. Major strikes broke out at Coventry and Birmingham in July. The attempt to impose conscription on Ireland united the revolutionary and constitutional wings of Irish opposition and was met with a general strike on 23 April. The government's ability to conscript Irishmen continued in theory. It was quietly abandoned in practice. Britain was paying the price for manpower budgeting after the manpower had already been spent.

Haig's reinforcement was achieved at the cost of a ruthless 'comb out' of men in industry. This would have had a damaging effect on industrial production if the war had continued into 1919. By October not only the army but also the country was scraping the bottom of the manpower barrel. The war did not end a day too soon.

Besides men, the main demand created by the war was for munitions. These were in very short supply by the spring of 1915. Battlefield expenditure had been greater than any of the belligerents anticipated. The British were particularly badly affected. Pre-war production of guns and ammunition had been on the same small scale as the rest of Britain's military arrangements. Stockpiles rapidly diminished. Fresh supplies were dependent upon the state-owned arsenals and small-arms factories and a limited number of private manufacturers, chief among which was Vickers. Their efforts seemed increasingly inadequate. The struggle to increase output became a major political issue and a centre-piece of the history of the war.

Armaments procurement was the responsibility of the War Office Ordnance Department under the direction of its Master-General, Major-General Sir Stanley von Donop. Lloyd George long ago consigned the reputation of von Donop and his department to the dustbin of history. He was – as usual – less than just. Von Donop cannot be blamed either for the state of British munitions production or the failure to remedy it. This was quite beyond the power of a middle-ranking soldier. Lloyd George knew this. The real target of his attacks was not von Donop but von Donop's political chief, Kitchener.

Kitchener undoubtedly possessed the political power and prestige which von Donop lacked. Lloyd George charged him not only with failing to put this behind the mobilization of a 'war economy' but also of using it to prevent others from doing so. The charge is groundless.

Asquith was a fairer judge. He recognized that accusations of apathy or lethargy were unfounded.[52] Kitchener's War Office presided over a nineteen-fold increase in the supply of munitions during the first six months of the war. Orders placed by the Ordnance Department were primarily responsible for supplying the army in the field until well into 1916. Guns and ammunition ordered by the Ministry of Munitions did not become available at all until the end of October 1915 and not in quantity until the following spring. Much of these were sub-standard.[53]

Kitchener's administration was not without faults. His other responsibilities as Secretary of State left him with insufficient time to devote to munitions.[54] He was reluctant to delegate. This resulted in a certain amount of caution and delay. New ideas were not taken up as quickly as they might have been. Pressure

---

52. The Earl of Oxford and Asquith, *Memories and Reflections* (2 vols., London, Cassell, 1928), II, pp. 76–9.
53. See above, p. 63.
54. See above, p. 139.

on the manufacturers to complete orders which had been placed with them was not always maintained.[55]

These failings, however, were hardly fundamental. Kitchener was not the real problem. It is doubtful whether anyone else could have done better in the circumstances. The simple fact was that the production of munitions on the scale required by the army necessitated massive changes in British industrial practices, labour relations and government power. These could not be left to a sub-department of the War Office. The transfer of munitions production to a separate department of state with enhanced powers was inevitable. Asquith appreciated this. His inability to effect the transfer painlessly owed something to Kitchener's reluctance to lose part of his 'empire', but most to the intrigues of Sir John French.[56]

Kitchener also understood the need for new ways of doing things. He himself introduced businessmen into the management of the Ordnance Department, despite Asquith's reservations. One of them, George Booth, wrote Kitchener's political epitaph: 'Kitchener was a great man. He was inexplicable at times, but he really knew the big things.'[57] The same may be said of Lloyd George.

Lloyd George was Minister of Munitions for just over a year (May 1915–July 1916). During that time he laid the foundations of his reputation as 'the man who won the war'. The challenge which confronted him was a great one. On 7 July 1915 Kitchener made a formal announcement of British intentions to place a 70-division army in the field. Existing supplies of guns and ammunition were inadequate even for an army of less than half this size. There were sufficient 18-pdr guns – staple of the British artillery – to equip only 28 divisions and enough 4.5-inch and 5-inch howitzers for only 17 divisions. War Office regulations stipulated the maintenance of an ammunition reserve of 42-days supply. That for 18-pdrs was a mere 12 days. Small arms were no better provided for. There were rifles for only 33 divisions. Delivery to the army of hand grenades – a vital weapon in trench warfare – was at the rate of 2,500 a day. Seventy thousand a day were required. The demand for machine-guns was estimated at 26,000 a year. Orders had been placed for less than 5,500. Orders for trench mortars stood at less than 15 per cent of estimated need.[58]

Lloyd George set himself to transform this situation. There can be no doubt of his galvanizing effect on munitions production. By the time he left the Ministry in July 1916 a year's production of 18-pdr ammunition at the 1914–15 rate was being achieved in three weeks, a year's production of heavy howitzer ammunition in four days. Ten million 18-pdr shells were delivered to the army between January and June 1916, 23M between June and December.[59] One-thousand-one-hundred-and-five guns, 94 of them 'heavies', were manufactured between August 1914 and June 1915. During the first year of the Ministry of Munitions' existence the figure rose to 5,006, including 894 'heavies'. Output of

55. C. Wrigley, 'The Ministry of Munitions: an Innovatory Department', in K. Burk, ed., *War and the State: The Transformation of British Government, 1914–1919* (London, Allen & Unwin, 1982), pp. 37–8.
56. See above, pp. 36, 107–8.
57. Quoted in D. Crow, *A Man of Push and Go. The Life of George Macaulay Booth* (London, Hart-Davis, 1965), p. 138.
58. R.J.Q. Adams, *Arms and the Wizard. Lloyd George and the Ministry of Munitions, 1915–1916* (London, Cassell, 1978), pp. 53–4.
59. Adams, *Arms and the Wizard*, p. 244.

grenades increased from 68,000 to 27M, trench mortars from 312 to 4,279,[60] machine-guns from 1,486 to 17,679.[61] And there was much more to come.

Lloyd George's lack of generosity in claiming the whole of this achievement for himself and the Ministry of Munitions, when some of it properly belonged to the War Office, should not detract from its importance. Production of guns and ammunition in such quantities compelled a break with traditional practices on the part of employers, labour and government. The Ministry of Munitions was the principal instrument of change. By the end of the war it had assumed a burden of responsibility and a scale of operations unequalled in the history of any government department. Its headquarters staff alone employed 25,000 people.[62]

The activities of the Ministry were far ranging. The Munitions of War Act, 1915, granted it unparallelled and extensive powers over all armaments factories which the Minister chose to control. Manufacturers could be forced to undertake government work. Skilled men and machinery could be compulsorily transferred from private to State-owned factories. The Act also gave legal sanction to the provisions of the 'Treasury Agreement' prohibiting strikes, instituting compulsory arbitration, suspending restrictive practices and controlling profits.[63]

The exercise of these powers was not confined to munitions factories. It spread throughout the economy as a whole. The Ministry soon turned its attention to questions of manpower planning,[64] power supply and the control of raw materials. This extension of the Ministry's influence made it the most important single directing force in the British war effort on the home front.

In the 'controlled establishments', which eventually amounted to several hundred factories, the Ministry's aim was to encourage good industrial practice. The latest machinery and methods were introduced. The use of electricity increased enormously. Provision of extra generating capacity was beyond the financial resources of local government. The Treasury was forced to intervene.[65] Arc furnaces began to replace Bessemer converters in the steel industry. This allowed the exploitation of indigenous supplies of low-grade iron ore and the greater use of scrap and waste. The steel–scrap ratio rose from 15 per cent to 50 per cent during the course of the war.[66] Mass-production techniques of standardization, simplification and the use of machine tools began in earnest.[67] Industrial specialization and research and development were encouraged. Modern systems of financial control and production analysis made a tentative appearance. Private employers seized the opportunity to effect changes which had previously foundered on trade-union opposition.[68]

The Ministry was also a susbtantial employer in its own right. A large number of factories were built from public funds on land specially acquired for the

60. Lloyd George, *War Memoirs*, I, pp. 389–90.
61. Adams, *Arms and the Wizard*, p. 245. The figures include Vickers, Lewis and Hotchkiss guns.
62. Wrigley, 'Ministry of Munitions', p. 42.
63. See above, p. 185.
64. See above, pp. 184–5.
65. Wrigley, 'Ministry of Munitions', pp. 47–8.
66. S. Pollard, *The Development of the British Economy 1914–1950* (London, Edward Arnold, 1962), p. 57.
67. Wrigley, 'Ministry of Munitions', p. 48.
68. Notably Vickers, see *op. cit.*, p. 50.

purpose. These included fifteen National Projectile Factories for the production of heavy shells, fifteen National Filling Factories where empty shell cases were filled with explosive, and four National Cartridge Factories to augment the supply of rifle ammunition.

The Ministry took its rôle of industrial employer seriously. Much attention was paid to questions of employee health and welfare. Provision was made for decent catering, washing and recreational facilities, a task made more urgent by the large-scale employment of women. Standards were set in State-owned factories which private employers were obliged to follow. A limited amount of housing was also built to provide displaced munitions workers with cheap and respectable accommodation. Two of the largest estates – at Gretna in Dumfries-shire and Eltham in south-east London – were of exceptional quality.[69]

Industrial efficiency required a disciplined workforce. The Ministry took the kind of paternal interest in the morals of its employees familiar during the early years of the factory system. Shoddy workmanship, bad timekeeping and absenteeism were severely frowned upon and punished by fines and dismissal. Female welfare officers were appointed to supervise and advise women workers. A substantial force of women police was recruited to superintend the munitions factories. Whether they were intended to protect women workers from the surrounding male population or vice versa was unclear. Munitions girls attracted an unsalubrious reputation for financial extravagance, sexual promiscuity and smoking in public.[70] Sobriety was encouraged by the restriction of licensing hours. The mid-afternoon closure of public houses became a distinctive feature of British social life.

Posterity has been kind to the Ministry of Munitions.[71] There is no doubt that it was effective. Lloyd George had criticized the War Office for its failure to comprehend the magnitude of the demand for munitions. He was determined not to make the same mistake himself. The Ministry planned on the basis of what Lloyd George thought the military would need in 1917 not on what the military said they needed in 1915. In the short term, as von Donop predicted, this meant some sacrifice of quality to quantity, but in the long term Lloyd George's judgement was vindicated. The ability of British industry to supply the army with the prodigious quantities of munitions which it expended in 1917 and 1918 was due in no small measure to decisions taken by Lloyd George in the early days of the Ministry's existence. This was not his only contribution. He also realized that it was not enough for the Ministry merely to produce greater numbers of established weapons. Innovation was necessary. The amount of resources devoted to research and development owed much to Lloyd George's

---

69. The Well Hall Estate at Eltham excited a great deal of contemporary interest. The January 1918 issue of *Country Life* devoted a 17 page article to its charms.

70. Prejudice of this kind was common whenever women attained a degree of financial independence. Similar complaints were made about Nottingham lace workers before the war. J.B. Priestley commented on the phenomenon during his visit to Nottingham in 1933, see *English Journey* (1934; Harmondsworth, Penguin, 1977), p. 131.

71. Accounts have often been laudatory, not least Lloyd George's own (*War Memoirs*, I, Chapter XIX). See G. Dewar, *The Great Munitions Feat 1914-18* (London, Constable, 1921) and C. Addison, *Politics from Within 1911–1918* (2 vols., London, Herbert Jenkins, 1924) and *Four and a Half Years* (2 vols., London, Herbert Jenkins, 1934). The most recent study, Adams's *Arms and the Wizard*, is remarkably uncritical of Lloyd George.

personal initiative. There were rich dividends, including improvements in high-explosive chemistry and fuse and detonator design, and the adoption of the Stokes mortar, one of the most important and effective weapons of the war.[72]

Whether the Ministry of Munitions was efficient is less certain. Lloyd George was a contemptible administrator. His willingness to cut corners and ignore established procedures shocked civil service opinion and was productive of much muddle and confusion. Only after his departure did the Ministry's organization assume any semblance of system and coherence. During the first year of its existence the Ministry was held together principally by the driving force of Lloyd George's personality. He was a man in a hurry. His aim was specific and short-term: to produce the materials of war in sufficient quantities to make a British victory possible. How this was accomplished was of secondary importance. What mattered was that it was done. This conception of the Ministry as an 'emergency department of state', and the expedients to which it gave rise, had lasting consequences for the future of industry, labour relations and government power.

Transformation?

'War,' declared Trotsky, 'is the locomotive of history.' In August 1914 the British government set the signals at red. Its aim was 'business as usual'. The hope proved vain. Lloyd George coined the phrase on 4 August. Three days later it was bankrupt. Kitchener's call to arms changed everything. The nation began its faltering progress down the road to 'total war'. It has never been quite the same since.

Britain's political inheritance on the eve of the Great War was utilitarian, liberal and individualist. England, in particular, was an old country whose development had been uninfluenced by foreign conquest or domination. Most constitutional problems had long been resolved. Government was valued for its utility not for its embodiment of some greater good or mystical national aspiration. English politics were about bread and butter issues. The State was almost invisible by Continental standards. Administration was largely amateur, local, self-regulating and small-scale. Britain did not possess a bureaucracy. It had civil servants. There were very few of these and most of them were in London. There was no national police force, no compulsory military service and no state control of education. Advocates of 'national organization' were confined to a small group of radical Imperialists. The working class looked to self-help for the amelioration of its condition. The idea of an ominpotent State – even a beneficent one – found no favour. Protection had been abandoned in 1846. Free trade remained for many an article of faith. Private enterprise dominated the economy. Government interference was slight. Personal taxation was extraordinarily low. Most wage earners were totally exempt from income tax. Salaries between £160 and £500 a year were charged at the rate of 9d in the pound, those above £500 a year at the rate of 1s 3d. Individual rights, especially those relating to the ownership of property, were deeply entrenched in the common law and fiercely guarded by an independent judiciary. The tradition of collective action was well established,

---

72. Lloyd George, *War Memoirs*, I, pp. 366–81.

but – as in the case of the trade unions – existed principally for the pursuit of individual ends.

Obstacles to the growth of state control were therefore both numerous and severe. Political attitudes, however, were not fossilized. The possibility of accommodation to the demands of war was real. Signs of change were apparent before the war began. Political Liberalism was itself evolving. The governments of Campbell-Bannerman and Asquith were not inhibited by doctrinaire Classical Liberalism. Their welfare reforms increased significantly the scope of the State. The number of government employees rose from 116,413 at the turn of the century to 280,900 by 1914. Lloyd George's 'People's Budget' of 1909 threatened the upper classes with the spectre of redistributive taxation. Government intervention in labour disputes became an accepted feature of political life.

This 'new Liberalism' was a response to the social problems and aspirations generated by a mature urban and industrial economy and a prudent adjustment to the political reality of the 'rise of labour'. It involved no ideological conversion to social engineering, economic planning and the benefits of a powerful State either on the part of government or on the part of the masses who benefited from the fruits of reform.

British wartime experience followed the same course. The advance of state control between 1914 and 1918 was cautious, pragmatic, limited and, above all, temporary.

State interference was immediate. Control of the railways was planned in advance and written into the provisions of the War Book.[73] The purchase of sugar – widely regarded as an essential foodstuff, vital to civilian morale – began as soon as the war broke out.[74] Guarantees were given to banks and discount houses in order to prevent a breakdown of the world system of credit based on the City of London. The Defence of the Realm Act, which became law on 8 August, empowered the government to try by courts martial civilians charged with contravening regulations designed to effect 'public safety'.

The nature of this interference was characteristic. It involved a series of *ad hoc* responses to specific problems. These were made because of necessity and not through choice. There was no overall plan and no philosophy of action.

Future difficulties were tackled in the same piecemeal fashion. The evolution of government powers required for coherent and systematic manpower planning was not completed until the summer of 1918 and achieved then only by the threat of military defeat. The need to extend state control to the munitions and clothing industries was accepted relatively early, but elsewhere things took longer. There was no Shipping Controller until January 1916 and no Ministry of Shipping until the following December. A Food Controller was appointed only during the same month. Concerted measures to increase food production did not begin until February 1917, when a Coal Controller was also appointed. Food rationing was introduced on a local basis at the end of the year, but a national system did not come into operation until 8 July 1918.

Governments were rarely willing to proceed at a pace faster than that which they believed public opinion would tolerate. This was as true of Lloyd George's

---

73. See above, pp. 16–17.
74. This is considered below, Chapter 9.

government as it was of Asquith's. The consequences are apparent. Property rights were carefully respected. The State took over the railways and the mines. Milk supplies were controlled and 3M acres of land brought under the plough. But neither the railways nor the mines nor the land were nationalized. Co-operation between businesses in the name of efficiency was encouraged. But amalgamation – except in the case of the railways and, to some extent, the mines – was not imposed. The power to direct labour was used with great circumspection. There were no industrial conscript armies in wartime Britain. Trade-union co-operation was always contingent upon a return to 'normalcy' at the end of the war. Fears that the government intended to break this agreement provoked instant and invariably successful resistance either from the trade-union leadership or the rank-and-file. The trade-unions were not alone in their fears or in the effectiveness of their resistance. The farmers' lobby demanded the lifting of coercive orders and restrictions even before the war ended.[75] This agitation was but a prelude to the post-war 'bonfire of controls' which undid much of the innovative work of the Ministry of Munitions in reforming labour relations and industrial practices.[76]

The degree of state control eventually achieved during the course of the war was striking and impressive. It encompassed all Britain's basic industries. The British people showed a remarkable readiness to accommodate themselves to the fact of this change. This readiness was not, however, extended to the question of principle. State control was not an idea whose time had come, but an exceptional measure for exceptional circumstances, to be abandoned when the world returned to its senses. The power and responsibilities of government increased, but the nature of the State was not transformed.

Neither was British industry, though the effects of the war were considerable and permanent. New techniques were fostered.[77] Organization and combination among manufacturers was encouraged. The advantages of rationalization were made apparent. The demand for protective tariffs for 'key' industries was strengthened.[78] A climate of urgency and enterprise was created. This was reflected in the establishment of virtually new industries. These included the making of scientific instruments and glassware, ball bearings, tungsten, benzol, toluol and liquid ammonia.[79] Infant industries such as motor vehicles, wireless and aircraft grew to lusty manhood through the stimulus of military demands. Scientific research was rescued from prejudice and neglect. Physicists, chemists and engineers were recognized as national assets. They made a fundamental contribution to the war effort through the development of tanks, chemical weapons, synthetic materials and underwater detection apparatus.[80] Most important of all, perhaps, industry was habituated to the need for constant innovation and adaptation to change.

The sector which experienced the greatest changes was engineering. Its importance to the war effort compelled rationalization. Manufacturing

75. Hurwitz, *State Intervention*, pp. 221–2.
76. See R.H. Tawney, 'Abolition of Economic Controls, 1918–21', *Economic History Review*, XIII (1943), pp. 1–30.
77. See above, p. 189.
78. Tawney, 'Abolition', p. 8.
79. Pollard, *Development of the British Economy*, p. 54.
80. See G. Hartcup, *The War of Invention. Scientific Developments 1914–1918* (London, Brassey's, 1988).

processes were standardized. Automatic and semi-automatic machines were introduced, making possible the use of mass-production techniques and reducing traditional reliance on skilled labour. The expansion of motor vehicle, aircraft and machine tool production promised a rosy future in the post-war world.

Elsewhere, fortunes were mixed. The first industry to be affected by the war was railways. There were 130 companies in 1914. The government took over all of them. The advantages of this were too great to ignore. There could be no return to wasteful pre-war practices. Nationalization was resisted, but the Railway Act of 1921 restricted the control and management of the national network to four companies.[81]

The coal industry also experienced *de facto* nationalization, but this produced no lasting benefits. There were no significant technical innovations. Attempts to improve productivity failed. Output declined towards the end of the war. Labour relations remained bitter and strikes were frequent. The wartime legacy of over-capacity and high wages was an explosive combination which finally ignited in 1926.[82]

Shipbuilding ended the war with a hugely and artificially inflated capacity which had to compete with even more greatly inflated capacity in other countries, particularly the United States. Iron and steel suffered similar problems to a lesser degree.

Farmers traditionally do well out of war. The Great War was no exception. Prices rose considerably more than costs. Profits increased five-fold between 1914 and 1917.[83] Longer-lasting changes, however, were comparatively few. Agriculture certainly became more mechanized. American tractors began to appear in the rural landscape from 1916 onwards. Government policy was subordinated to the need for short-term increases in food production. The difficulties were immense. Farmers were expected to produce more food with fewer workers. Many farms were small and undercapitalized. There were chronic shortages of feedstuffs and fertilizers. These problems were tackled systematically only after the formation of the Lloyd George Coalition in December 1916.[84] Substitute labour was arranged. By the end of the war there were, 84,000 soldiers, 30,000 prisoners of war and 16,000 members of the Women's Land Army working on Britain's farms.[85] Three million acres of pasture were ploughed up to provide wheat, barley, oats and potatoes. Good farming practice was encouraged. The results were disappointing. The calorific value of food production in 1918 was 21.2 billion calories. This compared favourably with the figure of 19.4 billion calories in 1916, but was 0.2 billion calories lower than the figure for 1914.[86] The farming community was suspicious of government intervention. Its co-operation was often only grudgingly given. Government

81. See E.A. Pratt, *British Railways and the Great War* (2 vols., London, Selwyn & Blount, 1921).
82. See R.A.S. Redmayne, *The British Coal Mining Industry During the War* (Oxford, Oxford University Press, 1923), and W.H.B. Court, 'Problems of the British Coal Industry Between the Wars', *Economic History Review*, XV, 1st series (1945), pp. 1–24.
83. P.E. Dewey, 'British farming profits and government policy during the first world war', *Economic History Review*, XXXVII, 2nd series (1984), pp. 374–8.
84. See above, pp. 127–8.
85. J. Brown, *Agriculture in England. A Survey of Farming, 1870–1947* (Manchester, Manchester University Press, 1987), p. 65.
86. P.E. Dewey, 'Food production and policy in the United Kingdom, 1914–1918', *Transactions of the Royal Historical Society*, 5th series, XXX (1980), pp. 71–89.

was reluctant to push its powers too far. Few farmers were dispossessed. Improvements in food production were not enough to feed the country without massive imports. Starvation was prevented principally not by the efforts of the nation's farmers, but of her merchant seamen and their Royal Naval escorts. Food control policy also made a vital contribution. The raising of the extraction rate in milling flour and the diversion of barley and oats from animal feed to baking flour ensured that available grains were efficiently used. This was in marked contrast to the German experience.[87] Government showed little interest in the long-term needs of agriculture. Post-war farming returned to the doldrums.[88]

The trades union movement emerged from the war with enhanced status, self-confidence and power. The demands of the war had compelled a temporary retreat from cherished positions, but no ground was permanently yielded. The war established the national importance of the unions for all to see. Without their co-operation no victory would have been possible. Individual union leaders found themselves holding high political office, including membership of the War Cabinet itself.[89] The unions had become 'an estate of the realm'. Their power was not going to go away. No one appreciated this more than Lloyd George.[90]

The war also increased the authority of the unions among working people. Membership soared from 4.1M in 1914 to 6.5M by 1918. The pre-war pattern of a large number of small unions began to change through a process of amalgamations and combinations similar to that which affected the engineering industry, the railways, the mines and the banks. The Iron and Steel Trades Confederation was established in 1917, to be followed after the war by the Amalgamated Engineering Union (1920) and the Transport and General Workers Union (1921). Big unions joined big business and big government in deciding the shape of the post-war world.

Whether the unions knew what to do with their new-found power is more doubtful. The ideology of labour was unchanged by the war. The unions remained an uneasy coalition of interest groups, pursuing often contradictory ends. The willingness of their leaders to participate in government was constrained by the open hostility of much of the rank-and-file, articulated by a radical shop stewards' movement which was itself the prisoner of old prejudices and fears.

The other principal group in British society which improved its position during the war was women. Their contribution to the war effort is well known. By November 1918 947,000 were employed on munitions work.[91] This was often unpleasant and sometimes dangerous. More than 300 lost their lives as the result of TNT poisoning and explosions.[92] Lloyd George paid a handsome tribute to

87. The Germans made the mistake of feeding grain to animals rather than eating it themselves. This is wasteful. Germany suffered severe food shortages as early as the winter of 1916–17, the notorious 'turnip winter'.
88. Brown, *Agriculture in England*, pp. 76–106.
89. See above, p. 128.
90. See C. Wrigley, *David Lloyd George and the British Labour Movement: Peace and War* (Hassocks, Harvester, 1976).
91. A. Marwick, *Women at War 1914–1918* (London, Fontana, in association with the Imperial War Museum, 1977), p. 166.
92. The War Memorial in Victoria Square, Bolton, Lancashire, is dedicated to the 'men *and* women' of the town who died in the war. This is fitting, but very unusual.

12 Doing their Bit: Women at War (*The Trustees of the Imperial War Museum, London*)

their spirit of patriotism and self-sacrifice.[93] Women also served with the military forces. There were 40,850 in Queen Mary's Auxiliary Army Corps by the end of the war. Some 17,000 women were employed with the British Expeditionary Force in August 1918.[94] Many of these were nurses, but they also included cooks, waitresses, mechanics, drivers, clerks, telephonists and shorthand typists.

In all , the number of women in paid full-time employment rose during the course of the war from 5,966,000 in 1914 to 7,311,000 by 1918. Some changes were particularly striking. The number employed in metal working rose from 170,000 to 594,000,[95] in transport from 18,200 to 117,200, in commerce from 505,200 to 934,500 (including an increase from 1,500 to 37, 600 in banking), in national and local government from 262,000 to 460,200 (including 15,000 on the headquarters staff of the Ministry of Munitions alone).[96]

93. Lloyd George, *War Memoirs*, I, pp. 352–4.
94. Marwick, *Women at War*, p. 168.
95. Hurwitz, *State Intervention*, pp. 132, 35.
96. Marwick, *Women at War*, p. 166.

The significance and effects of these changes are much disputed. Some things are clear. The employment of women was not new. It was a familiar feature of many pre-war industries, including textiles, pottery, clothing and domestic service. The overall increase in the number of women workers was not especially impressive. The mobilization of women barely started before the autumn of 1915 and gained real momentum only after the imposition of general male conscription in the spring of 1916. It is also doubtful whether many truly 'new' workers were brought into the labour force. Some who entered employment between 1914 and 1918 would have done so even if there had not been a war. Some were married women who took the opportunity to return to work. Others were women who were already employed in poorly paid 'traditional' female trades attracted to munitions and other 'war work' by higher wages and better prospects. The number of women employed in the clothing trade fell from 612,000 in 1914 to 556,000 by 1918, the number in domestic service from 1,658,000 to 1,250,000.[97] Many women were employed on work which was by definition temporary and which would terminate with the war. Two-thirds of women who entered employment during the war had left it by 1920. There was a feeling that women's work was done. The Ministry of Reconstruction's Committee on Women's Employment went so far in 1918 as to recommend that the employment of married women be discouraged.[98] Commerce and government were exceptions to the post-war decline. These were sectors where the recruitment of men for military service bit deepest[99] and where the employment of women was most enduring. Wage rates certainly improved. The average rose from 13s 6d a week in 1914 to 35s a week by 1918.[100] The difference between male and female wage rates was also eroded. In 1914 women earned, on average, half as much as men. By 1918 they earned two-thirds as much. The principle of equal pay for equal work, however, was not established. Male trades unionists remained as hostile as ever to the aspirations of women.

Parliament was more generous. The Representation of the People Act of February 1918 extended the franchise to all women aged 30 and over. Lloyd George portrayed this as a fitting reward for their war service.[101] The actual process by which women received the vote was less straightforward.[102] Some have argued that the victory was a hollow one.[103] This is not how the suffragists themselves felt. Astute women, like Mrs Fawcett,[104] recognized that it was only a matter of time before women obtained the vote on the same terms as men. Other changes also followed. The Sex Disqualification (Removal) Act 1919 opened jury service, the magistracy and the legal profession to women. The National Insurance Acts of 1918, 1920 and 1921 made women wage earners eligible for national insurance benefits. Nursing was granted full professional status in 1919.[105]

97. *ibid.*
98. *Parliamentary Papers* (1918), Vol. XIV, Cmd. 9239-1919, pp. 68-9.
99. Dewey, 'Military recruiting', p. 220.
100. Hurwitz, *State Intervention*, p. 136.
101. Lloyd George, *War Memoirs*, II, p. 1172.
102. See M. Pugh, *Women's Suffrage in Britain 1867-1928* (London, Historical Association, 1980), pp. 30-5.
103. M. Pugh, 'Politicians and the Woman's Vote 1914-1918', *History*, LXIX (1974), pp. 358-74.
104. Dame Millicent Garrett Fawcett (1847-1929), President of the National Union of Women's Suffrage Societies, 1897-1918.
105. Marwick, *Women at War*, p. 162.

These changes were hardly revolutionary. The position of women in British society did not change overnight. Many prejudices remained. The costs of the war to women were also high. As wives and mothers they bore the brunt of the nation's suffering. The proportion of widows per 1,000 people rose from 38 to 43. This represented not only an enormous personal loss but also continuing economic hardship, especially for working-class women. Vera Brittain may have found the University of Oxford more welcoming to women when she went up to Somerville after the war, but the 'price' she paid for this was the loss of her sweetheart, her brother and all her close male friends.[106]

An assessment of the consequences of the war for British women depends on calculating short-term gains and losses and balancing them against long-term ones.[107] Some of the short-term gains were very short indeed. High wages, equal pay and access to skilled industrial work were the product of wartime expediency. They disappeared with the need which gave them birth. Fresh opportunities were created in clerical work – where change was apparent even before the war – and in the higher professions, some of which were opened to women for the first time. Health and welfare provision for pregnant women and nursing mothers improved.[108] Most important of all, perhaps, women's belief in what they could do and society's belief in what they might be required to do changed significantly. The consequences of this are still with us.

106. See V. Brittain, *Testament of Youth* (London, Victor Gollancz, 1933).
107. Marwick, *Women at War*, p. 162.
108. Winter, *Great War and the British People*, especially pp. 188–204.

9

Comradeship, Discipline and Morale[1]

Unless we have the nation with us, and believing in us, we may just as well give up at once.

Brigadier-General John Charteris[2]

The morale of the soldier is the greatest single factor in war.

Field-Marshal Viscount Montgomery[3]

Modern wars are wars of the masses. The armies which fight them are not self-contained corporations remote from their parent societies. Only a small number of soldiers are professional specialists. The majority are 'citizens in uniform'. They retain ties of affection and sentiment with civilian life. They depend for their equipment, armaments and supplies on the co-operation and efficiency of workers at home. Their fate is viewed with interest and anxiety by those they leave behind.

This means that all modern wars are fought on two fronts. The home front is not only as important as the war front but also inseparable from it.

In 1870 France suffered a crushing military defeat by Prussia. The French Army collapsed. France did not. A Republic was proclaimed. Leon Gambetta organized provincial resistance. The Prussian Army was forced to lay siege to

1. For the Home Front, A. Marwick, *The Deluge. British Society and the First World War* (London, Bodley Head, 1965; Harmondsworth, Penguin, 1967) remains indispensable, but must now be supplemented by B. Waites, *A Class Society at War: England 1914–1918* (Leamington Spa, Berg, 1987) and J.M. Winter, *The Great War and the British People* (London, Macmillan, 1986). See also, C. Haste, *Keep the Home Fires Burning; Propaganda in the First World War* (London, Allen Lane, 1977). M. Macdonagh, *In London During the Great War: The Diary of a Journalist* (London, Eyre & Spottiswoode, 1935); Mrs C.S. Peel, *How We Lived Then, 1914–1918: A Sketch of Social and Domestic Life in England During the Great War* (London, John Lane, 1929); and C.E. Playne, *Society at War, 1914–1916* (London, Allen & Unwin, 1931) and *Britain Holds On, 1917, 1918* (London, Allen & Unwin, 1933) are interesting accounts by contemporaries with a metropolitan perspective. For a view from the shires, see A. Clark, *Echoes of the Great War. The Diary of the Reverend Andrew Clark* ed, J. Munson (Oxford, Oxford University Press, 1985). For military morale, see T. Ashworth, *Trench Warfare, 1914–1918; The Live and Let Live Sustem* (London, Macmillan, 1980); J. Baynes, *Morale: A Study of Men and Courage: the Second Scottish Rifles at the Battle of Neuve Chapelle, 1915* (London, Cassell, 1967; repr. Leo Cooper, 1987); Lord Moran, *The Anatomy of Courage* (London, Constable, 1945); and J. Brent Wilson, 'The Morale and Discipline of the British Expeditionary Force, 1914–1918' (Unpublished MA thesis, University of New Brunswick, 1978).
2. J. Charteris, *At GHQ* (London, Cassell, 1931), p. 97. The date is 11 June 1915.
3. F-M Viscount Montgomery, *The Memoirs of Field-Marshal the Viscount Montgomery of Alamein* (London, Companion Book Club, 1955), p. 74.

Paris. French partisans waged a costly campaign of harassment against the Prussian lines of communication. The war dragged on.

In 1954 a small force of French Foreign Legionnaires and paratroopers suffered a trifling military defeat by the Viet Minh. French military capacity was little impaired. The French Army did not collapse. The French Empire in Indo-China did.

The difference between the two events was one of political will. Even a crushing military defeat may not prove decisive if the political will to resist remains. Even a trifling military defeat may prove decisive if the political will to continue is exhausted.

Political will is not simply about the resolve of politicians. It is a reflection of national morale. Maintenance of this is a cardinal element of success in modern war.

One Nation?

The preservation of national morale through the vicissitudes of war depends on many things. Time is a major consideration. Short wars make less demand on national morale than long ones (though, paradoxically, the stronger the morale among adversaries the less likely wars are to be short). The European Great Powers showed a keen awareness of this in the years before 1914. They all planned quick victories (but the actual strength of morale among them prevented any quick victories from being achieved).

Wars which are perceived as legitimate acts of defence against aggression are more likely to rally public support than those which are not. The success of armies in the field can be fatally undermined by lack of approval for their actions at home, as the Americans found to their cost in Vietnam. The belligerents in 1914 were anxious to legitimize their resort to arms by portraying it as defensive in nature. This was particularly true of Britain and Germany, countries which were not directly attacked and whose territory was not invaded.

All societies experience social and political tensions. These can easily be exacerbated by war, especially if sections of the population appear to be evading their fair share of responsibilities or to be profiting from their positions at the expense of others. Enemy propagandists will seek to exploit the gulf between the privations of the combat soldier and the comfortable life of the 'shirker' at home.[4] This makes it difficult to create even the impression of equality of sacrifice without the implementation of compulsory military service.

British governments before 1914 were fully aware of the importance of national morale in the event of war. They were less certain that they could maintain it. They had good cause. The 'condition of England' was very worrying. The level of political disaffection was unusually high. Ireland teetered on the brink of civil war. The campaign for women's suffrage took on a new militancy. Parliamentary politics were bitter and unruly. Investigative sociology revealed the true depths of urban poverty. The working class was restless. This was a major concern. The working class comprised 80 per cent of the population. Their morale *was* the national morale. Working-class co-operation in any future war was clearly vital. Whether it could be secured was less obvious.

4. I am grateful to Dr R.J. Oakland for showing me examples of such propaganda material from his collection.

The working class achieved an unprecedented degree of political prominence in the years before the outbreak of the Great War. A Labour Representation Committee was formed in 1900. This became the Labour Party in 1906. Its electoral fortunes fluctuated, but by August 1914 it had 36 MPs. The trades union movement grew in size and authority.[5] Widespread industrial unrest demonstrated not only its determination to protect working-class living standards but also its formidable capacity for disruption. The 'labour question' was high on the political agenda.

Despite this, the working class remained a mystery. Theirs was 'a life apart',[6] remote from the world of metropolitan high politics. They made few demands on government. Their chief desire was to be left alone. This was not encouraging.

It became commonplace among the political élite to doubt the working class's willingness to make 'sacrifices' for the 'common good' in time of war.[7] This pessimism influenced even strategic thinking.[8] It was firmly believed that the working class would not accept conscription, providing powerful reinforcement for those who favoured the traditional 'British way in warfare'.[9] Governments hoped for a short war. They planned a naval one. Maritime supremacy would not only limit the risk of high military casualties but also preserve the nation's food supplies – and with them the working-class diet, reduction of which it was believed would result in a disastrous collapse in morale.

There were also those who doubted the capacity of the working class to fight a war. The experience of the South African War was disturbing. Many thousands of working-class volunteers were rejected as physically unfit for military service. This caused something of a panic in official circles. Fashionable theories of Social Darwinism drew attention to working-class manpower as a strategic asset in the international struggle for survival. Britain's appeared to be in an advanced state of deterioration. A quest for 'national efficiency' began. Its aims informed many of the Liberal governments' social reforms after 1906, especially those which dealt with working-class child health and welfare.[10]

A decade's governmental reflection on the 'problem' of national morale was thus somewhat negative in its results. The preservation of national morale seemed to depend principally on avoiding certain things. There was a clear set of 'don'ts' – do not become embroiled in a long war, do not incur excessive military casualties, do not allow the working-class standard of living to fall, do not introduce conscription, do not antagonize organized Labour.

There was no equivalent set of 'do's'. The need for the government to 'lead' public opinion was little understood. The 'public opinion' which the political élite recognized was itself extraordinarily narrow. Working-class opinion was dismissed as irrational and sectarian and completely excluded.[11] Governments

5. See above, p. 195.
6. The phrase is from S. Meacham, *A Life Apart. The English Working Clas 1890-1910* (London, Thames & Hudson, 1977).
7. See, for example, C.F.G. Masterman, *The Condition of England* (London, Methuen, 1909), pp. 132–3. The chapter 'The multitude' is very revealing.
8. See A. Offer, 'The working classes, British naval plans and the coming of the Great War', *Past and Present*, CVII (1985), pp. 204–26.
9. See above, pp. 133–5.
10. See G.R. Searle, *The Quest for National Efficiency* (Oxford, Oxford University Press, 1971).
11. B. Waites, 'The government of the home front and the "moral economy" of the working class', in P.H. Liddle, ed., *Home Fires and Foreign Fields. British Social and Military Experience in the Great War* (London, Brassey's, 1985), pp. 190–1.

had few resources of their own with which to publicize themselves and to conduct official propaganda. There was no 'Ministry of Information' and no desire to create one. Presentation of the government case depended on the ability of politicians to 'manage' the Press. This was problematical. Since the 1890s newspapers had become increasingly dominated by the personal whims and ambitions of powerful and irresponsible Press Barons. The tone of the popular Press – especially after the outbreak of the Boer War – was strident and jingoistic. There was considerable hostility to the Liberal Party in general and to Asquith in particular. Governments also suffered from their inability to obtain an independent assessment of the attitudes of the working class. They tended to view the working class through the distorting prism of the trades unions. These were dominated by the interests of skilled male workers and were not necessarily representative of the working class as a whole. If the war did not end quickly, if British casualties became excessive, if food supplies were threatened, if the working-class standard of living began to fall, if conscription had to be introduced, if the industrial *status quo* could not be maintained, governments would have to re-think their whole attitude to the mobilization of popular opinion or risk a catastrophic national defeat.

Keeping the Home Fires Burning

That a catastrophic national defeat was avoided was due in no small part to the resilience of civilian morale. This surprised many people at the time. It has appalled some people since. The gradually increasing sophistication of government propaganda is only part of the explanation. Much was also owed to the underlying cultural values of British society, to the war's unintended beneficial effects, to civilian ignorance of the appalling privations which many soldiers had to endure, and to a persistent belief in the justice of Britain's cause.

Government attempts to control public opinion proceeded by the same gradual and *ad hoc* methods which characterized other aspects of state intervention.[12] Early government propaganda was concentrated on enemy and neutral opinion. This was the responsibility of the Secret War Propaganda Bureau established at Wellington House in London in September 1914.[13] The Foreign Office, War Office and Admiralty retained their rôles of information distribution and intelligence collection. Constant inter-departmental bickering was the inevitable result. This was only partly resolved by the creation of a co-ordinating authority – the Department of Information – in February 1917. Despite this, British 'overseas' propaganda was a conspicuous success.[14] Its aims were to maintain friendly relations with neutrals and allies, to arouse neutrals against the enemy and to undermine the enemy's will to resist.[15] The techniques

12. See above, pp. 180–95.
13. For this and other aspects of British 'overseas' propaganda, see M. Sanders and P. Taylor, *British Propaganda in the First World War* (London, Macmillan, 1982).
14. M.E. Occleshaw, 'The "Stab in the Back" – Myth or Reality?' *Journal of the Royal United Services Institute for Defence Studies*, CXXX (1985), pp. 49–54, emphasises the role of British Military Intelligence propaganda in the collapse of German civilian morale in 1918. Occleshaw's *Armour Against Fate: British Military Intelligence in the First World War* (London, Columbus, 1988) appeared too late to be taken account of in writing this book.
15. For the rôle of propaganda in general, see H.D. Lasswell, *Propaganda Technique in World War I* (1927; Cambridge, Mass., Massachusetts Institude of Technology Press, 1971).

which were developed for these purposes were eventually applied to the domestic scene.

The government entered the war without a conscious propaganda policy for the home front. The mobilization of opinion behind the war effort – like recruiting[16] – was left to the voluntary activities of well-intentioned individuals and groups. Some attempt to co-ordinate these was made with the formation of a Central Committee of National Patriotic Organizations. This – like voluntary recruitment – could not last. By mid-1917 a combination of war-weariness, disaffection and dissent among sections of the population finally forced the government to take the initiative. A National War Aims Committee (NWAC) was established in June. Under its direction 'home' propaganda became more systematic and coherent.

The first step was to create an effective national organization. This was done quickly. The fullest use was made of what lay to hand. The Central Committee of National Patriotic Organizations, complete with its local network, was absorbed in July. The constituency organizations of the political parties were also obliged to co-operate on a bi-partisan basis. This ensured that the NWAC's message could be carried into every significant population centre in the country.

Much of the work of the NWAC was traditional. Propaganda 'offensives' were organized in the manner of election campaigns. Rallies were held, speeches made, thousands of leaflets distributed. Effort was concentrated in areas where morale was most suspect. But this was not all. There were also two important innovations.

The first of these was the attempt not only to use propaganda techniques to create a sense of national purpose but also to use the sense of national purpose so created as weapon of moral ostracism against 'shirkers' and dissenters. This required a more populist approach to 'public opinion' than that which obtained before the war. The government began to take working-class opinion seriously and to investigate it independently. The implications for the future relationship between government and the 'masses' were significant.[17]

The second was the use of a new and potent medium – film.[18] This was a natural development. Propaganda was already becoming less literary. The experience of 'overseas' propaganda demonstrated the effectiveness of visual images harnessed to catchy phrases. The initial attitude to film was, however, characteristically tentative. It took the enormous public response to the release of the 'Battle of the Somme' in August 1916 to awaken official interest in the possibilities of the medium. This remarkable film, the first of its kind in the history of the cinema and the history of war, contained scenes of actual fighting, including British dead and wounded.[19] It was very far from being propaganda. Its 'message' was stark: modern war is brutal and destructive. Feature-length films which followed – on the 'Battle of the Ancre' and the 'Battle of Arras' – displayed greater reticence, but it was not until 1917 that genuine propaganda films

16. See above, p. 158.
17. Waites, 'Government of the Home Front', p. 191.
18. N. Reeves, *Official British Film Propaganda During the First World War* (London, Croom Helm, with the Imperial War Museum, 1986) is an excellent account.
19. The film is now available on video from the Imperial War Museum. An accompanying pamphlet, *Viewing Guide: The Battle of the Somme*, compiled by C. McCarthy *et al.*, provides a scene-by-scene analysis. See also the account by one of the two cameramen who shot the original film, G. Malins, *How I Filmed the War* (London, 1920).

began to be produced. These were mostly 'shorts'. They were directed at aspects of the war on the home front. Their aim was to publicize the contribution to the war effort made by the 'sacrifice' of munitions workers, nurses, Land Army girls, thrifty housewives and others who were 'doing their bit' and to shame and isolate others who were not.

The development and application of these techniques was a recognition on the part of government that morale was not an inexhaustible commodity. It had to be cherished and protected. The function of propaganda was to cherish and protect it. Propaganda could do no more than this. It certainly could not 'create' morale. The working class was not an inert mass waiting to be shaped by the will of government. It had views of its own. These were complicated and paradoxical.

The British urban working class was the oldest industrial workforce in the world. Its class consciousness was very strong. It was well organized. It had a sharp awareness of its industrial strength. It was quite remarkably strike-prone.[20] It was also riven with divisions, petty snobberies and subtle distinctions. It was disciplined and deferential, conformist and hedonistic, patriotic and loyal. It showed little interest in radical ideologies.[21] It had a vast fund of goodwill towards Britain's national institutions, especially monarchy and parliament. From the point of view of a hard-pressed government in time of war, the working class was far from intractable. There was, however, a sticking point. This was 'fairness', a concept deeply rooted in Anglo-Saxon culture. Government could ignore 'fairness' only at its peril. Propaganda could not make up for its absence. Appeals to the 'national interest' and the 'spirit of sacrifice' were doomed without it.[22]

Working-class attachment to national institutions was not immediately undermined by the war. In the short term it may even have been strengthened. The King set the tone. He committed himself and his Court to total abstinence from alcohol for the duration of the war. Many of his subjects followed his example. Few of them were in the Cabinet. The traditional ruling class led from the front. The list of peers and sons of peers killed during the war runs to sixty-four pages of the *Complete Peerage*. The political élite itself was not spared. Asquith lost a son. Bonar Law lost two. Military enlistment was highest among the middle and upper classes.[23] Casualty rates among the officer corps – solidly middle- and upper-class throughout the war – were roughly double those of their men.[24] Restrictions were placed on the 'excess profits' of munitions manufacturers and others who were 'doing well out of the war'.[25] Bonar Law's proposal to introduce a tax on 'luxuries' in April 1918 met with widespread approval.[26]

There were also material factors at work. Government was sensitive to the

20. For the 'industrial strategy' of the working class, see P. Joyce, *Work, Society and Politics. The Culture of the Factory in Later Victorian England* (Hassocks, Harvester, 1980).
21. R.I. McKibbin, 'Why was there no Marxism in Great Britain?' *English Historical Review*, XCIX (1984), pp. 297–331.
22. Waites, 'Government of the Home Front', p. 191.
23. Winter, *Great War and the British People*, p. 37.
24. *op. cit.*, p. 87.
25. For the Excess Profits Duty, see J.R. Hicks *et al.*, *The Taxation of War Wealth* (Oxford, Oxford University Press, 1941).
26. Sir E.L. Woodward, *Great Britain and the War of 1914–1918* (Oxford, Oxford University Press, 1967), p. 519.

need to ensure adequate supplies of food and fuel at affordable prices.[27] This led eventually to rationing.[28] The science of nutrition was encouraged.[29] The working-class diet improved despite an aggregate national food shortage.[30] This contributed mightily to the maintenance of civilian morale, in marked contrast to Germany (and to Russia), and was a major element in the British and Allied victory. It owed much to improvements in the working-class standard of living.

The war was expensive.[31] Extra monies had to be raised to pay for it. Revenue was increased four-fold. A high proportion of this came from direct taxation. Income tax rose steadily. By 1918 it stood at 6s in the pound. This was an eight-fold increase since 1914. Many workers were required to pay income tax for the first time. The traditional distinction between the taxed and the untaxed, between the 'classes' and the 'masses' began to blur.[32] The reliance on direct taxation helped keep down the cost of living for working-class families and made the tax system more redistributive.[33]

The war also provided a temporary respite from the great evils of working-class life, poverty and unemployment. Wages improved significantly, especially during the second half of the war. By 1918 they were twice the 1914 level.[34] The army's insatiable demand for men transformed the labour market within weeks of the outbreak of war.[35] By 1916 unemployment had virtually disappeared.

The combined effect of these changes was to reduce social inequalities. Working-class males who remained in civilian employment improved their life expectancy compared with pre-war trends. The mortality levels of the poorly paid improved in relation to the better-paid. Nutrition-related diseases declined. Infant and maternal mortality declined sharply, especially in the overcrowded and impoverished urban slums.[36]

All this was very different from the fate which awaited the working class on the battlefield. Social amelioration at home was purchased at a high price abroad. The quite disproportionate attention paid to officer casualties and to the 'lost generation' of public schoolboys should not be allowed to disguise the true nature of Britain's war losses. Almost 94 per cent of British dead belonged to the 'Other Ranks'. These were overwhelmingly working class.

The huge scale of the casualties made curiously little impact on national morale during the war itself. Lloyd George had no hesitation in attributing this to censorship.[37] He was only partly right. Deaths were too numerous to hide. No attempt was made to hide them. Official Figures were available in the form of

---

27. S. Pollard, *The Development of the British Economy 1914–1918* (London, Edward Arnold, 1962), p. 60.
28. See above, p. 284. The adoption of rationing owed much to the activities of working-class Food Vigilance Committees, see Waites, *Class Society at War*, p. 32.
29. See J.G. Stark, 'British Food Policy and Diet in the First World War' (Unpublished PhD thesis, University of London (LSE), 1985).
30. Winter, *Great War and the British People*, pp. 215–29.
31. Woodward, *Great Britain and the War of 1914–1918*, pp. 514–20.
32. Marwick, *Deluge*, p. 137.
33. Pollard, *Development of the British Economy*, p. 65.
34. Winter, *Great War and the British People*, p. 232. There was considerable variation between trades.
35. See above, p. 184.
36. Winter, *Great War and the British People*, pp. 103–53.
37. D. Lloyd George, *War Memoirs* (2 vols., London, Odhams, [1938]), I, p. 229.

weekly lists published by His Majesty's Stationery Office. The press gave them wider currency. Among national newspapers, the *Daily Telegraph* and the *Morning Post* published casualty lists until the end of 1916. *The Times's* lists were particularly extensive.[38] They included the names of all ranks until the end of 1917, but for the remainder of the war only officer casualties were recorded. These restrictions owed little to concern for the effect on public opinion. They were determined by journalistic considerations. Once the grim novelty of the Somme was over casualties were no longer 'news'.

This did not apply to the provincial press. Local newspapers published casualty lists throughout the war. These were often accompanied by photographs of the victims and by short obituaries. Despite an element of voyeurism – and appalling lapses of taste which placed accounts of men's deaths alongside advertisements for undertakers and pork pies[39] – this made them more poignant and affecting. Death was personalized and allowed to assume its individual tragic significance.

The provincial press's unconcern to shield its readers from the realities of war extended beyond the obituary columns to coverage of actual combat. '7TH NORTHAMPTONS CUT UP' was the uncompromising headline in the *Northampton Daily Chronicle* during the Battle of Loos.[40] Provincial newspapers maintained their links with local men on active service. This gave them access to a more vivid and truthful source of information than that afforded by the bland official communiques which were the staple of national press reports. 'I have lost my right leg,' Private W. Hartness told readers of the *Barnsley Chronicle* on 15 July 1916. 'It is something awful . . . I am very sorry to say that the Barnsley lads have caught it. It was like hell let loose, and I never thought I should get through it alive.'[41]

Censorship of the press was in other respects also astonishingly lax. The possible military consequences of press reports were not carefully considered. The exploits of New Army battalions were followed with avid interest. Their establishment, training and eventual deployment were reported in considerable detail. German intelligence officers concerned with the British Order of Battle would have found rich pickings in the provincial press during the first two years of the war. Reports of Arthur Henderson's speech in the spring of 1916, in which he explained to munitions workers that their Whitsun holiday would have to be delayed until July, alerted the Germans to the probable date of the British attack on the Somme. Although openly subversive publications of the revolutionary Left were ruthlessly controlled and suppressed, as was left-wing political activity in general, the freedom of mass circulation newspapers to comment on political issues was little impaired. The press was Asquith's major and most consistent opponent. It played a central part in the political crises of May 1915 and December 1916 and was instrumental in his downfall.[42] Press willingness to

38. See, for example, 16 November 1916.
39. The *Barnsley Chronicle* ran an astonishing series of advertisements, promising 'slaughter at the sales', alongside news of real slaughter throughout July 1916, see J. Cooksey, *Pals. The 13th and 14th Battalions York & Lancaster Regiment. A History of the Two Battalions Raised by Barnsley in World War One* (Barnsley, Barnsley Chronicle, 1986), p. 220.
40. I owe this reference to Mr Dominic Luke.
41. Cooksey, *Pals*, p. 222.
42. See J.M. McEwen, 'The Press and the fall of Asquith', *Historical Journal*, XXI (1978), pp. 863–83.

publish General Maurice's charges in May 1918 also provided the one real moment of political unease in Lloyd George's wartime prime-ministership.[43]

This laxity owed something to a tradition of political liberalism. But it owed most to naivety. Official recognition that 'walls have ears' and 'careless talk costs lives' was conspicuous only by its absence. Problems began at the top. Kitchener's reluctance to confide military details to his civilian colleagues is usually dismissed as another manifestation of a pathologically morose and suspicious personality, but it was well founded. Gossip is the lifeblood of politics. Politicians found it difficult to forego their regular draughts. Cabinet ministers discussed public business with their wives. Lloyd George discussed it with other men's wives. Asquith discussed it with Venetia Stanley.[44] The military were little better. Arrangements for the Gallipoli landings were fatally compromised by a criminal lack of secrecy.[45] There was no greater gossip than Henry Wilson, except perhaps for Nivelle, who paraded his intentions through the salons of London in the Spring of 1917.[46] Haig himself kept a diary full of sensitive information while on active service, a privilege denied to his men by King's Regulations under threat of court martial.

There was, however, another side to the rôle of the press, and one which was ultimately more important to the prosecution of the war. Despite the inadequacies and imperfections of government control, the press undoubtedly helped to sustain the war effort. 'The press has done more than its share to win this war,' wrote the soldier-poet Gilbert Frankau, without intended irony, in 1918.[47] There were two reasons for this.

The first was that the press in general, and the mass circulation dailies and their owners in particular, believed newspapers had a duty to maintain civilian morale at home and support for the army abroad. This made censorship virtually unnecessary. The results are clear.

Belief in the justice of Britain's cause was a principal source of both civilian and military morale.[48] The press did nothing to undermine this and much to enhance it. Newspapers offered no challenge to the war's perceived legitimacy. They denied a platform to individuals and groups who did. They were hostile to aliens, pacifists, conscientious objectors, socialists, strikers and other 'shirkers' and contributed to an atmosphere which made it difficult during the second half of the war for dissenters to rent premises for their meetings or to hold meetings outdoors without fear of violent disruption.

The press viewed the war – especially the relationship between civil and military power – in simplistic terms. The rôle of politicians was to take all steps necessary to provide the army with everything needed to win the war and then stand back and allow the soldiers to get on with it. 'Moderation' became regarded as a kind of treason. The press's mounting hostility to Asquith was occasioned by his alleged inability to take the war seriously. The spirit of criticism with which the press greeted his actions was entirely absent from its

---

43. See above, p. 152.
44. See M. and E. Brock, eds., *H.H. Asquith. Letters to Venetia Stanley* (Oxford, Oxford University Press, 1982).
45. See above, p. 45.
46. Sir E.L. Spears, *Prelude to Victory* (London, Jonathan Cape, 1939), p. 41.
47. G. Frankau, 'The Other Side' (first published 1918). I owe this reference to Dr. R.W. Bushaway.
48. This point is developed below.

treatment of the military. With the exception of the Australian journalist Keith Murdoch's attempt to expose and discredit the handling of the Gallipoli campaign, which included a personal attack on Sir Ian Hamilton, the press barely questioned the military conduct of the war. This had important consequences.

When the war began the army treated the press with suspicion and contempt. Even accredited war correspondents were allowed nowhere near the front until May 1915. But this attitude did not last. The High Command gradually realized the advantages of a 'favourable press' and took steps to cultivate journalists and newspaper magnates. No one understood the need better than Haig, who possessed a degree of political shrewdness which his many detractors have consistently failed to appreciate. A sort of military lobby system ensued. Senior officers met and briefed correspondents. Journalists and other 'opinion-formers' were taken on specially-arranged 'Cook's tours' of the trenches under the supervision of 'conducting officers' who were carefully instructed in the proper management of their charges. A cosy intimacy and community of purpose was engendered. 'I must say that the correspondents have played up splendidly,' Haig wrote to his wife on 18 November 1916, and commended Northcliffe for being 'such a help ... to the Army and myself'.[49]

The General Staff view of the progress of the war was retailed to the public without demur. Although casualty lists were published, there was no proper accounting, no attempt to measure men lost against ground gained or damage done to the enemy. German casualties were consistently exaggerated. A curtain of unreality descended between the war and public perceptions of it. A *Times* headline describing the first day on the Somme read 'The Day Goes Well'.[50] However reprehensible this may appear in retrospect, and whatever its long-term effects,[51] there can be little doubt that in the short term it prevented a more serious erosion of morale than that which actually occurred in the final two years of the war.

The second reason for the press's 'positive' contribution to the maintenance of civilian morale lay as much in its inability as in its unwillingness to convey the true nature of the war. Although the innovative editorship of W. T. Stead at the *Pall Mall Gazette* in the 1880s ushered in an era of 'new journalism', later taken up by Northcliffe's *Daily Mail*, with its use of banner headlines, photographs and contrived sensation, the British press remained throughout the Great War an essentially 'cool' medium. Even popular newspapers could hardly be described as populist. Few concessions were made to the idea of 'mass culture'. Editorials were magisterial and intellectual. Reporting was literary in style and reflective in tone. War news, already hamstrung by the constraints of military censorship, was thus further denuded of impact by the way in which it was presented. The 'message' was lost in a mass of dull verbiage.

Photography did nothing to remedy this situation. Front-line combat photo-journalism of the kind later practised by Robert Capa and Don McCullin was unknown. Photographs of any kind were difficult to come by in the first months of the war. Newspapers fell back on the conventional imagination of the graphic

49. F-M Earl Haig, *The Private Papers of Douglas Haig 1914–1919* ed. R.N.W. Blake (London, Eyre & Spottiswoode, 1952), p. 180.
50. *The Times*, 3 July 1916, p. 10.
51. See below, Chapter 10.

artist for their illustrations.[52] Later photographs were strictly censored. Pictures of British dead and wounded were systematically and ruthlessly excluded. Very few of the Imperial War Museum's collection of 250,000 photographs of the war contain scenes of 'horror' or 'action', though these are the ones that are continually reproduced.[53] The war's imagery was as staid and comforting as its reporting. It would have been a very different story, and a very different war, had television cameras and satellites been invented.

Civilian morale, especially that of the working class, could never be taken for granted. Age-old fears and animosities simmered beneath the surface of events, erupting from time to time in open displays of disapproval and complaint. Strikes were commonplace in all major industries. The strain mounted from mid-1916 onwards. It is not difficult to understand why. The Munitions of War Acts and the Military Service Acts began to bite. Working hours lengthened. The pace of production increased. The progress of the war brought no comfort. All the news was bad: Jutland, Kitchener's death, the Somme's massive casualties. There was no victory in sight. War-weariness set in.

Discontent came to a head in 1917 after a very severe winter in which food and fuel shortages intensified and became harder to bear. A massive wave of industrial unrest broke in the spring. Munitions workers at Barrow struck on 21 March. Two weeks' work was lost. An even more serious and damaging dispute began at a small engineering firm in Rochdale in April. By May it had spread to 48 towns, involving 200,000 men, with the loss of 1.5M working days.

The strikes were ended by a mixture of firmness and concession. Many strike leaders felt the full weight of state power and were arrested and imprisoned for 'impeding the production of war material' according to Regulation 42 of the Defence of the Realm Act. Lloyd George recognized, however, that the workers could not be crushed and that no lasting settlements could be achieved which did not address the substance of the men's grievances. Attacking and isolating strike leaders and placating their men became the basis of the government's tactics for the rest of the war.

None of these strikes was 'official'. They were led by committees of shop stewards. The collaborationist policies of the trades unions' national leaders were often bitterly resented by ordinary working people. It fell to local representatives to articulate their grievances. In some parts of the country, notably Clydeside, the 'shop stewards' movement' had a strong Marxist influence.[54] Scotland Yard and Special Branch worked themselves up into a frenzy of concern about 'socialist agitators' and pressed for draconian measures. Lloyd George was sufficiently perturbed to order a Commission of Inquiry under the Chairmanship of the Minister of Labour, George Barnes. His report made reassuring reading.

Barnes dismissed 'feelings of a revolutionary nature' as a significant cause of the unrest. He offered more pragmatic explanations. Three principal grievances were identified. The first, and most important, was the high price of food and its unequal distribution. Pre-war anxieties about the relationship between food and morale were thus fully justified, and the importance of maintaining an

---

52. See above, p. 27.
53. I am grateful to Lyn Silford of the Imperial War Museum's Department of Photographs for clarifying the nature of the Museum's photographic holdings.
54. For the shop stewards' movement, see J. Hinton, *The First Shop Stewards' Movement* (London, Allen & Unwin, 1973). For a critique, see I. McLean, *The Legend of Red Clydeside* (Edinburgh, John Donald, 1983).

atmosphere of equality of sacrifice clearly demonstrated. The other two major grievances concerned the operation of the Munitions of War and Military Service Acts, and in particular the restrictions imposed upon the mobility of labour by the need for workers to obtain 'leaving certificates' from their employers before they could change jobs. There were also many other lesser and more localized grievances, including housing, the restrictions on drink, industrial fatigue and distrust of the government's post-war intentions, but neither individually nor together did they constitute a rejection of the war or an attempt to undermine its prosecution.

The 'shop stewards' movement' was not only the cutting edge of working-class unrest but also its prisoner. Working-class agitation focused on traditional trade union grievances about the rights of skilled workers, piece rates and free collective bargaining. There was nothing distinctively socialist about these concerns. Many of them were directed as much at other workers as at employers and government. The 'shop stewards' movement' failed – even on Clyde-side – to invest working-class unrest with a serious socialist purpose. Shop stewards were valued for their ability as negotiators and admired for their success in extracting concessions from those in authority. Few of the 'rank and file' showed a willingness to follow them down the road to revolution. Trades unionism was ever an albatross round the neck of British socialism.

At the Labour Party conference in Manchester in January 1917 a resolution in favour of a 'fight to the finish' against Germany was passed by an overwhelming majority. The feeling which this reflected – that whatever else was desirable, the defeat of Germany was essential – was strong and widespread. The feeling was a real one and not just the product of government propaganda and the chauvinist ravings of the press. An appreciation of it is central to an understanding of the resilience of both civilian and military morale.

Perhaps Britain's greatest asset in a war against Germany was Germany herself. The Germans were in many ways the perfect enemy. Their conduct throughout the war seemed almost designed to offend British liberal sensibilities and to galvanize public opinion in support of the war effort.

The impressive and unexpected display of national unity which greeted British entry into the war was itself largely a German creation. German violation of Belgian neutrality must rank as one of the worst political miscalculations of the century. Opposition to British intervention, which enjoyed considerable support on the parliamentary Left and among Liberal newspapers such as the *Manchester Guardian* and the *Daily News*, collapsed overnight in the face of it.

British morale thereafter continued to be fuelled with moral outrage. Whenever it began to flag there was always another German 'atrocity' waiting round the corner ready to refresh the national resolve – the policy of 'frightfulness' towards the civilian populations of France and Belgium, the bombardment of Hartlepool, Scarborough and Whitby, the sinking of the *Lusitania*, the use of poison gas, the execution of Nurse Edith Cavell, the Zeppelin – and, later, the Gotha – bombing raids on civilian targets, unrestricted submarine warfare, the imposition of a punitive peace on Russia and Romania.

The 'justice' of the British cause was an easy case to defend. It never lacked advocates. One of the most impressive things about the war was the degree of support for it found among intellectuals. The post-war attention paid to the views of intellectual dissenters like Gilbert Murray and Bertrand Russell and the

13 Patriotic labour: Ramsay Macdonald sits forlornly on the dockside after British sailors refuse to convey him to Stockholm for the international socialist conference (*Punch, 20 June, 1917*)

enormous influence of the war poets' disillusionment has tended to disguise this. The Great War witnessed no *trahison des clercs*.

Dissent was given no focus on the nation's campuses. Voluntary recruitment and then conscription emptied the universities of their male students. Kitchener's call-to-arms met with a ready response from undergraduates and the younger dons. They supplied thousands of officers to the New Armies as well as providing many of the war's outstanding scientists, engineers and administrators.[55]

The academic community as a whole, like the press, saw its duty to support the war and to bolster morale. Historians led the way. Six members of the Oxford University Faculty of Modern History produced *Why We Are at War, Great Britain's Case*. This was followed by the famous series of 'Oxford Pamphlets'. These were intended to placate the consciences and assuage the doubts of the chattering classes. British intervention was given the seal of academic approval. Traditional academic concern for objectivity was set aside.

The wider intelligentsia also played their part. Major literary figures, such as Bennett, Kipling and Masefield, lent their pens and their reputations to the national effort. The churches gave it their blessing.

Opponents of the war were too weak to breach this formidable wall of support.

Dissent was characterized by its heterogeneity. The voice of Liberal reason was never completely stilled. The formation of the Union of Democratic Control in August 1914 provided a platform for those who believed that British involvement in the war was mistaken – the result of 'secret diplomacy' – and who wished to see a negotiated peace. They looked forward to a 'new era' in which foreign policy would be subjected to democratic control and war would become a thing of the past. The UDC's leaders were distinguished and well connected. They found access to the press comparatively easy. They were listened to. They enjoyed some influence. The post-war Labour Party absorbed many of their ideas and most of their number.[56] But they were not the men to lead an open challenge to established order or to articulate the working-class sense of grievance which became increasingly apparent from 1917 onwards.

Nor were the small band conscientious objectors.[57] The imposition of conscription turned pacifism into a political issue and pacifists into political dissidents. The Military Service Acts anticipated this. They allowed exemption from millitary service on grounds of conscience and established a system of tribunals to vet applications. The Acts' recognition of 'conscientious objection' was in the best tradition of British liberalism. The actual operation of the tribunals was not. The local big-wigs and military representatives who manned them were invariably unsympathetic to the objectors if not openly hostile. Nevertheless, the majority of the 16,500 conscientious objectors co-operated with the tribunal system and 90 per cent eventually accepted some form of alternative service.[58] Only 1,298 refused all service and were imprisoned. The majority of these so-called 'absolutists' were Christians. A few were Socialists. Many were men of

55. Academe and the war is the subject of Stuart Wallace's *War and the Image of Germany. British Academics 1914–1918* (Edinburgh, John Donald, 1988). Appendix 5 provides a list of 'Academics in Wartime Whitehall'.

56. See M. Swartz, *The Union of Democratic Control in British Politics During the First World War* (Oxford, Clarendon Press, 1971).

57. Conscientious objection has attracted a great deal of attention. The best study is M. Ceadel, *Pacifism in Britain 1914–1945* (Oxford, Clarendon Press, 1980). See also D. Boulton, *Objection Overruled* (London, MacGibbon & Kee, 1967), J.W. Graham, *Conscription and Conscience* (London, 1922; USA, Kelley, 1969) and J. Rae, *Conscience and Politics. The British Government and the Conscientious Objector to Military Service, 1916–1919* (London, Oxford University Press, 1970).

58. Ceadel, *Pacifism*, p. 41.

high principle and great moral courage. Some were cranks. All were subjected to treatment which was frequently brutal and occasionally fatal.[59] In retrospect, they exerted a moral influence out of all proportion to their numbers. Posterity has acclaimed them as heroes. Contemporaries were less impressed. 'Conshies' were thoroughly despised.[60] Popular feeling was well summed up in the Representation of the People Act, 1918, which disfranchised them. This remarkable act of spite was, perhaps, somewhat ingenuous. Far from undermining support for the war, conscientious objectors provided convenient whipping boys, useful in bringing society as a whole to a renewed recognition of its obligations. They were, in a perverse way, good for morale.

The same cannot be said for the Irish. The 'condition of Ireland' was one of the British government's greatest concerns when the war broke out. Two of the British Expeditionary Force's six infantry divisions were held back from France for several weeks in anticipation of Irish 'unrest'. But none arose. Instead, Irishmen, north and south, rallied to the cause of 'freedom'. The poisonous issue of Irish Home Rule disappeared temporarily from the centre stage of British politics.[61] Irish units of the 'old' and 'new' armies fought with customary gallantry. Attempts by the Irish Nationalist, Sir Roger Casement, to recruit an Irish Legion from among Irish prisoners of war in Germany was a signal failure. It was all too good to last.

The Military Service Act of January 1916, which introduced conscription for single men, did not apply to Ireland. This was a candid admission of the precariousness of British rule. In Britain 'history' had forged a workable political consensus; in Ireland it had succeeded only in manufacturing conflict. Further proof of this was soon forthcoming.

On Easter Monday 1916 a group of Sinn Féin militants seized the General Post Office in Dublin and proclaimed the Irish Republic. The British response was military and indiscriminate. More than 500 people were killed in five days of heavy fighting, including 100 British soldiers. The self-styled Provisional Government of the Irish Republic surrendered on 29 April. The British Commander-in-Chief, Sir John Maxwell, was left in charge of events for a further two weeks. During that time he had fourteen of the 'rebels' shot. This was a fatal mistake. Their martyrdom changed the course of Irish history. Irish public opinion shifted perceptibly in favour of Sinn Féin. Asquith's subsequent failure to carry Home Rule doomed the parliamentary Nationalists and completed the *débâcle*.[62] There could be no further pretence that this was also Ireland's war.

The consequences for British morale, however, were slight. Irish republicanism found few adherents in England. Those who did exist were soon interned. Irish units in the British Army became the subject of official suspicion, but – on the whole – their conduct gave no cause for alarm. Individual Irishmen, such as the fighter 'ace' 'Mick' Mannock, continued to serve with conspicuous valour.[63]

---

59. Some seventy men died as a result of their treatment in prison. See Graham, *Conscription and Conscience*, p. 312.
60. For a more generous front-line perspective, see S. Rogerson, *Twelve Days* (London, Arthur Barker, 1933), pp. 161–3.
61. See above, p. 106.
62. See above, p. 122.
63. Mannock was not only Irish but also an Irish Nationalist. See J. Dudgeon, *Mick – The Story of Major Edward Mannock, VC* (London, Robert Hale, 1918). A volume entitled *Irish Heroes in the War* was published in 1917 by Everett & Co., with a foreword by the leader of the Irish

Irish exemption from the Military Service Acts did cause resentment, especially in the right-wing press, but this was subsumed in a more general feeling that the Irish were a 'bad lot' who had 'ratted' on the Empire in its hour of need. If the war could not be won with them, it would have to be won without them.

From the middle of 1916 onwards it also became increasingly and painfully apparent that the war could only be won by the British Army. This was no longer the small, elite force of Regulars who had embarked for France in August 1914. It was a mass, citizen army. On the morale of the 'British working man in uniform'[64] the fate of the Empire and of the Entente would ultimately rest.

'The British Working Man in Uniform'

What sustains the morale of soldiers in combat is seen by some as simply inexplicable. At the heart even of Churchill's celebrated tribute to the selfless devotion of ordinary British soldiers during the Great War there lies a sense of wonder and incomprehension.[65] Why do men fight? For soldiers themselves finding an answer to this question, or – more properly, perhaps – to the question 'Why do men stop fighting?' is more than an exercise in metaphysical speculation. It is a practical necessity upon the successful resolution of which may turn victory or defeat.

Some men enjoy war and find in it an excitement and sense of purpose often denied them in civilian life.[66] Most men do not. This is understandable. War is disorientating. It takes you away from the places you know and the people you love to fight for your life in places you do not love against people you do not know. War is boring. Most of it consists of sitting around waiting for orders over which you have no control and whose purpose you do not understand. War is tiring. It tests body, soul and mind to the point of exhaustion and beyond. War is frightening. Fear is its chaperon. Fear of being killed, fear of killing, fear of being blinded, maimed, disfigured, gassed, burned, buried alive, fear of pain, fear of fear.[67] War is also very, very dangerous, modern war especially so. Death is omnipresent. During the Great War it took a thousand forms. It could come from close up or far away, delivered through the primitive brutality of the bayonet or the sophisticated ingenuity of the chemical engineer. It could come slowly through shock, loss of blood, gangrene or quickly through

---

National Party, John Redmond. See also M. MacDonagh, *The Irish at the Front* (London, Hodder & Stoughton, 1916).

64. The phrase, which sums up Kitchener's army for this author, is based on Sir William Orpen's description of the soldiers in the wartime paintings of C.R. Nevinson as 'the British workman in disguise'. See Sir W. Orpen, *The Outline of Art* (London, George Newnes, n.d.), p. 374. I owe this reference to Dr R.W. Bushaway.

65. W.S. Churchill, *The World Crisis 1911–1918* (abridged and revised edition, London, Thornton Butterworth, 1931), pp. 654–5:'. . . no word of complaint ever arose from the fighting troops. No attack however forlorn, however fatal, found them without ardour. No slaughter however desolating prevented them from returning to the charge. No physical conditions however severe deprived their commanders of their obedience and loyalty . . .'

66. See, for example, A.C. Borton, *My Warrior Sons* ed. G. Slater (London, Peter Davies, 1973) and G. Greenwell, *An Infant in Arms: War Letters of a Company Officer, 1914–1918* (London, Dickson & Thompson, 1935). See also N. Nicolson, *Alex. The Life of Field Marshal Earl Alexander of Tunis* (London, Weidenfeld & Nicolson, 1973), pp. 23–46.

67. E.J. Leed, *No Man's Land. Combat and Identity in World War I* (Cambridge, Cambridge University Press, 1979), pp. 163–92 contains a moving analysis of the tragic subject of 'war neuroses'.

the instant annihilation of high explosive. For the front-line infantryman, in particular, there was no escape.[68] His destiny was to lie 'on the litter or in the grave'.[69]

The only rational response to these appalling existential realities is to escape from them. This finds powerful reinforcement from the primeval mechanisms of biology. The purpose of military morale is to get men to stay and die when all reason and every instinct tells them to flee and live. Its essence is the 'organized abnegation of self'.

This was well understood by the pre-war British Regular Army. Morale was its business. The army had evolved principally to satisfy the military needs of the Empire. These called for a small, highly trained force capable of operating with limited resources in environments which were often politically as well as climatically hostile. Its effectiveness was largely a question of morale. The maintenance of this was crucial. It was seen to depend, above all, on the successful inculcation of military values. These were based on regimental pride, leadership by example and discipline.[70]

The most important thing in the life of the Regular soldier was his battalion. This housed him, clothed him, fed him, trained him, chastised him. It contained the friends upon whose support and community he would depend for survival in battle. It was his home. Its history was that of past deeds of heroism to which he was expected to aspire. It became the focus of intense loyalties, sharpened by calculated rivalries with other battalions and other regiments.[71]

The most important man in the battalion was its Commanding Officer. 'There are no bad regiments,' Napoleon asserted, 'only bad Colonels.' Leadership by example began at the top. The Colonel was the 'father' of his regiment. He was expected to set the standards of personal behaviour and professional competence for his subordinate officers. It was not enough that the men should fear him. He had also to win their respect. A good Colonel knew his men individually. He put their welfare before his own and was firm but fair in matters of discipline. 'A fine man, my Colonel,' recalled one Old Contemptible, 'a grand gentleman and a great sportsman. He was the first to the heights of the Aisne and the first to be killed.'[72] Battalion commanders required immense reserves of mental and physical strength and emotional resilience. The war took an enormous toll of them.[73]

The Regular Army's 'Other Ranks' also had their obligations. They were expected to be fit, to know their trade, to take individual responsibility for their actions, to display cheerfulness in adversity and unquestioning obedience at all times. They were kept to these standards by a disciplinary code of

---

68. One of the best contemporary accounts of the infantryman's war is *The War the Infantry Knew 1914–1919* (London, King, 1939), an account of the Royal Welch Fusiliers compiled by one of their medical officers, Captain J.C. Dunn. The book was happily reprinted by Jane's in 1987, with an Introduction by Keith Simpson. J. Ellis, *The Sharp End of War. The Fighting Man in World War II* (Newton Abbot, David & Charles, 1980) is also a vivid and compelling account of combat, which has equal relevance for the Great War.
69. General Omar Bradley, quoted in Ellis, *Sharp End*, p. 52.
70. See Baynes, *Morale, passim*.
71. See the Appendix 'The British Regiment' in B. Farwell, *Queen Victoria's Little Wars* (London, Allen Lane, 1973), pp. 354–63.
72. From a tape recording in the possession of Mrs Helen Higgs.
73. J.L. Jack, *General Jack's Diary* ed. J. Terraine (London, Eyre & Spottiswoode, 1964), pp. 159–260, is a vivid account of the strains of battalion command.

uncompromising severity. Military crime – petty theft, drunkenness, insubordination, misuse of equipment, malingering, untidiness – was met with instant and frequently painful retribution. Cowardice, desertion and sleeping on duty could be capital offences.

Such values and traditions owed little to those of British civilian society. The army's preliminary training was carefully designed to break recruits of their civilian perceptions and to remould them in the army's image. The length of time which recruits were required to enlist, the fact that they tended to come from the most deferential and malleable sections of society and the cultural isolation of overseas service made this a relatively simple proceeding. The Great War, however, was another matter.

Kitchener's decision to raise a mass army was not greeted with universal approbation on the part of his fellow professionals. Henry Wilson was especially critical.[74] His scorn reflected a deep unease felt by the Regular Army towards Kitchener's 'experiment'. The sudden influx of a million civilians from all walks of life threatened to revolutionize the army's sociology and destroy its long-established methods of operation.

The civilians, for their part, were puzzled by the Regular Army. They often came to admire its discipline and its exemplary courage, but there was neither a real understanding of its values nor a desire to share them.[75] This sometimes made for conflict.[76]

The Regular Army's understanding of morale had been acquired through two centuries' practical experience of war. It was not going to be surrendered easily. Much of it was validated by events.

Throughout the war, in élite units such as the 1st and 2nd Royal Welch Fusiliers, regimental pride continued to be instilled. Not only the officers and NCOs but also the men were expected to learn the regimental history and did so.[77] Elsewhere, things were more difficult. The expansion of the army was rapid.[78] By the end of 1915 some regiments had grown ten-fold. The influence of regimental lore became rather diluted by the time it percolated down to the 23rd battalion. But this was not the end of the story. The value of pride in the military community was apparent. Where no traditions existed, they were simply invented. The Royal Flying Corps, the Machine Gun Corps and the Tank Corps, as well as many Dominion infantry battalions, founded new regimental traditions on a functional importance and success in battle which, in most cases, was considerably more recent even than the war itself.

There was also no official relaxation in the expected standards of discipline. The army hierarchy remained convinced that the death penalty was essential to the maintenance of morale.[79] There are reasons to doubt this. Most veterans of the war recall the existence of capital punishment – and the humiliating Field Punishment No 1[80] – with loathing and contempt rather than fear and respect.

74. Sir C. Callwell, *Field-Marshal Sir Henry Wilson, His Life and Diaries* (2 vols., London, Cassell, 1927), I, p. 178.
75. See Sidney Rogerson's 'Foreword' to *General Jack's Diary*, pp. 13–15.
76. See Robert Graves's poem 'Sergeant-Major Money'.
77. R. Graves, *Goodbye to All That* (4th edn, London, Cassell, 1966), pp. 78–9.
78. See above, pp. 155–57.
79. For capital punishment, see A. Babington, *For the Sake of Example: Capital Courts Martial 1914–1920* (London, Leo Cooper: Secker & Warburg, 1983).
80. This consisted of lashing men to a gun-wheel by their wrists and ankles for one hour in the morning and one in the evening for up to twenty-eight days.

Kitchener's men, in particular, were acutely conscious that they had volunteered for military service. They were there of their own accord by deliberate choice. They were deeply resentful of the belief that they could only be kept to their duty by the threat of being shot by their own side for any dereliction of it. Some British troops were exempt from the death penalty. The Australian Government refused to let it be applied to their men. This was a source of irritation and alarm to the High Command, not least to Haig himself. He frequently pointed out the higher incidence of military crime, especially insubordination, drunkenness and absence without leave, in Australian units.[81] But this did not seem to affect their morale or combat efficiency. The ANZAC Corps became used increasingly as 'shock' troops and even Haig was eventually compelled to pay tribute to their contribution as spearhead of the victories of 1918.

Discipline was one of the principal functions of what has been called the army's Formal Command Structure, those successive layers of organization stretching from the front-line soldier, through his company, battalion, brigade, division, corps and army to the Commander-in-Chief at GHQ.[82] This structure was clearly important and could not be ignored. The ordinary soldier received his orders down its chain of command. His superiors exercised their authority in the name of it. The behaviour of all of them was prescribed by its laws and regulations. But it was not the only structure that affected morale. There were other – informal – structures. These owed little to the values and traditions of the Regular Army, but in understanding the morale of Kitchener's men they are equally, if not more, important.

The preparation of the 'common man' for war is a well worn theme of much twentieth-century writing and popular entertainment. The new recruit is first stripped, literally and metaphorically, of his civilian identity. He is examined, classified, allocated, uniformed, tagged and numbered. Foul-mouthed and brutal NCOs then rob him of the last vestiges of individualism and humiliate him into submission and conformity. He becomes a small cog in a great death machine. In battle he is no more than a terrified statistic fighting for survival by someone else's rules in a meaningless, murderous nightmare.

There was more to British experience in the Great War than this. Kitchener's army was one of the most extraordinary there has ever been. It was an army of men who would never normally have contemplated a military 'career': the self-styled social and physical élites of provincial commerce who thronged the Territorial and 'Pals' battalions, working-class intellectuals who had already discovered *The Ragged Trousered Philanthropists*, skilled craftsmen with a keen sense of privilege and self-worth, tough miners proud of their strength and earning power, tee-total Methodists steeped in *The Pilgrim's Progress*, city clerks fired by the lyrics of Francis Thompson. It was an army of ranker poets and Classical scholars, of the self-educated and curious. 'Hallo, Evan, you've got a pretty bloody job,' David Jones commiserated with a fellow private carrying two full latrine buckets. 'Bloody job – bloody job indeed,' came the

81. F-M Earl Haig, *The Private Papers of Douglas Haig* ed. R.N.W. Blake (London, Eyre & Spottiswoode, 1952), pp. 290, 291. Haig's distrust of the Australians went back to the South African War.
82. See Major C.M. St G. Kirke, 'Social Structures in the Peninsular Army', *Journal of the Royal United Services Institute for Defence Studies* (Summer, 1988), p. 66. The whole article is suggestive and I derived much encouragement from it.

unexpected reply. 'The army of Artaxerxes was utterly destroyed for lack of sanitation.'[83] It was, above all, an army of trades unionists.

The volunteers who flocked to Kitchener's call were not social blanks waiting for the army to write its will upon them. They remained remarkably impervious to the 'inculcation of military values'. 'The pride of arms was ... an abiding source of strength in the Regular Army during the early part of the last war,' recalled Lord Moran. 'But it never took root in the citizen force upon which the brunt of the struggle [later fell].'[84] Instead, the 'citizen force' took a perverse pride in being unmilitary. Its self-image was consciously self-deprecating. They were 'Fred Karno's Army',[85] a bunch of cack-handed misfits, a permanent 'awkward squad'. They had chosen to be soldiers, but only for the 'duration'. When the 'lousy war' was over there would be 'no more soldiering' for them.[86]

The consequences of this for morale could have been disastrous. That they were not owed much to the strength of the loyalties which Kitchener's volunteers carried with them into the army from civilian life, and to the new loyalties which evolved in response to the experience of war quite independent of official encouragement.

Chief among these civilian loyalties was, of course, patriotism. This is a concept which disturbs many people. It is easily confused with jingoism, though the two are not the same: patriotism is about love, jingoism about hate. The confusion has resulted in ideological, even aesthetic, suspicion. It is now commonplace to regard patriotism as nothing more than a cynical device through which the interests of the 'masses' are manipulated in favour of 'élites'. For the volunteers of 1914 and 1915, however, it was a very real feeling. Contemporary correspondence leaves little doubt about this.[87]

For the minority of men who were able to put their feelings into words patriotism was a reasoned and coherent idea. Recent research has shown that the response to Kitchener's call-to-arms was not a simple 'knee-jerk' reaction.[88] Many factors were involved. Local economic conditions, the attitudes of employers, the desire to escape the boredom and responsibilities of humdrum lives, peer-group pressure, bravado were all important,[89] but so was the belief that volunteering served a purpose. The peak of voluntary recruitment came not in the immediate aftermath of the outbreak of war but in the middle of September 1914 when dramatic reports of the German advance through France and Belgium first reached the public. Men volunteered because they felt that they were needed and that without them the nation's sovereignty, the liberal values for which it

83. D. Jones, *In Parenthesis* (London, Faber, 1982), p. 207.
84. Lord Moran, *The Anatomy of Courage* (London, Constable, 1945), p. 184.
85. Fred Karno was a music-hall comedian whose act was based on 'imbecility and absurd incompetence', see J. Brophy and E. Partridge, *The Long Trail. Soldiers' Songs and Slang 1914–1918* (London, Sphere, 1969), p. 28. I am indebted to David Betts for a copy of this book.
86. Brophy and Partridge, *Long Trail*, p. 50.
87. For a general collection, see M. Moynihan, ed., *Greater Love – Letters Home 1914–1918* (London, W.H. Allen, 1980). See also E.H.W. Hulse, *Letters Written from the English Front in France between September 1914 and March 1915* (1916) and L. Housman, ed., *War Letters of Fallen Englishmen* (London, Gollancz, 1930).
88. J.M. Osborne, *The Voluntary Recruiting Movement in Britain 1914–1916* (New York, Garland, 1982), especially pp. 73–105.
89. M. Middlebrook, *The First Day on the Somme* (London, Allen Lane, 1971), pp. 1–28, is a vivid portrayal of the mixture of motives.

stood, possibly even its very existence would be overwhelmed by 'German militarism'.[90] This belief was very important. It gave the war meaning. It helped sustain men when they confronted the instinctive individual terrors of the battlefield. Its loss could have a catastrophic effect on morale.[91]

The patriotism of the majority of men who did not articulate their feelings was more subliminal[92] and varied. It is more accurate, perhaps, to speak of 'patriotisms'. This was inevitable in an army where colonial pioneers, men who had travelled the world and tamed the wilderness, rubbed shoulders with Batley weavers who thought folk from Dewsbury had two heads.[93] The public schoolboy infused with a heady mixture of Kiplingesque Imperialism and Christian chivalry viewed things differently from the Northumberland pitman labouring in the dark 600 feet below the North Sea. They may both have been 'patriotic' but the country they loved was not the same place. In the end this did not matter. What was important was that they were each true to what they loved.[94]

The highly localized recruitment pattern of the Kitchener armies, deliberately cultivated by the Voluntary Recruiting Movement, tapped this rich vein of local patriotisms. Not only individuals but also entire communities were recruited. There were dockers' battalions, clerks' battalions, public schools' battalions, transport workers' battalions, sportsmen's battlions, 'City' battalions and 'Pals'' battalions. There was even a stockbrokers' battalion. There was no place and no need for the inculcation of traditional regimental pride.

These patriotisms were the product of centuries of British history. They were not easily eroded. They certainly survived the war. Among a dwindling band of veterans they endure still. They gave to the Kitchener armies before the Somme an aspect of crusading ardour seen in no British army since Cromwell's Ironsides. This did not endure. No one can pretend that things were the same after the Somme.[95] But neither should one assume a descent into cynicism and disillusionment.[96] Rather the mood became one of stoical resignation and dogged determination, best captured by the war's most faithful interpreter, the cartoonist Bruce Bairnsfather.[97]

Idealism and combat efficiency are not necessarily connected. After the

90. This point is developed below, Chapter 10.
91. Siegfried Sassoon's famous Letter of Protest against the continuance of the war was occasioned by his belief that 'this War, upon which I embarked as a war of defence and liberation, has now become a war of aggression and conquest'. *Siegfried's Journey, 1916–1920* (London, Faber & Faber, 1945) p. 53.
92. F. Scott Fitzgerald, *Tender is the Night* (Harmondsworth, Penguin, 1958), p. 125, is suggestive.
93. This conceit is based on Rogerson's *Twelve Days*, an account of the 2nd West Yorks (which had several 'colonial' officers) and a lifetime's observation of English parochial rivalries.
94. P. Parker, *The Old Lie: the Great War and the Public-School Ethos* (London, Constable, 1987), pp. 16–17, gives the astonishing casualty figures suffered by many public schools. The book, as a whole, is bitter in tone and seems to me to overstate the case against public school militarism.
95. C.E. Carrington, 'Kitchener's Army: The Somme and after', *Journal of the Royal United Services Institute for Defence Studies*, CXXIII (1978), pp. 15–20.
96. This point is explored further below, Chapter 10.
97. For a collection of Bairnsfather's cartoons, see T. and V. Holt, comps. and eds., *The Best of Fragments from France* (Cheltenham, Phin Publishing, 1978). See also T. and V. Holt, *In Search of the Better 'Ole. The Life of Bruce Bairnsfather* (Portsmouth, Milestone Publications, 1985).

Somme the BEF became less idealistic but more combat efficient. The moral resilience which made this possible came increasingly to be derived from values emanating from the circumstances of the war itself. These circumstances were not new to the working class.

The British working class was well adapted to the challenge of war. This owed nothing to its supposed 'militarization'.[98] It owed everything to its sense of community, its social cohesiveness, its capacity for endurance. The predominant values of the working class were very similar to those of front-line soldiers and for the same reason: solidarity in adversity. For the working class the trenches were a familiar and recognizable environment.[99] Material poverty, physical hardship, unpredictable and disruptive authority were already facts of life. The 'strategy' for surviving them was equally tried and tested. Sharing, comradeship, conformity to social norms, self-deprecating humour and cheery vulgarity proved their utility in war as they had in peace. The strike was no longer available, but traditional trade union practices of the 'go slow' ('ca'canny'), the 'work to rule' and 'live and let live' could still be used to restrain the over-zealous, circumvent the intentions of higher authority and soften the brutalities of war.[100]

Working-class solidarity was the product of shared experience and the need for mutual support. So, too, was that of the soldier. Military solidarity was felt at many levels of the army's formal command structure. Divisional, battalion and company loyalties were undoubtedly important, those to army, corps and, perhaps, brigade less so. But the most important loyalties of all were forged where the shared experience was most intense and the need for mutual support most compelling. This was among small informal and functional groups: men who worked together, played together, ate together, slept together and, but for one another's help, would certainly die together.

The investigations of American military sociologists have long since identified the formation and cohesion of these 'primary groups' as vital to combat morale.[101] Modern military training is based on them. During the last two years of the Great War, when idealism alone was no longer enough and the casualties mounted with no end in sight, they became the strongest element in the BEF's morale. Comradeship made the war's privations and dangers bearable. For some, it made the war worthwhile. Veterans remember the intensity of its loyalties and mourn its loss. Some have written about it with embarrassing candour.[102] Men like Sassoon and Owen returned to the front when they need not have done, and after they had lost all faith in the war's higher purposes, because of its force. It cost Owen his life.

The army hierarchy showed a poor understanding of the importance of 'primary group membership'. Rather, they tended to regard it as subversive of military authority. This was understandable. Intense loyalties produce intense

98. See above, p. 179.
99. I am grateful to Dr R.W. Bushaway for suggesting this line of thought and hope that one day he will find the time to write up his own ideas on the subject at greater length than is possible here.
100. Ashworth, *Trench Warfare*, is a brilliant study of the relationship between these values and the war.
101. Serious research began with S.L.A. Marshall, *Men Against Fire* (New York, William Morrow, 1947). See also A.L. George, *The Chinese Communist Army in Action* (New York, Columbia University Press, 1967).
102. Rogerson, *Twelve Days*, pp. 59–60.

animosities. Many of these were directed towards the army itself. Regimental officers were hostile to the Staff. Ordinary infantrymen reserved a special venom for the 'specialists', especially trench mortar men, who appeared intermittently in the front line, stayed just long enough to bombard the Germans and then departed swiftly, leaving the trench's 'innocent' occupants to suffer the inevitable retaliation.[103] All loathed the disembodied 'them', whose orders brought frequent misery and confusion. The army's attitude, however, was also misconceived. The morale which 'primary group membership' generated may have made casualties easier to bear, but it also made them more keenly felt. The result was hatred of the enemy and a thirst for revenge. This was entirely suited to the intentions of the High Command.[104] The strength of these feelings has often been overlooked in many modern accounts of the war which emphasize only the community of suffering between front-line soldiers of both sides.

Besides comradeship, the other key element in the human dynamics of the 'primary group' was leadership. Here, the army hierarchy was on firmer ground. The Regular Army entered the war with a clear idea of what was expected of its officers. They were to be gentlemen. They were to put the welfare of their men before their own. And they were to lead by example.

This stereotype had its faults. It tended to place 'character' above 'technical ability'. There was a heavy price to pay for this, especially in the early stages of the war. Young officers often made themselves too conspicuous. They committed foolhardy acts of courage which frequently got them killed and jeopardized the lives of their men.[105] The stereotype also placed too much responsibility on officers. The leadership potential of Non Commissioned Officers was neglected. Their quality became a cause for concern as early as 1915. The establishment of training schools in all commands after February 1916 did something to remedy this,[106] but British NCOs certainly remained inferior to their German counterparts and never attained anything like the degree of professional authority of modern Royal Marine or Parachute Regiment NCOs whose performance was such a feature of the Falklands War. 'Other Ranks' were regarded almost as children. They were molly-coddled and denied the exercise of initiative. As a result, when their officers were killed, they were often at a loss how to act. Attacks stalled or fell back.[107]

Despite this, the stereotype had many virtues. These outweighed its defects. It ensured, above all, that the British army avoided the 'managerial style' of leadership which cost the Americans so dearly in Vietnam. British regimental officers lived too close to their men to regard them as 'assets'. They shared the same privations and dangers. They were the caring face of authority. This was vital for morale. Quite simply, British soldiers continued to follow because they continued to be led.

This vindication of the traditional stereotype does not mean that the officer corps remained unchanged throughout the war. It did not. This often seems

---

103. Ashworth, *Trench Warfare*, pp. 82–3.
104. *op. cit.*, pp. 176–203, it is argued that the High Command's 'raiding policy' was deliberately designed to maintain the 'martial spirit' by provoking the desire for revenge and retaliation. There is no doubt that unsuccessful trench raids had a damaging short-term effect on morale.
105. See the comments recorded by the Reverend Andrew Clark, *Echoes of the Great War*, pp. 87–8.
106. B. Williams, *Raising and Training the New Armies* (London, Constable, 1918), pp. 118–19.
107. See above, p. 171.

barely to have been noticed. The war has become embalmed in a public-school idiom. R.C. Sherriff has a lot to answer for.[108] In fact, there is little evidence to show that the Territorial Army and the New Army chose to recruit public schoolboys as officers out of preference. Even if they did, there were simply not enough to go round. The officer corps was certainly never 'democratized'. Working-class officers were very few and far between. But it attained a degree of professional competence and technical ability to go with its courage. This was a necessary response to the problems which the war presented. It was recognized in February 1916 by the decision that henceforward temporary commissions would only be granted to men who had served in the ranks.[109] Officers became less conspicuous. They began to wear the same uniform as their men, to carry rifles instead of pistols and canes, and to hide their insignia of rank.[110] Their casualty rate fell.[111] They became wise in the ways of war and fit to command the men in their charge.

The Regular Army saw the maintenance of morale as a regimental problem. The rôle of High Command was ill defined and little understood. Bernard Montgomery complained that he had served on the Western Front throughout the Great War under two Commanders-in-Chief, French and Haig, and had never laid eyes on either of them. This was, perhaps, surprising in the case of French, who liked to 'get around the army'.[112] It is less surprising in the case of Haig. His army was vast. He had no talent as a showman. He preferred to exercise his influence and authority through his subordinates along the chain of command. Unlike Montgomery, he made no attempt to impose his personality on his troops direct. 'No doubt Haig's character did influence those immediately around him,' argued Lord Moran. 'But we in France knew nothing of [him] . . . with us [he] was not even a legend.'[113]

If the High Command contributed little in terms of 'charisma' to the maintenance of morale, its contribution in other respects was immense. It is difficult to see how morale could have been maintained for five minutes without Staff work of a very high order. The British Army Staff during the Great War has had a bad press. It has been little studied. The first thing to notice about it is its size. It was very small. There were only 300 officers on the General Headquarters Staff at Montreuil, with a further 240 in the outlying Directorates.[114] A division had six Staff officers, a brigade two.[115] They all lived lives of wearisome endeavour, working long hours under tremendous pressure. Many broke under the strain.[116] Their achievement was to construct and operate an administrative system of great complexity and remarkable efficiency.

108. R.C. Sherriff, *Journey's End* (1928) is a play about public school officers. It ran for 594 performances when first staged and was later made into a successful film. It was recently revived. See also R.C. Sherriff, 'The English Public Schools in the War', in G.A. Panichas, ed., *The Promise of Greatness* (London, Cassell, 1968).
109. Williams, *New Armies*, pp. 98–9.
110. See, for example, Jack, *General Jack's Diary*, p. 233.
111. Winter, *Great War and the British People*, p. 87.
112. See above, p. 28.
113. Moran, *Anatomy of Courage*, pp. 203–4.
114. 'GSO', *G.H.Q. (Montreuil-sur-Mer)* (London, Philip Allan, 1920), pp. 35–6.
115. Williams, *New Armies*, p. 111.
116. J. Charteris, *At GHQ* (London, Cassell, 1931), p. 244. For Charteris's working day, see pp. 74, 131. Williams, *New Armies*, pp. 111–12, lists the considerable duties of a Staff Captain.

This system kept the troops well fed.[117] It supplied them with the huge quantities of stores and ammunition they needed when they were in the line and arranged their accommodation and entertainment when they were resting. It supervised their 'relief' and leave arrangements.[118] It organized refresher courses and training schools for an array of military skills. It brought the best available medical attention within reach of the battlefield.[119] It salvaged the debris of war and re-cycled it. It employed a direct labour force of 270,000 men, including tens of thousands of Chinese coolies.[120] It grew and cut timber, printed millions of maps, forecast the weather, chastised the wrongdoer, buried the dead. It carried the precious mail from home. And it did all these things well.

The positive benefits to morale of this administrative triumph must be set against the darker side of the High Command: the willingness to incur casualties for training purposes, the stubborn insistence in holding captured ground irrespective of its tactical value, the waste of irreplaceable trained troops by persisting in the continuation of offensives long past their usefulness. These were damaging to morale. 'The secret of success in war is success,' wrote Lord Moran.[121] Too often the BEF was expected to maintain its morale on a diet of failure.

How good was the army's morale? The final answer must be 'good enough'. There is abundant evidence of the problems. There were 25,000 courts martial for absence without leave, 20,000 for disobedience and insubordination and 4,000 for self-inflicted wounds. Drunkenness was rife. More than 3,000 men were sentenced to death, mostly for cowardice, desertion in the face of the enemy or sleeping on duty but sometimes for 'civil' crimes such as murder and rape: 346 were actually executed.[122] Discipline in front-line infantry regiments did break down from time to time with the resort to extreme measures of summary execution in order to quell panic and restore order.[123] There were two periods of particular concern. The first was in the winter of 1914–15, when an army psychologically and materially unprepared for positional warfare, had to endure some of the worst physical miseries, including the agonizing 'trench foot'. The second was in the winter of 1917–18 after two years' savage fighting which brought unprecedented casualties and no victory. The incidence of 'crime' rose alarmingly. The spectre of Bolshevism danced before the High Command. An increasing proportion of a diminishing manpower was devoted to 'policing' the army. But there was no mutiny. The few major outbreaks of collective indiscipline took place away from the front line in base camps and workshops, where the solidarities and imperatives of 'primary group membership'

117. Rogerson, *Twelve Days*, pp. 140–1.
118. It was recognized that constant exposure to front-line duties was destructive of morale. A typical pattern was to spend four days in the front line, four in support, eight in reserve, with the remainder of the month 'in rest'. 'Rest' often involved large amounts of physical effort.
119. J. Keegan, *The Face of Battle* (London, Jonathan Cape, 1976), pp. 266–7, gives a typically incisive summary. See also L. MacDonald, *The Roses of No Man's Land* (London, Michael Joseph, 1980).
120. See M. Summerskill, *China on the Western Front: Britain's Chinese Work Force in the First World War* (London, Michael Summerskill, 1982).
121. Moran, *Anatomy of Courage*, p. 207.
122. Wilson, 'Morale and discipline of the BEF', pp. 50, 59.
123. See, for example, F.P. Crozier, *A Brass Hat in No Man's Land* (London, Jonathan Cape, 1930), pp. 109–10, and Jack, *General Jack's Diary*, pp. 277–8.

did not apply, or after the conclusion of hostilities.[124] So long as the war lasted the majority of British soldiers obeyed their superior officers, kept faith with their mates and saw it through.

124. See D. Gill and G. Dallas, 'Mutiny at Etaples Base in 1917', *Past and Present*, LXIX (1975), pp. 88–112, and A. Killick, *Mutiny! The Story of the Calais Mutiny, 1918* (Brighton, n.d.) See also A. Rothstein, *The Soldiers' Strikes of 1919* (London, Macmillan, 1980).

10

Values and Ideas[1]

I had entered the holocaust still childish and I emerged
tempered by my experience, but with my illusions intact,
neither shattered nor cynical.

The Earl of Avon[2]

No difference between victors and vanquished. A foolish fable.
The Germans didn't believe it after 1918. We shouldn't have
believed it if they had won. We shan't believe [it] if they win
next time.

Hugh Dalton[3]

This book began with the casualties.[4] It must end with the poets. The Great War
is unique in being apprehended and remembered chiefly through its poetry.
Poets had always written about war, but it was not until the Great War that
there were 'war poets'. Their work is seen not only as a landmark in the history
of literature,[5] but also as a valuable source of insight into the history of the war.
The validity of this is much disputed.[6]

It is true that a long process of literary selection has brought to prominence
poets whose work may not only be unrepresentative of general attitudes
towards the war but also unrepresentative of the bulk of its poetry as well.[7]
'Bulk' is the appropriate word. One of the most notable features of the war's
poetry is its volume. The public demand for poetry and its popularity as
a medium of expression ran at unprecedented levels. Catherine Reilly has

1. The best general account is still A. Marwick, *The Deluge. British Society and the First World
   War* (London, Bodley Head, 1965; Harmondsworth, Penguin, 1967). In a lighter vein, E.S.
   Turner's *Dear Old Blighty* (London, Michael Joseph, 1980) contains a feast of follies.
2. The Earl of Avon, *Another World 1897–1917* (London, Allen Lane, 1976), p. 150.
3. Quoted in B. Pimlott, *Hugh Dalton* (London, Cape, 1985), p. 253.
4. See above, p. 1.
5. For this, see P. Fussell, *The Great War and Modern Memory* (Oxford, Oxford University
   Press, 1975). Fussell argues that the war created a new kind of literature, characteristic of
   twentieth-century writing since.
6. See, for example, A.J.P. Taylor, *English History 1914–1945* (Harmondsworth, Pelican,
   1970), p. 96 and J. Terraine, 'Introduction' to G. Greenwell, *An Infant in Arms* (London,
   Allen Lane, 1972), p. xiii. For war literature in general, see D. Jerrold, *The Lie About the War*
   (London, Faber & Faber, 1930); C. Barnett, 'A Military Historian's View of the Great War', in
   Essays by Divers Hands, XXXVI (1970), pp. 1–18 and 'Of Horrors and Scapegoats. Ending
   World War I Legends', *Encounter*, L (1978), pp. 66–74.
7. For a more representative selection, with a historical sense of chronology, see D. Hibberd and
   J. Onions, eds., *Poetry of the Great War: An Anthology* (London, Macmillan, 1986).

identified 2,225 poets who were published between 1914 and 1918.[8] The most popular at the time, John Oxenham, is now entirely forgotten. Among those who later emerged as major figures, Owen was unknown and largely unread during the war, Sassoon barely known and only marginally more widely read.

It is also true that many anthologies have selected their material not on the criterion of representativeness or even of literary merit but in order to serve the needs of their period's dominant mythology. In the case of anthologies compiled during the war and in its immediate aftermath this was the mythology of 'heroism' and the 'just war'.[9] In the case of later anthologies, especially those compiled during periods of political idealism like the 1930s and 1960s, it was the mythology of the poet as a 'warning voice' recalling men to a recognition of their common humanity amid purposeless violence.[10]

There is no doubt that these later anthologies have helped shape modern perceptions of the war. There is also no doubt that they have misled. They have often been arranged so as to portray the development of attitudes towards the war as a progression from idealism, through experience, to realism, disillusionment and protest.[11] This model fits quite well – though no more than that – the military career and work of Siegfried Sassoon,[12] but in general it is untenable. To be sustained it requires not only a highly selective choice of poets but also a complete disregard for chronology.[13]

'Idealistic' poems were written long after 1914, indeed long after familiarity with what Gilbert Frankau called 'This loathliest task of murderous servitude' became the daily lot of the 'citizen army'. Rupert Brooke's lyrics lost none of their popularity or power to move. His collection *1914 & other Poems*, which included 'Peace' and 'The Soldier', first published in May 1915, went through twenty-three impressions by the end of the war, twelve of which appeared after the opening of the Somme offensive. The war did not end on the muddy slopes of Passchendaele. During 1918 there was a marked revival of idealism and patriotic endeavour in the aftermath of the German Spring Offensive. This is almost entirely ignored in most anthologies.[14]

'Realistic' poems, which did not flinch from an unsentimental depiction of the horrors of war, were also written before the Somme, indeed even before the war

8. See C. Reilly, *English Poetry of the First World War: A Bibliography* (London, Prior, 1978). Many of these poets were women, see C. Reilly, *Scars Upon My Heart. Women's Poetry and Verse of the First World War* (London, Virago, 1981).

9. See, for example, E.B. Osborn, *The Muse in Arms* (London, John Murray, 1917) and J. Trotter, *Valour and Vision: Poems of the War 1914–1918* (London, Longmans, 1920).

10. See, for example, B. Gardner, *Up the Line to Death* (London, Methuen, 1964) and I.M. Parsons, *Men Who March Away* (London, Heinemann, 1965).

11. Parsons's *Men Who March Away* is divided into sections entitled 'Visions of Glory', 'The Bitter Truth', 'No More Jokes', 'The Pity of War', etc.

12. For Sassoon, see *Collected Poems 1908–1956* (London, Faber & Faber, 1961), *Memoirs of an Infantry Officer* (London, Faber & Faber, 1932), and *Siegfried's Journey 1916–1920* (London, Faber & Faber, 1945). Sassoon's war did not end with his famous 'Protest'. He returned to his regiment and saw out the war on active service.

13. See Hibberd and Onions, *Poetry of the Great War*, p. 4.

14. This is, perhaps, understandable. The last year of the war is the least reflected in the war's poetry and prose. It was the only year of the war that did not produce a great memoir. The majority of the war's most famous memorialists were either dead, *hors de combat* or otherwise silent by 1918.

began.[15] 'Realistic' imagery and 'anti-war' sentiments were not synonymous. Some of the war's most 'realistic' poets, not least Robert Graves, were counted among those who were determined to carry the war through to a successful conclusion. The number of poems that were overtly critical of the military conduct of the war was very few, perhaps no more than Sassoon's 'The March-Past' and 'The General'. 'Protest' was more often directed at those who were inhibiting rather than encouraging prosecution of the war – strikers, pacifists and 'shirkers', both civilian and military.[16]

These criticisms do not, however, lessen the importance of the war's poetry as a whole. They merely emphasize the complexity and diversity of the feelings which it reflects. They also demonstrate the gulf between many contemporary perceptions of the war and those which have commonly obtained since. These, too, were a product of the war and cannot be excluded from any assessment of it.

The Last Crusade

The Great War is rarely remembered as a conflict of ideologies. Correlli Barnett summarized the feelings of many people when he wrote that 'the First World War had causes, but no objectives'.[17] This is understandable. It is now virtually impossible to view the First World War other than through the experience of the Second. For the British this experience was much more satisfactory than that of the First. Its memory continues to evoke both nostalgia and pride. It was a war which the British people did not seek and which their government tried strenuously to avoid, but one – once embarked upon – which they themselves wanted to win, if necessary 'at all costs'. The country united behind issues which appeared overwhelming and clear-cut: good versus evil, humane decency versus murderous barbarity, national survival versus national extinction. It was also a war with a happy ending. Abroad, a despicable régime was utterly crushed. The liberation of Buchenwald and Belsen, the revelations of Dachau and Auschwitz set the seal of moral approval on a military triumph. At home, the 'people's war' was rewarded with a 'people's peace' which promised full employment and 'fair shares for all'.[18] The exhilaration of it has disguised the war's darker side: the long and dispiriting chain of British military defeats with which it began, the moral ambiguities of some of the methods with which it was prosecuted, the disintegration of British power and the division and enslavement of much of Europe which followed it. It has also disguised the moral imperatives of the earlier struggle. For many, this, too, was a 'noble crusade'.

The Great War has been described as the 'Holy War of English Liberal idealism'.[19] There is much truth in this. It is richly ironic. The very idea of war was

15. See, for example, M. Van Wyck Smith, *Drummer Hodge. The Poetry of the Anglo-Boer War* (Oxford, Clarendon Press, 1978). I owe my awareness of this interesting body of work to Dr Iain R. Smith.
16. Hibberd and Onions, *Poetry of the Great War*, p. 24.
17 C. Barnett, *The Swordbearers. Studies in Supreme Command in the First World War* (Harmondsworth, Penguin, 1966), p. 35.
18. These comments are based on the magisterial and magnificent last paragraph of Taylor's *English History*, p. 727.
19. See Irene Cooper Willis, *England's Holy War: A Study of English Liberalism During the Great War* (New York, Alfred Knopf, 1928).

anathema to Liberal opinion. Its outbreak was a shock. 'Then suddenly, like a chasm in a smooth road, the war came,' wrote Virginia Woolf.[20] The 'smooth road' was that of 'rational progress'. It seemed to have by-passed war as an instrument of international relations. This view is currently unfashionable. It has been replaced by the portrait of a Europe somehow ready for war after long years of peace and suburban boredom. It is true that Edwardian England was rife with the literature of apocalypse. Salons rang to the 'voices prophesying war'.[21] But 'reason' also has a good case. There was much to encourage cooler spirits. The inauguration of the modern Olympic Games in 1896 reflected a growing belief in the 'community of nations'. Postal agreements, international submarine cables and wireless communication provided practical proof of co-operation and interdependence. The first Hague Conference, in 1901, established an International Court to arbitrate disputes. The second, in 1907, produced a series of conventions designed to limit the horrors of war. There was a marked decline in international tensions after 1912. War seemed increasingly unlikely, at least between civilized nations. And no nation seemed more civilized than Germany.

Responsibility for the war was little doubted. Sir Edward Grey deployed his formidable array of rhetorical skills to prove it.[22] Popular opinion concurred. Wilfred Owen described the war as 'The foul tornado, *centred at Berlin*'.[23] The source was as shocking as the outbreak. Evidence of mounting animosities between Britain and Germany at all levels is not difficult to find.[24] Some Englishmen anticipated war with Germany. A few relished the idea. For many years before the war began Admiral Lord Charles Beresford greeted his officers at breakfast with the toast 'Well, gentlemen, one day nearer the German war'. But Germany was also widely admired, not least as an exemplar of the achievements of 'rational progress' advocated by Liberals or even Fabian Socialists. Germany was 'a civilized country that led the world in many departments of art, and science, and national and municipal life', a speaker in Northampton Market Square reminded his audience on 2 August 1914.[25] Two days later there was no one to listen. German violation of Belgian neutrality robbed her of the last vestiges of moral decency. She became an international pariah. Liberal idealism found a new just cause.

That cause was the defeat of 'militarism'. War was to be waged on the causes of war. It was all terribly English. 'A sour, soiled, crooked old world [was] to be rid of bullies and crooks and reclaimed for straightness, decency, good-nature,' wrote C.E. Montague, formerly of the *Manchester Guardian*.[26] The Germans immediately did their best to live up to the rôle in which they had been cast. The destruction of the great medieval library at Louvain, the shelling of Rheims cathedral, even the murder of Belgian civilian hostages now seem small beer in comparison with the twentieth century's catalogue of inhumanities, but they

20. V. Woolf, 'The Leaning Tower', in *The Moment* (London, Hogarth Press, 1947), p. 111.
21. For a study of these, see I.F. Clarke, *Voices Prophesying War* (London, Oxford University Press, 1966).
22. See above, p. 7, and 5 Hansard, LXV, 1809–1827.
23. W. Owen, '1914'. My emphasis.
24. See P.M. Kennedy, *The Rise of the Anglo-German Antagonism 1860–1914* (London, Allen & Unwin, 1980).
25. *Northampton Chronicle*, 3 August 1914. I owe this reference to Mr Dominic Luke.
26. C.E. Montague, *Disenchantment* (London, Chatto & Windus, 1924), p. 3.

were enough to outrage 'civilized' opinion. Revulsion was not confined to Liberals. Lord Moran recalled the feeling of shock and disbelief which ran through the British Expeditionary Force after the German gas attack at Ypres in April 1915.[27] Little more was heard about the 'land of Bach and Beethoven'. The cultured, rational, modern, progressive, scientific German was dead. The 'Evil Hun' was born.

British public opinion camped throughout the war on the moral high ground. Asquith pitched the first tent. 'I do not believe any nation ever entered into a great controversy ... with a clearer conscience and a stronger conviction that it is fighting ... in the defence of principles the maintenance of which is vital to the civilization of the world,' he told the House of Commons on 6 August 1914.[28] Less famous chambers echoed to the same theme. At a meeting in the Stafford Street Drill Hall in Wolverhampton successive speakers emphasized the 'justice of England's cause', how she had not sought war, but how it was now essential that she play her part – as the personification of 'Liberty' and 'Democracy' – in the defeat of an autocratic Germany which aimed at trampling Europe under a 'vile military dictatorship'. 'In the whole history of England,' declared Father Darmonay, the High Church Vicar of St Peter's, 'she had never gone to war with cleaner hands than she did now.'[29] British propaganda shamelessly exploited this belief.[30] Governments were careful not to compromise it. Clarification and specification of British policy was avoided. There were no further declarations of war aims until January 1918, at a low point for both civilian and military morale, when Lloyd George felt compelled to reiterate before an audience of trades unionists the disinterested idealism of Britain's cause and her renewed determination to effect a just and lasting peace based on the sanctity of treaties, the right of self-determination and the creation of an international organization to 'limit the burden of armaments and diminish the probability of war'.[31]

Liberal idealism also embraced the war for reasons other than the opportunity of establishing a new international order capable of preventing future wars. Chief among these was the idea of 'renewal'. The attractions of this were not confined to Liberals. It had a wide appeal and many meanings.

Poets interpreted renewal as an opportunity to achieve personal fulfilment. Rupert Brooke, a Socialist, captured the feeling in his famous sonnet 'Peace'. War would strip away the petty frustrations and distractions of ordinary life. It would cleanse the soul and exalt the spirit. It would free the intellectual from the enervating habit of introspection, the clerk from the desiccating toil of the office, the workman from the mind-numbing tedium of the factory. In answering its challenge they would discover their true selves among the values that really mattered – love of country, love of duty, love of one's fellow men.

For moralists, too, renewal meant a return to the 'old values'. Everywhere these seemed forgotten or abandoned. They saw about them only decay, decadence and degradation. The upper classes wallowed in luxury and the arrogant display of wealth and neglected their responsibilities. The lower classes were

27. Lord Moran, *Men and Courage* (London, Constable, 1945), p. 60.
28. 5 *Hansard*, LXV, 2079.
29. *Wolverhampton Express and Star*, 10 August 1914.
30. See C. Haste, *Keep the Home Fires Burning. Propaganda in the First World War* (London, Allen Lane, 1977), pp. 77–107.
31. D. Lloyd George, *War Memoirs* (2 vols., London, Odhams, [1938]), II, pp. 1492–3. These war aims also coincided, significantly, with those of the United States.

like dangerous children, concerned only with the pursuit of sensual gratification and the fleeting pleasures of frivolous entertainment.[32] These were the 'evils of too-long peace'. War would be the stern schoolmaster teaching again the lessons of the past to pupils who would have to listen.

For a minority of Milnerite radicals, advocates of 'national organization', renewal meant an increase in the power and authority of the State, the imposition of a greater social discipline through the medium of conscription, closer Imperial co-operation, more efficient exploitation of the Empire's economic resources and an enhanced military capability which would guarantee security to the Empire in a world in which it was threatened not only – or even primarily – by Germany but also by the United States and Japan. War would 'ring out the feud of rich and poor'. The imperial ideal would replace class prejudice and 'ancient forms of party strife'.[33]

For a majority of Liberals – and some Socialists – renewal meant an opportunity to build a new order at home as well as one abroad. This would be based on social reform, political democracy, economic prosperity and education.[34]

These neat, artificial divisions disguise many ambiguities, complexities and contradictions. They also disguise some common themes. One of the most important was the recognition that the price of 'renewal' would be 'sacrifice'.

The speed and fervour with which the British embraced the idea of sacrifice is difficult to understand. It was not the result of mass casualties. It began long before the citizen armies took the field. On 19 September 1914 Lloyd George addressed a gathering of the London Welsh at the Queen's Hall. In an astonishing speech, which encapsulated many of the ideas discussed above, he identified 'the great pinnacle of Sacrifice', 'clad in glittering white' and pointing 'like a rugged finger to Heaven' as one of the 'everlasting things that really matter to a nation'.[35] This struck a chord which resounded throughout the war. 'The Great Sacrifice' became a theme of countless postcards.[36] Poetry was suffused with it. War cemeteries commemorated it.[37]

Religious influence is unmistakable. This is less difficult to understand. If England's cause was just, if the war was a struggle between good and evil, then it followed that England's cause was also God's. The concepts of suffering, redemption and renewal lay at the heart of Christian faith. Their imagery came naturally to people brought up on the Bible, the Book of Common Prayer, the Protestant hymnal and *The Pilgrim's Progress*. The Church, too, for its part, had long made use of the imagery of war. The idea of the 'Christian Soldier' assumed a new meaning and significance. Christ's example was the war's inspiration and justification. 'Greater love hath no man than this, that a man lay

32. Professional football, both those who played it and the hundreds of thousands who watched, were a favourite target of moralists. The football programme was not abandoned until the end of the 1914–15 season. Everton won the Championship and Sheffield United the FA Cup. Competition was not resumed until 1919–20.
33. See above, pp. 128–9.
34. For a scintillating treatment of Liberal ideology, see P.F. Clarke, *Liberals and Social Democrats* (Cambridge, Cambridge University Press,1978).
35. *War Speeches of British Ministers 1914–1916* (London, Unwin, 1917), pp. 211–26.
36. 'The Great Sacrifice' was the title of a painting by James Clark. Colour reproductions were given free as a supplement to the Christmas 1914 edition of the *Graphic*. For postcards, see J. Laffin, *World War I in Postcards* (London, Alan Sutton, 1988).
37. The principal icon of every British war cemetery is the 'Sword of Sacrifice'.

down his life for his friends.'[38] Christ's suffering offered many parallels with that of the soldier. The war's poetry is full of them.[39] 'He stood before me there,' Sassoon wrote of an ordinary Tommy. 'I say that He was Christ.'[40]

The power of these ideas and images to inspire or console was not confined to one particular class or group. Nor were they made to serve one particular view of the war. But for a generation of public schoolboys, perhaps, they were especially deep and poignant. Many public schools had a strong Christian ethos. Their Headmasters were usually clergymen. Chapel was a focal point of school life. The Christianity they taught was of the 'militant' or 'muscular' variety. The concepts of 'sacrifice' and 'service' were very much to the fore. They mingled with similar ideals of self-denial, comradeship and loyalty derived from medieval chivalry and the ethic of team sports to form a potent mixture. The soldier was not only Christ but also Galahad; the war not only a Calvary but also a search for the Holy Grail. To the 'Great Sacrifice' was added the 'Great Adventure' and the 'Great Game'.[41] 'If wounded, Blighty,' Donald Hankey – like Rupert Brooke, an old Rugbeian – shouted to his men as they went over the top, 'if killed, the Resurrection.'[42]

The Uprooting

Belief in the 'just war', 'renewal' and the 'nobility of sacrifice' gave meaning within a traditional framework to unprecedented events. These ideas displayed a remarkable resilience during the war itself. Some erosion was inevitable. Idealism, although often still deeply felt, was spoken of less openly. Sassoon and others protested that the war was no longer just. Cheery athleticism ground to a halt on the rolling hills of Picardy. Even public schoolboys began to distinguish between the battlefield and the sports field. Dribbling footballs across No Man's Land lost its appeal. There was an end to 'innocence'. But there was no mass collapse into cynicism and disillusionment, much less into dissent. The 'war generation' kept faith with the beliefs which had inspired it. The same could not be said for the generation which followed. The war lit a slow fuse under the values which had done most to sustain it. When the explosion came they suffered near mortal damage.

There was another side to the Liberalism which underpinned British belief in the just war. This is the side that is now remembered: chauvinism, racism, bloodlust. The atmosphere of righteous anger in which the war was fought seemed to legitimize behaviour which was the very antithesis of the spirit of

38. Christ's saying to his disciples before the Crucifixion (John 15:13).
39. Hibberd and Onions, *Poetry of the Great War*, p. 17.
40. S. Sassoon, 'The Redeemer', in *The War Poems of Siegfried Sassoon* (London, Faber & Faber, 1983) p. 16.
41. For this, see P. Parker, *The Old Lie: the Great War and the Public School Ethos* (London, Constable, 1987). For the influence of games, see J.A. Mangan, *Athleticism in the Victorian and Edwardian Public Schools* (Cambridge, Cambridge University Press, 1981) and C.R. Veitch, 'Sport and War in the British literature of the First World War, 1914–1918', Unpublished MA thesis, University of Alberta. I owe the last reference to Mr R.M.Y. Shackleton.
42. Quoted in R. Pound, *The Lost Generation* (London, Constable, 1964), pp. 264–5. Hankey was the brother of the Secretary to the War Cabinet and the author of the influential *A Student in Arms* (London, Melrose, 1916). He was killed in action on 12 October 1916 on the Somme.

rational progress. British propaganda against the 'Evil Hun' quickly abandoned itself to an uninhibited campaign of exaggeration and vilification. Respect for the truth became the war's first casualty. The Germans were portrayed as beasts who crucified enemy soldiers, raped nuns and bayoneted pregnant women. They were even rumoured to process their own dead to make fertilizers and glue.[43]

It is hardly surprising that the British public's response was tinged with hysteria. The cry of 'hang the Kaiser' soon went up.[44] There was a demand for 'aliens' to be interned.[45] The architect Charles Rennie Mackintosh's Scottish accent rendered him an object of suspicion to his new Suffolk neighbours and he was forced to 'explain himself' to the authorities.[46] German waiters were dismissed, German shops boycotted, German brass bands silenced. Dachshunds were stoned in the streets. (German Shepherds avoided this by becoming ideologically acceptable 'Alsatians'.) Lord Haldane was harried from public life because of his admiration for German philosophy. Prince Louis of Battenburg suffered the same fate because of his German name. The movements of D.H. Lawrence and his German wife were closely monitored by the police. They were eventually charged with espionage and exiled from Cornwall to prevent their signalling to German submarines in the Atlantic. The Quaker pacifist Arnold Rowntree was similarly accused of placing lights on the family Cocoa works to guide German Zeppelins.[47]

Hysteria, however, was not the only response. The sinking of the liner *Lusitania* in May 1915 was followed by outbreaks of serious public disorder. German shopkeepers were beaten up and their premises ransacked. The shooting down of a Zeppelin at Cuffley in Hertfordshire in October 1915 was greeted with ecstatic cheers from a largely middle-class crowd, their faces radiant with hate.[48] The Gotha bomber raids on London in June 1917 provoked widespread public demand for reprisals against German cities and the formation of a British strategic bombing force.[49] Soldiers were often shocked and disgusted by the ferocity of civilian bellicosity. Siegfried Sassoon was moved to bitterness,[50] C.E. Montague merely to contempt.[51]

Britain entered the war to defend proclaimed principles of international law, but its outbreak was greeted with a display of extreme chauvinism. The Union

43. British soldiers who crossed the Hindenburg Line in 1918 claimed to have found such a 'corpse factory'. The disreputable nature of this propaganda is sometimes said to have occasioned disbelief of claims that a later generation of Germans were building real 'corpse factories'.
44. See, for example, H.A. Stewart, *From Mons to Loos. Being the Diary of a Supply Officer* (Edinburgh & London, Blackwood, 1916), p. 164. It seems strange that wanting to 'hang the Kaiser' should be held against the generation that fought the First World War, when the generation that fought the Second clearly would have hung Hitler and did hang many of his associates, including even those as lowly as radio announcers.
45. Haste, *Keep the Home Fires Burning*, pp. 108–39.
46. T. Howarth, *Charles Rennie Mackintosh and the Modern Movement* (2nd edn, London, Routledge, 1977), p. 196.
47. I owe this to Miss Geraldine Shaw.
48. I owe this to Mr Colin Roberts of St John's College, Oxford, who witnessed the event as a boy and was deeply shocked by it.
49. See B.D. Powers, *Strategy Without Slide Rule. British Air Strategy 1914–1939* (London, Croom Helm, 1976), pp. 75–106.
50. See his poem 'Blighters', *War Poems*, p. 68.
51. Quoted in P. Vansittart, *Voices from the Great War* (London, Cape, 1981), p. 45: 'Hell hath no fury like a non-combatant'.

14 An Ideological War:
The Evil Hun (Drawing
by Edmund J. Sullivan
in *The Kaiser's Garland*)

Flag began to appear everywhere. The 'National' Anthem, previously rather neglected and despised, became obligatory at public entertainments and events.[52] Arrogant assumptions of racial superiority surfaced. These were natural to an Imperial people fed on a diet of a century's cheap victories over native troops. 'Look here, Dick, there is only one way to treat foreigners from Hong Kong to France,' Frank Richards was solemnly advised by one of his mates, 'and that is to knock hell out of them.'[53] Young men of military age were subjected to intense pressure to show their 'patriotism' by joining in the knocking about. This was not confined to the antics of teenage girls with white feathers. Will Dobbie, the York Labour leader, encouraged women to walk on the other side of the road when passing a man not in uniform.[54]

52. Turner, *Dear Old Blighty*, p. 30. For the history and ambiguities of the National Anthem, see K. Robbins, *Nineteenth-Century Britain: England, Scotland and Wales, The Making of a Nation* (Oxford, Oxford University Press, 1989), pp. 169–70.
53. F. Richards, *Old Soldiers Never Die* (London, Faber & Faber, 1933), p. 12.
54. A.J. Peacock, 'History of conscientious objection and its opposition in the city of York', *York Historian*, V (1984), pp. 39–40.

Post-war opinion recoiled from these excesses. Among the very young a pacifist reaction set in even before the war ended. 'To be as slack as you dared on OTC parades, and to take no interest in the war, was considered a mark of enlightenment,' George Orwell recalled of his schooldays at Eton. 'For years after the war, to have any knowledge of or interest in military matters . . . was suspect in "enlightened" circles. . . . I have often laughed to think of that recruiting poster, "What did you do in the Great War, daddy?" . . . and of all the men who must have been lured into the army by [it] and afterwards despised by their children for not being Conscientious Objectors.'[55] In 1933 the 'enlightened circles' of the Oxford Union declared – famously – in favour of the motion 'this House will not fight for King and Country'. This was not necessarily a pacifist statement, but it was clearly a rejection of the perceived values of the Great War. Patriotism was not enough. There had to be a better cause. Some found this in support for the Liberal ideal of the League of Nations. A small number of public schoolboys found it in allegiance to the Soviet Union and International Communism. The 'old lie' succumbed to a new.

No British institution recoiled further from chauvinist excess than the Church of England. The Church had been in the forefront of support for the war. A legend grew up round its involvement. Clergy were accused of having turned their churches into recruiting stations and of having preached hate from their pulpits. Robert Graves's *Goodbye to All That* (1929) pictured Anglican Chaplains as ineffective and cowardly and ignored by the men. Many Anglicans were shocked that the war had not brought men to a closer awareness of God. There had been no religious revival. At the front, the soldiers seemed to find all they needed in fatalism. At home, the bereaved found consolation in spiritualism, which enjoyed a tremendous boom. The Church had failed.

This portrait was, of course, a caricature.[56] It did no justice to the clergy whose outspoken opposition to reprisals and championing of a just peace brought them public ridicule and contempt or to the courageous Chaplains who risked their own lives to bring spiritual succour to the wounded and dying. But the impression that the Church had been fatally compromised remained, that its readiness to see God's cause in the nation's had resulted in the abandonment of its true vocation, an undermining of its authority to speak and be heard on religious and moral issues and a corruption of the Christian message.

The idea of the 'just war' rests, in part, on the observance by combatants of certain restraints on the exercise of violence. It was Germany's willingness to breach these conventions which gave the British war effort much of its moral force. But, by the end of the war, Britain had embraced all the violations which Germany began. How could any war be 'just' which gassed men and starved women and children into submission or killed them in their beds with bombs from the air? How could any war on such a scale, with such horrors and such disruptions even be useful? 'One thing is sure,' wrote Brigadier-General John Charteris. 'The dread of war will be with us so long as we live, like the fear of plague, or even of death.'[57] The over-riding feeling of the British people, looking

---

55. G. Orwell, 'My Country Right or Left', in *The Collected Essays, Journalism and Letters of George Orwell* (4 vols., Harmondsworth, Penguin, 1970), I, p. 589.
56. For a corrective, see A. Wilkinson, *The Church of England and the First World War* (London, SPCK, 1978).
57. J. Charteris, *At GHQ* (London, Cassell, 1931), p. 318.

back on the war, was 'never again'. This feeling was entirely shared by their governments.

By the 1920s the much hoped-for 'renewal' was also looking threadbare. The war disappointed expectations at all levels. 'You can no more take the glamour out of war than you can take it out of sex or the Rolling Stones,' the combat-photographer Tim Page once remarked.[58] This may be true. But there is no doubt that the Western Front created a new moral landscape of war which had no place for chivalry or romance. 'I've said good-bye to Galahad,' wrote Sassoon at the end of 1916.[59] War has never been looked at in the same way since. It was no longer about personal fulfilment or honour or even heroism. It was about survival.

Moralists were also frustrated. There was no return to the 'old values'. On the contrary, the war had unwonted effects. There was a perceptible loosening of sexual constraints. Chaperons disappeared from polite society. 'It is difficult to recall that fifty years ago a young lady of good position could not walk in the street alone without damage to her reputation,' wrote Harold Macmillan. 'To walk down St James's Street was to put her beyond the pale.'[60] These conventions became relaxed during the war. They collapsed entirely in the 1920s. Some increase in sexual permissiveness was probably inevitable. War exposed the fragility of human happiness. Those who did not love today might not be able to love tomorrow. Sex became a celebration of life in the midst of death. Virginity was a depreciating asset. The results were plain to see. The illegitimacy rate soared. The Registrar-General attributed this in 1916 to the 'freedom from home restraints of large numbers of both sexes'.[61] Pregnancies were not the only consequence. Venereal disease was incapacitating the equivalent of an infantry division a day (*c*. 10,000–15,000 men) by 1918.[62] Attempts to control prostitution were inhibited by memory of the widespread opposition to the Contagious Diseases Acts in the 1880s,[63] but a new prag-matism did descend on sexual matters. Contraceptives became much more widely available by the end of the war. The changing climate of opinion made possible the publication of Marie Stopes's prescription for sexual fulfilment, *Married Love*, five days after the opening of the German Spring Offensive.[64]

Manners changed as well as morals. Smoking increased in popularity. The humble 'Woodbine' was one of Britain's war-winning weapons. Men – and women – not only smoked more but also more publicly. Swearing took its first tentative steps down the road to social acceptability. The degree of fleeting financial independence and greater self-respect achieved by women was reflected in fashion. Hemlines shortened. Hair-styles became more practical – and more mannish. Some women even wore trousers. They were

---

58. Before an audience at the Institute for Contemporary Arts, London, 1979.
59. See his poem 'The Poet as Hero', *War Poems*, p. 61.
60. H. Macmillan, *Winds of Change* (London, Macmillan, 1966), p. 103.
61. Quoted in Marwick, *Deluge*, p. 115.
62. I.F.W. Beckett, 'The Nation in Arms, 1914–1918', in I.F.W. Beckett and K. Simpson, eds., *A Nation in Arms. A Social Study of the British Army in the First World War* (Manchester, Manchester University Press, 1985), p. 19.
63. S. Buckley, 'The failure to resolve the problem of venereal disease among the troops in Britain during World War One', in B. Bond and I. Roy, eds., *War and Society: A Yearbook of Military History* (London, Croom Helm, 1977), pp. 65–85.
64. M. Stopes, *Married Love* (London, Putnam's, 1918). It was reprinted four times before the end of the war.

able to enter public houses alone without being thought 'loose'. Make-up ceased to be the prerogative of the whore.

The mood of moral earnestness and the desire for self-improvement so apparent in the Second World War was less marked in the First. London, in particular, was a temple built to indulgence. For most of the war it was a blaze of lights, vital and energetic. The music-hall – vulgar, boisterous and celebratory – widened its appeal across all classes. Theatres were full. Plays were romantic and sentimental, revues sophisticated and frivolous. Night clubs appeared on the social scene. Good food in good restaurants was always available for those who could pay. The Ministry of Food's injunction at the beginning of 1918 to 'eat slowly, you will need less food' was treated with derision in the West End.[65] Troops in the front line dreamed of women who were 'soft, silken and scented'. 'It is not without significance that the song "The girl I love is on a magazine cover" was popular,' recalled Captain Sidney Rogerson.[66] There was a longing for the sensuous. The Western Front bred a hedonism greater even than that against which Edwardian moralists had inveighed. The Great War gave birth not to a new Puritanism but to the Roaring Twenties.

The 'English Prussians', too, suffered a defeat. This is, perhaps, surprising. The war provided much encouragement for them. The nation did become more 'organized'. The power and authority of the State did increase. Conscription was introduced. The Empire did rally to the Mother Country in her hour of need. Former enemies, like Jan Christian Smuts, took their place in the forefront of events. Impressive improvements in industrial productivity and in the exploitation of human and natural resources did occur. British military capability was enhanced. Britain ended the war with the largest army, the largest navy and the largest air force in the world. A community of national purpose did form round the need to defeat Germany. But it was not enough.

These changes were regarded by most people, including most politicians, as temporary expedients.[67] The State achieved no mystical significance. Its machinery of control was rapidly dismembered after the collapse of the Lloyd George coalition in 1922, itself an event which owed much to the persistence of traditional attitudes. Conscription ended in 1920. The basic underlying values of British – and, particularly, English – society underwent no transformation.[68] The British people were not 'militarized'. Wartime excesses of chauvinism, anger and hate became regarded with incredulous embarrassment and were then forgotten. Patience, tolerance and generosity returned.

The war produced no effective instruments of Imperial government. It did, however, increase the self-awareness and self-definition of the great Dominions, especially Australia and Canada. 'I began the war as a colonial,' one veteran declared. 'I ended it as an Australian.'[69] The legend of Australian bravery betrayed by British upper-class incompetence created a corrosive legacy. No Australian troops fought in Europe during the Second World War. The one South African division fought as part of the American Army.

No British institution experienced the 'deluge' of war more than the British

65. See M. MacDonagh, *In London During the Great War* (London, Eyre & Spottiswoode, 1935).
66. S. Rogerson, *Twelve Days* (London, Arthur Barker, 1933), p. 148.
67. See above, p. 193.
68. See above, pp. 12, 191–2.
69. On BBC television, January 1988.

army. None was less affected by it. The army changed enormously during the war,[70] but very few of the changes were carried over into the peace. The greater tactical awareness apparent by 1918 and an understanding of the need to recruit and train technical specialists did survive, but so did the ethos of the pre-war officer corps. The return to colonial policing duties was welcomed. The army could get back to 'real soldiering'.[71]

When the war ended the army's reputation stood higher than at any time in its history. Haig was a national hero. The Christian name 'Douglas' achieved a fleeting popularity. Haig's lying-in-state and funeral in 1928 attracted large and reverent crowds in both London and Edinburgh. This soon changed. The 'mud and blood' school of debunking memoirs which began to appear in large numbers from the end of the 1920s provoked uncomfortable questions about the military conduct of the war. Some veterans required no such encouragement for their scepticism. 'The events of those two years of war had slowly eaten away my faith in the infallibility of authority,' wrote Lord Moran.[72] Publication of the volume of Official History dealing with 'Passchendaele' had to be postponed on the eve of the Second World War lest it should further undermine public confidence in the military before the coming struggle.[73] In the long run the most important British soldier of the Great War was Colonel Blimp.

There can be little doubt that the working class and the nation came closer together as a result of the war, but this owed more to changes in what the ruling élites were prepared to regard as the 'nation' than it did to changes in the attitudes of the working class itself.[74] The British class system did not yield to a 'national' – much less an 'Imperial' – ideal. The class structure was simplified and strengthened by wartime developments. 'Dilution' had the effect of homogenizing working-class experience and of enhancing and consolidating working-class confidence.[75] The working class ended the war not only more powerful and cohesive but also more ambitious than ever before. There was much that it wished to see change. The war left not only a legacy of improvement but also of bitterness – about high prices, long hours, poor housing, unequal access to food, education and opportunity. Its continued membership of the 'moral community of patriotism' would depend on a successful resolution of these complaints.

Liberalism, itself, was soon regarded as one of the war's principal victims. The Liberal party was clearly damaged by the war.[76] There were 261 Liberal MPs in August 1914 and only 163 after the general election of December 1918. The Liberal party's competitors, in contrast, both improved their positions. The Conservative party did especially well out of the war.[77] The issues on which

70. See above, Chapter 7.
71. For the post-war army, see K. Jeffrey, 'The Post-war Army', in Beckett and Simpson, eds., *Nation in Arms*, pp. 211–34.
72. Moran, *Anatomy of Courage*, p. 74.
73. It was finally published in 1948.
74. For this, see B. Waites, *A Class Society at War. England 1914–1918* (Leamington Spa, Berg, 1987) and 'The effect of the First World War on class and status in England, 1919–20', *Journal of Contemporary History*, II (1976), pp. 27–48.
75. See A. Reid, 'Dilution, trade unionism and the state in Britain during the First World War', in S. Tolliday and J. Zeitlin, eds., *Shop Floor Bargaining and the State* (Cambridge, Cambridge University Press, 1985), pp. 46–74.
76. See above, p. 127.
77. See, in particular, J. Stubbs, 'The Impact of the Great War on the Conservative Party', in

pre-war Unionism had floundered – Ireland, Welsh disestablishment, the power of the House of Lords – became things of the past. The Conservative party ceased to be a party of landowners and became a party of businessmen. These may have been 'hard-faced', but they were much more closely attuned to the mood and needs of the electorate. The party was also fortunate that among its post-war leadership were men like Baldwin and Chamberlain who had experienced the war's harrowing losses personally and whose principled determination to render 'sacrifice' worthwhile by building a better world did much to restore Conservatism's moral authority. The Labour party's advance was less spectacular. The war effected few changes in the ideology of Socialism,[78] but improvements in organization and self-confidence were immense.[79] The party began the war as little more than a trade union pressure group which flourished electorally only through the patronizing condescension of the Liberal party. It ended the war as a national party capable of government.

The precise rôle of the war in these developments and their responsibility for the disastrous post-war decline in Liberal electoral support is much disputed.[80] It is also unclear whether the damage sustained by the Liberal party was suffered equally by the Liberalism which underpinned it. Pre-war Liberalism was itself evolving. It had departed considerably from the Gladstonian certainties by 1914.[81] Social Democracy was beckoning even before the war broke out. Liberalism of this kind was not confined to the Liberal party. Many who espoused it found a congenial home in the post-war Labour party, including Lloyd George's ertswhile 'political manager' Christopher Addison.[82] Nor was it confined to parliament. In the realm of ideas Liberalism successfully resisted the challenge of Socialism. In the persons of Keynes and Beveridge it exercised a decisive influence on economic and social policy and was instrumental in the foundation of the post-Second World War Welfare State.

As for the belief in the 'nobility of sacrifice', George Orwell spoke for the post-war generation when he dismissed it in a sentence: '1914–1918 was . . . a meaningless slaughter, and even the men who had been slaughtered were . . . in some way to blame.'[83] By the early 1930s it was commonplace to see the war as 'futile'.[84] The frustrations of the liberal democracies when confronted with the rise of Fascism and the subsequent outbreak of another war did nothing to arrest this trend. The war's enduring images – stretcher-bearers up to their thighs in liquid mud, crocodiles of the blinded like some grim parody of a school procession, soldiers clambering over barbed wire and disappearing into the

---

G. Peele and C. Cook, eds., *The Politics of Reappraisal 1918–1939* (London, Macmillan, 1975), pp. 14–38.

78. See J.M. Winter, *Socialism and the Challenge of War. Ideas and Politics in Britain, 1912–18* (London, Routledge, 1974).

79. See, in particular, R.I. McKibbin, *The Evolution of the Labour Party, 1910–1924* (Oxford, Oxford University Press, 1974).

80. See T. Wilson, *The Downfall of the Liberal Party 1914–1935* (London, Pan, 1968); H.C.G. Matthew, R.I. McKibbin and J.A. Kay, 'The franchise factor and the rise of the Labour party', *English Historical Review*, XCI (1976), pp. 723–53; and M. Hart, 'The Liberals, the war and the franchise', *English Historical Review*, XCVII (1982), pp. 820–32.

81. See P.F. Clarke, *Lancashire and the New Liberalism* (Cambridge, Cambridge University Press, 1971).

82. See above, p. 125.

83. Orwell, 'My Country', p. 589.

84. See C. Barnett, *The Collapse of British Power* (London, Eyre Methuen, 1972), pp. 424–38.

smoke, young men old before their time staring wide-eyed at the camera – provide ready material for anyone from philosophers to pop video producers who wish to make a point about the 'horrors of war'. The comment 'such a waste' is frequently found in the visitors' books at British war cemeteries.[85] Many veterans came to share the view that the war had achieved nothing or that its achievements had been gained at too great a cost or that they had been frittered away. Many more did not. For them the First war as much as the Second was one of freedom's battles. The threat to the 'safety of our homes' was not an insincere rhetorical abstraction.[86] It seemed very real in the spring of 1918, just as it did in 1940. They did not seek the war. They did not doubt that it had to be won. They won it. The only thing worse than a war won is a war lost. They spared us that.

Backwards into the Future?

The Great War was a great event. Its precise effects, however, are difficult to chart. History does not stand still. The world was changing before the war began. Einstein revealed a universe of exploding galaxies and collapsing stars in which the only constant was the speed of light. Freud discovered in the inner space of the human psyche a maelstrom of suppressed desires and violent fantasies remote from traditional assumptions of the rational intellect maximizing pleasure and minimizing pain. Picasso and Kandinsky inaugurated a revolution in the visual arts which captured the dilemma of the individual in the age of the machine. Tsarist autocracy was already exhibiting signs of social and political strain resulting from rapid industrialization. The awesome economic and industrial power of the United States was already apparent. Only the political will was required to make her a 'super-power'. Japan's defeat of Russia in 1905 was the 'French Revolution of Asia'. Britain was not exempt. Her relative industrial decline was already well advanced, the effortless supremacy of the Royal Navy under threat. Edwardian society was not one long garden party on a summer afternoon. Frustration and discontent with the way things were was everywhere apparent.

Much of this was unclear in 1918. To many of those who lived through it the Great War seemed cause rather than effect, putting an emphatic final full stop to a golden age of British domination, of liberalism and humane rationality, and ushering in a new dark age of industrialized brutality, systematic cruelty and mass murder. 'Science With Art Reads Nature's Book,' the Victorians had confidently declared.[87] There now entered the nagging fear that what was written there was the stuff of nightmares.

The war cut a gash, deep and unlovely, across the nation's history. There were few who did not feel that something of infinite value and importance had

---

85. A veteran of the Second War once pointed out such a comment to me in a cemetery on the Somme. Underneath it was written 'No country has the right to demand this of its young men'. Both comments were written by university students. 'How can anyone write this stuff?' he said. ' "No country has the right to demand this of its young men!" If it wasn't for them lads out there, there wouldn't be no bloody England!'
86. The phrase was Haig's. He certainly believed it.
87. From a mosaic in the entrance hall of the Wedgwood Institute, Burslem, Staffordshire. The building's foundation stone was laid by Gladstone in October 1863. It was opened in 1869.

been lost.[88] The look back was wistful and full of regret, the view forward fearful and uncertain. Would anything be the same again? Could the old world be restored? Some thought so. In economic policy there was a headlong flight back into nostalgia for the pre-war order in which sterling was tied to the price of gold and the London money markets ruled the world. Others dreamed of building anew. 'War cannot change,' wrote Lord Moran, 'it exposes.'[89] The Great War had exposed many evils at home and abroad. There was much to do. It was difficult to fit the war into the 'onward march of progress'. The march would have to be resumed all the same.

88. One was Ezra Pound, under whose spell English poetry fell after the war. He dismissed the pre-war world as a 'botched civilization', 'an old bitch gone in the teeth'.
89. Moran, *Men and Courage*, p. 170.

Epilogue[1]

9 p.m. Clouded sky. Subdued moonlight. Air damp.

Diary Entry of Rev. Andrew Clark,
11 November 1918[1]

Have you forgotten yet?

Siegfried Sassoon[2]

The Great War ended with dramatic suddenness. The announcement of an Armistice was greeted at home with ecstatic relief. Factories stopped work. Children were sent home from school. Crowds spilled on to the streets. Social inhibitions were cast aside. Sexual restraint collapsed. It had been a long, long way to Tipperary. Now it was time to rejoice. Death had been dethroned.

The government, too, had much to celebrate. At home, the working class had, after all, proved willing to make 'sacrifices' for the 'common good'. There had been significant improvements in the scale, organization, enterprise and quality of British manufacturing industry. Old industries, such as coal, iron, steel and textiles, had revived. New ones, such as aeroplanes, cars, chemicals and wireless, with a potential for ensuring future national prosperity, had been created. A new spirit of realism had entered industrial relations. 'Tripartism' – the co-operation of business, unions and government – promised a political climate favourable to continued economic regeneration. The 'condition of England' had also improved. The worst extremes of poverty and wealth had been flattened out. The working-class standard of living had risen. Continued partnership with 'patriotic Labour' could be expected. The Lloyd George Coalition submitted itself to the test of public opinion at a General Election on 14 December and received overwhelming approval. Coalition candidates won 472 seats. The Asquithian Liberal party was reduced to a rump. Asquith himself was repudiated by the electors of East Fife. All his senior colleagues were also defeated. Labour won only sixty seats.

Abroad, there was a triumph. Britain ended the war as the most powerful country in the world. Admiral Beatty received the surrender of the German High Seas Fleet on 21 November. The Royal Navy tightened its blockade. Germany was compelled to sign a humiliating peace treaty at Versailles in June 1919. German military power was emasculated. The German Army was limited

---

1. A. Clark, *Echoes of the Great War. The Diary of the Reverend Andrew Clark* ed. J. Munson (Oxford, Oxford University Press, 1985), p. 259.
2. S. Sassoon, 'The Aftermath', in *The War Poems of Siegfried Sassoon* (London, Faber & Faber, 1983) p. 143.

to 100,000 men, with no general staff, no compulsory military service, no tanks, no heavy artillery, no chemical weapons and no aircraft. The German Navy was restricted to surface vessels of less than 10,000 tons. No submarines were to be built. The Saar, heartland of German heavy industry, was subjected to French occupation for fifteen years. The Rhineland became a demilitarized zone. Severe financial indemnities – 'reparations' – were imposed. Britain also exacted her traditional colonial tribute. The German Empire in Africa and the Pacific was dismembered. Britain established an hegemony of the Arabian peninsula and the oil-rich Middle East. The liberal pieties which accompanied the British declaration of war were not forgotten. Tsarist autocracy, the real *bête noire* of pre-war Liberalism, was one of the war's principal victims. So, too, were the Austro-Hungarian and Ottoman empires. 'Self-determination' took their place. New states – Czechoslovakia, Finland, Yugoslavia – were created. Old ones – Estonia, Latvia, Lithuania, Poland – were restored. A League of Nations was established to provide a forum for arbitration and conciliation and render war obsolete as a method of settling international disputes.

The 'price' of all this, when calculated according to the amoral arithmetic of geo-politics, was not 'excessive'. British casualties *were* unprecedented, but the aggregate effect of their demographic consequences was remarkably slight. The well-established pre-war trend towards smaller families was not arrested. The proportion of the population between the ages of 15 and 64 continued to increase. In terms of casualties relative to total strength, Austria-Hungary, France, Germany, Italy, Romania, Russia and Serbia all fared worse than Britain. British territory was not invaded. Britain suffered neither loss of sovreignty nor economic reparations. Her merchant shipping losses were severe, but recovery was swift. The loss of foreign investments was less than one-thirteenth of the total. Some export markets were surrendered, but France and Germany both lost more.

The official British victory celebration took place in London on 19 July 1919. Contingents came from all parts of the Empire. Every race and creed was represented. Africans and Asians, Hindus and Sikhs, Moslems and Jews, Canadians and Australians, black men and white marched in step through the streets of the Imperial capital of the greatest empire the world had ever seen. 'The British Empire seemed firm and solid, strengthened rather than undermined by the experience of war,' recalled Harold Macmillan.[3] It was the end of an era.

Things quickly began to fall apart. The mood of rejoicing was short-lived. It gave way to a numbing contemplation of the human costs of 'victory'. Throughout the 1920s the nation as a whole struggled to come to terms with its bereavement.[4] The response was paradoxical. At the official – and unofficial – level remembrance was ritualized. The Cenotaph[5] in Whitehall was unveiled in 1919, the Shrine of the Unknown Warrior in Westminster Abbey in 1920. The Imperial War Graves Commission began to lay out the 2,000 distinctive British war cemeteries on the Western Front. The tradition of wearing replica blood-red Flanders' poppies – cruelly, made out of paper and

---

3. H. Macmillan, *Winds of Change 1914–1939* (London, Macmillan, 1966), p. 102.
4. See D. Cannadine, 'War and death, grief and mourning in modern Britain', in J. Whaley, ed., *Mirrors of Mortality* (London, Europa, 1981), pp. 187–242.
5. Literally, 'empty tomb', evocative of Christ's resurrection.

wire by disabled soldiers – was established. Every city, every town, almost every village in Britain commissioned its own memorial. So did many railway and insurance companies and factories. Many of the simple street shrines which grew up spontaneously during the war took on a permanent form.

Some people now find the iconography and language of remembrance offensive and insincere and dismiss it as a tasteless manifestation of militarism. This was not perceived at the time. The purpose of remembrance was not to glorify war but to mourn the dead. During the 1920s Armistice Day, with its two-minutes' silence, wreath laying, sounding of the Last Post and Reveille and absence of speechifying evoked profound respect and emotion. As late as the 1930s it was commonplace for men to remove their hats when passing the Cenotaph.

At the personal level the war also provoked another response to bereavement. Among some survivors of the war, and more especially among the younger generation that followed them, the 1920s saw the growth of a self-conscious hedonism, a rejection of Victorian morbidity and a fierce determination to enjoy the good things of life while they lasted. This represented a significant break with the past.

The 'moral community of patriotism' was already showing signs of strain before the war ended. Within a few years it looked completely threadbare. The demobilization of the army was as confused as its recruitment. The pent-up frustrations of four years of war exploded in outbreaks of violent resentment. Many soldiers returned home to poor housing, dead end jobs or no jobs at all. The post-war economic boom soon collapsed, exposing the precarious prosperity of Britain's traditional industrial communities. In February 1919 the miners, railwaymen and transport workers resurrected their pre-war 'triple alliance' which had been threatening the government with a general strike when war broke out in 1914. During the same month tanks, which had played such an important part in the military victories of 1918, were used on the streets of Glasgow to suppress what the government clearly feared was a workers' rising. Industrial relations entered the downward spiral which led to the General Strike and bitter six-months-long miners' strike of 1926. Labour's arch-conciliator, Lloyd George, could do nothing about it. In 1922 he fell victim to the suspicion and hostility of the Conservative backbenches. He was only 59. He never held public office again.

Britain's international position also gave early cause for alarm. The outcome of the Great War undoubtedly resulted in the achievement of some of Britain's principal war aims. The importance of the prevention of a German hegemony of Europe and the preservation of the independence of Belgium should not be underestimated. But Britain's wider aim of ensuring the long-term security of the Empire in a dangerous world was not achieved. On the contrary, it was undermined. The war was extremely costly. Britain ended the war heavily indebted to the United States. Financial necessity dictated reductions in public expenditure. The attempt to remain a major military power was speedily abandoned. The army was reduced to its pre-war size and expectations. More ominously, traditional British concern for the maintenance of maritime supremacy was also sacrificed. At the Washington Naval Conference in 1922 Britain accepted parity in capital ships with the United States and a superiority of only 5 to 3 over the Japanese. The run-down in the number of cruisers and destroyers continued throughout the 1920s. The Royal Navy's ability to police the world was severely compromised.

Germany's humiliation at Versailles destroyed her military power in the short-term but it also encouraged a dangerous spirit of revenge. Hatred of the Versailles Settlement was the one thing that united Germans floundering amid the poisonous animosities of the Weimar Republic. The imposition of economic reparations not only saddled German democracy with a crushing burden but also impeded the recovery of Europe as a whole. The annexation of the German Empire added further to Britain's Imperial obligations without contributing anything material to her resources. British hegemony of the Middle East became a diplomatic and strategic minefield which she could neither abandon nor defuse. The collapse of Tsarist autocracy raised the frightening spectre of Bolshevism and removed the Soviets from normal diplomatic consideration. The dismemberment of the Austro-Hungarian and Ottoman empires left a series of weak successor states, often riven with petty territorial ambitions, which would provide poor counterweights to a resurgent Germany or an expansionist Soviet Union.

Neither the League of Nations nor the Empire offered respite from these uncertainties. The United States Congress repudiated the Covenant of the League of Nations and refused to ratify the Treaty of Versailles. The Soviet Union was not a member of the League, and neither for some years was Germany. The only effective military force available to it was the French Army and this could not always be relied upon. The pomp and circumstance of British Imperialism continued to beguile but it was without substance. The Empire remained a massive drain on Britain's depreciating military power and contributed little to its own defence. The abandonment of the Anglo-Japanese Alliance in 1922 under American pressure was a sinister development, pregnant with danger.

The General Election of 1918 was not only a triumph for Lloyd George but also for Sinn Féin, which won seventy-three seats. Ireland had disavowed the Union. An Irish Free State was officially proclaimed on 6 December 1922. It remained part of the Empire in name only. The 'Third World' also began to stir. The Great War was essentially a European civil war. It struck a damaging blow to European pretensions to superior civilization. 'Natives' became restless with their rôle as political and cultural inferiors. On 10 April 1919 a large crowd gathered at Amritsar in the Punjab in order to demonstrate for Indian independence. Three hundred and seventy nine of them were shot by British troops and another 1,200 injured. The slow unravelling of the 'second British Empire' had begun. The last thing Britain could afford was another war.

Five million soldiers served in the British Army during the Great War. Few of them were untouched by it. For some the war's special comradeship was deeply felt. They could never be truly intimate with anyone who had not shared in it. But this feeling remained private. It was never translated into social or political form. British ex-servicemen's organizations enjoyed little influence. It is difficult to imagine anything more apolitical than the British Legion. The war was a relative experience. Only the dead experienced it absolutely. Frank Richards was a pre-war Regular called back to the colours in 1914.[6] He fought in virtually

6. See above, pp. 17–18.

every major battle on the Western Front, lived side by side with death for four years and suffered nothing worse than piles.[7] Charles Henry Hirst was a Kitchener volunteer. He gave up his job as a barman to join the 1st Barnsley Pals in the Autumn of 1914. His war was a short one. The preliminaries – a camping holiday, followed by a Mediterranean cruise – were not unpleasant. The real business of war began at 7.30 a.m. on 1 July 1916 and ended a few seconds later in a hail of German machine-gun bullets before the village of Serre.[8] Frank Vodrey was a conscript. His father volunteered – over-age – in 1915. His brothers soon followed. Frank was told to stay at home and mind the family shop, but the military authorities were unimpressed by his obligations. During his induction at Whittington Barracks, Lichfield, he was asked which regiment he would like to join. His fellow recruits expressed a preference for famous regiments such as the Black Watch or the Grenadier Guards, possibly because they were the only ones they had heard of, and were sent to join the North Staffords in the Ypres Salient. Frank chose the Royal Engineers and was sent to work on the Palestine Military Railway at Kantara in Egypt. His was the dull routine of lines of communication troops, broken only by sight-seeing, brothel visiting and pilfering from supply trains in the hope of finding something sweet to eat. He was lucky. As he watched the shores of Egypt fade away from the deck of the S.S. *Caledonia* in 1919 he offered up a silent prayer 'Thank God I am leaving in the same condition as when I arrived'.[9] Others were less fortunate. By 1928 the government was issuing 4.2 M disability pensions. Limbless men were a constant reminder of the war's toll for years to come. The war cast a long shadow. As late as the 1960s Coroners' reports regularly drew attention to war service, especially gassing, as a contributory cause of death. Some men were permanently traumatized by their experience.[10] Many more suffered recurring nightmares throughout their lives.[11] The sight of rats or flies, the smell of quicklime or decaying food or even nail varnish could bring back unwonted memories with all the sharp awareness of remembered fear.[12] Three-quarters-of-a-million gave their lives. Many of them also gave their posterity. Some gave their peace of mind. All gave their youth. It was their war. We will remember them.

---

7. See F. Richards, *Old Soldiers Never Die* (London, Faber & Faber, 1933).
8. See J. Cooksey, *Pals. The 13th & 14th Battalions York and Lancaster Regiment. A History of the Two Battalions Raised by Barnsley in World War One* (Barnsley, Barnsley Chronicle, 1986), pp. 11–215.
9. F.L.J. Vodrey, 'The Autobiography of Frank L.J. Vodrey', typescript in the possession of the author, pp. 28–60.
10. See, for example, the Parish Notes of Weston-sub-Edge, Gloucestershire, Christmas 1984.
11. See, for example, J. Cloak, *Templer, Tiger of Malaya. The Life of Field Marshal Sir Gerald Templer* (London, Harrap, 1985), pp. 28–9.
12. I owe the example of nail varnish to Mr E.R. Syme, whose father-in-law banned his daughter from using it as it reminded him of the trenches.

Index